OXFORD ISLAMIC LEGAL STUDIES

Series Editors:
Anver M. Emon, Clark Lombardi, and Lynn Welchman

DOMESTIC VIOLENCE AND THE ISLAMIC TRADITION

Dear Joan,
this book is by a
young scholar of Islam
whose voice is
both present & weighty
in the critique she
brings to a tradition &
its legacy. I hope
you enjoy it, despite
the somberness of the
topic. Cordially,
Anver

Domestic Violence and the Islamic Tradition

Ethics, Law, and the Muslim Discourse on Gender

AYESHA S. CHAUDHRY

OXFORD
UNIVERSITY PRESS

OXFORD
UNIVERSITY PRESS

Great Clarendon Street, Oxford, OX2 6DP,
United Kingdom

Oxford University Press is a department of the University of Oxford.
It furthers the University's objective of excellence in research, scholarship, and education by publishing worldwide. Oxford is a registered trade mark of Oxford University Press in the UK and in certain other countries

First Edition published in 2013

Impression: 1

Published in the United States of America by Oxford University Press
198 Madison Avenue, New York, NY 10016, United States of America

British Library Cataloguing in Publication Data
Data available

Library of Congress Control Number: 2013947083

ISBN 978-0-19-964016-4

Printed and bound in Great Britain by
CPI Group (UK) Ltd, Croydon, CR0 4YY

For Rumee,

Who inspires me
to be the best version of myself.

In you I have found at last
a Refuge,
a Haven,
a Sanctuary.

Series Editors' Preface

The Oxford Islamic Legal Studies Series promotes scholarship that speaks to a broad scholarly audience. The books in this series are designed to speak to specialists in the field. They are also selected with an eye to non-specialists, and are written in a manner that allows non-specialists to engage in a nuanced way with cutting-edge topics regarding Islamic law. The current volume exemplifies this type of nuanced, accessible, and provocative text.

Perhaps no topic in Islamic law has as broad ranging an audience as those related to the field of Islam and gender. As editors, we recognize that concerns about gender justice in the Muslim world have contributed to policies and agendas all too often associated with empire. Yet, we also acknowledge that cultures of patriarchy—which are not limited to the Muslim world—continue to perpetuate limits on the scope of freedom and self-fulfillment that women continue to experience. Calling patriarchy to account through sustained, rigorous scholarship provides a model of engagement that elevates conversation from the mere polemical or apologetic trends that often appear in the popular media.

Ayesha S. Chaudhry's *Domestic Violence and the Islamic Tradition* offers such a model. In this book, Chaudhry closely examines the historical and contemporary "Islamic tradition", and illuminates the legal and theological paradigms that enable patriarchy to regulate the bodies of Muslim women. Chaudhry focuses attention on the historical debates around a specific Qur'anic verse. Q 4:34, the so-called "beating verse", often engenders extreme reactions, whether of outrage, discomfort, or defensiveness. Recognizing how this verse plays out in popular and often politicized debates about Islam and Muslims, Chaudhry takes the reader step-by-step through the historical commentary on that verse. Her analysis proceeds from the pre-modern period into the modern one, with a review of contemporary sources in Arabic, Urdu, and English, whether in print or audiovisual. Reading the first page of her book, the reader will immediately encounter the distinctive and stirring voice of a scholar working through the implications of a tradition for which she cares, but who does not shy away from critique. Her analysis reveals the way in which patriarchy informs what she calls an "idealized cosmology", an optative "as if" world that provides an interpretive lens of gendered hierarchy. She shows that if there is to be a tradition of gender egalitarianism in Islamic thought, more than piecemeal reform is required. Nothing short of a refashioned cosmology—which touches upon law, theology, exegesis, and text criticism—is required.

Anver M. Emon
Clark B. Lombardi
Lynn Welchman

Acknowledgments

I am grateful to many amazing people whose goodwill and kindness sustained me through the many years that were devoted to this book. First and foremost, I acknowledge the great debt I owe my dear husband, Rumee Ahmed, whose patience and generosity have been ceaseless and whose kindness and compassion seem inexhaustible. This book would simply not exist without his constant love and support. He played multiple roles through the process of this project, including friend, critic, chef, editor, interlocutor, research assistant, nursemaid, travel agent, driver, therapist, and entertainer. Most of all, I am thankful that he has chosen to walk with me in this journey through life, showing me how to delight in its joys and persevere through its sorrows. I cannot imagine a more perfect life partner and am truly honored by this tremendous privilege.

In writing this book, I have had the great fortune of working with an excellent editorial team. I am especially lucky to have worked with Anver M. Emon, who guided me through the publication process with great sagacity. He has been accommodating, patient, and constructive, and made the publication experience thoroughly enjoyable. In addition, he introduced me to an ethos of collegiality that separates scholarly critique from personal attack and in the process has reaffirmed the human dignity of a scholar. I am also fortunate to have had the privilege of working with Lisa Y. Gourd as my copy-editor. Her corrections, comments, and insights were meticulous, painstaking, and brilliant. They greatly improved the quality of this manuscript. Most of the current version of this book was written at Bel Café and Revolver in Vancouver, where I was treated with exceptional hospitality and graciousness. I am particularly indebted to Bel Café, where I sometimes worked for ten hours at a time, right through the afternoon rush hour. Anna Heyd and Parker McLean were sunshine on rainy days.

Although it has turned out to be a rather different book, this project began during my graduate studies in the Department of Middle Eastern and Islamic Studies at New York University. At NYU I had the good fortune to meet and work with extraordinary scholars, friends, and colleagues, who deeply influenced my personal and intellectual trajectory. I am thankful to those who went above and beyond the call of duty to lend a kind word, sympathetic ear, and helping hand. Thank you, Khaled Fahmy, Michael Gilsenan, Bernard Haykel, Zachary Lockman, and Catharine

R. Stimpson. I am also thankful to my dissertation committee, namely Kecia Ali, Marion H. Katz, and Everett K. Rowson, for reading through the many drafts of the dissertation and encouraging me to be a better scholar. I am also grateful to the external readers Fiona J. Griffiths and Kristin Z. Sands. Kecia Ali deserves special thanks. Her dissertation inspired mine, and she took on this project as an external advisor, providing feedback at every stage and acting as a mentor as I have transitioned to a career in teaching. Now that I am an assistant professor myself, I have renewed appreciation for the magnitude of her commitment. I am also grateful to my intellectual mentors at the University of Toronto who helped shape my scholarly trajectory, particularly Robert Gibbs, Sebastian Günther, James A. Reilly, Walid Saleh, and Janice Stein.

I must also thank the foremothers in the field of Gender and Islamic Studies who cobbled together this field with their intellectual curiosity, commitment to justice, and courageous spirit. Without their pioneering work, a project like this would be unimaginable. The women whose work most directly shaped and influenced my personal intellectual journey include Leila Ahmed, Asma Barlas, Fatima Mernissi, Ziba Mir-Hosseini, and Amina Wadud.

I have been blessed with fabulous and nourishing friends who have supported me through the process of writing this book, sometimes enabling and other times rejecting my hermit-like tendencies. Special thanks to Sarah Abdullah, Charlie Bergstrom, Menka Berry, Jeff Bary, Craig Bohlken, Doug Brockway, Lale Can, Allyssa Case, Aryeh Cohen, Elliott Colla, Valerie Cooper, Amanullah De Sondy, Vivette Elfawal, Barney Ellis-Perry, Farid Esack, Neal Ferrazani, David Fushtey, Leah Greenstein Ferrazani, Benjamin Goold, Tom Greggs, Noah Haiduc-Dale, Susan Hardy, Irfana Hashmi, Suzanne Holland, Matthew Ingalls, Steven Kepnes, Meher Khan, Nadia Mahdi, Mahan Mirza, Ebrahim Moosa, Rachel Muers, Noor Najeeb, Sarah Namer, Martin Nguyen, Peter Ochs, Vanessa Ochs, Krisjon Olson, Kristian Petersen, Moura Quayle, Aadia Rana, Randi Rashkover, Nevin Reda, Deena Rymhs, Mohammed Rustom, Maher Samra, Sa'diyya Shaikh, Mary Simonson, Anjali Thomas-Bohlken, William Twaddell, Homayra Ziad, and Laurie Zoloth.

And last but certainly not least, I am thankful to my family: my father, Abdul Ghafoor, for his unconditional pride; my mother, Noor Fatima, for instilling a desire to seek knowledge; Omar, for starting off my doctoral career in style with my first computer; Amena for holding my hand as I jumped into the abyss of independence; Tayyab, for sharing in the endeavor of self-improvement; Khadijah, for showing me the humor in things; and Maryum, who knows when words are unnecessary and hugs are better. I am appreciative of my siblings' spouses—Ayesha, Ahmed, Rachel, and Ozair—and my in-laws for adding light to our lives. May the world be bright and vibrant for my nephews, niece, and godson: Abdur-Rauf, Zainab, Abdullah, Hamza, Ibrahim, and Hafez. Dearest Sibghatullah, may you rest in peace.

Ayesha S. Chaudhry

Vancouver, BC
January 28, 2013

Contents

Introduction

> I speak only one language, and it is not my own.
>
> Jacques Derrida, *Monolingualism of the Other: Or, the Prosthesis of Origin*

There is no aspect of Islam that is gender-neutral; everything is gendered, from sacred texts, theology, ethics, legal theory, jurisprudence to mystical expressions and the embodied experiences of believers. So although the topics of "Islam and women," "the treatment of women in Islam," and "the role of women in Islam" are often bracketed out as special topics in seminars and lectures, as if "Islam" as a discrete entity must be made to speak to or about "gender", in fact, Muslim men and women the world over can interact with Islam only in a gendered way. A gendered Islam pervades the entirety of a believer's experience with Islam, as much as gender affects his or her identity.

Like most intellectual pursuits, this book emerges from a personal journey. Growing up in Canada as the daughter of Pakistani immigrants with conservative Muslim values, I found myself balancing conflicting demands that stemmed from embodying multiple identities—Muslim, Canadian, modern, second-generation immigrant, Western, Pakistani, female—a process that was as painful as it was enlightening. For me, this often brought into sharp relief opposing values that could not be reconciled, no matter how much I tried; one often had to be chosen over the other. Ultimately, I found that I was unable to perfectly fit the models of ideal femininity that were celebrated in either of my primary educational settings—my local mosques and public schools. I could not conform to a vision of womanhood presented by patriarchal religious leaders in the mosque while growing up in a country in which gender egalitarianism was—at least rhetorically—a national value. Nor could I be a blithely independent feminist unconstrained by the visions of the gracefully modest female with which I was raised.

My relationship with one particular verse in the Qur'ān helps to illustrate what it means to navigate these multiple, inherited identities. This verse is found is Chapter 4, verse 34 of the Qur'ān. It is a verse that describes the relationship of men to women, catalogues the behavior of good and bad women, and then advises husbands on how to discipline and rectify the bad behavior of their wives. The verse reads:

> Men are *qawwāmūn* (in authority) over women, because God has preferred some over others and because they spend of their wealth. Righteous women are obedient and guard in [their husbands'] absence what God would have them guard. Concerning those women from whom you fear *nushūz* (disobedience/rebellion), admonish them, and/or abandon them in bed, and/or *wa-ḍribūhunna* (hit them). If they obey you, do not seek a means against them. God is most High, Great. (Q. 4:34)

When I first encountered this verse, while reading a translation of the Qur'ān in middle school, I was both unsettled and defensive. It was the first time I found myself disturbed by a verse in the Qur'ān, a scripture that I considered to be literally sacred and true, to the exclusion of all others. What did it mean that men were in authority over women? Weren't men and women equal? Why should men be in charge of women based on their gender; shouldn't authority be based on one's knowledge and qualifications? And shouldn't spouses be partners, rather than hierarchically and asymmetrically related to one another? And what was this business about husbands being allowed to hit their wives? What exactly was *nushūz*, and why did righteous women need to be obedient? Weren't there other, more valuable qualities that could be expected of humans? And didn't both women *and* men need to be obedient to God? So why single out the obedience of women here and not men?

But I also felt defensive. This verse made it look as if Muslims did not believe in gender equality, that they thought men were better than women, and that they were okay with husbands hitting their wives. I did not believe any of these things to be true about Islam; men and women were equal, and each was rewarded according to his or her deeds. Didn't the Qur'ān after all say, "The human has nothing but what he strives for; and his striving will soon come in sight?"[1] And the Qur'ān could not sanction husbands to hit their wives. I sincerely believed this, but Q. 4:34 disrupted this belief. Most importantly, Prophet Muḥammad, who was "a walking Qur'ān" never hit his wives, and Muslims were meant to follow his example. Still, someone might read this verse and, without understanding the complexity of the Islamic tradition, think that Islam condones violence against women. This was thoroughly distressing. I did not want Islam's image to be tarnished, especially in comparison to Judaism and Christianity. As someone who devoutly believed in a supersessionist vision of Islam, in which Islam

[1] Q. 53:39–40. This translation is based on Yusuf Ali's *The Holy Qur'an* (trans. Abdullah Yusuf Ali) (Chatham: Wordsworth Editions Ltd, 2000).

was the new and improved version of both Judaism and Christianity, the thought of Islam looking worse than the other two Abrahamic faiths was worrisome. It is not as if the Hebrew Bible and Gospels treat men and women equally; besides, at least the Qur'ān treats men and women *more* equitably than the Bible. Islam had given women all sorts of rights they did not have before Islam, and which the Western world only recently gave to women, such as the right to own property, to be a witness, or to inherit. The Qur'ān was against female infanticide. At first, then, my concern was more for the religion and less for the well-being of Muslim women, whom I was certain would not have to worry about domestic abuse from God-fearing husbands. I found an uneasy settlement in this line of evasive reasoning, and for a while I was content in this place.

Yet Q. 4:34 remained where it was, as it was, and people continued to read it and speak about it. And I wished that they would just stop and talk about something else. There were thousands of other verses in the Qur'ān, why was everyone obsessed with this verse? By the time I finished high school, my defensiveness toward Q. 4:34 had turned to alarm. I was old enough to have heard stories of women in my community whose husbands hit them and justified their behavior on the basis of Q. 4:34. I had heard women use this verse as an explanation for their choice to remain in physically abusive relationships. I had heard women ask religious leaders if their husbands really had the right to hit them, if they would be sinning by calling the police, or if seeking help from secular authorities would incur God's wrath. I had heard religious leaders ask these women why their husbands hit them, what did they do wrong? They counseled patience and obedience to wives before telling husbands that it was better to avoid hitting their wives. The best men followed the example of Prophet Muḥammad, who never hit his wives. And if the men absolutely had to hit their wives, they were to do so lightly, without violence, without leaving a mark, with a toothbrush or perhaps even a rose. So while discouraging husbands from hitting their wives, these scholars nevertheless upheld their right to physically discipline their wives as divinely ordained. They could not, after all, deny God's word or disagree with Him. Whatever their moral and ethical compunctions, they could not be more wise, just, or loving than God.

During my undergraduate years at the University of Toronto, the prescription to hit wives became increasingly central to my moral problems with Q. 4:34. Why are men allowed to hit their wives at all, however lightly? Why is violence ever the correct answer to marital dispute? And why had God interrupted human history to divinely sanction the right of husbands to hit their wives? It did not help to think about the specific context of seventh-century Arabia; the argument that Q. 4:34 was progressive for its time was not compelling. The logic here was that prior to Islam, husbands could hit their wives without any restrictions at all, and so Q. 4:34, in a mode of progressive justice, actually limited the reasons and procedure for hitting wives. A related argument is that, given the historical and social context of seventh-century Arabian bedouin society in which women were basically treated like a chattel, it would have been too naive, unrealistic, and socially disruptive to expect men to stop hitting their wives altogether. Arguments such as these only intensified my discomfort. If ever women needed protection from any kind of physical discipline, it would have been in a patriarchal society in which they were so grievously disempowered that female babies were buried alive. Moreover, the Qurʾān prohibits believers from lying, cheating, backbiting, and gossiping. Were these prohibitions not "too naive, unrealistic, and socially disruptive" for seventh-century Arabian society?

Armed with university-honed analytic skills, I began to ask these questions of various religious leaders. Surely, some scholars might have some perspective on this verse that would vindicate it. I was looking for someone who would say that Q. 4:34 had been completely misunderstood or mistranslated, and that it did not allow husbands to hit their wives. Since I had a specific answer in mind, I began approaching scholars who appeared amenable to my point of view. I approached younger scholars dressed in Western attire, who were converts to Islam or second-generation immigrants. I assumed such scholars would better understand the need to deny Qurʾanic sanction for husbands to hit their wives under any circumstance, and that they would presuppose that men and women were equal. Unfortunately, the scholars I spoke to were stuck in a bind; on the one hand, they felt it was necessary to justify and defend the violent wording of Q. 4:34, and on the other hand, they tried to restrict the violence permitted by it. They regularly began their answers by saying that Q. 4:34 had been misunderstood by Muslims and non-Muslims alike. It did not actually condone violence against women. Each time one of these scholars appeared sympathetic, I was naive enough to get excited. But each time I was disappointed, because the scholars I spoke to regularly defended a violent reading of Q. 4:34. Mind you, the scholars I am speaking about would never describe their defense this way. They were adamant that husbands were only allowed to hit their wives lightly, that they could not hit their wives for minor infractions but only for gross disobedience, or perhaps for adultery; this verse did not sanction domestic violence. The contradictory nature of these claims did not seem to bother them. The hitting in question was not supposed to be harmful, but how could you hit someone without harming them, physically, psychologically, and emotionally?

Asked about why men had disciplinary privileges at all if indeed men and women were equal, the scholars I spoke to offered a theory of the complementarity of genders. Men and women are spiritually equal, where it really counts. In this lower life, men and women are created different, biologically and socially. Accordingly, it is better to think about their roles as complementary rather than equal. After all, what does "equal" mean, if it does not account for differences in biology? The equality of genders in all things is a modern, Western (meaning colonialist and corrupt) value that twists human nature to fit into an unnatural mold. In contrast, Islam embraces human nature, revealed as it was by the Creator of humans, and thus it accounts for and accommodates the differences between men and women. According to these Muslim scholars, its beauty lies in the fact that it allows men to be men and women to be women, and values them both in their own ways.

As a Muslim woman who believes in gender egalitarianism and the non-essential nature of gender, it was disheartening to hear popular religious leaders of my community speak this way about women—especially the ones who appeared to be the most moderate, the ones who should have known better than to say such things. I developed a keen sense of suspicion based on these conversations, and whenever I encountered a shiny, new scholar who was especially charming and compelling, I used Q. 4:34 as a litmus test to see if he or she really was as moderate as they made themselves out to be. Was it ever okay for a husband to hit his wife, I would ask, and time and again I found myself dismayed by the response.

Reflecting back on this time, I know now that most of the scholars I encountered drew their authority from the "Islamic tradition" of which they spoke; they situated themselves and their opinions in long chains of historical, authoritative Muslim scholars. In following this tradition uncritically, they were willing to blind themselves to the concerns and needs of their immediate community. They understood well that if they broke from the tradition and espoused an opinion that they could not root in that tradition, then they would lose authority within the Muslim community. Their very legitimacy was at stake. And these stakes were high enough that they rationalized a marital hierarchy in which husbands had the power of physical discipline, resulting in marital counsel that gave some credence, however qualified, to abusers and some blame to victims. These scholars were thus willing to neglect the pain of real members of their present community in order to belong to an imagined historical community.

Invariably, accompanying these defensive, violent interpretations of Q. 4:34 were lengthy lectures about the wisdom of God and the "complexity of the Islamic tradition." These were both dismissive moves.

The "wisdom of God" talk was intended to cast doubt on my value system and to encourage me to formulate a value system based on a more literal reading of the divine text. If I was troubled by a verse, then the problem was on my end, not with the text. The "complexity of the Islamic tradition" talk was intended to breed humility and faith: humility in the face of the thousand-plus years of Muslim scholarship on related issues, and faith that the eminent Muslim scholars of the past had provided satisfactory, authoritative answers—if only one read their works. "All the questions that you are raising have already been answered by scholars in the Islamic tradition. These scholars were well-educated in the Islamic sciences, they were brilliant, had photographic and encyclopedic memories; they were qualified to ask and answer these questions. If you want to ask such questions, you must first study the illustrious Islamic tradition, which has all the answers." I heard various versions of this response from different scholars. It was and continues to be used to stifle critical inquiry and to delegitimize new positions, perspectives, and criticisms that seek to make Islam relevant to contemporary concerns.

But what is the "Islamic tradition," I wondered, and what does it say about Q. 4:34? For all the talk of the "Islamic tradition," it is not easily defined. Modern rhetorical overtures to the "Islamic tradition" are tempered by the historical, emotional, and psychological experiences of colonialism. The topic of gender egalitarianism is especially fraught because the colonialist project was justified at home and abroad through the inconsistent rhetoric of women's emancipation and de-veiling. Individuals like Lord Cromer exemplified the disingenuousness of this justification; he promoted de-veiling in Egypt under the banner of female emancipation while heading up the anti-suffragist movement in England.[2] As a result of its entanglement with the experiences of colonialism, feminism became and remains highly politicized in the Muslim world; championing a call to feminism can be tantamount to collaborating with colonialists and thus betraying "traditional" Muslim values. The alignment of feminism and colonialism produced a religious counter-rhetoric that sought to "save" Muslim women from corrupting Western and modern influences.

In this framework, the pre-colonial era came to represent a mythic golden age in which Muslims ruled empires and commanded the respect

[2] Leila Ahmed, *Women and Gender in Islam: Historical Roots of a Modern Debate* (New Haven: Yale University Press, 1992) 152–3. Lila Abu-Lughod makes a similar point regarding Laura Bush's justification for the invasion of Afghanistan. She argued that Afghan women needed to be "saved". Lila Abu-Lughod, "Do Muslim Women Really Need Saving?," *American Anthropologist*, 104(3) (2002) 783–90. See also, Lisa Hajjar, "Religion, State Power, and Domestic Violence in Muslim Societies: A Framework for Comparative Analysis," *Law & Social Inquiry*, 29(1) (2004) 15.

of the world, in stark contrast to the humiliation and suffering brought about by colonialism. The logic here is that political fortunes are a reflection of the spiritual grandeurs of its leaders. Thus, the conquest of the Arabian peninsula was the reflection of God's favor upon Muḥammad, the expansion into empire mirrored the spiritual ascendency of Muḥammad's companions, and the flourishing of Islamic civilization thereafter resulted from the majesty of the scholarly elite. The link between Muḥammad and the scholars is made explicit in the prophetic tradition, "The scholars are the inheritors of the prophets (*al-ʿulamāʾ wārithatu al-anbiyāʾ*)," such that the grandeur of the Muslim condition would be a testament to the greatness of the community's religious scholars. Thus, the Muslim humiliation at the hands of the colonists was understood at least partly to be a result of the spiritual degradation of colonial-era Muslim scholars and the dismantling of their scholarly institutions. Colonial and post-colonial religious scholarship continues to be viewed—in some circles—with contempt as tainted, corrupt, and in all ways inferior to pre-colonial scholarship. The pinnacle of Islamic thought, therefore, is usually seen to lie in the pre-colonial age, when the scholars were able to curry God's favor and came to represent a pristine, spiritually ascendant "Islamic tradition."

The scholars I spoke with about Q. 4:34 called upon the authority of the "Islamic tradition," speaking about it as a vague and disembodied concept. For them, the "Islamic tradition" is legendary. Being so mythologized, the "Islamic tradition" has taken on an overblown and overbearing authoritative status.[3] Its canonical powers are invoked to defend interpretations of the Qur'ān that might not accord with modern values, including Q. 4:34, and also to assuage modern Muslim anxieties about the relevance of the text to the modern world. The "Islamic tradition" is invoked as the solution to all modern problems, even if the content of those solutions is never clear.

Frustrated by the obstacle that the "Islamic tradition" posed to finding an egalitarian interpretation of Q. 4:34, I decided to study this tradition. I would read Qur'anic commentaries and Islamic legal works and find answers for myself and others. Everyone said that the "Islamic tradition" was complex, multivalent, and pluralistic; that it not only tolerated but celebrated and respected various scholarly positions on every topic imaginable. All my life, I had been regaled with stories of how Muslim

[3] Lama Abu-Odeh relies on Joan W. Scott's scholarship to call this the "fantasy effect," where "fantasy is the means by which real relations of identity between past and present are discovered and/or forged." Lama Abu-Odeh, "The Politics of (Mis)recognition: Islamic Law Pedagogy in American Academia," *American Journal of Comparative Law*, 52(4) (2004) 792. See also, Joan W. Scott, "Fantasy Echo: History and the Construction of Identity," *Critical Inquiry*, 27(2) (2001) 284, 287.

scholars in the glorious past were able to disagree with each other and also respect one another. The phrases "In this, there is a difference of opinion" and "God knows best" are peppered throughout Muslim scholarly works. Pre-colonial Muslim scholars knew that no one had a monopoly over truth, so they accommodated multiple interpretations of each verse in the Qurʾān. I was thrilled at the prospect of studying the "Islamic tradition" to find all the different positions on Q. 4:34 and at the prospect of bringing to light egalitarian interpretations that treat men and women with equal human worth, without intrinsic moral and disciplinary privileges over each other. I was confident that I would find egalitarian voices amidst the patriarchal ones. Since justice was a central value of Islam, and hitting wives was blatantly unjust, it was impossible for me to imagine an Islamic tradition in which no one challenged the right of husbands to hit their wives.

Yet this is exactly what I found. Not a single pre-colonial Islamic jurist or exegete interpreted Q. 4:34 in a way that forbids husbands from hitting their wives. This does not mean that they did not have ethical concerns about the disciplinary privileges of husbands. They mitigated the physical abuse of wives by restricting the procedure and extent of violence permissible. Pre-colonial scholars disagreed with one another about whether husbands needed to follow the three disciplinary steps outlined in Q. 4:34—admonishment, abandonment in bed, and hitting—sequentially and exhaustively, or if they could apply all three steps simultaneously, or if this matter was best left to a husband's discretion. They also debated about the extent of violence permitted to husbands in marriage. While most agreed that the hitting should be non-extreme (*ghayr mubarriḥ*), for some, non-extreme hitting included rather severe beatings. In the end, Muslim exegetes and jurists created acceptable space for hitting wives that encompassed symbolic hitting with a handkerchief or toothbrush, as well as beating with one's hands, sandal, switch, or whip. And while husbands could be legally liable for hitting their wives, this was only in the case of extreme beatings that resulted in observable injuries such as broken bones and open wounds. I was shocked to find that not a single pre-colonial Muslim scholar objected to the disciplinary privilege of husbands; they instead treated this privilege as a basic marital right. How was it possible that all these scholars arrived at similar conclusions about an ideal marital structure, in which men and women were asymmetrically related to each other, and husbands' morally authoritative position afforded them disciplinary privileges over their wives? These scholars lived in vastly disparate social, political, and historical contexts, spanning centuries and diverse geographic locations; each had his own personal and subjective experiences with the women who surrounded him and with whom he interacted. Why didn't their conclusions account for these differences?

Some will find my shock deeply naive. How could I expect scholars who, despite their contextual differences, all belonged to patriarchal societies to come up with egalitarian visions of Islam? Wasn't that too much to ask of these men, who belonged to their times as fully as I belong to mine? I was nevertheless surprised because it was difficult to confront an "Islamic tradition" that failed to offer just interpretations of a Qur'anic verse. I had believed in the myth of the "Islamic tradition," of the greatness of its scholars, their nobility and relentless pursuit of justice, their ability to challenge and fight an oppressive status quo. This was the framing story when Muslim scholars spoke of racial and economic distinctions, so why was this not true for gender distinctions? In the case of domestic violence in particular, it astonished me that pre-colonial scholars had not challenged the right of husbands to hit their wives, that they had not disagreed with each other on this most obvious point of social justice. Never mind hitting wives, I was confounded by the fact that they had not questioned the assumed moral superiority and disciplinary privileges of husbands at all, considering that before God, all humans were as "equal as the teeth of a comb."[4]

My research did yield a pleasant surprise. As my investigation expanded into the modern period, I found that modern Muslim scholars and activists had, in fact, proposed non-violent, gender-egalitarian interpretations of Q. 4:34. These interpretations challenge the moral and disciplinary privileges of husbands over wives and forbid husbands from hitting their wives, regardless of circumstance, procedure, or extent. The ethical discussions of these scholars centered around exactly the issues of justice that Q. 4:34 raised for me. It turns out that contemporary Muslim scholarly discourse surrounding Q. 4:34 is in fact sophisticated and complex. Their discourse encompasses multiple differing perspectives, and these Muslim scholars are engaged in a relentless pursuit of justice, challenging and fighting against an oppressive status quo. It is just that I had been looking in the wrong places for this discourse. Rather than the pre-colonial period, these conversations are happening in the post-colonial period; they are happening now.[5] But why had I never heard of these positions before, during all those years when I was seeking answers from scholar after scholar?

[4] This is a *ḥadīth*, or prophetic report. The full text reads, "People are as equal as the teeth of a comb; they are differentiated only by piety." For more on this *ḥadīth*, see Khaled Abou El Fadl, *Speaking in God's Name: Islamic Law, Authority and Women* (Oxford: Oneworld, 2001) 262.

[5] See the work of contemporary figures such as Leila Ahmed, Kecia Ali, Laleh Bakhtiar, Asma Barlas, Sarah Eltantawi, Farid Esack, Azizah al-Hibri, Laury Silvers, Ziba Mir-Hosseini, Ebrahim Moosa, Fatima Mernissi, Nevin Reda, Sa'diyya Shaikh, Amina Wadud, and Homayra

The answers to these questions lie in what I call the "egalitarian-authoritative dilemma," which is created by the contemporary endeavor to reconcile two competing idealized cosmologies (discussed in further detail later).[6] In this impossible space, the "Islamic tradition," defined by pre-colonial Islamic scholarship, obfuscates rather than facilitates a gender-egalitarian vision of Islam. The nature of the relationship between modern Muslims and their tradition is at the heart of this book. The imagined past of the Muslim community is central to identity-formation in certain Muslim communities and is thus foundational to their claims of authority.

The "Islamic tradition" is invoked to support innovative religious positions but also to stifle creativity and delegitimize innovative hermeneutical strategies. Hence, in order to speak authoritatively, Muslim scholars attempt to anchor their positions in the Islamic tradition. The question "where is the historical precedent for this new position amongst the illustrious scholars (*'ulamā'*) of the past?" is one to which all Muslim scholars must respond when submitting new interpretations, views, or perspectives that address the needs and concerns of their immediate communities. This question raises the issue of authority: do modern scholars display arrogance and hubris when they propose new interpretations or positions in face of a multitude of qualified pre-colonial scholars? Since the "Islamic tradition" is the first obstacle that Muslim scholars must overcome in rethinking any given issue, it is understandable that Muslim scholars preemptively appeal to its authority when devising new opinions. However, resorting to the "Islamic tradition" means that this tradition is privileged and sets the terms of the ensuing discussion. Since the Islamic tradition is fundamentally patriarchal, its idealized

Ziad. In addition, see the work of organizations such as Musawah for Equality in the Family, Women's Islamic Initiative in Spirituality and Equality (WISE) and the Canadian Council for Muslim Women (CCMW).

[6] Ziba Mir-Hosseini describes this as creating an "epistemological crisis." She writes, "The idea of gender equality, which became inherent to global conceptions of justice in the course of the twentieth century, has presented Muslim legal tradition with an 'epistemological crisis.'" In the footnote to this note, she explains, "I borrow this concept from the philosopher Alasdair MacIntyre, who argues that every rational inquiry is embedded in a tradition of learning, and that tradition reaches an epistemological crisis when, by its own standards of rational justification, disagreements can no longer be resolved rationally. This gives rise to an internal critique that will eventually transform the tradition, if it is to survive. It is then that thinkers and producers in that tradition of inquiry gradually start to respond and assimilate the idea that is alien to the tradition." Ziba Mir-Hosseini, "Justice, Equality and Muslim Family Laws: New Ideas, New Prospects" in Ziba Mir-Hosseini, Kari Vogt, Lena Larsen, and Christian Moe (eds.), *Gender and Equality in Muslim Family Law: Justice and Ethics in the Islamic Legal Tradition* (London: I.B. Taurus, 2013) 26. See also, Alasdair MacIntyre, *Whose Justice? Which Rationality?* (Notre Dame: University of Notre Dame Press, 1988) 350–2.

cosmology gains normative status. In this framework, gender-egalitarian visions of Islam are especially disadvantaged, since they challenge the authority of the ubiquitously patriarchal "Islamic tradition," thereby inviting anti-colonialist ire.

The problem, then, lies in the tension between gender-egalitarianism and traditionalist authority. Modern Muslim scholars who seek gender-egalitarian readings of Islamic texts confront a serious and unique difficulty: given the ubiquitous patriarchy of pre-colonial Muslim scholarship, how can one interpret the Qurʾān to promote gender-egalitarianism without losing the authority that comes from recourse to the pre-colonial Islamic tradition? Since authority in many religious communities is derived in large part from their traditions, breaking from tradition results in a loss of authority in the eyes of the community. The flipside of this dilemma is that if scholars rely on the patriarchal tradition in order to maintain authority and legitimacy, then they must compromise their commitment to gender-egalitarianism. In this way, the relationship of modern progressive scholarship with the "Islamic tradition" has come to be a central issue in Muslim feminist religious discourse.

The egalitarian–authoritative dilemma, as a quintessentially modern quandary, arises from tensions caused by two competing idealized cosmologies. By "idealized cosmology" I mean a representation of a perfect world, a vision of the world as it should be rather than merely as it is; in the case of the Muslim scholars under study, idealized cosmologies are visions of the universe as it would exist if all humans submitted entirely to God's laws. It is the world as God intended it, as it should be, unpolluted by mundane realities. I use the term "idealized" as opposed to "ideal" in order to emphasize the act of making perfect, since Muslim scholars actively imagine and create idealized cosmologies.[7] Narrowly defined, the term "cosmology" refers to theories that explain the origin of the universe; however, in the humanities and social sciences, cosmologies are also descriptions and justifications for a particular ordering of the universe.[8] In religious studies, a cosmology is a worldview that not only

[7] In using the term "idealized," I am drawing on and relying upon the theoretical frame offered by several modern theorists. In particular, I take inspiration from, among others, Benedict Anderson's "imagined communities," Mohammed Arkoun's "*imaginaire*," and Charles Taylor's "social imaginary." Benedict Anderson, *Imagined Communities: Reflections on the Origin and Spread of Nationalism* (London: Verso, 2003); Mohammed Arkoun, "Discours islamiques, discours orientalistes et pensée scientfique" in "As Others See Us: Mutual Perceptions, East and West Bernard Lewis" (ed. Edmund Leites and Margaret Case), *Comparative Civilizations Review*, 13–14 (1985–6); Charles Taylor, *Modern Social Imaginaries* (Durham, NC: Duke University Press, 2004).

[8] Ebrahim Moosa argues that "there is cosmology underlying Muslim juristic theology or legal theory (*uṣūl al-fiqh*). This cosmological narrative enables us to bridge the discursive divide between the empirical and transcendental realms." Ebrahim Moosa, "Allegory

accounts for the ranking amongst human beings, but also places them in a larger context assigning them a role in the universe vis-à-vis God and other metaphysical realities.[9] I use the term "idealized cosmology" then, to refer to a vision of the universe which expresses normative religious constructions of gender, social relations, the human-divine relationship, and descriptions of the divine (theology) through the language of law and Qur'anic exegesis.

Scholars who promote patriarchal and egalitarian visions of Islam hold two competing idealized cosmologies that are fundamentally irreconcilable. In the patriarchal idealized cosmology, God sits atop a hierarchy, followed by his creations, according to their ontological rank. In this ranking, humans are privileged over all other creations, and men rank above women. As such, men have direct, unfettered access to God, but women's relationship to God is mediated by men, who must oversee their wives' moral well-being. In contrast, in the egalitarian idealized cosmology, men and women possess equal human worth before God, so every individual has an independent relationship to the divine. This distinction is illustrated in Figure 1.

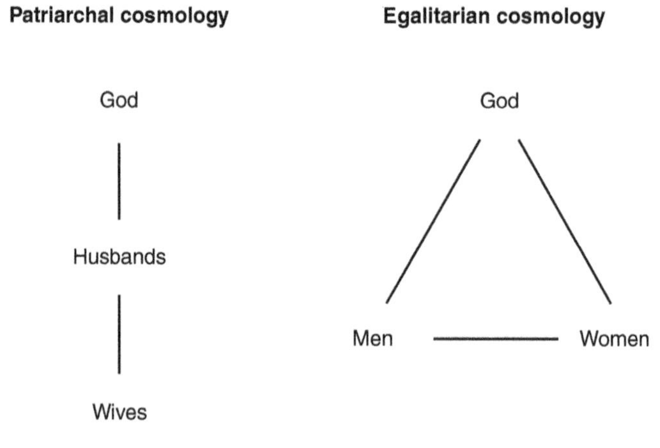

of the Rule (Hukm): Law as Simulacrum in Islam," *History of Religions*, 38(1) (August 1998) 1–24. See also, Nancy J. Davis and Robert V. Robinson, "The Egalitarian Face of Islamic Orthodoxy: Support for Islamic Law and Economic Justice in Seven Muslim-Majority Nations," *American Sociological Review*, 71(2) (2006) 167–90.

[9] For examples of the use of "cosmology" in religious studies works, see Adele Berlin, "Cosmology and Creation" in Maxine Grossman and Adele Berlin (eds.), *The Oxford Dictionary of the Jewish Religion* (New York: Oxford University Press, 2011) 188–9. See also, David Aune, "Cosmology" in *Westminster Dictionary of the New Testament and Early Christian Literature* (Louisville: Westminster John Knox Press, 2003) 118–19.

The clash of these two competing cosmologies is the driving force of tension in the egalitarian–authoritative dilemma. Pre-colonial interpretations of Q. 4:34 were consistently patriarchal, despite the various cultural and historical differences in centuries, geographic regions, juridical and theological schools. The monolithic nature of pre-colonial approaches to Q. 4:34 can be accounted for by their unvaried patriarchal cosmology. This is why pre-colonial concerns with Q. 4:34 were about the correct hierarchical placement of women, and why the discussion surrounding physical discipline was procedural rather than ethical when women upset this hierarchy. Scholars who advocate an egalitarian vision of Islam are seen not as offering a new interpretation of a particular text or legal ruling but rather as threatening the stability of the entire patriarchal cosmological order. Hence, discussions of gender in the modern period have serious theological and cosmological ramifications for the relationship that modern Muslims have to the "Islamic tradition."

The right of husbands to physically discipline wives presents an ideal case study for the purpose of exploring the egalitarian–authoritative dilemma that results from the clash of egalitarian and patriarchal idealized cosmologies. The question of whether husbands have the right to discipline their wives at all, even leaving aside the question of violence, raises clear ethical issues concerning morality and justice. And the husbandly privilege to hit wives is a reliable litmus test for ascertaining where particular scholars stand vis-à-vis the egalitarian–authoritative dilemma. The modern ethical concerns raised by granting husbands disciplinary privilege over wives are straightforward and difficult to equivocate. Scholars are forced to take a side on this issue—is it ethical or immoral to hit one's wife? Yes, or no? Those committed to gender egalitarianism would argue that men should not be considered disciplinarians of their wives, regardless of circumstance. However, honest adherence to the "Islamic tradition" and a patriarchal cosmology opens an ethical space in which the right of husbands to hit their wives is acceptable.

On its surface, Q. 4:34 does not pose an insurmountable problem. Since all Arabic words are conjugations of trilateral roots, each Arabic word lends itself to multivalent meanings. Some meanings of the trilateral root of *ḍ-r-b* include to walk, to run, to rape, to whip/flog, to slap, to present an example, to behead, to play the *daff*, to knock on a door, to wear a *hijāb*, to pitch a tent, and to apply a poll tax. The verb *ḍ-r-b* does not have most of these meanings without a specific direct object, preposition, or other verbal indicator. In this way it is very much like the English verb "to strike," which can be used in the phrases "strike a pose," "strike a bargain," "strike a similitude," etc.—but never has these meanings in isolation. Pro-gender-egalitarian scholars could simply reject violence against wives in this text by opting for a different translation for *wa-ḍribūhunna*. However, because this term was interpreted ubiquitously to mean "hit them" in pre-colonial eras, modern scholars find themselves hamstrung by the traditional meaning given to the verb in its context. As a result, Muslim scholars who may appear to espouse gender-egalitarian values find themselves justifying the right of husbands to hit their wives in increasingly restrictive and symbolic ways. Why can't modern Muslims simply go back to the Qur'anic text and re-interpret it to have non-violent meanings? Because time and again, the 'Islamic tradition' proves to be a hurdle that they are not able to overcome in order to make this move.

The main question here is this: How does a believer derive egalitarian ethics from revealed sources, such as the Qur'ān, while still remaining a member of the believing community whose "tradition" holds a contradictory theology? In his recent article, Mohammad Fadel argues that even to attempt to do so is folly. Citing Andrew March's "Reformer's Dilemma", he asserts that for a religious reformer, altering foundational doctrines such as theology is more "costly" and less effective than reforming applied doctrine in the form of jurisprudence. So in the case of the husbandly privilege to discipline wives, Fadel proposes that it is better for reformers to "deny the moral relevance" of such a verse without denying "the moral integrity of the traditional interpretations" of this verse.[10] I argue that such a believer already espouses a different theology and cosmology than that which was espoused by the Islamic tradition. For her, it is not a question of coming up with a new theology to find a way to deal with such divine texts but rather to acknowledge that such a theology is already informing the subjectivity of such a believer and her relationship to the text. A theological approach to ethics is required not so much to reform how texts ought to be read but rather fully to conform to how texts are already being read in practice.[11]

Ebrahim Moosa has argued that the Muslim community must have a performative relationship with the Qur'anic text in order to avoid "text fundamentalism."[12] According to Moosa, "Text fundamentalism . . . perpetuates the fiction that the text actually provides the norms, and we merely 'discover' the norms."[13] This view of the text marginalizes "the community of the text" and views the text as "sovereign" and

[10] Mohammad Fadel, "Is Historicism a Viable Strategy for Islamic Legal Reform? The Case of 'Never Shall a Folk Prosper Who Have Appointed a Woman to Rule Them,' " *Islamic Law and Society* (2011) 5, 6, and 44.

[11] Ayesha S. Chaudhry, "The Ethics of Marital Discipline in Pre-Modern Qur'anic Exegesis," *Journal of the Society of Christian Ethics* 30(2) (2010) 123–30.

[12] Ebrahim Moosa, "The Debts and Burdens of Critical Islam" in Omid Safi (ed.), *Progressive Muslims: On Justice, Gender and Pluralism* (Oxford: Oneworld, 2003) 111–27.

[13] Moosa (n 12) 125.

independent of its interpretive communities.[14] In fact, the text is only meaningful in its relationship with various interpretive communities, and its meanings cannot be discovered in a void but only through interaction. Acknowledging the performative relationship that interpretive communities already have with the Qur'anic text will grant Muslim communities a legitimate voice in shaping the interpretations of the Qur'ān, thereby making the text meaningful and relevant.

I agree with Moosa, but moreover, since the weight of the authoritative "Islamic tradition" is used to critique any new approach to the Qur'ān, it is necessary for the Muslim community also to have a performative relationship with the Islamic tradition. In order to have this performative relationship, Muslims must critically examine this vast tradition beyond simple overtures. The Islamic tradition is indeed complex and varied, and includes disciplines such as theology, jurisprudence, mysticism, lexicology, philology, exegesis, philosophy, legal theory, and more. For the purposes of this study, we will examine the two most relevant disciplines, Qur'anic exegesis and Islamic law, since we are primarily concerned with the moral and ethical issues raised by Q. 4:34.

This book addresses the intersecting concerns of a rarefied Islamic tradition, competing idealized cosmologies, the ethical problems raised by difficult scriptural texts, and the hermeneutical negotiations between allegiance to a religious community and dissent from its inherited tradition. The first three chapters shed light on the Islamic tradition by exploring pre-colonial exegetical and legal positions on the right of husbands to hit their wives. The last two chapters bring modern voices into the picture in order to compare and contrast modern perspectives with those of the "Islamic tradition," illustrating the malleability of source texts and the role that imaginations of the Islamic tradition play in the modern discourse of gender.

Chapter 1 is devoted to studying pre-colonial exegetical texts in order to disclose the idealized cosmology held by pre-colonial scholars and to demonstrate its influence on their interpretations of Q. 4:34. Chapter 2 continues exploring these same texts to scrutinize the scope and limits of pre-colonial exegetical and ethical discussions on the right of husbands to hit their wives. What did pre-colonial scholars think about this Qur'anic prescription? Did they limit or expand its scope, and did any exegetes offer alternative, non-violent readings of the verse? In Chapter 3, we shift focus to pre-colonial jurisprudential texts. How did legal discussions regarding the right of husbands to hit their wives compare with exegetical considerations? Since the disciplines of Qur'anic exegesis and Islamic law

[14] Moosa (n 12) 123.

were not hermetically sealed off from one another, it is worth asking if legal scholars were more or less concerned with protecting wives against violence and abuse. In Chapter 4, I examine and categorize modern Muslim discussions on domestic violence, paying close attention to the way modern scholars balance their claims to authority, their relationship with the Islamic tradition, and their proposals for creative hermeneutics. In Chapter 5, we investigate the influence of competing idealized cosmologies on interpretation and analyze the ways in which the Qur'anic text and prophetic reports can be used to argue for discrete idealized cosmologies.

A few points must be noted before we continue. First, since the "Islamic tradition" is an abstract concept rather than a historical reality, it is difficult to pinpoint the exact dates to which it is confined. However, since internal Muslim discussions presume that the "Islamic tradition" was untainted by the incursion of colonists, the sources in this study are divided by the event of colonialism. It is a known fact that colonialism changed Muslim discourse, especially with regard to gender. This book uses the distinction of "pre-" and "post-colonial" as a useful heuristic device.[15] It is not my intention here to pinpoint a specific date for the event of colonialism, which was experienced in various regions at different times and in different ways. My concern here is about how Muslim scholars speak about colonialism. Certainly, colonialism had a tangible impact on the historical, political, economic, and social structures of the Muslim world; however, my use of the term is conditioned by the fact that "colonialism" is also used as an intellectual construct in contemporary Muslim religious discourse. This book is most concerned with this construct of colonialism and its rhetorical weight in debates surrounding contemporary Qur'ān interpretations. In order to limit the scope of this project, the pre-colonial works are restricted to existing printed Arabic sources from the earliest centuries of Islam to the seventeenth century.[16] Arabic was the language of the religious elite and was used by both Arab and non-Arab religious scholars throughout the Muslim world. For this reason, the exegetical and legal writings surveyed will be representative of the religious elite in the Muslim world. In the post-colonial period, I study sources from the twentieth and twenty-first centuries, which are characterized by the decolonization and self-determination of Muslim

[15] Abu-Odeh (n 3) 792; Ebrahim Moosa, "Colonialism and Islamic Law" in Muhammad Khalid Masud, Armando Salvatore, and Martin van Bruinessen (eds.), *Islam and Modernity: Key Issues and Debates* (Edinburgh: Edinburgh University Press, 2009) 161.

[16] As mentioned previously, the exact date of colonialism proper differs from place to place. I decided to consider sources up to the seventeenth century in order to mitigate the earliest estimations of colonialist endeavors in Muslim lands. This ensures that the pre- and post-colonial sources belong to two distinct historical, political, and social periods.

peoples. In the modern era, the scope of this monograph is expanded to Muslim scholars and activists writing in Arabic, Urdu, and English, in three mediums—written, audio, and video, reflecting the significant changes in methods of religious education with the advent of colonialism. English is the new global language spoken by Muslims around the world. Proficiency in Arabic continues to be expected of the scholarly elite, and Urdu is, in one form or another, understood by approximately five hundred million people, making it the most commonly understood Islamicate language in the world today. In this way, this monograph is limited by language rather than geographic region. This allows for enough geographical diversity without it becoming overwhelming.

Second, in this book I exclusively examine pre- and post-colonial normative Sunni Muslim scholarship on marital violence. This work is a study of text, not an anthropological or sociological study. I do not explore what actually happens in Muslim marriages.[17] Written texts are a lens through which we learn about aspects of the social and historical context of their authors; we also learn about their imaginations of an ideal world, which need not be connected to their lived experiences. So while texts are naturally connected to social experiences, it is difficult to make definitive claims about people's lived experiences based on written texts alone. Hence, this project makes no claims about how Muslims interact with this verse of the Qur'ān in their daily lives. Nevertheless, through the study of texts, we will learn about how Muslims think and argue about their scripture and how they make ethical demands on their religious texts, on their own tradition, and on each other. The voices contained in this book reveal that Muslims do not speak with one voice about Islam, but rather that the Muslim scholarly discourse is spirited and animated, full of opposing and dynamic positions. Furthermore, the voices of contemporary Muslim scholars tremendously enrich and enhance the diversity and scope of the "Islamic tradition."

Finally, writing this book has been an angst-ridden experience because the subject of domestic violence and, more specifically, the treatment of wife-beating in historical and contemporary Muslim religious discourse are highly controversial topics. There are those who feel that given the especially vulnerable situation of Muslims globally, it is best to leave off topics that expose Muslims to further criticism and scrutiny. Many

[17] Others have done excellent work on this topic. See, eg, Lisa Hajjar (n 2) 1–38; Julie Macfarlane, *Islamic Divorce in North America: A Shari'a Path in a Secular Society* (Oxford: Oxford University Press, 2012); Judith Tucker, *In the House of the Law: Gender and Islamic Law in Ottoman Syria and Palestine* (Berkeley: University of California Press, 1998); Judith Tucker, *Women, Family, and Gender in Islamic Law* (Cambridge: Cambridge University Press, 2008).

Muslims believe that in this charged atmosphere, only Islam's best face should be put forward, and people of conscience ought to strive to promote a "public relations" (PR) image of Islam. The PR approach highlights only positive and unproblematic elements of Islam, chalking up any troublesome religious doctrines or rulings to misinterpretation and cultural bias. This perspective is seen most prominently in recent attempts to portray Islam as "a religion of peace." Such proponents reject any reference to religious violence as a misreading of the Qur'anic text and/or the Islamic tradition by Muslims and non-Muslims alike.

Promoting a "PR version" of Islam is not without its merits, especially given the contemporary political climate in countries across Europe and North America. In the United States alone, since September 11, 2001, several laws have been enacted that strip American Muslims of civil liberties and cast them as de facto suspect citizens. More recently, at least twenty-one of the fifty states in the U.S. have introduced bills to ban "Sharia," which some Americans claim is menacingly "creeping" into their legislative systems. In some cases, the "creeping Sharia" movement seeks to criminalize common Muslim ritual practices, such as the daily prayers. Concurrently, the American Muslim community is confronted with revelations that the New York Police Department conducted surveillance of Muslim student associations across several New York university campuses, even joining students on a whitewater rafting trip. Similar trends have developed in Europe as well. France and Belgium have each passed anti-*burqa* legislation that prohibits Muslim female citizens from wearing the face veil (*niqāb*). Swiss citizens voted favorably in a referendum to ban the building of new minarets in Switzerland. And in anti-Muslim protests organized from Orange County, California to Vancouver, British Columbia, neo-conservative and Christian fundamentalists portray Muslim men as "wife-beaters." In the face of these and similar developments, it is understandable that some Muslims worry about the image of Islam and are anxious that if Muslims discuss less savory aspects of their tradition, these will be manipulated by anti-Muslim forces to demonize and dehumanize Islam and Muslims globally.

While I appreciate these concerns and have personally struggled with them over the years, I believe that shying away from difficult discussions and controversial topics in order to "save" Islam and Muslims from unwarranted criticism is a bad idea. People can and always have found ways to misrepresent and misread intellectual projects. Using the work of a scholar to promote causes from which said scholar would recoil is not a new phenomenon. Once intellectual property is created and disseminated, it is in the hands of a large and varied public, who are free to use it for multiple, sometimes conflicting, purposes. While scholars have a responsibility to produce intellectually rigorous and honest work, they do not bear responsibility for the numerous, unanticipated ways in which their work is received and utilized. At some point, those who misconstrue and misrepresent scholarly works must bear responsibility for their own actions. In the case of wife-beating in particular, Islamophobes have regularly used Qur'anic verses and prophetic reports to argue that Islam is inherently misogynistic and violent. I hardly think that this book will change their attitude or give them ammunition that they do not already have. Furthermore, it is problematic to cater one's research agenda and intellectual interests around anxieties about the actions and rhetoric of small-minded bigots, who search for any and all excuses to smear Islam, presenting it as a uniquely flat, one-dimensional religion.

Interestingly, the PR image of a presentable and palatable Islam also reproduces a sterile, sanitized, monotonous, and dehumanized version of Islam, one that depicts a complex religion only in shades of black and white. This vision does a disservice to the study of Islam since it lacks the complex, varied, rich, and vibrant picture of Muslim experiences of Islam. In order to maintain its monolithic image, PR Islam quells exciting, intellectually rigorous, and stimulating conversations about Islam within Muslim communities, resulting in stagnant communities that cannot honestly and openly discuss their ethical and moral concerns. The reactionary nature of PR Islam, borne out of fear, is part of the problem; it is not helpful to Muslim communities negotiating multiple identities in the contemporary world. It stifles the dialogue, internal criticism, and self-reflective thinking that is necessary for individuals and communities to grow and thrive.

And so, to be clear, I am writing this book to showcase the complexity and diversity of the Muslim intellectual tradition on the topic of marital violence. The fact that the pre-colonial Islamic tradition was patriarchal is unsurprising given the socio-historical context of that time. Nor was patriarchy unique to Islam; adherents of all living religious traditions rooted in patriarchal social and historical contexts struggle to find ways to reconcile gender-egalitarian values with religious traditions that primarily served the interests of men.[18] However, as each religious tradition is different, its adherents must do so in their own distinctive way, speaking to their various communities and navigating multiple allegiances. This book investigates (a) the ways Muslims engage the Qur'anic text, (b) the

[18] See, eg, Rachel Adler, *Engendering Judaism: An Inclusive Theology and Ethics* (England: Jewish Publication Society, 1998); Rachel Adler, *Standing Again at Sinai: Judaism from a Feminist Perspective* (New York: HarperCollins, 1991); Phyllis Trible, *Texts of Terror: Literary-Feminist Readings of Biblical Narratives* (Philadelphia: Fortress Press, 1984).

patriarchal Islamic tradition, and (c) how a community of believers who value gender-egalitarianism addresses a concrete ethical problem—domestic violence. It is my hope that this book will bring to light the very real and high stakes involved in creating a performative relationship with the Islamic tradition and the Qur'anic text. This journey is painful and difficult, but we will see that it is one that Muslim scholars and activists are beginning to embark on with great courage, vision, and grit.

Part I

Historical Roots of a Contemporary Debate

Life can only be understood backwards; but it must be lived forwards.

Soren Kierkegaard

1

The Multiple Contexts of Q. 4:34

The treatment of women often takes center stage in debates about Islam's compatibility with modernity. In these debates, the Qur'anic text is often used as a starting point by those on either side to argue for fundamentally egalitarian or patriarchal visions of Islam. Within the Qur'anic text, one verse in particular has received a great deal of attention. This is the thirty-fourth verse of Chapter 4, the latter commonly known as the "Chapter of Women." This verse has been used by conservative Muslims to defend patriarchal institutions and by right-wing Islamophobes to argue that Islam and modernity are irreconcilable because of the verse's indubitable patriarchy. This same verse has been a thorn in the side of Muslim feminists and modernists, who must find a way to reconcile the verse with a vision of a gender-egalitarian Islam that presents Islam and modernity as fully compatible.

The debates surrounding this verse, hereafter referred to as Q. 4:34, have had tangible legal impact. In the last five years, Q. 4:34 was used in a German court by Judge Datz-Winter to deny a German-Moroccan woman an expedited divorce from her physically abusive husband. The judge reasoned that the Qur'ān, specifically Q. 4:34, permitted her husband to hit his wife.[1] In a different vein, this same verse was used by a judge in the United Arab Emirates (UAE) to fine a man £85 for hitting his wife and daughter so hard as to damage the wife's lower lip and teeth and bruise the daughter's hand and knee. The defendant claimed that he had legitimately exercised his right of physical discipline, enshrined in "the *sharīʿa*" through Q. 4:34. The judge countered that the defendant abused the right to engage in physical discipline given to him in Q. 4:34 by exceeding the boundaries of acceptable discipline.[2] These cases illustrate that the

[1] Mark Lander, "Germany Cites Koran in Rejecting Divorce," *The New York Times* (Mar. 22, 2007). See also Ayesha S. Chaudhry, "The Problems of Conscience and Hermeneutics: A Few Contemporary Approaches," *Comparative Islamic Studies*, 2(2) (2006) 158.

[2] Dan Newling, "Men ALLOWED to Beat Their Wives and Young Children (As Long as They Don't Leave Any Marks), Rules UAE Court," *Daily Mail* (UK) (Oct. 18, 2010).

relevance of Q. 4:34 extends beyond its implications for various theoretical positions to affect the lived experiences of women around the world.

In order to fully appreciate the modern discourse on Q. 4:34 it is important first to understand the historical backdrop for such conversations. Since the "Islamic tradition" plays a major role in how modern Muslim scholars situate themselves when advocating various positions, we must begin with the treatment of Q. 4:34 in pre-colonial exegetical and legal texts. In this chapter, we will study three contexts that influenced pre-colonial readings of Q. 4:34. These contexts are textual, historical, and cosmological. The textual context, meaning the verses surrounding Q. 4:34, influences its potential plain-sense meanings. The seventh-century historical context within which Q. 4:34 was revealed, whether real or imagined, illustrates how exegetes and jurists understood this verse affecting the early Muslim community. Disclosing the idealized cosmology of pre-colonial exegetes and jurists will help us to understand the expectations that pre-colonial scholars had of the Qur'anic text and how these assumptions determined the meanings they derived from Q. 4:34. Together, these three contexts provide a framework for understanding the breadth and boundaries of ethical and legal discussions about the right of husbands physically to discipline wives in the pre-colonial Islamic tradition.

TEXTUAL CONTEXT: THE POLYSEMIC POTENTIAL OF Q. 4:34

A robust study of pre-colonial exegetical interpretations of Q. 4:34 requires careful consideration of the surrounding Qur'anic text in which Q. 4:34 is situated. In this section, we will engage in an exegesis exercise of Q. 4:32–5 in order to assess the interpretive potential of these verses. Taking into account the subjectivity of a reader of the Qur'ān, as committed to either a patriarchal or egalitarian idealized cosmology, we will explore the polysemic nature of these texts.[3] Verses 32–5 of Chapter 4 read:

> *4:32* And in no wise covet those things in which Allah hath bestowed His gifts (*faḍḍala*) more freely on some of you than on others: to men is allotted what they earn, and to women what they earn: but ask Allah of His bounty: for Allah hath full knowledge of all things.

[3] In doing so, I draw inspiration from Asma Barlas's work, *"Believing Women" in Islam: Unreading Patriarchal Interpretations of the Qur'an* (Austin: University of Texas Press, 2002).

4:33 To (benefit) everyone We have appointed sharers and heirs to property left by parents and relatives. To those also to whom your right hand was pledged give their due portion: For truly Allah is Witness to all things.

4:34 Men are the protectors and maintainers (*qawwāmūn*) of women, because Allah has given (*faḍḍala*) the one more (strength) than the other, and because they support them from their means. Therefore the righteous women (*ṣāliḥāt*) are devoutly obedient (*qānitāt*), and guard in (the husband's) absence what Allah would have them guard. As to those women on whose part ye fear disloyalty and ill-conduct (*nushūz*), admonish them (first), (next) refuse to share their beds, (and last) beat them (lightly) (*wa-ḍribūhunna*); but if they return to obedience (*aṭaʿnakum*), seek not against them means (of annoyance): for Allah is Most High, Great (above you all).

4:35 If ye fear a breach between them twain, appoint (two) arbiters, one from his family, and the other from hers; if they wish for peace, Allah will cause their reconciliation: for Allah hath full knowledge, and is acquainted with all things.[4]

Q. 4:34 appears in a set of verses that address legal issues such as inheritance, domestic conflict, and court adjudication of marital conflict—all set in the structure of a gendered cosmology. Verse 32 begins with a general prohibition against coveting God's preference (*faḍḍala*) of "some over others." This prohibition is potentially directed at all believers regardless of gender, since the masculine plural referring to those who should not covet can grammatically include both men and women. The opening prohibition also clarifies that the advantage (*faḍl*) that some people have over others is not a result of chance or effort but is rather a function of God's preference, which is conferred by God to some as opposed to others. The substance of God's preference is unspecified and could be interpreted as referring to wealth, social status, children, etc.

However, the next phrase of Q. 4:32 introduces gender and earning as differentiating categories, even though it speaks of them in the language of parity. Men and women are differentiated from each other, perhaps even preferred by God one over another, based on their gender and further based on what they earn. Still, the text assures the reader that both men and women will be rewarded in proportion to what they earn. Will the earnings of men and women be apportioned regardless of gender? The text answers this question affirmatively and negatively. One could argue that earnings and rewards are differentiated based on gender, since the

[4] In general, I rely on Abdullah Yusuf Ali's translations of the Qur'ān. There are many translations of the Qur'ān, each with its own merits. I have found that, despite its sometimes stilted writing, Yusuf Ali's translation is faithful to both the tone and content of the original Arabic. Abdullah Yusuf Ali, *The Meaning of the Holy Quran* (Beltsville: Amana Publications, 1997) Q. 4:32–5.

text brings up gender as a significant disparity. After all, why bring up this distinction if it is not relevant to earnings and reward? Alternatively, it can be reasoned that this verse states that men and women will be rewarded regardless of gender, since it ends with an exhortation to "ask God for his favor (*faḍl*)," indicating that God's favor might be earned, that it is not ontologically related to either gender but can be gained based on merit.

The second, more egalitarian reading of verse 32 can be strengthened through a reading of verse 33 that emphasizes the inheritance right of wives, who are described as those to whom your "right hand has pledged" (*alladhīna ʿaqadat aymānukum*).[5] This verse exhorts believers to ensure that they apportion part of their inheritance to their wives. If one were worried about how this might affect the inheritance rights of children and other relatives, the verse reminds the reader that God himself has appointed shares for children and relatives. Read in this light, this verse can be seen as projecting an ethos of social equality by raising the status of wives, dedicating a portion of inheritance to them, even if this portion is unspecified. However, this verse also offers a reading that sanctions a social hierarchy that would be in line with a gender-differentiated reading of verse 32. If verse 32 offers a hierarchy based on gender differentiation, verse 33 confirms this hierarchy by leaving the exact portion of wives' inheritance unspecified. Taken in the context of inheritance laws outlined in the Qurʾān, which allot different portions to each gender, this verse can be seen as ratifying unequal legal gender norms.[6]

Q.4:34, appearing in this succession of verses, clarifies the questions of gender differentiation raised by verse 32. The plain-sense meaning of verse 34 supports a patriarchal reading of verse 32. In contrast to the previous two verses, verse 34 offers little potential for a gender-egalitarian reading. This verse begins with a general, unrestricted declaration or descriptive statement that men are *qawwāmūn* over women. The term *qawwāmūn* has various shades of meaning that connote authority, dominance, or maintenance.[7] Any reading of this declaration creates a hierarchy wherein

[5] Several Qurʾān translators interpret this phrase as "husbands and wives." See, eg, M.A.S. Haleem, *The Qurʾān: A New Translation* (Oxford: Oxford University Press, 2004) and Muhammad Asad, *The Message of the Qurʾan* (London: E.J. Brill, 1980).

[6] "They ask thee for a legal decision. Say: Allah directs (thus) about those who leave no descendants or ascendants as heirs. If it is a man that dies, leaving a sister but no child, she shall have half the inheritance: If (such a deceased was) a woman, who left no child, her brother takes her inheritance: If there are two sisters, they shall have two-thirds of the inheritance (between them): if there are brothers and sisters, (they share), the male having twice the share of the female. Thus doth Allah make clear to you (His law), lest ye err. And Allah hath knowledge of all things." Q. 4:176, Yusuf Ali (n 4).

[7] In the modern period, scholars have offered more egalitarian interpretations of the word *qawwāmūn* to mean that men are the "caretakers" of women, arguing that this role is not necessarily hierarchal. For more on this, see Chapter 4.

men rank above women in one way or another. The verse explains that men are *qawwāmūn* over women for two reasons: one, depending on how one interprets the verb *faḍḍala*, because God has preferred or caused some to excel over others; and two, because they (masculine plural) spend of their wealth. The reference to preference (*faḍl*) here should bring to mind verse 32, which mentioned God's preference of "some over others." In verse 34, men's economic advantage over women appears to be a function of divine preference. A patriarchal reading of this passage might be mitigated by highlighting the descriptive nature of this statement and confining this description to seventh-century Arabia, which is the immediate social and historical context of this verse. That is to say, that this text can be understood as a description of how things were in the past, not a prescription for how they should be in the present or future. This is a compelling reading for modern readers not least because in the contemporary period the ubiquity of male economic privilege is increasingly challenged by women entering the workforce.

The compelling descriptive reading of the first half of verse 34 is compromised, however, by the second half of the verse, which describes two types of women: righteous (*ṣaliḥāt*) and rebellious (*nāshizāt*). Righteous women are those who are obedient (*qānitāt*) and guard in their husbands' absence "what God would have them guard."[8] As with the previous verses, this description of righteous women can be read in both patriarchal and egalitarian fashions. An egalitarian reading takes the statement about men's social rank over women as descriptive of seventh-century Arabian society, and righteous women are described as obedient to God rather than to their husbands. Furthermore, the ability of women to manage themselves and handle their affairs in their husbands' absence, without male supervision, can be read as progressive for the seventh-century Arabian context. Read from a patriarchal perspective, a husband's financial dominance is interpreted as a function of divine ordinance, and women are religiously obligated to obey their husbands in return for financial maintenance and to guard themselves and their husband's property in his absence.

The next part of the verse limits the interpretive possibilities of Q. 4:34 significantly, since it grants husbands disciplinary privileges over their wives and can be further read as permitting them to hit their wives. This passage reads, "As for those women on whose part you fear *nushūz*, admonish them, abandon them in their beds and hit them." *Nushūz* can be and has been interpreted to have various meanings—including disobedience, sexual refusal, lewdness, or adultery—but regardless

[8] This is a literal translation of the Arabic.

of the definition of *nushūz*, it is difficult to find a gender-egalitarian interpretation of husbandly disciplinary privilege that justifies the right of husbands to hit wives in any circumstance. The problem with this plain-sense meaning of Q. 4:34 has led some modern Muslim scholars to translate *wa-ḍribūhunna*, which literally means "hit them", non-violently, such that it means "to walk away from" or "to have sex with" wives.[9] The very difficulty inherent in incorporating Q. 4:34 into a gender-egalitarian vision of Islam serves as the driving force of this study. The manner in which Muslims address this verse says a great deal about how they relate to and understand the Qur'anic text as part of a larger idealized cosmology.

The way one interprets Q. 4:34 has ramifications for the interpretations of other Qur'anic verses. For instance, the following verse, Q. 4:35, can also be read as both egalitarian and patriarchal. On the one hand, Q. 4:35 can be read assuming a patriarchal cosmology, in that it provides a husband with directives for proceeding when the prescriptions in Q. 4:34 fail to rectify a wife's behavior. If a marital conflict cannot be resolved internally—through admonishment, abandonment, and hitting—then a process for adjudication should be orchestrated in which each party must have representation. In the end, if the parties desire reconciliation, then God will help them to be harmonious. On the other hand, Q. 4:35 can be read assuming an egalitarian cosmology if it is seen as a stand-in or replacement for verse 34. When faced with marital conflict, rather than trying to address the issue internally through punitive measures, it is best to find external adjudication. The provision for both parties, the husband and the wife, to have representation in this adjudication may well have been revolutionary in the patriarchal society of seventh-century Arabia, where women had little or no legal rights. Q. 4:35 may be read as taking power away from the husband by according wives legal representation and can thus be seen as promoting a gender-egalitarian marital structure.

This exercise of thinking of Q. 4:32–5 alternately in a patriarchal and egalitarian light demonstrates that scriptural texts have numerous plain-sense meanings that are deeply influenced by the cosmology and expectations of their readers. Despite the potential for such verses to have multiple plain-sense meanings, living Muslim communities place these interpretations in conversation with the pre-colonial Islamic tradition. As mentioned in the Introduction, a mythologized and abstract pre-colonial

[9] See Ahmed Ali, 'Al-Qur'an: A Contemporary Translation,' <http://www.studyquran.org/Ahmed_Ali_Al_Quran.pdf> (last accessed Dec. 17, 2012); Laleh Bakhtiar, *The Sublime Quran* (Chicago: Kazi Publications, 2007) xxv–xxvi; and Edip Yuksel, Layth Saleh al-Shaiban, and Edip Yuksel, *Qur'an: A Reformist Translation* (USA: Brainbow Press, 2007) 20. The various modern translations of *wa-ḍribūhunna* as other than "hit them" are explored further in Chapter 4.

"Islamic tradition" plays a significant role in the present discussions of Q. 4:34. So what did pre-colonial Muslim scholars think about this verse? Did they endorse the right of husbands to hit their wives, or did they restrict this right? Were there ethical conversations surrounding this verse, and if so, what did they look like? What was the legal import of this verse? Was it used by judges to keep women in abusive relationships? Was this verse used as a proof text for the right of husbands to hit wives? In answering these questions, we must begin with pre-colonial Qur'ān commentaries, which provide a useful framework for interpreting legal verses in the Qur'ān.

HISTORICAL CONTEXT: *ASBĀB AL-NUZŪL* OF Q. 4:34

Qur'ān commentaries form a genre of traditional Islamic literature known as *tafsīr*, which is devoted to the interpretation or exegesis of the Qur'ān. In their commentaries, exegetes used various methodological tools to explicate the meaning(s) of Qur'anic verses. Norman Calder offers three defining characteristics of the *tafsīr* genre: analysis of Qur'anic texts in short units; incorporation of polyvalent readings of the Qur'anic text; and the connection of Qur'anic text to other Islamic disciplines. The majority of exegetical works offered interpretations of the entire Qur'ān through close analysis of each verse. Exegetes often meticulously addressed the meanings of individual verses through close analysis of their constitutive words, particles, pronouns, and prepositions.[10]

When offering interpretations of the Qur'anic text, they cited authoritative sources to buttress their interpretations.[11] Prophetic practice (*sunna*), as related through prophetic reports (*ḥadīth*) and prophetic biography (*qiṣaṣ al-anbiyā* and *sīrat al-nabī*), figured prominently as authoritative sources. Reports from Companions of the Prophet (*ṣaḥāba*), the generations of the Successors, and the opinions of previous scholars from various Islamic disciplines also carried authority. The Qur'ān's polyvalence was a defining feature of *tafsīr*, illustrating the genre's ability to embrace multiple perspectives.[12] Exegetes connected the Qur'anic text

[10] Norman Calder, "*Tafsīr* from Ṭabarī to Ibn Kathīr: Problems in the Description of a Genre, Illustrated with Reference to the Story of Abraham" in G.R. Hawting and Abdul-Kader A. Shareef (eds.), *Approaches to the Qur'ān* (London: Routledge, 1993) 101.

[11] Calder (n 10) 103.

[12] Calder (n 10) 103–4. According to Calder, polyvalent readings embody the theological message that the Muslim community and the Qur'anic text "could contain multiplicity while remaining one community and one text."

to other Islamic disciplines such as *ḥadīth*, philology (*lugha*), speculative theology (*kalām*), jurisprudence (*fiqh*), and mysticism (*taṣawwuf*), among others.[13] This frequent reference within *tafsīr* to other Islamic disciplines is important to consider for our study because it helps us to determine whether particular interpretations of Q. 4:34 emerge from linguistic analysis of the text itself or from the perceived relation between the Qur'anic text and some extra-Qur'anic framework of religious understanding.

Exegetes therefore had many tools at their disposal when explaining the meaning(s) of specific verses in the Qur'ān. The tools they relied upon depended not only on the stylistic approach of particular exegetes but also on the category that they accorded the specific verse being interpreted. Many exegetes divided verses of the Qur'ān into the broad categories of legal and non-legal verses. This division is heuristically helpful for the present study, despite the fact that legal verses form a minority of verses in the Qur'ān. The overwhelming majority of verses are not legal but rather narrative, allegorical, exhortative, etc. However, because of its imperative nature and content, exegetes treated Q. 4:34 as a legal verse.

Identifying the *sabab al-nuzūl*, or "occasion of revelation," of a verse was an essential tool that pre-colonial exegetes used to help to explain the meaning of a verse. The Qur'ān is considered to have been revealed over a period of roughly twenty-two years, which span Muḥammad's prophetic career. The historic moment of revelation of a given verse is significant for the interpretative enterprise because the Qur'anic text is believed to have been responsive to specific historical circumstances. *Asbāb al-nuzūl* (sing. *sabab al-nuzūl*), literally "causes" or "occasions of revelation," is the science devoted to identifying the specific historical moment that prompted the revelation of a particular verse. This literature records the historical context into which particular verses were revealed and identifies the problems to which a verse might have been responding.[14] Hence, *asbāb*

[13] Calder (n 10) 106.

[14] According to Rippin, *sabab al-nuzūl* literature also attempts to answer the question of "why" the Qur'ān mentioned a specific issue, or it can "adduce the *jāhilī* 'foil', where things were worse off before Islam." Pre-colonial exegetes were limited by the *asbāb al-nuzūl* reports that were circulated in the second Hijri/eighth C.E. century, and these reports did not address all Qur'anic verses. Thus, exegetes could not always rely on *asbāb al-nuzūl* reports to provide stories/events surrounding legal verses. For those verses that did have corresponding *asbāb al-nuzūl*, Wansbrough explains that the reports describe two types of revelation: "spontaneous" (*ibtidā'an*) and "in response to an event or query" (*'aqiba wāqi'a aw su'āl*). For the purpose of exegesis, *sabab al-nuzūl* that describes the second type of revelation sheds light on the legal thrust and scope of the verse. Andrew Rippin, "The Function of *Asbāb al-Nuzūl* in Qur'anic Exegesis," *Bulletin of Oriental and African Studies*, 51(1) (1988) 1–20 and John Wansbrough, *Quranic Studies: Sources and Methods of Scriptural Interpretation*, London Oriental Series 31 (Oxford: Oxford University Press, 1977) 178.

al-nuzūl are historical reports that claim to describe a moment in the life of the early Muslim community that occasioned the revelation of a particular verse to Muḥammad.[15] Given their importance, many *asbāb al-nuzūl* gained currency amongst exegetes and legal scholars despite being related through weak or non-existent chains of transmission (*isnād*).[16]

Q. 4:34 has two documented *asbāb al-nuzūl* (hereafter referred to as "*sabab*"), which helped exegetes to explain the verse's legal import. The two reports connect Q. 4:34 to two other Qur'anic verses, namely Q. 4:32 and Q. 20:114,[17] and each *sabab* emphasizes different aspects of the verse. The less frequently invoked *sabab* was narrated by Umm Salama, a wife of Muḥammad. She narrated that the women in Medina asked Muḥammad why men had preference (*faḍl*) over women in inheritance. This query prompted the revelation of two verses; Q. 4:32 was the primary revelation, followed by Q. 4:34.[18] According to this *sabab*, Q. 4:32 affirmed the privilege of men over women in matters such as inheritance and also admonished women to be content with their reduced share of inheritance.[19] Read through the lens of this *sabab* and Q. 4:32, Q. 4:34 can be seen to emphasize the preference of men over women and to explain the consequences of this

15 Saleh considers *asbāb al-nuzūl* a separate sub-category in his discussion of "fictive narratives." Walid Saleh, *The Formation of the Classical Tafsīr Tradition* (Boston: Brill, 2004) 162.

16 In the case of Q. 4:34, for example, the preeminent *sabab al-nuzūl* is *mursal* in its transmission, meaning that its chain of transmission could not be traced back to the generation of the Companions of Muḥammad. Rather, this *sabab al-nuzūl* is traced to the generation of the Successors, specifically in this case al-Ḥasan al-Baṣrī (d. 110/728). Moreover, this report cannot be found in any major *ḥadīth* collection. Nevertheless, exegetes used this report in the exegesis of Q. 4:34 without any mention of its authenticity. It may be that the historical context and Prophetic sanction provided by this *sabab* was so hermeneutically fruitful that to exclude this context would be to forfeit an exegetical tool that was at the same time historically accessible and authoritative. Regardless of the motivation behind exegetes' according an authoritative status to otherwise dubious reports, *asbāb al-nuzūl* played a central role in Qur'anic exegesis in general and Q. 4:34 in particular.

17 Many of the commentaries considered in this survey referred to the occasion of revelation of Q. 4:34 explicitly and used it to define the discourse surrounding this verse. For a list of exegetes who considered the *asbāb al-nuzūl* for Q. 4:34, see Appendix 1 (A1).

18 Marín argues that Q. 4:34 was revealed in response to the *sabab* of Umm Salama. However, I argue that according to exegetical literature, Q. 4:32 was revealed in direct response to the Umm Salama *sabab*, and Q. 4:34 was connected to this *sabab* through the mediation of Q. 4:32. Manuela Marín, "Disciplining Wives: A Historical Reading of Qur'ān 4:34," *Studia Islamica* (2003) 11–12. Exegetes such as Muḥammad ibn Yūsuf Abū Ḥayyān, *Tafsīr al-baḥr al-muḥīṭ* (Beirut: Dār al-Kutub al-ʿIlmiyya, 1993) 3:248; Ibn ʿAṭiyya (A1) 2:44–6; al-Qurṭubī (A1) 5:162; and al-Rāzī (A1) 4:70 directly connected Q. 4:34 with the proclamation in Q. 4:32.

19 Al-Qurṭubī explained that women benefitted from men's priority in inheritance. Although men received double the inheritance of women, they were required to pay the dower (*mahr*) and maintenance (*nafaqa*). Al-Qurṭubī (A1) 5:162. Al-Rāzī also saw the partiality towards men in inheritance law as being balanced out through their obligation to pay the dower and maintenance. Of course, men also benefitted from these financial obligations, since they, in turn, compelled wives to obey their husbands. Al-Rāzī (A1) 4:70. See also Ibn ʿAṭiyya (A1) 2:44–6 and Abū Ḥayyān (n 18) 3:248.

preference in marriage. In this context, the primary point of Q. 4:34 is to instantiate a gendered hierarchy, in which, secondarily, husbands have a disciplinary prerogative in marriage.

In contrast, according to the second, more frequently cited *sabab*, Q. 4:34 was revealed for the purpose of granting husbands disciplinary power over their wives.[20] Here, the gendered hierarchy was not the stand-alone point of the verse but rather justified the disciplinary privilege of husbands. As such, this *sabab* significantly narrowed the interpretive possibilities of Q. 4:34. The basic narrative of the second *sabab* is that a prominent Medinan woman was struck by her husband. The woman in this story was most commonly identified as Ḥabība bt. Zayd b. Abī Zuhayr, wife of one of the leaders of the Anṣār named Sa'ad b. Rabī' b. 'Amr.[21] When describing Sa'ad's physical assault on Ḥabība, exegetes generally used the verbs *laṭama* (to slap, to strike) or *ṣakka* (to strike, to beat) interchangeably with *ḍaraba* (to strike) and *jaraḥa* (to wound, to injure).[22] After being assaulted and, in some cases, carrying the impressions of the slap on her face, Ḥabība—or her father or brother—took her case to Muḥammad. He ruled in her favor and offered her retribution.[23] Q. 4:34 was revealed at this moment, forcing Muḥammad to revoke his verdict.[24]

[20] This *sabab* was cited by all exegetes who considered the cause for the revelation of Q. 4:34 in their exegesis, including exegetes who cited the *sabab* regarding Umm Salama's question. See A1 for a list of exegetes in this study who considered this *sabab*.

[21] She was also referred to as 'Umayra (and in some cases Ḥabība) bt. Muḥammad b. Muslim, wife of As'ad or Sa'id b. al-Rabī'. She was least commonly denoted as Jamīla bt. 'Abdallah b. 'Ubayy, wife of Qays b. Shimās. For the sake of clarity, I will refer to the couple as Ḥabība and Sa'ad, given the predominance of those names in the narrations. A good number of exegetes mentioned that the couple was from the Anṣār and that Sa'ad belonged to the leaders (*nuqabā'*) of the Anṣār. The fact that the couple was Medinan may have been significant because Medinan women were characterized as less submissive, more uppity than Meccan woman. In the next chapter we will encounter a *ḥadīth* in which 'Umar sought permission to hit wives in response to the altered behavior of Meccan women, who, after mingling with the women of Medina (Anṣārī women), became ill-behaved in 'Umar's eyes. Eg, see al-Khāzin (A1) 1:374 and al-Rāzī (A1) 4:72.

[22] Al-Jaṣṣāṣ related a version of the *sabab* wherein Ḥabība complained to Muḥammad after her husband wounded her (*jaraḥa*). By making Q. 4:34 about wounding rather than slapping, al-Jaṣṣāṣ was able to argue more persuasively for the legal position that there was to be no retaliation between a husband and wife except in the case of loss of life. Al-Jaṣṣāṣ (A1) 2:188. See also Mujāhid (A1) 274 and al-Ṣan'ānī (A1) 1:157.

[23] The various words used to describe Ḥabība's behavior were that she complained (*tashkī*), appealed for assistance against (*tasta'dī*), or sought (*taltamis/ṭalabat*) retaliation against her husband. In various narrations of this report, either Ḥabība represented herself to Muḥammad (al-Māwardī (A1) 1:481 and al-Qurṭubī (A1) 5:162) or she was accompanied by her father (al-Qurṭubī (A1) 5:161 and al-Ṭabarī (A1) 4:60–1) or an unnamed man from her tribe (Ibn Kathīr (A1) 1:601 and al-Suyūṭī (A1) 2:151).

[24] Perhaps because Muḥammad realized after his ruling that Ḥabība was married to an Anṣārī chieftain, who must have been influential in Medina. Mohamed Mahmoud, "To Beat or Not to Beat: On the Exegetical Dilemmas over Qur'ān Q. 4:34," *Journal of the American Oriental Society*, 126(4) (2006) 539.

It is unclear whether this *sabab* caused the exegesis of Q. 4:34 to be focused on physically disciplining wives or whether, as Andrew Rippin might argue, this *sabab* provided a means for exegetes to make Q. 4:34 about the physical discipline of wives, *ex post facto*.[25] This *sabab* allowed exegetes to make marital discipline their central hermeneutic concern. Physical discipline was a fundamental husbandly privilege, and for pre-colonial exegetes, Q. 4:34 encapsulated the legal dictum that wives could not claim compensation from their husbands for physical assault, barring extreme circumstances such as death or serious injury. This *sabab* raised theological and legal questions for pre-colonial exegetes. Why did Saʿad hit Ḥabība? How hard did he hit her? Had Muḥammad already ruled in Ḥabība's favor when Q. 4:34 was revealed? How did Muḥammad respond to his ruling being revoked? Was Muḥammad out of line for making a decision in Ḥabība's case without consulting God? And what was the legal implication of this *sabab* coupled with the verse? Were wives entitled to retribution from their husbands on grounds of physical violence? As these questions illustrate, pre-colonial exegetes did not overtly display compassion or concern for Ḥabība's fate—they did not wonder about her situation after this story, whether she was returned to her physically abusive husband, or how she felt about the revelation of Q. 4:34.

Interestingly, many exegetes did not speculate as to why Saʿad struck Ḥabība. They might have found this detail irrelevant because they were less concerned with the marital conflict and more interested in the theological and legal issues following Muḥammad's adjudication of this case. The fact that Muḥammad did not ask Ḥabība why Saʿad hit her could indicate that he considered the act of hitting one's wife worthy of retribution, regardless of the husband's reasoning. Those exegetes who did speculate about Saʿad's reasoning offered vague vignettes that avoided placing blame. For instance, Abū Jaʿfar Muḥammad ibn Jarīr al-Ṭabarī (d. 311/923) related from al-Suddī that the domestic violence occurred after "words" (*kalāmun*) were exchanged between the couple.[26] However, some exegetes added a detail in their narration of this *sabab* that changed Ḥabība's status from a victim of domestic violence seeking justice to a disobedient wife who complained to Muḥammad when she was justifiably disciplined by her husband.[27] Plotting the marital drama prior to the

[25] Rippin argues that in addition to playing a "central role in supporting exegetical decisions regarding the establishment of context," *asbāb al-nuzūl* was often used by exegetes to support their interpretation of a verse *"ex post facto"* with a *sabab*. Rippin (n 14) 8.

[26] Al-Ṭabarī (A1) 4:61.

[27] Al-Thaʿlabī (d. 427/1035) (A1) 3:302. Marín also notes this shift in blame from the abusive husband to rebellious wife, but she places it later, with al-Wāḥidī (b. 468/1075). See Marín (n 18) 10. Most exegetes after al-Thaʿlabī mentioned Ḥabība's disobedience (*nushūz*) as the cause for Saʿad striking her. However, it is difficult to make a chronological argument

revelation of Q. 4:34, their narrations stated that Saʿad struck Ḥabība as a result of her general disobedience or recalcitrance (*nushūz*) or specifically because she was disobedient in bed. For example, Abū al-Suʿūd wrote that Ḥabība "committed *nushūz* against her husband, so he slapped her."[28]

The contrasting prophetic and divine responses to Ḥabība's case raised a theological problem for exegetes. How could Muḥammad be so out of sync with his Lord that he would offer a legal opinion that was the exact opposite as that intended by God? Would he not have intuitively anticipated a ruling somewhat closer to the divine intention? Appending Ḥabība's *nushūz* to the narrative of this *sabab* served to soften this tension: had Muḥammad known that Saʿad had hit Ḥabība for her *nushūz*, he might have issued the correct ruling. By transforming Saʿad's slap from an act of unwarranted abuse to physical discipline,[29] God's revocation of Muḥammad's ruling could be seen as explaining Ḥabība's marital circumstances rather than censuring Muḥammad. Some exegetes further ameliorated prophetic and divine tension by creating a space that had Muḥammad and God responding to different aspects of Ḥabība's case. If exegetes could demonstrate that Ḥabība had been seriously injured by her husband, that would explain why Muḥammad was moved to rule in her favor. To this end, some exegetes included versions of the story in which Ḥabība complained to Muḥammad

here, since earlier scholars also mentioned that Ḥabība was slapped because of her *nushūz*. Eg, see al-Jaṣṣāṣ (A1) 2:188.

[28] Abū al-Suʿūd (A1) 1:339. See also al-Ḥaddād (A1) 2:249 and al-Shirbīnī (A1) 1:346. In the exegetical work attributed—falsely, according to Rippin—to al-Fīrūzābādī (d. 817/1414), the narration reads that Ḥabība was slapped specifically because of "her disobedience in bed." See Rippin, "Ibn Abbās and Criteria for Dating Early *Tafsīr* Texts," *Jerusalem Studies in Arabic and Islam*, 18 (1994) 38–83 and al-Fīrūzābādī (A1) 92. Al-Rāzī offered a particularly interesting version of this *sabab* in which he held that Ḥabība did in fact commit *nushūz*, but only after her husband had already slapped her, narrating that Saʿad "slapped her so she rose (*nashazat*) from his bed, went to the Prophet and relayed her complaint." In his narration, the impression of the slap remained on her face when she complained to the Prophet. It is possible though unlikely that al-Rāzī was simply using the term "*nashazat*" literally, to say that Ḥabība raised herself from her husband's bed to complain to Muḥammad. However, this explanation is implausible given that this *sabab* appears in the exegesis of Q. 4:34, where the *nushūz* of wives is deserving of punitive measures. Rather, it is more likely that al-Rāzī considered Ḥabība's *nushūz* to be either that she rose from her husband's bed at all—thereby refusing herself to him sexually—or that she complained against her husband to the Prophet. Since al-Rāzī gave her a very solid case for her complaint (that the impression of the slap remained on her face), he probably did not think that her complaint was an act of *nushūz*. That leaves the explanation that he thought her rising from her husband's bed, even after being slapped, was a form of *nushūz*. This is nevertheless confounding because whereas Q. 4:34 speaks of physical discipline as a result of wifely *nushūz*, al-Rāzī's narration of this story removes the possibility that Saʿad's slap was disciplinary because it precedes Ḥabība's *nushūz*. Al-Rāzī (A1) 4:70.

[29] Of course, any type of physical discipline of a wife is abusive, but pre-modern exegetes differentiated between abuse and physical discipline. They understood abuse as unwarranted physical violence against a wife, whereas physical discipline included what they considered "justifiable" violence.

while still carrying the impressions of Saʿad's strike on her face.[30] The fact that Saʿad had hit his wife on her face and left an impression was compelling evidence against him, given that prophetic reports (*aḥādīth*) forbade both of these actions explicitly. This scenario actually rehabilitates the believers' trust in Muḥammad's judgment, casting his decision-making as operating on a higher moral level. Still, although this incriminating evidence against Saʿad made Muḥammad's initial reaction appear justifiable, it ultimately enhanced rather than resolved the tension between the prophetic and divine judgments. According to this version of the *sabab*, Q. 4:34 granted husbands legal permission to hit their wives in the face hard enough to leave marks, overriding Muḥammad's own moral disapproval of such behavior.

Pre-colonial exegetes dealt with the tensions created by the disparate prophetic and divine rulings through either acceptance or denial. Some exegetes conceded that Muḥammad should have sought guidance before making his decision. In this case, he was reprimanded by God for acting out of turn, prompting the revelation of both Q. 20:114 and Q. 4:34.[31] Q. 20:114 instructed Muḥammad to await revelations instead of making hasty decisions, and Q. 4:34 offered a ruling on the case at hand. Alternatively, some exegetes denied any tension altogether by citing alternate versions of the *sabab* in which Muḥammad had not actually ruled in Ḥabība's favor but was in the process of making a decision when Q. 4:34 was revealed.[32]

In the first case, exegetical accounts of this *sabab* illustrate that Muḥammad's initial adjudication was strongly in Ḥabība's favor. Although the exact retribution offered to Ḥabība is not mentioned, we can speculate that it was monetary or maybe even physical.[33] Muḥammad's decision was so definitive that Ḥabība left the scene to seek retaliation against her husband[34]—in some accounts with her father in tow. In other narrations,

[30] In one narration, Ḥabība is reported to have said to Muḥammad, "My husband struck my face (*inna zawjī laṭama wajhī*)." Al-Qurṭubī (A1) 5:162. Ibn Kathīr and al-Suyūṭī mentioned a variant of this *sabab*, wherein an unnamed man from the Anṣār complained on behalf of an unnamed woman that she was struck in the face by her husband and that the impression of the strike remained on her face (*innahū ḍarabahā fa-aththara fī wajhihā*). Ibn Kathīr (A1) 1:601 and al-Suyūṭī (A1) 2:151. See also al-Rāzī (A1) 4:70.

[31] "High above all is Allah, the King, the Truth! Be not in haste with the Qur'an before its revelation to thee is completed, but say 'O my Lord! Increase me in knowledge.'" Yusuf Ali (n 4) Q. 20:114. See, eg, Ibn al-ʿArabī (A1) 1:493; Ibn ʿAṭiyya (A1) 2:47; and al-Suyūṭī (A1) 2:151.

[32] According to one variation of this *sabab*, Muḥammad "wanted" to grant the woman retaliation, but then Q. 4:34 was revealed. Al-Suyūṭī (A1) 2:151.

[33] The Mālikī Ibn ʿAṭiyya mentioned that Muḥammad ordered Ḥabība to "strike/slap him [ie her husband] as he had struck/slapped her." Ibn ʿAṭiyya (A1) 2:47. Al-Ḥaddād also considered the nature of the retaliation to be physical, as he understood *qiṣāṣ* to include "a slap (*laṭama*), a skull fracture (*shajja*) or a wound (*jirāḥ*)." Al-Ḥaddād (A1) 2:249.

[34] Exegetes who mentioned that Ḥabība and her father set out to seek retaliation from Saʿad include al-Thaʿlabī (A1) 3:302; al-Baghawī (A1) 5:422; al-Qurṭubī (A1) 5:161; al-Khāzin (A1) 1:374; and al-Ḥaddād (A1) 2:247–51.

she returned with her husband to Muḥammad, in order to retaliate in Muḥammad's presence.[35] Coming on the heels of such strong prophetic support, the revelation of Q. 4:34—nullifying Muḥammad's initial ruling—is especially jarring.

Furthermore, the dramatic nature of the scene created by first the prophetic ruling and then the contrary divine ruling put Muḥammad in an embarrassing situation. After having already ruled in Ḥabība's favor, he was forced to revoke his ruling and backtrack from his personal intuitive approach to the case. In narrations wherein Ḥabība and her father had already set out to seek retaliation from Saʿad, they are called back and told about the revelation of Q. 4:34.[36] As a consequence, the retaliation was lifted (*rufiʿa al-qiṣāṣ*),[37] the first command was abolished/annulled (*naqiḍa al-ḥukm al-awwal*),[38] or Ḥabība returned without retaliation (*fa-rajaʿat bi-ghayr al-qiṣāṣ*).[39] In the narration wherein Ḥabība returned with her husband for retaliation, they were both sent away without any retaliation for Ḥabība. Once Q. 4:34 was revealed, Ḥabība was left without a recourse that Muḥammad initially judged her as deserving.

The Ḥanafī jurist Aḥmad b. ʿAlī al-Jaṣṣāṣ (d. 370/981) believed that Muḥammad was wrong to have decided in Ḥabība's favor and as a result was reprimanded through the Qurʾanic text. Al-Jaṣṣāṣ recorded two variations of the *sabab* concerning Ḥabība, which in his opinion made two complementary legal points. In the first *sabab*, an unnamed woman was wounded (*jaraḥa*) by her husband. Her brother brought her case to Muḥammad, who ruled in her favor. However, his verdict was revoked by the revelation of Q. 4:34. For al-Jaṣṣāṣ, the legal principle that can be derived from this *sabab* is that there was no retaliation (*qiṣāṣ*) in marriage except in the case of death. A husband was permitted to hit his wife such that he wounded her, without any liability, unless he killed her.[40]

[35] Exegetes who mentioned that Ḥabība returned with her husband to receive retaliation from him in Muḥammad's presence and that they were sent away after the revelation of Q. 4:34 include Muqātil (A1) 1:235 and al-Ṭabarī (A1) 4:60–1. This account does not surface in later commentaries.

[36] Eg, al-Thaʿlabī (n 27) 3:302; Ibn ʿAṭiyya (A1) 2:47; al-Qurṭubī (A1) 5:161; and al-Khāzin (A1) 1:374.

[37] This wording is used by, among others, Abū Ḥayyān (n 18) 3:248; al-Baghawī (A1) 5:422; al-Khāzin (A1) 1:374; al-Rāzī (A1) 4:70; al-Shirbīnī (A1) 1:346; al-Thaʿlabī (A1) 3:302; and al-Zamakhsharī (A1) 1:495.

[38] Ibn ʿAṭiyya (A1) 2:47 and al-Qurṭubī (A1) 5:161.

[39] Narrations with this wording include those by Ibn Abī Ḥātim (A1) 3:940; Ibn Kathīr (A1) 1:601; and al-Suyūṭī (A1) 2:151.

[40] Al-Jaṣṣāṣ (A1) 2:188. This is a good example of an intersection between exegesis and Islamic law. Al-Jaṣṣāṣ' position here is representative of the Ḥanafī school's position on the right of husbands to discipline wives. See also al-Ṣanʿānī (A1) 1:157.

In al-Jaṣṣāṣ' second *sabab*, a woman approached Muḥammad for help against her abusive husband. When Muḥammad ruled in her favor, he was reprimanded for making his decision before waiting to hear from God.[41] This chastisement is captured in Q. 20:114, which reads:

> Be not in haste with the Qur'ān before its revelation to thee is completed, but say "O my Lord! Increase me in knowledge."[42]

Following this reprimand, Q. 4:34 was revealed, granting husbands the right to physically discipline their wives, and Muḥammad was forced to revoke his earlier decision.[43] This story clarified the appropriate prophetic etiquette required from Muḥammad when faced with legal decisions. For al-Jaṣṣāṣ, this *sabab* also established the legal injunction that husbands were permitted to hit their wives if the latter committed *nushūz*.[44]

[41] For evolving Ḥanafī positions on God reprimanding Muḥammad, see Rumee Ahmed, "The Ethics of Prophetic Disobedience: Q. 8:67 at the Crossroads of the Islamic Sciences," *Journal of Religious Ethics*, 39(3) (2011) 440–57.

[42] Yusuf Ali (n 4) Q. 20:114.

[43] For a list of exegetes who mentioned this account, see Appendix 2 (A2). Al-Qurṭubī wrote that after the revelation of Q. 20:114, Muḥammad waited (*amsaka*) for the revelation of Q. 4:34. Al-Qurṭubī (A1) 5:162. See Abū Ḥayyān (n 18) 3:248; Ibn al-ʿArabī (A1) 1:493; Ibn ʿAṭiyya (A1) 2:47; Ibn Kathīr (A1) 1:601; al-Khāzin (A1) 1:374; al-Māwardī (A1) 1:481; al-Suyūṭī (A1) 2:151; and al-Ṭabarī (A1) 4:60. See also Karen Bauer, "Room For Interpretation: Qur'ānic Exegesis and Gender," Ph.D. diss. (Princeton University, 2008) 115.

[44] The full text of al-Jaṣṣāṣ reads: "Chapter Concerning the Obedience of a Wife to her Husband. God said, 'Men are *qawwāmūn* over women, with that in which God has preferred some over others and because they spend of their wealth.' It is related from Yūnus [b. ʿUbayd (d. 140/757)] from al-Ḥasan [al-Baṣrī, d. 110/728] that a man wounded/injured (*jaraḥa*) his wife, so her brother complained to the Prophet of God, peace and blessings be upon him, who called for retaliation (*al-qiṣāṣ*). Then God revealed 'Men are *qawwāmūn* over women' (Q. 4:34) and the Prophet said, 'we wanted one thing and God wanted another' (*aradnā amran wa-arāda allāhu ghayrahu*). It is related from Jarīr b. Ḥāzim from al-Ḥasan that a man slapped (*laṭama*) his wife, so she sought help against him (*fa-staʿadat ʿalayhi*) from the Prophet of God, who said, 'you owe retaliation' (*ʿalaykum al-qiṣāṣ*). Then God revealed, 'Do not make haste with the Qur'ān before its revelation is made complete to you' (Q. 20:114). Then God revealed, 'men are *qawwāmūn* over women' (Q. 4:34). Abū Bakr [al-Jaṣṣāṣ] argued that the first (narration) proves that there is no retaliation (*qiṣāṣ*) between [married] men and women except in the case when a life [is taken]. Similarly, [Ibn Shihāb] al-Zuhrī (d. 124/741–2) narrated that the second *ḥadīth* is proof that it was permissible for the husband to slap his wife because she had committed *nushūz* against him. God has permitted (*abāḥa*) hitting her (*ḍarbahā*) when she commits *nushūz*, by saying, 'concerning those women from whom you fear *nushūz*, admonish them, abandon them in their beds and hit them.' If it is said: if hitting her was permitted because of her *nushūz*, then why did the Prophet impose retaliation? It should be said to such a person that the Prophet said this before the revelation of this verse which permitted hitting with the presence of *nushūz*, because God revealed, 'men are *qawwāmūn* over women' to 'beat them' afterward. As a result, husbands were no longer liable in any matter [concerning their wives] after the revelation of this verse. The statement 'Men are *qawwāmūn* over women' implies that men are in authority [over wives] concerning their moral education (*taʾdīb*), management (*tadbīr*), protection (*ḥafẓ*) and maintenance (*ṣiyāna*). [This is] because God has preferred men over women in their intellect (*ʿaql*) and opinion (*raʾy*), and God has charged them with spending their wealth [on wives]." Al-Jaṣṣāṣ (A1) 2:188.

Those exegetes who denied any contradiction between Muḥammad and God in Ḥabība's case offered versions of the *sabab* with a slightly altered timeline. According to these exegetes, Q. 4:34 was revealed before Muḥammad had made up his mind. In a narration mentioned by al-Ṭabarī, Q. 4:34 was revealed during the process of adjudication, before Muḥammad had issued a verdict in Ḥabība's favor (*fa-baynā hum ka-dhālik nazalat āya*).[45] Fakhr al-Dīn al-Rāzī (d. 606/1209) mentioned an account which stated that although Muḥammad's instinctive response was in favor of Ḥabība, he chose to wait for divine guidance before making his decision, saying "Be patient until I decide [on the matter]." By delaying Muḥammad's decision, exegetes were able to remove any conflict between prophetic and divine opinion. In this case, rather than overturning his decision, the revelation of Q. 4:34 simply aided Muḥammad's decision-making process.

In the scenario in which Q. 4:34 did in fact revoke Muḥammad's ruling in Ḥabība's case, one cannot help but wonder how Muḥammad felt about being contradicted by God. In some narrations, Muḥammad responded disagreeably or with resignation, saying "I desired one thing and God desired another" (*aradtu amran wa-arāda allāhu ghayrahu*).[46] Some commentators were comfortable with the disagreement between prophetic and divine judgments captured in this wording. Others tried to diminish the disparity by adding the phrase "and what God desired is better" to the end of Muḥammad's comment. Putting this phrase in Muḥammad's mouth was important, as it gave him space to acknowledge that although he might have initially disagreed with the divine ruling in Ḥabība's case, he now deferred to the divine command by accepting its superiority. In this version of the narration, Muḥammad's comments read, "I desired one thing, God desired one thing, and what God desired is better" (*aradtu amran wa-arāda allāhu amran wa-l-ladhī arāda allāhu khayr*).[47]

[45] Al-Ṭabarī and al-Huwwārī also mentioned a narration in which Muḥammad "wanted" to rule in her favor, but then Q. 4:34 was revealed. Al-Huwwārī (A1) 1:377 and al-Ṭabarī (A1) 4:60. See also al-Suyūṭī (A1) 2:151.

[46] Or "I desired one thing and God desired *one thing*" (*aradtu amran wa-arāda allāhu amran*). Exegetes who mentioned the narration in which Muḥammad said "I wanted one thing and God wanted another" without following it with "And what God wanted was better" include Abū Ḥayyān (n 18) 3:248; Ibn ʿAṭiyya (A1) 2:47 (mentioned both variations); Ibn Kathīr (A1) 1:601; al-Jaṣṣāṣ (A1) 2:188; al-Qurṭubī (A1) 5:161; al-Suyūṭī (A1) 2:151 (although he mentioned four variations of this *sabab*, he never included "and what God wanted was better" in any of them); and al-Ṭabarī (A1) 4:61.

[47] Exegetes who mentioned the *sabab* with "And what God wanted was better" include Abū al-Suʿūd (A1) 1:339; al-Baghawī (A1) 5:422; al-Bayḍāwī (A2) 1:85; al-Ḥaddād (A1) 2:249; Ibn ʿAṭiyya (A1) 2:47 (mentioned both variations); al-Khāzin (A1) 1:374; Mujāhid (A1) 274; Muqātil (A1) 1:235; al-Qurṭubī (A1) 5:161; al-Rāzī (A1) 4:70; al-Shirbīnī (A1) 1:346; al-Thaʿlabī (A1) 3:302; and al-Zamakhsharī (A1) 1:497.

Muḥammad's verbal approval of God's correction helped to smooth over any perceived uneasiness about his reception of Q. 4:34.

The basic legal point Ḥabība's *sabab* offered to exegetes was that Q. 4:34 provided divine justification of a husband's right to physically discipline his wife. Exegetes argued that—barring death and severe injuries—wives could not claim retaliation (*qiṣāṣ*) for abuse from their husbands.[48] This legal maxim is unsettling even for its seventh-century Arabian context, in which Medinan women—who previously might have expected external recourse to retaliation if they suffered violence at the hands of their husbands—were now denied retaliation.[49] After all, why did Ḥabība take her case to Muḥammad? She must have been hopeful of a positive outcome, either because of existing pre-Islamic tribal laws that she expected Muḥammad to apply to her case, or because of her perception—or the perception of those who produced this anecdote—that Muḥammad was receptive to the grievances of women. If she was relying on Muḥammad's application of pre-Islamic tribal laws, then this *sabab* illustrates that women lost recourse to these laws in a post-Qur'anic context, where the power of husbands over their wives increased. If, however, she was counting on Muḥammad's compassion despite her contextual realities, then Medinan women might not have lost status but rather failed to experience an anticipated gain in status.

The various ways in which Ḥabība's story is discussed in Qur'ān commentaries demonstrate that pre-colonial exegetes were not concerned for Ḥabība's welfare, security, or protection. Rather, they were primarily concerned with the theological issues raised by the discrepancy between Muḥammad's response to Ḥabība's plight and the divine decree captured in Q. 4:34. Their unease with this *sabab* lay not in ethical concern for Ḥabība but with Muḥammad's alleged discontent with Q. 4:34. Interpretive energy was devoted to relieving tensions between the prophetic judgment for retaliation and divine revocation of this decision.[50] In this maneuvering, the hierarchy of men over women in Q. 4:34 was used to justify the right of husbands to physically discipline their wives.

[48] We will investigate the legal limits on hitting wives in the four Sunnī schools of jurisprudence in Chapter 3.

[49] Marín argues that Muḥammad's judgment for retaliation was based on pre-Islamic tribal law. Marín (n 18) 9.

[50] For more discussion on relieving the tension between the prophetic judgment for retaliation and divine revocation of this decision, especially from a Shāfiʿī perspective, see Kecia Ali, "The Best of You Will Not Strike," *Comparative Islamic Studies*, 2(2) (2006) 143–55.

HIERARCHY AND JUSTIFICATION: THE EXEGETES' COSMOLOGICAL FRAME

According to pre-colonial exegetes, the rank of men over women, which is mentioned in the beginning of Q. 4:34, justified the disciplinary privileges of husbands. The asymmetrical marital relationship constructed by these scholars had theological underpinnings and was part of a larger idealized cosmology. This cosmology was comprised of a divinely mandated, gendered social ordering in which God stood atop a hierarchy, followed by husbands, and then wives. The relationship of wives to God and, by extension, to their own salvation was mediated through their husbands. Wives pleased God by pleasing their husbands and incurred His wrath when they angered their husbands. Q. 4:34 played a crucial role in defending and explicating this cosmology.

Several recent studies have demonstrated that despite the variance on technical points, pre-colonial exegetes offered consistently and monolithically patriarchal interpretations of Q. 4:34. This is especially significant since the pre-colonial scholars under study belonged to different cultural, social, and historical contexts, separated by centuries, geographic regions, and juridical and theological schools.[51] This uniformity in the face of varying contexts can be accounted for by a cosmology that was both reflective of the socio-historical patriarchal milieu and the scholars' own idealized cosmologies. That is to say, the cosmology gleaned from the study of exegetical works on Q. 4:34 reveals an ideal, divinely ordered universe, describing the world as it *should* be rather than how it was. In this idealized cosmology, the relationship between God and man parallels the relationship between husbands and wives.[52] Pre-colonial exegetes defended these parallel hierarchies by interpreting Q. 4:34 to make three related normative claims: first, God preferred (*faḍḍala*) men over women; second, men ought to be in a position of authority (*qawwāmūn*) over women; and, third, the superiority and authority of men over women resulted in husbandly financial and disciplinary privileges and responsibilities. These claims were interwoven into the commentaries of Q. 4:34, and we will now turn our attention to uncovering the idealized cosmology of pre-colonial exegetes through their exegesis of this verse.

[51] Marín (n 18) 5–40; Bauer (n 43) 24, 177, and 188; Ayesha S. Chaudhry, "Wife-Beating in the Pre-Modern Islamic Tradition: An Inter-Disciplinary Study of *Ḥadīth*, Qur'anic Exegesis and Islamic Jurisprudence," Ph.D. diss. (New York University, 2009) chs 2 and 3; Hadia Mubarak, "Breaking the Interpretive Monopoly: A Re-Examination of Verse 4:34," *Hawwa*, 2(3) (2005) 261–89; and Sa'diyya Shaikh, "Exegetical Violence," *Journal for Islamic Studies*, 17 (1997) 49–73.

[52] Shaikh (n 51) 61–3.

"Men are *qawwāmūn* over women..."

Qiwāma can have several meanings, all of which are hierarchical. Exegetes interpreted this word to mean that husbands are the managers, directors, guardians, protectors, in charge of and responsible for their wives;[53] some analogized the relationship to a shepherd tending his flock.[54] Others compared the marital relationship to that of a ruler and his subject, depicting the station of a husband as commander/chief (*amīr*),[55] head/chieftain (*ra'īs*),[56] judge/sovereign (*ḥākim*),[57] and legal guardian (*nāfidh al-amr*).[58] Husbands were in authority over (*musallaṭūn*)[59] and overseers (*muṣayṭir*) of their wives,[60] and their marital responsibilities included restraining their wives (*wa-l-akhdh ʿalā aydīhinna*).[61] Such descriptions of husbandly rank in marriage conferred upon husbands financial, social, religious, and moral authority over wives.

The *qiwāma* of husbands over wives was often discussed using the same language that exegetes used to describe the lordship of God over humans. Prophetic reports used by pre-colonial exegetes to support husbands' lordship over their wives effectively turned husbands into shadow deities. A commonly cited prophetic tradition (*ḥadīth*) reported Muḥammad as saying, "If I had commanded anyone to prostrate to another, I would have

[53] Some forms of the root word *qawwāmūn*, such as *qā'im*, *yaqūmu*, *qayyim*, or the word *qawwāmūn* itself, were used to describe the relationship between husbands and wives. For a list of exegetes who used some form of *q-w-m* to describe the relationship between husbands and wives, see Appendix 2 (A2).

[54] "*al-wilāya ʿalā al-riʿāya*." Exegetes who used this phrase to describe the relationship between husbands and wives include Abū al-Suʿūd (A1) 1:338; al-Bayḍāwī (A2) 1:85; al-Nasafī (A2) 1:354; al-Shirbīnī (A1) 1:346; and al-Zamakhsharī (A1) 1:495.

[55] Exegetes who used *amīr* to describe a husband's relationship with his wife include Ibn Abī Ḥātim (A1) 3:939; Ibn ʿAṭiyya (A1) 2:47; Ibn Kathīr (A1) 1:601; al-Rāzī (A1) 4:70; al-Suyūṭī (A1) 2:151; al-Ṭabarī (A1) 4:60; and al-Thaʿālibī (A2) 2:229.

[56] Eg, Ibn Kathīr (A1) 1:601.

[57] Eg, Ibn Kathīr (A1) 1:601. Al-Naḥḥās has described husbands as the arbitrators (*ḥukkām*) and commanders (*umarā'*) over their wives. Aḥmad ibn Muḥammad al-Naḥḥās, *Maʿānī al-Qur'ān al-karīm* (Mecca: Jāmiʿat Umm al-Qurā, 1988) 2:77. See also al-Qurṭubī (A1) 5:161.

[58] Eg, al-Ṭabarī (A1) 4:59 and al-Rāzī (A1) 4:70.

[59] For a list of exegetes who used *musallaṭūn* to describe a husband's relationship with his wife, see Appendix 3 (A3).

[60] Eg, al-Nasafī (n 54) 1:354 and al-Zamakhsharī (A1) 1:495. See use of *muṣayṭir* in "Thou art not at all a warder over them." Yusuf Ali (n 4) Q. 88:22.

[61] I take this translation of the expression from Bauer, who makes a compelling case for this translation. She writes, "Another expression used by the exegetes is *akhdh ʿalā yadayhā*: this (in masculine form) is described by Ibn Manẓūr as 'preventing someone from doing something which he wishes to do, as if you grabbed (*amsakta*) hold of his hand.' I translate this expression as 'restraining them.'" For more on this, see Bauer (n 43) 22. For a list of exegetes who used this expression, see Appendix 4 (A4).

commanded a wife to prostrate herself to her husband."[62] Another version of this report emphasized the unlimited rights of husbands over their wives. It reads:

> The rights of a husband over his wife [are so great] that if he were covered with a wound oozing blood and puss, she would be incapable of fulfilling his rights even if she were to lick his wound with her tongue. If it was appropriate for one person (*bashar*) to prostrate himself to another, I would have ordered the wife to prostrate herself to her husband when he enters upon her, as a result of God's preference for him (*faḍḍalahu*) over her.[63]

Portraying husbands as demi-gods over wives, with unlimited rights, raises the red flag of associating partners with God (*shirk*), which is considered to be Islam's only unforgivable sin. However, pre-colonial exegetes did not see this characterization as contradicting the undivided unity of God (*tawḥīd*) because the marital hierarchy was ordained by God and sanctioned by scripture.

As shadow deities, husbands mediated their wives' relationship with God.[64] They were responsible for ensuring that their wives fulfilled their obligatory religious duties, such as praying five times a day and fasting in the month of Ramaḍan. They could also prohibit their wives from undertaking

[62] "*law amartu aḥadan an yasjuda li-aḥadin la-amartu al-marʾa an tasjuda li-zawjihā.*" Exegetes who mentioned this *ḥadīth* include al-Baghawī (A1) 5:422; al-Ḥaddād (A1) 2:249, and 251; Ibn al-ʿArabī (A1) 1:496; al-Jaṣṣāṣ, (A1) 1:376; Ibn Kathīr (A1) 1:602; al-Khāzin (A1) 1:374, and 179–81; al-Qurṭubī (A1) 5:164. Another variation of this *ḥadīth* reads, "If I had commanded anyone to prostrate to another, I would have commanded a wife to prostrate herself to her husband due to the greatness of his rights over her. A woman will not taste the sweetness of faith (*ḥalāwat al-īmān*) unless she fulfills her husbands rights, even if he asks her of herself [sexually] while she is on the back of a camel." Al-Suyūṭī (A1) 2:154.

[63] This *ḥadīth* did not appear as commonly as the previous one but was present in exegetical discourse as early as al-Jaṣṣāṣ in the fourth/tenth century and was cited by al-Suyūṭī as late as the tenth/sixteenth century. Al-Jaṣṣāṣ (A1) 1:376 and al-Suyūṭī (A1) 2:152. Khaled Abou El Fadl has analyzed the prostration *ḥadīth*, the one of the wife licking her husband's wounds, as well as the *ḥadīth* in which angels curse a woman who refuses her husband. He has argued that the symbolic power of these reports disqualify them from being authentic positions of Muḥammad. He writes, "We observe a similar association between husbands and the symbols of Divinity in the submission tradition. A whole host of angels in the Heavens are aggrieved by the frustration of a man's libido. This only raises the question: what is it about a man's sexual urges that make them so fundamental to the pleasure of the Heavens? Does this include all forms of pleasure by men or only sexual? What if a man's pleasure consists of being breastfed by his wife or of being tied up and whipped by his wife? Do the Heavens maintain their enthusiasm for the male libido regardless of its many forms and regardless of the emotional consequences upon the wife?... [These traditions] contradict the theological notion of the undivided supremacy of God and God's Will." Khaled Abou El Fadl, *Speaking in God's Name: Islamic Law, Authority and Women* (Oxford: Oneworld, 2001) 214. I argue that exegetes were precisely making this point by citing these traditions—they did not see the traditions as contradicting the "undivided" unity of God, because the marital hierarchy was divinely ordained.

[64] A *ḥadīth* that connected women's marital behavior to their salvation was cited by al-Suyūṭī. According to this report, "Muḥammad said, 'The sinful (*fussāq*) are the people of

supererogatory devotional activities, such as fasting and praying outside the prescribed times. If wives wanted to engage in such supererogatory acts, they were first required to obtain their husbands' permission.[65] In addition to regulating the devotional life of their wives, husbands were also responsible for restricting their wives' access to public spaces.[66] This setup prevented wives from having a direct, unmediated connection with God; rather, a chain of command was instituted wherein women related to God through their husbands. If a wife undertook supererogatory devotional acts despite her husband's disapproval, such acts counted against her in the divine reckoning.[67] Thus, wives could not please God if they displeased their husbands, and exegetes explicitly stated that a wife's salvific fate depended on whether she could please her husband.[68] To this end, al-Jaṣṣāṣ cited a *ḥadīth* in which Muḥammad advised a woman to carefully consider where she stood with regard to her husband, for he was her "paradise or fire."[69] It

the Fire.' They asked, 'O Prophet of God, who are the sinners?' He replied, 'Women (*al-nisā'*).' A man said, 'O Prophet of God, are they not our mothers, our sisters and our wives?' He replied, 'Indeed, but when they are given (something) they are ungrateful and when they are tested, they are impatient.' " Al-Suyūṭī (A1) 2:152. See also Muḥammad Ibn Isma'īl al-Bukhārī, *Summarized Saḥīḥ al-Bukhārī* (trans. Muhammad Mohsin Khan) (Riyadh: Maktaba Dār al-Salām, 1994) 57.

[65] Exegetes used *aḥādīth* to argue that wives should restrain themselves from undertaking any independent action without their husbands' permission, including devotional activities such as fasting and mundane activities such as leaving the house. Eg, see al-Jaṣṣāṣ (A1) 1:375. Along these lines, Mahmoud writes, "The logic of the situation is as follows: inasmuch as obedience to the Prophet is ultimately obedience to God, a wife's obedience to her husband, in what does not violate the law, is ultimately obedience to God . . . This leads to the conclusion that outside the strictly prescribed domain of what is obligatory, a wife anxious to draw near to God by means of supererogatory works stands to incur the wrath of God if her husband does not approve of what she does." Mahmoud (n 24) 540. See also Bauer (n 43) 75.

[66] Al-Qurṭubī believed that a husband was required to "manage (*yaqūmu bi-tadbīrihā*) and discipline (*ta'dībihā*) [his wife], keep her in the house and prohibit her from emerging/being prominent. And it is her [responsibility] to obey him, accept his command, as long as he does not command disobedience to [God]. The rationale for this is [men's] superiority, maintenance, rationality, strength as seen in the command to fight *jihād*, [that they have been given] inheritance, and the [responsibility to] command right and forbid wrong." Al-Qurṭubī (A1) 5:162. Restricting a wife's social mobility was a central responsibility of husbands, who were supposed to keep their wives at home and forbid them from going out. Eg, see al-Jaṣṣāṣ (A1) 2:188. See also Bauer (n 43) 135.

[67] Kecia Ali, "Women, Gender, *Ta'a* (Obedience), and *Nushūz* (Disobedience) in Islamic Discourses" in Suad Joseph (ed.), *Encyclopedia of Women and Islamic Cultures* (Leiden: Brill, 2003) 310.

[68] Al-Suyūṭī cited a few *aḥādīth* to this end. In one, Muḥammad stated that the prayer of three people was rejected; the runaway slave, the wife who displeased (*sakhiṭa*) her husband, and the drunkard. In another, a woman whose husband is pleased with her enters paradise. In a third, Muḥammad says that the prayer of a disobedient woman is rejected. Al-Suyūṭī (A1) 2:153–4.

[69] *"fa-innamā huwa jannatuk aw nāruk."* Al-Jaṣṣāṣ (A1) 1:376. See also al-Suyūṭī (A1) 2:152.

is clear, then, that wives attained paradise by pleasing their husbands and evoked divine wrath by angering them.[70]

"Because God has preferred some over others…"

Pre-colonial exegetes generally understood a husband's authority (*qiwāma*) over his wife to be anchored in God's preference (*faḍl*) of men over women. The verbal form *faḍḍala*, as it appears in the Qur'anic text, can be interpreted to mean several things, such as to prefer, to like better, to give preference, etc. There is ambiguity in the text on the issue of *faḍl* in Q. 4:34 regarding who exactly God has preferred or caused to excel. "God has preferred some over others" does not specify the identity of "some" and "others," yet pre-colonial exegetes interpreted the "some" and "others" as men and women respectively.[71] This interpretive move was strengthened by the *sabab* concerning Umm Salama, wherein she questioned men's advantage over women in inheritance distribution. The response she received in this *sabab* was that men had preference (*faḍl*) in inheritance because God had preferred them (*faḍḍala*) over women and that she should not covet men's status.[72]

Pre-colonial exegetes offered several religious, legal, cultural, and philosophical reasons for male superiority. It was standard to argue that men were better than women due to primary and secondary reasons.[73] The primary reasons were that men had superior strength (*quwwa*) and intellect (*ʿaql*).[74] The secondary reasons included various circumstantial

[70] Two *aḥādīth* were used to argue this point. One reads, "A woman who dies enters paradise if her husband is pleased with her." Al-Khāzin (A1) 1:375. Abou El Fadl finds the notion of "God's pleasure contingent on the husband's pleasure" problematic. Abou El Fadl (n 63) 219. The second *ḥadīth* reads, "The Prophet of God, peace and blessings be upon him said: When a woman prays five times, fasts for a month, protects her chastity and obeys her husband, it will be said to her, 'Enter paradise from any of the Doors of Paradise that you desire.' " Ibn Kathīr (A1) 1:602.

[71] Pre-colonial exegetes were unambiguous about the fact that men had authority (*qawwāmūn*) over women because "God had preferred [men] over [women] (*bi-sabab tafḍīl allāhi taʿālā iyyāhum ʿalayhinna*)." Abū al-Suʿūd (A1) 1:338. Bauer discusses the rationale offered for the arguments of the superiority of men over women in the pre-colonial exegetical tradition. Bauer (n 43) ch 3.

[72] Many exegetes mentioned men's greater share of inheritance (*mirāth*) as an indication of their preferred status (*faḍīla*) with God. For one example, see Abū al-Suʿūd (A1) 1:338. Ibn Kathīr wrote explicitly that "men are better than women (*al-rijāl khairun min al-nisāʾ*)." Ibn Kathīr (A1) 1:602.

[73] Al-Shirbīnī divided these characteristics into essential (*wahbī*) and acquired (*kasbī*). Al-Shirbīnī (A1) 1:346. Mahmoud describes al-Zamakhsharī's argument for the superiority of men over women as divided into the categories of "intrinsic," "social," and "*sharīʿa*-based" prerogatives. Mahmoud (n 24) 540–1. See also Abū al-Suʿūd (A1) 1:339; al-Bayḍāwī (A2) 1:85; and al-Jaṣṣāṣ (A1) 2:188.

[74] Abū Bakr Ibn al-ʿArabī cited the *ḥadīth* in which Muḥammad is alleged to have said that women are deficient (*nāqiṣ*) in their intellect and their religion. Based on women's

arguments.[75] For instance, religious arguments for male superiority were that prophets and scholars were ubiquitously male, and men were charged with the duty of prophethood, commanding good and forbidding evil,[76] delivering Friday sermons, and leading Friday prayers.[77] Legal grounds for male advantage were that the testimony of two women was the equivalent of one man, men could marry up to four wives while women were restricted to one husband, men had exclusive rights to divorce, greater shares in inheritance, and they could hit and abandon their wives.[78] Political and cultural proofs for male superiority were that men could attain political and military leadership and that men were better at horsemanship and archery.[79] Some, such as Maḥmūd ibn ʿUmar al-Zamakhsharī (d. 538/1143),

intellectual deficiencies—a view derived from this *ḥadīth*—he argued that the testimony of one man was equivalent to that of two women, because women are prone to forgetfulness and therefore must remind each other. This is a good example of *ḥadīth* providing exegesis of Qur'anic verses, in this case of Q. 2:282. Ibn al-ʿArabī (A1) 1:494. Bauer discusses this *ḥadīth* in her dissertation (n 43) 124. See also Abū al-Suʿūd (A1) 1:339; al-Baghawī (A1) 5:422; al-Bayḍāwī (A2) 1:85; Ibrāhīm ibn ʿUmar al-Biqāʿī, *Naẓm al-durar fī tanāsub al-āyāt wa-l-suwar* (Hyderabad: Maṭbaʿat Majlis Dāʾirat al-Maʿārif al-ʿUthmāniyya, 1972) 5:269; al-Ḥaddād (A1) 2:249; Ibn ʿAṭiyya (A1) 2:47; Ibn al-Jawzī (A1) 2:74; al-Māwardī (A1) 1:480; and al-Nasafī (n 54) 1:355.

75 Some exegetes, such as al-Qurṭubī and al-Samarqandī, offered philosophical explanations for the superiority of men over women, arguing that men's nature was "hot," while women were "cold"; men were strong, women were weak. Al-Qurṭubī (A1) 5:162 and al-Samarqandī (A1) 1:351. See also Bauer (n 43) 127–8.

76 The decision of exegetes to entrust men exclusively with the responsibility to "order good and forbid evil" is in contrast to Q. 9:71, which makes it a point to make this a shared responsibility of men and women. Q. 9:71 reads: "The Believers, men and women, are protectors one of another: they enjoin what is just and forbid what is evil: they observe regular prayers, practice regular charity, and obey Allah and His Messenger. On them will Allah pour His mercy: for Allah is Exalted in power, Wise." Yusuf Ali (n 4) Q. 9:71.

77 See, eg, Abū al-Suʿūd (A1) 1:338–9; al-Baghawī (A1) 5:422; al-Bayḍāwī (A2) 1:85; al-Biqāʿī (n 74) 5:269; al-Ḥaddād (A1) 2:249–50; Ibn al-ʿArabī (A1) 1:494; Ibn al-Jawzī (A1) 2:75; Ibn Kathīr (A1) 1:602; al-Shirbīnī (A1) 1:346; al-Thaʿlabī (A1) 3:302; and al-Wāḥidī (A4) 1:263. That the ability to participate in Friday prayers and the right to deliver the Friday sermon are cited as indications of men's *faḍīla* over women is significant for the modern debates regarding authority in the Muslim community; it bolsters the claim of Muslim women who argue that being barred from addressing the congregation during the Friday prayers represents a lack of female authority and leadership of women in the community.

78 Al-Baghawī (A1) 5:422; al-Bayḍāwī (A2) 1:85; Ibn Abī Zamanīn (A1) 1:367; Ibn al-ʿArabī (A1) 1:494; al-Huwwārī (A1) 1:377; Al-Jaṣṣāṣ (A1) 1:376; al-Khāzin (A1) 1:374; al-Nasafī (n 54) 1:355; and al-Wāḥidī (A4) 1:263. Some exegetes also mentioned men's greater share in booty as proof of their superiority over women. Eg, see Ibn al-Jawzī (A1) 2:74 and al-Fīrūzābādī (A1) 91.

79 See, eg, al-Baghawī (A1) 5:422, (A2) 1:85; al-Biqāʿī (n 74) 5:269; al-Khāzin (A1) 1:375; al-Rāzī (A1) 4:70; and al-Zamakhsharī (A1) 1:495. The fact that ʿĀʾisha, Muḥammad's youngest wife, was a military leader when she led an army against ʿAlī in the Battle of the Camel was not considered here by exegetes. Al-Thaʿlabī cited Q. 33:33 to discourage women from being prominent in the public sphere. Although this verse addresses Muḥammad's wives specifically, al-Thaʿlabī considered it to apply to believing women in general. Al-Thaʿlabī (A1) 3:302. Al-Biqāʿī contrasted the Qur'anic command for women to "stay in [their] homes" (Q. 33:33) with the command to men to "Go forth, lightly and heavily armed" (Q. 9:41).

even argued that men were better than women because they could grow beards and wear turbans.[80]

The fact that exegetes drew on such an extensive array of sources in order to justify the superiority of men over women in the exegesis of Q. 4:34 indicates that the marital relationship was part of a larger complex structure of interconnected social, political, and juridical relationships.[81] All of these relationships were informed by theology, and an imbalance in one realm had ramifications for all other spheres. Hence, a gendered marital structure underpinned and was reinforced by a gendered hierarchy in the religious, political, cultural, and social realms.[82]

Al-Biqāʿī (n 74) 5:269. Q. 33:33 reads: "And stay quietly in your houses, and make not a dazzling display, like that of the former Times of Ignorance; and establish regular Prayer, and give regular Charity; and obey Allah and His Messenger. And Allah only wishes to remove all abomination from you, ye members of the Family, and to make you pure and spotless." Yusuf Ali (n 4) Q. 33:33. Q. 9:41 reads: "Go ye forth, (whether equipped) lightly or heavily, and strive and struggle, with your goods and your persons in the Cause of Allah. That is best for you if ye (but knew)." Yusuf Ali (n 4) Q. 9:41.

[80] The full text of al-Zamakhsharī reads: "Men are the commanders [of right] and forbidders [of wrong], just as a governor guides the people . . . The 'some' in some of them refers to all men and all women. It means that men are only in control over women because God made some of them superior, and those are men, to others, and they are women. This is proof that governance is only merited by superiority (*tafḍīl*), not by dominance, an overbearing attitude, or subjugation. Concerning the superiority of men over women, the exegetes mention rationality (*ʿaql*), good judgment (*ḥazm*), determination, strength, writing—for the majority of men—horsemanship, archery, that men are prophets, learned (*ʿulamāʾ*), have the duties of the greater and lesser imamate, *jihād*, call to prayer, the Friday sermon, seclusion in the mosque (*iʿtikāf*), saying the prayers during the holidays (*takbīrāt al-tashrīq*), according to Abū Ḥanīfa they witness in cases of injury or death (*ḥudūd* and *qiṣāṣ*), they have more shares in inheritance, bloodwit (*ḥimāla*), pronouncement of an oath 50 times which establishes guilt or innocence in cases of murder (*qasāma*), authority in marriage, divorce, and taking back the wife after a revocable divorce, a greater number of spouses, lineage passing through the male line, and they have beards and turbans." Al-Zamakhsharī (A1) 1:495 and Bauer (n 43) 137. Al-Nasafī and al-Shirbīnī mentioned both beards and turbans as a sign of men's acquired superiority over women. Al-Nasafī (n 54) 1:355 and al-Shirbīnī (A1) 1:346. While the beard was a sign of the *faḍīla* of men over women for some exegetes, al-Qurṭubī disagreed, arguing that the beard did not indicate the *faḍīla* of men over women. Al-Qurṭubī (A1) 5:162.

[81] Kecia Ali, *Marriage and Slavery in Early Islam* (Cambridge, MA: Harvard University Press, 2010) 190.

[82] According to Ibn Kathīr, the political consequence of the preferred status of men over women was that women were ill-suited to receive prophethood and be rulers of nations. To this end, he cited the *ḥadīth* related by al-Bukhārī in which Muḥammad is reported to have said, "A nation led by a woman will never succeed." Ibn Kathīr (A1) 1:602. See also Fatima Mernissi, *The Veil and the Male Elite: A Feminist Interpretation of Women's Rights in Islam* (New York: Basic Books, 1991) 49. Single women also upset this cosmological order, because they were without the oversight of men. To this end, al-Thaʿlabī mentioned a *ḥadīth* in which Muḥammad said, " 'A woman without a husband is poor (*miskīna*).' The [Companions] said, 'O Messenger of God, even if she has wealth (*māl*)?' He said, 'Even if she has wealth, men are *qawwāmūn* over women.' " Al-Thaʿlabī (A1) 3:302–3.

"And because they spend of their wealth..."

The disciplinary power of husbands was structurally supported through their economic advantage. Wives were more likely to be obedient to their husbands if they were also financially dependent on them. Pre-colonial exegetes interpreted the phrase "they spend of their wealth" in Q. 4:34 in a legal manner. Men were financially responsible for their wives, through payment of dower (*mahr*) and maintenance (*nafaqa*). In exchange, they gained financial and social control of their wives, who owed them obedience and sexual access. A few exegetes such as Muḥammad ibn Aḥmad al-Qurṭubī (d. 671/1273) went as far as to argue that the financial dominance of husbands over wives was so essential that a husband's inability to provide maintenance nullified the marriage contract.[83]

"Righteous (*ṣāliḥāt*) women are obedient (*qānitāt*) and guard in their husbands' absence what God would have them guard..."

The literal wording in Q. 4:34, which describes righteous wives as "obedient," does not specify the object of women's obedience. Women might be required to be obedient to God, their husbands, or both. Most pre-colonial exegetes preferred the latter interpretations, seeing the two as intertwined.[84] They described wifely obedience as "obedience to God with respect to their husbands (*al-muṭīʿāt li-llāh fī azwājihinna*)".[85] However, a minority of exegetes seriously considered that righteous women were obedient to God alone.[86] For the majority of exegetes, though, an ideal

[83] Al-Qurṭubī explained "with what they spend of their money" as follows: "When [a husband] is incapable of paying maintenance then he is not *qawwām* over [his wife], and when he is not *qawwām* over her, the marriage is annulled (*fasakha*) because the purpose for which the marriage was legislated vanishes. This is a clear proof pertaining to the annulment of the marriage in cases of nonpayment for maintenance and clothing. This is the opinion of the schools of Mālik and Shāfiʿī. Abū Ḥanīfa says it is not annulled." Based on Bauer's translation, Bauer (n 43) 135 and al-Qurṭubī (A1) 5:162.

[84] For a list of exegetes who used the descriptor *qānitāt* or *ṭāʿa* to describe *ṣāliḥāt* wives, see Appendix 5 (A5).

[85] Variations of this phrase are used by al-Huwwārī (A1) 1:377; Ibn al-Jawzī (A1) 2:74; al-Māwardī (A1) 1:481; and al-Thaʿālibī (A2) 2:229. Abū al-Suʿūd wrote that "*qānitāt*" wives were "obedient to God and in charge (*qāʾimāt*) of their husbands' rights." Abū al-Suʿūd (A1) 1:339. See also al-Ḥaddād (A1) 2:249.

[86] Ibn ʿAṭiyya and Abū Ḥayyān cited al-Zajjāj as interpreting *qānitāt* wives in Q. 4:34 as women who are devout in prayer. Ibn ʿAṭiyya rejected this interpretation, describing it as "far-fetched." Ibn ʿAṭiyya (A1) 2:47 and Abū Ḥayyān (n 18) 3:249. However, in his *Maʿānī al-Qurʾān*, al-Zajjāj interprets "righteous women are obedient" as wives who "uphold the rights of their husbands." Abū Isḥāq Ibrāhīm ibn al-Sarī al-Zajjāj, *Maʿānī al-Qurʾān wa-iʿrābuhu* (Beirut: al-Maktaba al-ʿAṣriyya, 1973) 2:48. For a discussion on

marriage was one in which the authority of the husband over the wife was expressed through economic and sexual dominance. As discussed earlier, economic control was established through an asymmetrical marriage in which a wife relied on her husband for maintenance (*nafaqa*). The sexual dominance of husbands was instituted through the use of *aḥadīth* that lambasted wives who were sexually unavailable to their husbands. Such women were cursed by the angels and lost favor in God's eyes.[87] Jalāl al-Dīn ʿAbd al-Raḥmān al-Suyūṭī (d. 911/1505) brought this point home by citing the following *ḥadīth* in his discussion of Q. 4:34: "God does not look at a woman who is ungrateful to her husband when she is dependent on him."[88] In order to maintain their moral rectitude, wives were pressed to be sexually available to their husbands, even under extraordinary and inconvenient circumstances, such as while riding a camel[89] and baking at the oven.[90]

Obedience was an essential characteristic of a righteous wife. Al-Rāzī wrote, "Know that a woman cannot be righteous (*ṣāliḥat*) without being obedient (*muṭīʿat*) to her husband."[91] Wifely obedience was so meritorious that it rivaled male participation in military *jihād*.[92] Al-Suyūṭī cited a *ḥadīth* in which a woman questioned the disparity between men and women that resulted from male exclusivity in *jihād*. When men went on a military expedition, they were rewarded regardless of the outcome. If they won, they got booty; and if they were killed, they obtained paradise. In contrast, women suffered due to their husbands' participation in

the implications of this interpretation and the controversy surrounding al-Zajjāj's alleged position on the matter, see Chaudhry (n 51) 158.

87 Women were cursed for refusing their husbands' sexual advances, fasting without their permission, or leaving the house. One *ḥadīth* reads, "A woman who refuses herself to her husband and leaves his bed is cursed by the angels until morning." Another variation of this *ḥadīth* suggested that a wife would be cursed by the angels if she left home without her husband's permission and would be continuously cursed thereafter until she returned and "put her hand in his hand." Variations of this report are included in the commentaries of Ibn Kathīr (A1) 1:602; al-Jaṣṣāṣ (A1) 1:376; al-Khāzin (A1) 1:375; al-Qurṭubī (A1) 5:164; and al-Suyūṭī (A1) 2:152–3. A righteous wife did not leave her husband's house without his permission or undertake supererogatory fasts when he was present. Al-Jaṣṣāṣ (n 65) 1:375. See also Kecia Ali, *Sexual Ethics and Islam* (Oxford: Oneworld, 2006) 11.

88 Al-Suyūṭī (A1) 2:152.

89 "A woman should not refuse herself [to her husband] even if she is on the back of a camel." Eg, see Abū Ḥayyān (n 18) 251 and al-Suyūṭī (A1) 2:152, 154, and 156.

90 "When a man calls his wife to [fulfill] his need/desire, she should go to him even if she is at the baking oven." Al-Khāzin (A1) 1:375 and al-Suyūṭī (A1) 2:156.

91 Al-Rāzī (A1) 4:71. Pre-colonial exegetes described the "goodness/badness" of women based on how much ease or hardship they caused their husbands. Al-Suyūṭī mentioned a report in which good wives were described as "a gold-laden crown on a king's head," whereas bad women were "a heavy burden for a large man." Al-Suyūṭī (A1) 2:152.

92 In one prophetic report, obedient women who recognize their husbands' rights over them are rewarded in a manner comparable to participating in a military expedition (*ghazwa*). Al-Suyūṭī (A1) 2:153.

jihād—they tended to their husbands' duties when they were absent, cared for them if they were injured, and had to find a means to do without them if they were killed. In return, they received no compensation, most importantly spoils of war, for their troubles. "What is there for us in this?" she asked Muḥammad. He replied, "I have heard that a woman who obeys her husband and recognizes his rights over her will be rewarded the equivalent [of men participating in *jihād*]. And only a few of you will be able to do this."[93] This report strengthened the parallel nature of the God–man and husband–wife relationships. Just as men expressed their devotion to God by sacrificing their wealth and lives for Him, wives showed their devotion through a willingness to surrender their lives and forgo economic gains in obedience to their husbands.

According to pre-colonial exegetes, righteous wives were obedient to their husbands as long as their husbands did not ask them to violate God's commands.[94] For instance, if a husband asked his wife to abandon obligatory prayer, she could not obey him. When husbands ordered their wives to disobey a divine command, their own disobedience flouted the divine hierarchy. In all other matters, wifely obedience was a religious obligation.[95] To this end, the following text from Q. 4:34 offered exegetes two attributes of righteous wives: "Righteous (*ṣāliḥāt*) women are obedient (*qānitat*) and guard what God would have them guard in the absence [of their husbands] (*ḥāfiẓāt li-l-ghayb bi-mā ḥafiẓa allāh*)." The two qualities mentioned in this

[93] "A woman came to the Prophet of God and said, 'O Prophet of God, I come to you as a delegate for women (*wāfidat al-nisā'*). Concerning the *jihād* that God has prescribed for men; if they win (*yuṣībū*) they are rewarded, and if they are killed 'they live, finding their sustenance in the presence of their Lord' [Q. 3:169]. And we, the community of women, assume their burden, so what is there for us in this (*wa-naḥnu maʿshara al-nisā' naqūmu ʿalayhim fa-mā lanā min dhālika*)?' The Prophet replied, 'I have heard that a woman who obeys her husband and recognizes his rights over her will be rewarded the equivalent [of men participating in *jihād*]. And only a few of you will be able to do this.'" Al-Suyūṭī (A1) 2:152. For another version of this *ḥadīth*, see Appendix 6 (A6). The entirety of Q. 3:169 reads: "Think not of those who are slain in Allah's way as dead. Nay, they live, finding their sustenance in the presence of their Lord." Yusuf Ali (n 4) Q. 3:169. Al-Suyūṭī (A1) 2:152.

[94] Husbands were, however, responsible for ensuring that their wives obeyed divine commands as well as their own. Ibn al-ʿArabī wrote that husbands were required to "order her to obey God (*bi-ṭāʿat allāh*)," which included ensuring that she prayed and fasted. Ibn al-ʿArabī (A1) 1:494.

[95] Al-Ṭabarī quoted Ibn ʿAbbās explaining "Men are *qawwāmun* over women" as "meaning: [men are] commanders (*umarā'*) [over wives], so it is [a wife's] obligation to obey [her husband] regarding what God has commanded her." Al-Ṭabarī (A1) 4:60. Both Ali and Bauer note the correlation between obedience to husbands and God in exegetical and juridical works, as well as the obedience of wives being contingent on obedience to God. Ali writes, "Only if what her husband asks her is *maʿṣiya* [sinful disobedience] may she refuse him. Otherwise, her failure to obey itself becomes *maʿṣiya*, sinful disobedience. While *maʿṣiya* typically refers to sinful disobedience to God, through an interpretive maneuver it is made to come full circle: God has ordained that women must obey their husbands, and thus disobedience (*nushūz*) to one's husband is sinful disobedience (*maʿṣiya*) to God." Kecia Ali (n 67) 310 and Bauer (n 43) 76.

phrase corresponded to two circumstances in which a wife's behavior might be judged: when her husband was present, a righteous wife obeyed him,[96] and when her husband was absent, a virtuous woman protected her husband's property[97] and her own chastity[98]—both of which belonged to her husband.[99]

"As for those women from whom you fear *nushūz*, admonish them, abandon them in bed and hit them…"

A husband's responsibility to provide for his wives was closely connected to his trusteeship over his wives in the moral and social realms. To this end, a husband's disciplinary privilege in marriage was considered instrumental in fulfilling his marital duties. As the authoritative agent in marriage, a husband was charged with certain duties, including the discipline (*ta'dīb*), education (*taʿlīm*), management (*tartīb*), and/or regulation (*tadbīr*) of wives.[100] The term *ta'dīb* has various shades of meaning, which include discipline, education, and moral rectification,[101] and it was interpreted to mean chastising, correcting, disciplining, and punishing wives.[102] Abū

[96] Some exegetes mentioned additional qualities of a righteous wife, including her being kind to her in-laws. See, eg, Ibn Abī Ḥātim (A1) 3:939 and Ibn al-ʿArabī (A1) 1:494.

[97] For a list of exegetes who argued that wives were to protect their husbands' wealth/property in their absence, see Appendix 7 (A7).

[98] Eg, al-Rāzī wrote, "[A wife] should protect herself (*taḥfaẓ nafsahā*) from adultery (*al-zinā*), so that her husband is not afflicted with shame/disgrace (*al-ʿār*) as a result of her adultery, and so that a child is not attributed to him that is created by someone else's sperm (*nuṭfa*)." Al-Rāzī (A1) 4:70. See also al-Khāzin (A1) 1:374. Exegetes often described the chastity of wives by using the term "vulva" (*furūj*); wives should protect their *furūj* in their husbands' absence. See, eg, Ibn Abī Ḥātim (A1) 3:942. For a list of exegetes who argued that wives were to protect their chastity in their husbands' absence, see Appendix 8 (A8). Some exegetes also mentioned that wives were expected to keep their husbands' secrets. Eg, Abū al-Suʿūd (A1) 1:339; al-Baghawī (A1) 5:422; al-Khāzin (A1) 1:375; al-Nasafī (n 54) 1:355; and al-Zamakhsharī (A1) 1:496.

[99] A *ḥadīth* used to support this reads, "The best of women is one who makes you smile when you look at her, obeys when you order her, and in your absence preserves herself and your wealth. Then the Prophet of God, may peace and blessings be upon him, recited, 'Men are *qawwāmūn* over women' to the end of the verse." This *ḥadīth* sometimes began with the question "Shall I tell you about the best treasure a man can have?" For a list of exegetes who cited this *ḥadīth*, see Appendix 9 (A9). Bauer cites this *ḥadīth* to illustrate the selective use of *aḥādīth* by pre-colonial exegetes regardless of the authenticity of their chains of transmission. Although this particular *ḥadīth* is not found in any of the canonical *ḥadīth* sources, it was still quoted regularly be exegetes, even after the canonization of *ḥadīth* books. Bauer (n 43) 123–4.

[100] The term *taʿlīm* highlighted the husband's instructional role. Incidentally, permissible hitting was sometimes described as disciplinary hitting (*ḍarb al-adab*). See, eg, Ibn ʿAṭiyya (A1) 2:48.

[101] Bauer (n 43) 92 and 121–2.

[102] G.H. Hava, *Arabic-English Dictionary* (Beirut: Catholic Press, 1951) and Hans Wehr, *Arabic–English Dictionary: The Hans Wehr Dictionary of Modern Written Arabic* (Ithaca: Spoken Language Services, 1994). For a list of exegetes who use the terms *ta'dīb*,

Bakr Ibn al-ʿArabī (d. 543/1148) described husbandly responsibility as reforming, cultivating, and/or rectifying a wife's condition for the better (*yuṣliḥu fī ḥālihā*).[103] The general discussion of the disciplinary power of husbands over wives was inextricably tied to physical discipline. An example of this can be seen in al-Ṭabarī's interpretation of Q. 4:34, in which he wrote, "The man is the leader (*qāʾim*) of the woman, he commands her to the obedience of God, and if she refuses, he should hit her without causing extreme pain (*ghayr mubarriḥ*)."[104]

Prophetic reports were used by pre-colonial exegetes to reinforce the right of husbands to discipline their wives through physical chastisement. According to these prophetic reports, Muḥammad said, "Hang the whip where your wives can see it"[105] and "Do not ask a man about hitting his wife."[106] These *ḥadīth* reports were interpreted by pre-colonial exegetes to mean not only that the threat of physical discipline should be an ever-present reminder for wives but also that husbands who hit their wives were granted social, if not legal, immunity.[107] This left husbands unaccountable for how they treated their wives; a man's righteous standing in his community was not compromised by abusive behavior. To this end, several exegetes cited a report wherein Asmāʾ bint Abī Bakr al-Ṣiddīq narrated that when her husband, the Companion al-Zubayr b. al-ʿAwwām, "got angry [at one of his wives], he would hit her with a pole of a clothes rack (*ʿud al-mishjab*) until he broke it while hitting her."[108] An expanded version of this account reads:

> Asmāʾ bt. Abī Bakr complained to her father that al-Zubayr reprimanded her and her co-wife (*al-ḍarra*) for going out too much. He did this by tying their hair together and then hitting them intensely (*shadīdan*). Asmāʾ was hit more

taʿlīm, *tartīb*, or *tadbīr* to describe husbands' responsibility in disciplining wives, see Appendix 10 (A10).

[103] Ibn al-ʿArabī (A1) 1:493.

[104] Al-Ṭabarī (A1) 4:60. I follow Bauer's translation of *ghayr mubarriḥ*. She writes, "*Ghayr mubarriḥ* is often translated as 'non-violent', but hitting is intrinsically violent, despite the qualifications of not breaking bones, or seriously wounding. Given this context, 'without causing severe pain' is a better translation. Kazimirsky says that *mubarriḥ* is: 'very harsh, very painful, causing intense pain' (*très sensible, très-pénible, qui cause une douleur violente*)." Bauer (n 43) 111.

[105] "*ʿalliq al-sawṭ ḥaythu yarāhu ahl al-bayt*." Al-Thaʿlabī (A1) 3:303 and al-Zamakhsharī (A1) 1:497. I translate *ahl al-bayt* as "wives" rather than "households" because in the contexts surrounding this study, the phrase is consistently used to refer to wives rather than households.

[106] Ibn Kathīr (A1) 1:602–3; al-Khāzin (A1) 1:375; al-Qurṭubī (A1) 5:166; and al-Suyūṭī (A1) 2:156. See also Marín (n 18) 25.

[107] Another *ḥadīth* that made a similar point was one in which Muḥammad stated that it angered him when a woman complained against her husband. Al-Suyūṭī (A1) 2:153.

[108] Variations of this report were recorded by Ibn al-ʿArabī (A1) 1:496; al-Qurṭubī (A1) 5:164–5; al-Thaʿlabī (A1) 3:303; and al-Zamakhsharī (A1) 1:497.

> than her co-wife, leaving a mark, because she was less God-fearing than her co-wife. So she complained to her father, the Companion Abū Bakr, who said to her, "Be patient, my daughter, for al-Zubayr is a righteous man (*rajul ṣāliḥ*). It might be that he will be your husband in paradise, for I have heard that in paradise a man is married to the woman he deflowers (*ibtakara*)."[109]

Pre-colonial exegetes differed in their opinions about this account. Some, like Aḥmad ibn Muḥammad al-Thaʿlabī (d. 427/1035) and al-Zamakhsharī, felt that this narration confirmed that the physical chastisement of wives did not compromise a man's righteousness. The manner in which al-Zubayr executed his disciplinary power over his wives was his own business and was not meant to be regulated. However, other exegetes, such as al-Qurṭubī and Ibn al-ʿArabī, were troubled by the extent of al-Zubayr's physical violence. They argued that by hitting his wives in an extreme (*shadīd*) manner, al-Zubayr had violated the prophetic exhortation to hit wives in a non-extreme (*ghayr mubarriḥ*) fashion.[110]

"If they obey (*aṭaʿnakum*) you, do not find a means against them"

The last part of Q. 4:34 was also used to support a hierarchal marital structure. Pre-colonial exegetes understood this phrase to mean that husbands ought to be just overseers of their wives, treating them as they themselves desired to be treated by God.[111] They should not transgress

[109] This particular version was reported by Abū Ḥayyān (n 18) 3:252; Ibn al-ʿArabī (A1) 1:496–7; and al-Qurṭubī (A1) 5:164–5. Ibn al-ʿArabī expressed skepticism about this *ḥadīth* by referring to its chain of transmission (*isnād*) as one with limited corroboration (*gharīb*). According to Ibn al-ʿArabī, al-Ṭabarī's erroneous interpretation of *wa-hjurūhunna* to mean "tie them in beds" with a rope is probably based on this *ḥadīth*. However, he disagrees with al-Ṭabarī's interpretation and possibly with the credibility of the *ḥadīth* itself. Ibn al-ʿArabī (A1) 1:496–7. In contrast, Abū Ḥayyān mentioned this *ḥadīth* unproblematically alongside a report attributed to Ibn ʿAbbās in which he says that husbands are to hit wives with a "*siwāk* or something like it." He treated the beating of Asmāʾ as falling under the category of non-extreme (*ghayr mubarriḥ*) hitting. Marín mentions a variation of this *ḥadīth* recorded by Ibn Ḥabīb: "Al-Zubayr b. al-ʿAwwām arrived to his house, and he ordered his wife Asmāʾ bt. Abi Bakr and another of his wives to sweep the floor under his bed. When he later came again into the house, he found that his orders had not been carried out. Asma' said: He took both of us by our heads and beat us with his whip, hurting us. My co-wife accepted the punishment, but I did not; it affected me strongly. I went out and complained to ʿĀʾisha, who asked Abu Bakr to come to her and told him: What has this man done to my sister? Abī Bakr told me [Asmāʾ]: My little daughter, he is a pious man and he is the father of your children. God may marry him to you in Paradise. Now be patient and go back to your home." Marín (n 18) 15–16.

[110] This may be an instance where the juridical school of an exegete influenced his opinion of the legitimacy of a particular *ḥadīth* in his Qurʾanic exegesis. Al-Thaʿlabī was Shāfiʿī and al-Zamakhsharī was Ḥanafī, while both Abū Bakr Ibn al-ʿArabī and al-Qurṭubī were Mālikī.

[111] For a list of exegetes who drew a parallel between the God–man and husband–wife relationships, see Appendix 11 (A11).

against their wives, should not make unreasonable demands on them, and ought to forgive their wives as God forgives human failings.[112] Abū Isḥāq Ibrāhīm ibn al-Sarī al-Zajjāj (d. 311/923) instructed husbands to follow God's example and only hold their wives responsible for what was reasonable, since God did not excessively burden humans.[113] Consequently, husbands were not permitted to demand that their wives love them but rather simply that they obey them.[114]

In light of the previous discussions of husbandly disciplinary privilege, we can begin to discern that pre-colonial exegetes imagined an ideal, divinely ordered world wherein humans were crowned as the greatest of all of God's creation. Amongst humans, men ranked above women due to their inherent superiority, as manifested through their excellence in natural, social, political, cultural, and philosophical realms. This superiority came with responsibilities, making husbands responsible to God for the financial, moral, and social well-being of their wives. Wives, for their part in the cosmology, were responsible to God through their obedience to their husbands.[115] Disobedient wives challenged God's ordering of the world, and husbands were authorized to discipline them in order to set the marital—and cosmological—order straight.

CONCLUSION

Situating Q. 4:34 in its textual, historical, and cosmological contexts allows us to see the ways in which various frames of reference have influenced the interpretative scope of this verse. The textual context demonstrates that despite the constraints imposed by the words themselves, scriptural texts such as Q. 4:34 naturally lend themselves to multiple and potentially opposing meanings. With a little bit of hermeneutic maneuvering, Q. 4:34 can be compellingly read to support both egalitarian and patriarchal interpretations. The ambiguous spaces in this verse are filled in by the reader and profoundly influenced by the social and historical frameworks that surround the exercise of reading this text.

112 Al-Shirbīnī advised husbands to be fearful of God since He would punish them if they transgressed (*ẓ-l-m*) against their wives. Al-Shirbīnī (A1) 1:347.

113 Al-Zajjāj (n 86) 2:49.

114 For a list of exegetes who mentioned that it was not permissible to discipline a wife for not loving her husband, see Appendix 12 (A12).

115 While many exegetes interpreted *qānitāt* as "obedient to God and their husbands," some interpreted this as exclusively "obedient to their husbands," without reference to God. Eg, see Ibn Abī Zamanīn (A1) 1:367. Al-Jaṣṣāṣ described obedience as an essential quality of a righteous wife. Al-Jaṣṣāṣ (A1) 1:375.

While the textual context lends itself to both egalitarian and patriarchal interpretations of Q. 4:34, the historical context used by pre-colonial exegetes—as showcased in the occasions of revelation concerning Umm Salama and Ḥabība—significantly narrowed the interpretive range of Q. 4:34. Both stories determined the main thrust of Q. 4:34 in different ways. Read in light of Umm Salama's query about the disparity in the shares of inheritance apportioned to men and women, the main purpose of Q. 4:34 was to justify the unequal shares by asserting that men and women are essentially, socially, and religiously unequal. In this reading, the first half of the verse is the most important, and the second half simply explains the consequences of male superiority in the marital relationship. However, the focus of Q. 4:34 shifts significantly when it is understood as being revealed in relation to Ḥabība's complaint against her abusive husband. In this case, the main takeaway of the verse is the legal position that husbands may physically discipline their wives without retaliation. Here, the essential message of the verse lies in the second half, while the first half provides justification for this legal ruling. In both cases, the surrounding story about why exactly this verse was revealed and what question it was answering determines the thrust of the verse. The more popular *sabab* offered for the revelation of Q. 4:34 by pre-colonial exegetes is that it was revealed in response to Ḥabība's complaint. And although the main character of this story is an abused woman who is seeking retaliation against her husband, for pre-colonial exegetes this story highlighted the theological problem of prophetic and divine disagreement. Instead of attending to Ḥabība, these exegetes exerted their energies towards mitigating the tension between Muḥammad's judgment in Ḥabība's favor and the divine revocation of that ruling, supporting her husband against her.

The hierarchy of men over women, as posited by pre-colonial exegetes and jurists, helped to resolve this tension. If God had preferred men over women, then it followed that husbands had disciplinary duties and privileges in marriage. Hence, the purpose of Q. 4:34 was to introduce a new ruling, of which Muḥammad was understandably unaware. In studying the commentaries of Q. 4:34, we learn a great deal about the idealized cosmology of pre-colonial exegetes and jurists. Pre-colonial exegesis of Q. 4:34 consistently upheld an idealized God-centered cosmology, wherein a gendered social order reflected the wisdom of God. The asymmetrical marital relationship was reflective of a deliberate divine plan, and corresponded to men's and women's essential characteristics.[116]

[116] Ziba Mir-Hosseini writes, "It is no exaggeration to say that the entire edifice of family law in Muslim legal tradition is built on the ways in which classical jurists understood this verse [4:34] and translated it into legal rulings." Ziba Mir-Hosseini,

That the marital arrangement was a divinely ordained part of a larger cosmological order explains why pre-colonial discussions concerning physical discipline in marriage were about the correct placement of husbands and wives in an ideal marital hierarchy. It also helps us to understand why the discussion surrounding the *sabab* attributed to Ḥabība's complaint was about whether husbands could be liable for exercising their disciplinary power rather than about concern for Ḥabība's well-being. When wives disobeyed their husbands or demonstrated any form of recalcitrance, they threatened the entire cosmological order. Due to the high stakes involved in wifely disobedience, exegetes never questioned the husbandly right to physically discipline wives. Rather, their ethical discussions examined the procedure of hitting wives, which was a function of male superiority. Thus, when pre-colonial exegetes engaged in legal and ethical discussions about when and how husbands could physically discipline their wives, they predicated their ethical concerns on a patriarchal idealized cosmology. These discussions will be examined in greater detail in the next chapter, but for now it is important to understand how a patriarchal cosmology functions to create an ideal marital relationship, providing the necessary framework for the ethical and legal conversations in their larger context.

"Decoding the 'DNA of Patriarchy' in Muslim Family Laws," <http://www.musawah.org/decoding-dna-patriarchy-muslim-family-laws> (last accessed Dec. 20, 2012).

2

The Ethics of Wife-Beating

The Qur'ān is replete with commands in the imperative form, yet only some are interpreted to constitute legal rulings, while others are understood to be more akin to moral exhortations. What influenced Muslim legal decision-making to construe some Qur'anic imperatives as law and others as suggestions? When deciding whether imperatives should carry the weight of law or moral exhortation, pre-colonial jurists and exegetes invariably brought their cosmological commitments to bear on their interpretations. Scholars linked their cosmologies to law through ethical discussions that justified their particular interpretations. These ethical discussions reveal authorial preconceptions about how humans enact the law to be in fidelity with a divine cosmology. Thus, deriving ethics from Qur'anic imperatives is not merely an exercise in exegesis but one of eisegesis as well.[1] "Eisegesis" is the conceptual opposite of "exegesis": whereas exegesis refers to the activity of deriving meaning *from* a text, eisegesis describes the activity of reading meanings *into* a text.

The ethical discourse on disciplining wives in pre-colonial scholarly discussions is deeply conditioned by the patriarchal idealized cosmology outlined in the previous chapter. Without this cosmology, it is difficult to make sense of the ethical nature of the debate surrounding wife-beating. In fact, these same discussions sound decidedly unscrupulous when viewed through the lens of an egalitarian idealized cosmology. The measure of ethicality, then, changes based on differing idealized cosmologies. Many religious studies scholars have argued that it is unfair and unhelpful to be morally outraged at the patriarchal details of a patriarchal discourse. Indeed, in our disapproval of the patriarchal nature of patriarchal societies, we impose a modern, post-colonial, gender-egalitarian hegemony on a system that could not have imagined these norms. Furthermore, by privileging a post-colonial perspective over the pre-colonial one, we fail to see the ethical conversations that did exist in the pre-colonial period. For

[1] For more discussion on this, see Kristin Zahra Sands, *Ṣūfī Commentaries on the Qur'ān in Classical Islam* (London: Routledge, 2006) 5.

instance, when encountering a treatise about the limits on beating slaves, if we go no further than to feel appalled by the existence of slavery or by the fact that masters were permitted to beat slaves, then we entirely miss the interesting fact that pre-colonial scholars grappled with the question of justice in dealing with slaves at all. I argue that varying idealized cosmologies are a helpful way to appreciate the ethics of a particular discourse. In the case of wife-beating, this means that pre-colonial conversations about the procedures for disciplining wives can be read as simultaneously ethical and unethical. Discussions that might be justifiable in the framework of a pre-colonial cosmology can be unjust in a modern, post-colonial, egalitarian idealized cosmology.

The previous chapter outlined the ways in which pre-colonial scholars interpreted the first half of Q. 4:34 to set up a divinely-ordained idealized cosmology that justified the moral authority of husbands, granting them the right to physically discipline rebellious wives. This chapter will explore the ethical discussion surrounding the procedures for disciplining wives. This ethical dimension is often captured in juridical language, and the exegesis of the second half of Q. 4:34 is an excellent demonstration of the fluidity one often finds between the fields of Islamic jurisprudence and Qur'ān interpretation.[2] The relationship between Qur'anic text and jurisprudence in this case was further influenced by multiple external disciplines. As will be seen, exegetes incorporated philology, prophetic history, and cosmology into their legal and ethical discussions on the right and obligation of husbands to physically discipline rebellious wives.

Pre-colonial Qur'ān commentators, who were often masters of multiples sciences such as jurisprudence and theology, employed the genre of Qur'ān interpretation to expound on and defend particular idealized cosmologies. These idealized cosmologies, or visions of the world as it should be, can be gleaned from careful study of exegetical works, with a special focus on lexicology. Pre-colonial scholars deliberately interpreted specific words and technical terms to have precise contextual meanings, so their choice to interpret a term in a monolithic or varied manner speaks to their presuppositions and informs readers about the larger cosmological vision that exegetes brought to bear in their interpretation of the Qur'anic text.[3]

The sites for ethical discourse in Q. 4:34 centered around two terms and three disciplinary prescriptions. The two terms are *khawf* (literally, "fear") and *nushūz* (literally, "to rise"); and the three prescriptions are

[2] Karen Bauer, "Room For Interpretation: Qur'ānic Exegesis and Gender," Ph.D. diss. (Princeton University, 2008) 14.

[3] For an extensive study on how technical terms and their interpretations indicate varying underlying worldviews, see Rumee Ahmed, *Narratives of Islamic Legal Theory* (Oxford: Oxford University Press, 2012).

fa-ʿiẓūhunna (admonish them), *wa-hjurūhunna fī al-maḍājiʿ* (abandon them in beds), and *wa-ḍribūhunna* (hit them). The relevant passage of Q. 4:34 reads: "If you [husbands] fear *nushūz* from them [your wives] *fa-ʿiẓūhunna* (admonish them), *wa-hjurūhunna fī al-maḍājiʿ* (abandon them in beds), and/or *wa-ḍribūhunna* (beat them)." The interpretation of each of these terms and prescriptions has the potential for expanding or restricting male power in marriage.

Ethical considerations were further elaborated in the discussions of whether the three disciplinary steps—admonishment, abandonment, and beating—are meant to be followed simultaneously or sequentially. The question of sequence affects the legal right of husbands to resort to physical violence as a delayed or immediate reaction to wifely *nushūz*. Furthermore, the restriction placed on the otherwise unqualified Qur'anic prescription of physical discipline hinted at the (dis)comfort of pre-colonial exegetes and jurists with the right of husbands to physically discipline their wives. To this end, the *aḥādīth* that scholars chose to emphasize in their exegesis illustrated their hermeneutic and legal preferences. All of these reflections resulted in myriad hermeneutic opinions on the proper procedure for physically disciplining wives, the legality of which was assumed as fact.

KHAWF: DISTINGUISHING ETHICAL CONCERNS FROM TECHNICAL QUESTIONS

The seemingly straightforward task of defining the term *khawf* became a matter of ethical debate amongst Qur'ān commentators as a means of delimiting the amount of disciplinary power granted to husbands. Depending on how *khawf* is construed, husbands are permitted to discipline their wives either based on the mere suspicion of *nushūz* or only after manifest evidence of wifely *nushūz*. There was no debate that the denotive, plain sense meaning of *khawf* is "fear."[4] Interpreted in this way—as allowing husbands to discipline their wives based on their fear of wifely *nushūz*—Q. 4:34 grants husbands a great deal of leeway in disciplining their wives. This interpretation puts wives at a severe disadvantage since it exposes them to rebuke from potentially capricious, or at least suspicious, husbands. At first glance, then, it appears that interpreting *khawf* more restrictively and against its plain sense, connoting something closer to "certainty," would protect wives from

[4] I take the phrase "plain sense" from Peter Ochs, who defines it as "the exegetical practice of medieval Jewish scholars, for whom the 'plain sense' (*peshat*) of a text is its meaning within the rhetorical context of some body of received literature." Peter Ochs, *Peirce, Pragmatism and the Logic of Scripture* (Cambridge, Cambridge University Press, 1998) 5–6.

wanton disciplinary measures.[5] Yet the ethical discussions in pre-colonial Qur'ān commentaries were not so straightforward. Pre-colonial exegetes interpreted *khawf* in multiple ways, some maintaining the plain-sense meaning of *khawf* as "fear," while others interpreted *khawf* more restrictively as "knowledge" or "certainty." However, as will be seen, the interpretive choice of an exegete to define *khawf* more expansively or restrictively did not necessarily correspond to an increased or diminished ethical stance on the legitimacy of wife-beating.

Most pre-colonial exegetes interpreted *khawf* to mean "knowledge" (*ʿilm*),[6] while some further restricted the meaning to "certainty" (*yaqīn*).[7] This interpretation required a husband to have clear evidence of wifely *nushūz* before he could begin the disciplinary process.[8] The term *ẓann* was also used to describe *khawf*. *Ẓann* lends itself to a greater number of meanings than *ʿilm*, ranging from informed belief to mere speculation. Nevertheless, when exegetes used *ẓann* as a meaning for *khawf*, they emphasized its definitive rather than tentative nature. In most cases, a husband's *ẓann* was tantamount to his having knowledge (*ʿilm*) of his wife's *nushūz*. Thus, Abū al-Faraj ʿAbd al-Raḥmān ibn ʿAlī Ibn al-Jawzī (d. 597/1200) characterized *ẓann* as "what becomes apparent from

[5] Al-Samīn (d. 756/1355) wrote, "Some [scholars] say that '*wa-l-lātī takhāfūna*' means 'and concerning those women on whose part you fear *nushūz*, and then they commit *nushūz* (*wa-nashazna*)'. What is intended here is that it is impermissible to commence with admonishment and what comes after it [ie the disciplinary process] on the basis of fear alone. And some have said: this [interpretation of wives having committed *nushūz*] is unnecessary because *khawf* means *yaqīn* (certainty). Yet other [scholars] mention that probability [of *nushūz*] is sufficient." Aḥmad ibn Yūsuf al-Samīn, *al-Durr al-maṣūn fī ʿulūm al-kitāb al-maknūn* (Damascus: Dār al-Qalam, 1986) 3:673.

[6] Muqātil (d. 150/767) and al-Samarqandī (d. 375/985) wrote that the phrase "and on those women on whose part you fear *nushūz*" referred to those women on whose part husbands "knew of their disobedience (*taʿlamūna ʿiṣyānahunna*)." Along the same lines, al-Ṭabarī and al-Māwardī described *khawf* of a wife's *nushūz*, as "knowledge" of her *nushūz*. Muqātil ibn Sulaymān al-Balkhī, *Tafsīr Muqātil ibn Sulaymān* (Cairo: Mu'assasat al-Ḥalabī, 1969) 1:235; Naṣr ibn Muḥammad Abū al-Layth al-Samarqandī, *Tafsīr al-Samarqandī, al-musammā, Baḥr al-ʿulūm* (Beirut: Dār al-Kutub al-ʿIlmiyya, 1993) 1:352; Abū Jaʿfar Muḥammad ibn Jarīr al-Ṭabarī, *Tafsīr al-Ṭabarī: al-musammā Jāmiʿ al-bayān fī taʾwīl al-Qurʾān* (Beirut: Dār al-Kutub al-ʿIlmiyya, 1999) 4:64; and ʿAlī ibn Muḥammad Al-Māwardī, *al-Nukat wa-l-ʿuyūn: tafsīr al-Māwardī. Min rawāʾiʿ al-tafāsīr* (Beirut: Dār al-Kutub al-ʿIlmiyya, 1992) 1:481. For a list of additional exegetes who understand *khawf* as a cognate of *ʿilm*, see Appendix 13 (A13).

[7] Exegetes who offered *yaqīn* as a possible meaning of *khawf* include Muḥammad ibn Yūsuf Abū Ḥayyān, *Tafsīr al-baḥr al-muḥīṭ* (Beirut: Dār al-Kutub al-ʿIlmiyya, 1993) 3:250; Muḥammad ibn ʿAbd Allāh Ibn al-ʿArabī, *Aḥkām al-Qurʾān* (Cairo: Dār al-Manār, 2002) 1:495; Ibn ʿAṭiyya (A13) 2:48; and al-Qurṭubī (A13) 5:163.

[8] In al-Sulamī's (d. 660/1261) abridgment of al-Māwardī's (d. 450/1058) commentary, al-Sulamī explained that *khawf* as "knowledge" requires "evidence/proofs (*istidlāl*) of [wifely] *nushūz* as apparent bad actions (*sūʾ fiʿlihā*), and *nushūz* is from rising (*al-irtifāʿ*), as in her rising from her husband's obedience." ʿIzz al-Dīn ʿAbd al-ʿAzīz ibn ʿAbd al-Salām al-Sulamī, *Tafsīr al-Qurʾān: ikhtiṣār al-Nukat li-l-Māwardī* (Beirut: Dār Ibn Ḥazm, 1996) 1:321.

indicators (*dalāʾil*) of [a wife's] *nushūz*."[9] When observing this general trend of replacing the plain sense of the term "fear" with "knowledge," it is tempting to jump to the conclusion that this interpretive choice reflected a discomfort on the part of exegetes with the disciplinary power of husbands or perhaps an impulse to protect wives from arbitrary punishment at the hands of their husbands.

A closer examination demonstrates that many exegetes who required clear evidence of wifely *nushūz* before husbands could commence with disciplinary measures also maintained that once a husband had certain knowledge of his wife's *nushūz*, he was obligated to proceed with the disciplinary steps outlined in Q. 4:34.[10] The language of "obligation" (*wājib*) in the context of Q. 4:34 is important because it emphasizes the commanding nature of the imperatives to admonish, abandon, and hit wives. The imperatives in Q. 4:34 have the potential of being read as permissions or commands; in the latter case, husbands fall short of their own obligations (marital and religious) if they fail to discipline their wives, thereby jeopardizing their own moral well-being. If we remove the possibility that pre-colonial exegetes were conscientiously troubled by the disciplinary privilege of husbands, we are able to understand their choices in a different light. For example, it is possible that by interpreting *khawf* against its plain-sense meaning of "fear" to mean "knowledge," exegetes anticipated adjudication where husbands might need to provide evidence of wifely *nushūz* in court to defend their use of physical discipline.

This point is further highlighted when *khawf* was interpreted more vaguely to mean "fear," "suspicion" (*shakk*),[11] or "expectation" (*tawaqquʿ*).[12] Exegetes who allowed such expansive interpretations of *khawf* also restricted a husband's rebuke in other ways. For example, if husbands feared, suspected, or expected wifely *nushūz*, they were allowed to admonish their wives but not to abandon or hit them.[13] In order to proceed from admonishment to abandonment and hitting, husbands were required to have clear evidence of

[9] Eg, see al-Farrāʾ (A13) 1:265; and Ibn al-Jawzī (A13) 2:75.

[10] Ibn ʿAṭiyya wrote that the presence of *nushūz* itself made admonishment obligatory (*wuqūʿ al-nushūz huwa al-ladhī yūjib al-waʿẓ*). Ibn ʿAṭiyya (A13) 2:48.

[11] Exegetes who considered *shakk* as a possible meaning for *khawf* included Ibn ʿAṭiyya (A13) 2:48; al-Farrāʾ (A13) 1:265; and al-Ṭabarī (n 6) 4:64.

[12] For example, Ibn ʿAṭiyya (A13) 2:48.

[13] ʿAbd al-Razzāq al-Ṣanʿānī (d. 211/826), a teacher of Aḥmed Ibn Ḥanbal (d. 241/855), wrote, "When [the husband] fears [his wife's] *nushūz*, he should admonish her. If she does not accept this [by ceasing her *nushūz*] then he should abandon her. If she does not accept this, he should hit her in a non-extreme (*ghayr mubarriḥ*) manner." ʿAbd al-Razzāq al-Ṣanʿānī ibn Hammām al-Ḥimyarī, *Tafsīr al-Qurʾān* (Riyadh: Maktaba al-Rushd, 1989) 1:158. Exegetes who felt that husbands should admonish based on the fear of *nushūz* but proceed with abandonment and hitting only after a wife manifested her *nushūz* unambiguously include Ibn al-Jawzī (A13) 2:76; al-Khāzin, *Lubāb* (A13) 1:375; al-Māwardī (n 6) 1:483; and al-Sulamī (n 8) 1:322.

manifest wifely *nushūz*.[14] Fakhr al-Dīn al-Rāzī (d. 606/1209) preferred the plain-sense meaning of "fear" for *khawf*. He defined *khawf* as "a condition that enters the heart [of a husband when he] suspects [that his wife will commit] a reprehensible deed (*amr makrūh*) in the future (*fī-l-mustaqbal*)."[15] Although al-Rāzī preferred an expansive interpretation of *khawf*, granting husbands greater leeway for disciplining their wives, he also restricted their disciplinary rights. Adhering to the Shāfiʿī legal school's position that the imperative to hit wives in Q. 4:34 is merely a permission and not a command, he posited that although husbands are permitted to hit their wives, it is preferable for them to avoid physical discipline altogether. Furthermore, when husbands do exercise their disciplinary privilege to hit their wives, al-Rāzī mollified this right by recommending that husbands hit their wives with their hands or a folded handkerchief, avoiding the face and not using whips or sticks. Still, he did not propose that husbands hit their wives merely symbolically, since he believed the upper limit of blows permissible to husbands was between twenty and forty and further that they should be spread over the body rather than repeatedly hitting the same body part.[16] In sharp contrast, Muḥammad ibn Yūsuf Abū Ḥayyān (d. 745/1344) claimed that mere expectation (*tawaqquʿ*) of wifely *nushūz* was insufficient to begin any part of the disciplinary process, including admonishment.[17] Although he had more stringent requirements for setting the disciplinary process in motion, he granted husbands great leeway in hitting their wives. He believed that husbands were allowed to severely beat their wives, by punching (*laṭm*), kicking (*lakz*), and whipping (*sawṭ*) them in order to set them straight.[18]

[14] Fakhr al-Dīn al-Rāzī, *al-Tafsīr al-kabīr* (Beirut: Dār Iḥyāʾ al-Turāth al-ʿArabī, 1997) 4:71. He based his position on Al-Shāfiʿī's, who in his *Aḥkām al-Qurʾān*, stated that husbands could begin admonishment if they feared wifely *nushūz*. However, if husbands feared the persistence (*lajājatahunna*) of pre-existing *nushūz*—after it had already manifested itself—then they were permitted to combine the three disciplinary steps (admonishment, abandonment, and hitting). Muḥammad b. Idrīs al-Shāfiʿī, *Aḥkām al-Qurʾān* (Beirut: Dār al-Kutub al-ʿIlmiyya, 1975) 1:209–10. This work is attributed to him and compiled by Aḥmad b. al-Ḥusayn b. ʿAlī b. ʿAbdallāh al-Nīshapūrī (d. 458/1349). Interestingly, this is in contrast to al-Rāzī's position on the fear of husbandly *nushūz* in Q. 4:128, where he described fear as "the manifestation of the clear signs," such as a husband saying to his wife, "You are ugly (*damīma*) or old (*shaykha*) and I want to marry a young (*shābba*) and beautiful (*jamīla*) woman." Al-Rāzī (see earlier in this note) 4:128.

[15] Al-Rāzī (n 14) 4:71. Abū al-Suʿūd (d. 982/1574) used similar wording to describe *khawf*, but he did not adopt al-Rāzī's position of allowing men to discipline their wives—even with admonishment—as a result of expected future actions. He dubbed *khawf* "a condition that obtains in the heart [of a husband] with the presence of [his wife's] reprehensible actions." Here, *khawf* was not the husband's anticipation of his wife's future misdeeds but his feelings of disquietude upon observing the misdeeds, which might lead to wifely *nushūz*. Abū al-Suʿūd (A13) 1:339.

[16] Al-Rāzī (n 14) 4:72.

[17] "Admonishment and what follows [ie the disciplinary process] is permitted only after the persistent appearance of what one initially feared." Abū Ḥayyān (n 7) 3:251.

[18] Abū Ḥayyān (n 7) 3:252.

The preferred interpretations of *khawf* display some of the ethical concerns that pre-colonial scholars brought to bear on their interpretations of Q. 4:34. Some exegetes restricted husbands from beginning the disciplinary process without clear evidence of wifely *nushūz*, while others allowed husbands to admonish their wives based on mere suspicion. However, the preferred interpretation of *khawf* is insufficient for drawing conclusions about a given exegete's ethical stance on the husbandly privilege to physically discipline wives. To get a full picture, we need to determine the exegete's position on the extent of recommended physical discipline. Exegetes who restricted the meaning of *khawf* to "certain knowledge" might also obligate husbands to discipline their wives, and they might further permit husbands a great deal of violence. Exegetes who expanded the purview of husbands to begin admonishment based on their expectation of wifely *nushūz* might also limit the amount of hitting permissible. Just as interpretations of *khawf* influenced the disciplinary power of husbands, various interpretations of *nushūz* impacted the disciplinary license of husbands over wives.

WIFELY *NUSHŪZ*: WHY MIGHT A WIFE BE DISCIPLINED?

The trilateral root of the verbal noun *nushūz*, *n-sh-z*, appears twice in Chapter 4 of the Qur'ān, once in verse 34 and once in verse 128,[19] regarding the behavior of wives (*nushūzahunna*) and husbands (*nushūzan*) respectively.[20] In both cases, *nushūz* is a negative quality, something to be "feared" by the other spouse. The fact that the term *nushūz* is used to refer to the negative behavior of both husbands and wives in the marital relationship may at first glance suggest some parity between spouses—that they may transgress against one another in a similar manner and may be held to a similar standard of accountability. However, although pre-colonial exegetes acknowledged that in both cases the root of *n-sh-z* means "to rise"—describing its verbal noun form as a "hillock"—this rising

[19] "If a wife fears antipathy (*nushūz*) or desertion (*iʿrāḍ*) on her husband's part, there is no blame on them if they arrange an amicable settlement between themselves; and such settlement is best; even though men's souls are swayed by greed. But if ye do good and practice self-restraint, Allah is well-acquainted with all that you do." Abdullah Yusuf Ali, *The Meaning of the Holy Quran* (Beltsville: Amana Publications, 1997) Q. 4:128.

[20] Four conjugations of the verbal root *n-sh-z* appear in the Qur'ān: Q. 58:11, Q. 2:259, Q. 4:34, and Q. 4:128. For more on this, see Ayesha S. Chaudhry, "Marital Discord in Qur'anic Exegesis: A Lexical Analysis of Husbandly and Wifely *Nushūz* in Q. 4:34 and Q. 4:128" in S.R. Burge (ed.), *The Meaning of the Word: Lexicology and Tafsīr* (forthcoming).

was interpreted in completely different ways with regard to its application to and consequences for husbands and wives.[21]

Exegetes interpreted wifely *nushūz* to have four broad meanings: general disobedience, sexual refusal, rising out of one's place, and hatred for one's husband. In all of these cases, wifely *nushūz* necessitated disciplinary action. In contrast, husbandly *nushūz* was interpreted as literally rising out of bed, hatred for one's wife, sexual or monetary withdrawal, and roughness in speech or action (such as injuring a wife through physical violence).[22] Husbandly *nushūz* was always assumed to result from a husband's reaction to his wife's deficiencies. Pre-modern exegetes offered a potpourri of legitimate reasons for why a husband might commit *nushūz*, such as his preference for another, younger (*shābba*) and/or more beautiful (*jamīla*) woman (eg *atharatan ʿalayhā*), his repulsion or hatred for this particular wife (*bughḍ*), his dislike for her (*kirāha*) or her company, his not loving her (*lā yuḥibbuhā* or *raghaba ʿanhā*), her old age (*ʿajazat* or *kibarihā*), her ugliness/disfigurement (*damāmatihā*), her poverty (*faqrihā*), her bad etiquette (*sūʾ khuluqihā*), her inability to

[21] For a comparative analysis of husbandly and wifely *nushūz* in exegetical and legal sources, see Kecia Ali, "Obedience and Disobedience in Islamic Discourses" in Suad Joseph (ed.), *Encyclopedia of Women in Islamic Cultures* (Leiden: Brill, 2007) 309–13 and Chaudhry (n 20). In al-Ḥīrī's survey of the various meanings of *nushūz* in the Qur'ān, he designates "disobedience" as the meaning of wifely *nushūz* in Q. 4:34 and "sexual withdrawal" as the meaning of husbandly *nushūz* in Q. 4:128. Ismāʿīl ibn Aḥmad al-Nīsābūrī al-Ḥīrī, *Wujūh al-Qurʾān* (Mashhad: Majmaʿ al-Buhūth al-Islāmiyya, 2001) 562.

[22] Somewhat paradoxically, when husbandly *nushūz* was defined as sexual refusal it consisted of the very action husbands were authorized to undertake in order to discipline wives when they were guilty of wifely *nushūz*. Husbandly *nushūz* consisted of a husband's sexual antipathy towards her wife, treating her roughly (*khushūna*), injuring her (*yuʾdhīhā*), and hitting her (*ḍarabaha*). Thus, a husband may hit his wife in order to correct wifely *nushūz*, but his hitting might also be considered a form of husbandly *nushūz*. It can be argued that although they never explicitly stated it as such, exegetes reckoned that husbandly *nushūz* occurred when husbands withheld sexual intimacy and/or hit their wives without just cause—that is, apart from rectifying wifely *nushūz*. If wives were guilty of *nushūz*, then husbands would be warranted in withholding sexual intimacy and/or hitting them. But how is a wife to know that her husband's sexual abandonment or hitting are disciplinary measures for her own *nushūz* or constitutive of his *nushūz*? In both cases, the onus is on the wife to remove her husband's undesirable behavior by either changing her behavior so that she is no longer committing *nushūz* against him or appeasing him by relinquishing her marital rights. As anyone who is married knows, spouses often have different "truths" about what is happening in their relationship, so a wife may have a difficult time determining whether she should change her behavior or give up her marital rights. A wife may well be unaware as to exactly why her husband is abandoning or hitting her—whether it is because she is committing *nushūz* or because he no longer finds her attractive. Eg, see Abū Ḥayyān (n 7) 3:263; ʿAbd Allāh ibn Aḥmad al-Nasafī, *Tafsīr al-Nasafī, al-musammā bi-Madārik al-tanzīl wa-ḥaqāʾiq al-taʾwīl* (Beirut: Dār al-Qalam, 1989) 1:351; al-Rāzī (n 14) 4:235; and Maḥmūd ibn ʿUmar al-Zamakhsharī, *al-Kashshāf ʿan ḥaqāʾiq ghawāmiḍ al-tanzīl wa-ʿuyūn al-aqāwīl fī wujūh al-taʾwīl* (Beirut: Dār al-Kutub al-ʿIlmiyya, 2003) 1:499. For more on this, see Chaudhry (n 20).

bear children, his being bored by her (*ṭālat ṣuḥbatuhā*), and his general restlessness (*mulāl*).

Wives were encouraged to resolve husbandly *nushūz* by foregoing their marital rights, such as maintenance (*nafaqa*), dower (*mahr*), and/ or allotted nights for sexual congress (*qism*), in order to remain with their husbands.[23] By giving up the very rights that their husbands were denying them, such as their right to sexual congress and maintenance, wives freed their husbands from fulfilling their marital obligations. The disparate treatment of wifely and husbandly *nushūz* is best understood in light of the idealized cosmology of jurists and exegetes. Husbandly *nushūz* was not removed through disciplinary action because husbands ranked higher in the marital hierarchy. Whereas husbands could discipline wives in order to reclaim their spousal rights from them, wives could not in turn discipline their husbands. The fact that pre-colonial exegetes interpreted wifely and husbandly *nushūz* to have different meanings suggests that they were less concerned with maintaining a cohesive, consistent lexical definition of *nushūz* and were more concerned with interpreting *nushūz* to fulfill their vision of an appropriate marital relationship within a larger cosmological framework. In this framework, all the definitions of wifely (and husbandly) *nushūz* served to reinforce a hierarchal marital structure.[24]

As in the case of *khawf*, the definition of wifely *nushūz* could increase or decrease the power of husbands over wives. If the definition of *nushūz* were narrow and restricted to specific actions, then wives would be safeguarded from wanton disciplinary action. If the definition of *nushūz* were ambiguous and vague, then husbands' disciplinary power would be significantly increased. Pre-colonial exegetes interpreted wifely *nushūz* in Q. 4:34 to have four possible meanings. Overwhelmingly, they defined *nushūz* as a wife's disobedience to her husband.[25] While many exegetes

[23] Abū Ḥayyān (n 7) 3:363; Ibn al-Jawzī (A13) 2:218; Muḥammad ibn Aḥmad Ibn Juzayy, *Kitāb al-Tashīl li-ʿulūm al-Tanzīl* (Beirut: Dār al-Kitāb al-ʿArabī, 1973) 285; Ismāʿīl ibn ʿUmar Ibn Kathīr, *Tafsīr al-ʿaẓīm li-ibn Kathīr* (Damascus: Dar Ibn Kathir, 1994) 1:607; al-Māwardī (n 6) 1:533; al-Nasafī (n 22) 1:352; al-Qurṭubī (A13) 5:384; al-Ṭabarī (n 6) 4:308; Abū al-Ḥasan ʿAlī al-Wāḥidī Nīshābūrī, *al-Wajīz fī tafsīr al-Kitāb al-ʿazīz* (Damascus: Dār al-Qalam, 1995) 1:293; and al-Zamakhsharī (n 22) 1:559.

[24] Eg, al-Qurṭubī described husbandly and wifely *nushūz* in a contrasting manner. A wife committed *nushūz* when she became difficult (*istaṣʿabat*) for her husband, whereas a husband committed *nushūz* when he hit her (*ḍarabahā*) or treated her with cruelty (*jafāhā*). Al-Qurṭubī (A13) 5:163. For a detailed comparison of wifely and husbandly *nushūz*, see Chaudhry (n 20).

[25] For a list of exegetes who offered wifely disobedience as a possible meaning for wifely *nushūz*, see Appendix 14 (A14). The preponderance of *nushūzahunna* as *ʿiṣyānahunna* was partly based on the text of Q. 4:34, which states, "If [your wives] obey you, do not find a means against them." Some exegetes linked the definition of wifely *nushūz* as disobedience to this phrase. Eg, Abū Ḥayyān wrote, "'If they obey you'... suggests that [wives] become disobedient (*ʿāṣiyāt*) when they commit *nushūz*." Abū Ḥayyān (n 7) 3:252. See also Bauer (n 2) 155–6.

understood this to be unqualified disobedience, some limited it to sexual disobedience. Wifely *nushūz* was also characterized as her "rising" (*irtifāʿ*) against her husband[26] or her hatred/repulsion (*bughḍ* or *karāhiya*) for her husband.[27] For many scholars, these interpretations were interconnected and not mutually exclusive.

Defining wifely *nushūz* as the unqualified "disobedience" greatly expanded the range of behaviors for which a wife might be disciplined.[28] Although some exegetes described specific actions that would qualify as "disobedience," most interpreted this to mean a wife's refusal to obey the commands of her husband or God.[29] The meaning of *nushūz* was further broadened by some scholars to include the bad etiquette (*sūʾ al-khuluq*) of wives.[30] For instance, al-Rāzī argued that a wife could commit *nushūz* by altering any desirable behavior—whether in words or actions—to something less appealing. For example, if she was in the habit of standing when her husband entered a room, hurrying to his command, rushing to his bed, and rejoicing when he touched her and then she stopped these practices, she committed *nushūz*.[31] This description of *nushūz* as a wife

[26] For a list of exegetes who translate *nushūz* as "rising" by using *al-irtifāʿ* or a conjugation of *ʿalā*, see Appendix 15 (A15).

[27] Al-Suyūṭī disagreed with this definition of wifely *nushūz*. He argued that a wife was simply required to obey her husband—generally and especially sexually. If she obeyed her husband, even if she hated him throughout her obedience, then her husband should not find excuses against her. Al-Suyūṭī (A14) 2:155–6. Exegetes who considered *bughḍ* or *karāhiya* as possible definitions of wifely *nushūz* include Abū ʿUbayda Maʿmar ibn al-Muthannā al-Taymī, *Majāz al-Qurʾān* (Beirut: Dār al-Kutub al-ʿIlmiyya, 2006) 59; Ibn Abī Ḥātim (A14) 3:942; Ibn Kathīr (n 23) 1:602; Ibn al-Jawzī (A13) 2:75; al-Khāzin (A13)1:374; al-Māwardī (n 6)1:482; al-Qurṭubī (A13) 5:163; al-Ṭabarī (n 6) 4:64; and Abū Isḥāq Ibrāhīm ibn al-Sarī al-Zajjāj, *Maʿānī al-Qurʾān wa-iʿrābuhu* (Beirut: al-Maktaba al-ʿAṣriyya, 1973) 2:48.

[28] Al-Ṭabarī reported from Ibn ʿAbbās that wifely *nushūz* is a wife "reneging on her husband's rights and disobeying his commands (*wa-tastakhiff bi-ḥaqq zawjihā wa-lā tuṭīʿ amrahu*)." Al-Ṭabarī (n 6) 4:64. See also Ibn Abī Ḥātim (A14) 3:941; and al-Nasafī (n 22) 1:355. For a list of exegetes who simply replaced *nushūzahunna* with *iṣyānahunna*, see Appendix 16 (A16).

[29] The rights of husbands and God were intertwined and indistinguishable. Eg, Ibn Kathīr wrote, "God has made the husband's rights obligatory on [a wife], as well as obedience to him. And He has forbidden [a wife to] be disobedient to [her husband], since he has a preferred status (*faḍl*) and merit (*ifḍāl*) over her." Ibn Kathīr (n 23) 1:602. Some exegetes such as Ibn Abī Ḥātim argued that wifely *nushūz* included an abandonment of religious obligations, such as a wife's refusal to ritually purify herself after the end of her menstrual cycle, childbirth, or sex (*janāba*), or her refusal to perform her daily prayers. He argued further that if a wife reneged on her religious duties, a husband could ask a judge to grant him a wife-initiated divorce (*khulʿa*). The significance of this being a *khulʿa* as opposed to a husband-initiated divorce (*talāq*) is that the wife would have to compensate her husband for the divorce rather than vice versa. Ibn Abī Ḥātim (A14) 3:942.

[30] Al-Baghawī (A15) 5:423. Al-Māwardī described wifely *nushūz* as bad actions (*sūʾ fiʿlihā*). Al-Māwardī (n 6) 1:482. Al-Suyūṭī cited a *ḥadīth* that described the "best of women" as those with "excellent etiquette" and the "worst women" had "bad etiquette and a sharp tongue (*sayyiʾat al-khuluq* and *ḥadīdat al-lisān*)". Al-Suyūṭī (A14) 2:152.

[31] Al-Rāzī (n 14) 4:72. Al-Khāzin agreed with al-Rāzī's position, saying that the signs of a wife's *nushūz* are in speech and actions. Examples of such actions are a wife altering her

altering her behavior in some negative way is intriguing because it does not consider the reasons why a wife might change her behavior—is this a reaction to her husband's displeasing behavior? Is she too busy to stand up when he enters a room or too tired at the end of the day to "rejoice" when he touches her? Is she feeling ill? Has she had a bad day? There are myriad reasons why a spouse might alter her behavior. The lack of attention to this point in the exegesis of this verse is striking especially in comparison to the lengthy consideration of a husband's motivation for *nushūz* in the commentaries of Q. 4:128, as seen previously.[32]

Sexual disobedience, as opposed to general disobedience, also constituted wifely *nushūz*; this was described as a wife sexually refusing herself to her husband.[33] This interpretation is especially interesting in contrast to the explanation for husbandly *nushūz* in pre-colonial Qur'ān commentaries. Whereas a husband's sexual disinterest in his wife was interpreted as sexual antipathy with several potential legitimate causes, including his wife's old age, ugliness, or her bad etiquette, a wife's sexual disinterest indicated only sexual disobedience and deserved chastisement. Pre-colonial scholars did not try to ascertain or address the cause(s) of wifely *nushūz*; instead, they focused on the procedural elements of when and how a husband could discipline a wife who exhibited *nushūz*.

An equally prevalent definition of wifely *nushūz* in pre-colonial *tafsīr* was *al-irtifāʿ*, which can be translated as "rebellion," but "rising" is closer to its literal meaning. Of the Arabic equivalents for *nushūz* offered by pre-colonial exegetes, *al-irtifāʿ* is closest in lexical meaning to *nushūz*. Sometimes, *al-istiʿlāʾ* was used as a synonym, which denotes the same meaning of "rising."[34] On this definition, the rising of a wife was figurative and literal, and encompassed both general and sexual disobedience. Wives could rise literally, as in rising from their marital bed in sexual refusal—which counted as sexual disobedience.[35] In doing so, they also rose above their rank in the marital hierarchy.

behavior by no longer hurrying to his command, being deferential when he speaks to her, or standing when he enters upon her. Examples of verbal *nushūz* include a wife raising her voice at her husband and not answering his call. Al-Khāzin (A13) 1:374. See also Ibrāhīm ibn ʿUmar al-Biqāʿī, *Naẓm al-durar fī tanāsub al-āyāt wa-l-suwar* (Hyderabad: Maṭbaʿat Majlis Dāʾirat al-Maʿārif al-ʿUthmāniyya, 1972) 5:271 and al-Shirbīnī (A13) 1:346.

[32] Chaudhry (n 20).

[33] Al-Dīnawarī (d. 308/920) and al-Fīrūzābādī (d. 817/1415) held that *nushūz* occurred when wives disobeyed their husbands in bed (*ʿiṣyānahunna fī al-maḍājiʿ*). Al-Dīnawarī (A13) 1:151 and al-Fīrūzābādī (A13) 91. For a list of exegetes who considered wifely *nushūz* to include sexual disobedience, see Appendix 17 (A17).

[34] The notions of a wife rising against her husband and her rising against him in bed were intertwined for al-Ṭabarī. In addition to describing *nushūz* as disobedience, he described it as "the rising of wives (*istiʿlāʾahunna*) against their husbands, and their rising (*irtifāʿahunna*) from their husbands' bed in disobedience to them." Al-Ṭabarī (n 6) 4:64.

[35] For exegetes such as al-Qurṭubī, a wife's disobedience to her husband was the same as her rising against him. Al-Qurṭubī explained wifely *nushūz* as wives "raising themselves

The rising of wives against their husbands carried implications of rising against God as well. This is because the marital hierarchy, with men in a position of authority over women, was considered to be divinely ordained; when women rose above their station through disobedience to their husbands, they also rose against God, who had set up the hierarchy in the first place.[36] Some exegetes expressed this position by describing a wife's raising herself (*tasta'lī*) against her husband as raising her "nature" (*khuluq*), rising above the "rank assigned to [her] by God" and displaying arrogance (*takabbur*).[37] In these descriptions of wifely *nushūz*, marital hierarchy was an essential characteristic of an ideal marriage. In such a relationship, wives fulfilled their marital obligations and remained in their correct rank within marriage by being obedient to their husbands, whether sexually or otherwise. Any attempt to rise from their appointed rank in the marital hierarchy was considered an act of rebellion in need of discipline.

A final definition offered for wifely *nushūz* was the hatred/repulsion (*bughḍ*) or repugnance (*karāhiya*) of a wife for her husband.[38] For these exegetes, the hatred or repugnance for her husband was either the motivating factor for disobedience and rising, or it was constitutive of *nushūz* itself.[39] Like sexual disobedience, *bughḍ* for one's spouse was considered as a definition for husbandly *nushūz* as well and as such had the potential for a gender-neutral definition of husbandly and wifely *nushūz*, since hatred and repugnance—unlike disobedience—are not hierarchal by definition. One can hate a superior, a subordinate, or an equal.[40] However, a wife's *bughḍ* for her husband was considered to be an

(*ta'āliyahinna*) from what God has made obligatory upon them with regard to the obedience of their husbands." He also noted that a *nāshiza* wife was a wife who was "bad for companionship (*al-sayyi'a li-l-'ishra*)." Al-Qurṭubī (A13) 5:163. See also al-Rāzī (n 14) 4:72.

36 Al-Biqā'ī interpreted wifely *nushūz* as "rising against [their husbands] from the rank to which they were appointed by God." Al-Biqā'ī (n 31) 5:270–1.

37 Abū Ḥayyān wrote "*nushūz*: when a woman becomes crooked and raises her nature and rises against her husband (*wa-l-nushūz: an tata'awwaj al-mar'a wa-yartafi' khuluqahā wa-tasta'lī 'alā zawjihā*)." Al-Tha'ālibī (A13) 2:229. This description was later adopted verbatim by al-Tha'ālibī. Abū Ḥayyān (n 7) 3:25. Al-Khāzin incorporated a wife's evil/mischief (*shurūrahunna*) in his description of wifely *nushūz*. Al-Khāzin (A13) 1:374. See also al-Baghawī (A15) 5:423; al-Biqā'ī (n 31) 5:271; Ibn 'Aṭiyya (A13) 2:47–8; and Ibn Kathīr (n 23) 1:602.

38 Al-Naḥḥās described wifely *nushūz* as enmity or hostility (*'adāwa*). Al-Naḥḥās (A15) 2:78.

39 For Abū 'Ubayda (d. 209/824), *bughḍ* was the sole definition of *nushūz*. He wrote, "*nushūzahunna*: hatred for the husband (*bughḍ al-zawj*)." Abū 'Ubayda (n 27) 59. Ibn Abī Ḥātim al-Rāzī quoted al-Suddī as translating "*nushūzahunna*" as "*bughḍahunna*." Ibn Abī Ḥātim (A14) 3:942. See also al-Khāzin (A13) 1:374 and al-Ṭabarī (n 6) 4:64.

40 Al-Zajjāj (d. 311/923), eg, interpreted *nushūz* as the repugnance of one spouse for the other (*karāhiya li-ṣāḥibihi*), as opposed to only a wife's repugnance for her husband or vice versa (*al-nushūz karāhiya aḥadihimā li-ṣāḥibihi*). Al-Zajjāj (n 27) 2:48.

action warranting discipline, while a husband's *bughḍ* for his wife was resolved through a wife's relinquishment of her marital rights. When hatred was regarded as a motivating factor for wifely *nushūz*, it was treated as an irrational quality that emerged without just cause. Why a wife might hate her husband was not a question that any pre-colonial exegete asked, though as seen previously, they did explore in great detail the reasons why a husband might hate his wife.

All of the definitions offered for wifely *nushūz* in pre-colonial Qur'ān commentaries were hierarchal in nature, and they re-instantiated a patriarchal view of marriage. The fact that the definitions of wifely *nushūz* made it an act requiring disciplinary measures from husbands highlights the asymmetrical relationship between spouses. In this conception, wives ranked below their husbands and owed obedience to them. When wives disobeyed their husbands, they rose above their divinely appointed rank and thus disobeyed God as well. Wifely *nushūz* was interpreted in a manner that bolstered the unequal relationship between husbands and wives. When wifely *nushūz* was interpreted as general disobedience, its meaning was distinctly different than that of husbandly *nushūz*. However, in most cases the meanings of wifely and husbandly *nushūz* overlapped, but the implications of these actions were altered so that they required discipline in the case of wives and amicable settlement in the case of husbands.

THE FIRST IMPERATIVE: "ADMONISH THEM" (*FA-ʿIẒŪHUNNA*)

According to Q. 4:34, three disciplinary measures are available to husbands who fear wifely *nushūz*. The first is admonishment; the second is abandonment in bed; and the final step is hitting. The grammatical construction of these three steps is in the imperative form, and pre-colonial exegetes disagreed about whether they were meant to be understood as commands or recommendations. The exegetical discussion about the first imperative, admonishment, linked the idealized cosmology of scholars to the right of husbands to hit their wives. The purpose of admonishment was twofold: the first was to remind wives of a sanctified asymmetrical and hierarchal marital structure in which wives are required to be obedient to their husbands; the second was to threaten and frighten wives of the divinely ratified disciplinary privileges of husbands, who are allowed to beat disobedient wives.

Pre-colonial scholars agreed that admonishment was meant to be verbal;[41] however, the content of the verbal admonishment was somewhat contested. Exegetes offered a host of potential wordings that might achieve the desired end of admonishment. These wordings reflected a "carrot and stick" approach to admonishing wives;[42] some were loving and constructive, with the aim of rectifying behavior through persuasion;[43] and some were aggressive and threatening so as to affect the behavior of wives through fear.[44] Pre-colonial exegetes saw the ideal admonition as a balance between persuasion and threat. This was illustrated through the synonyms they used to describe admonishment as well as through the recommended content of the admonishment. All of their suggestions further underscored the idealized cosmology that pre-colonial exegetes brought to bear on their interpretation of Q. 4:34.

"Admonish them" (*fa-ʿiẓūhunna*) was most commonly interpreted to mean either "remind them" (*yudhakkirūhunna*)[45] and/or "warn them" (*khawwifūhunna*).[46] The content of the reminder and/or warning was the

[41] Al-Ṭabarī reported from Muḥammad b. Kaʿb al-Qarẓī (d. 117/735) that "When a man sees frivolity in [his wife's] eyes, and [sees] her coming and going [at will], he should say to her verbally, 'I have seen from you such and such, so stop! (*idhā raʾā al-rajul khiffatan fī baṣarihā wa-madkhalihā wa-makhrajihā, qāla yaqūlu lahā bi-lisānihi, "qad raʾaytu minki kadhā wa-kadhā, fa-ntahī!*).' " Al-Ṭabarī (n 6) 4:65. Exegetes who mentioned "verbal" in some form or other in their exegesis of this term include al-Baghawī (A15) 5:423; Ibn Abī Ḥātim (A14) 3:942; Ibn Abī Zamanīn (A14) 1:367; Ibn al-Jawzī (A13) 2:76; al-Khāzin (A13) 1:374; al-Qurṭubī (A13) 5:164; al-Rāzī (n 14) 4:72; al-Suyūṭī (A14) 2:155; and al-Wāḥidī (n 23) 1:263.

[42] Abū al-Suʿūd described admonishment as advice that included both the carrot (*targhīb*) and the stick (*tarhīb*). Abū al-Suʿūd (A13) 1:339. Al-Nasafī described admonishment as "speech that softens the hardened hearts (*al-qulūb al-qāsiya*) and inspires (*yuraghghib*) the aversive disposition." It was meant to "frighten [wives] of God's punishments (*al-ʿawāqib*)." Al-Nasafī (n 22) 1:355. Abū Bakr Ibn al-ʿArabī also encouraged husbands to use a mix of both positive and negative motivators when admonishing their wives. He interpreted "*fa-ʿiẓūhunna*" as the "remembering (*tadhkīr*) of God, in inspiring (*targhīb*) [wives] with reward and warning (*takhwīf*) them of His punishment (*ʿiqāb*)." Ibn al-ʿArabī (n 7) 1:496. See also al-Biqāʿī (n 31) 5:270.

[43] Eg, Ibn al-Jawzī noted that according to al-Khalīl b. Aḥmad (d. 170/786), the purpose of admonishment was a "goodly reminder," which would soften (*yuriqqu*) the heart of one's wife (*al-waʿẓ: al-tadhkīr bi-l-khayr fī mā yuriqqu lahu al-qalb*). Ibn al-Jawzī (A13) 2:75. According to Mohammad Fadel, his death date is contested. "Rules, Judicial Discretion and the Rule of Law in Naṣrid Granada" in *Islamic Law: Theory and Practice* (New York: I.B. Taurus, 1997) 78.

[44] Al-Biqāʿī advocated both approaches; he wrote that it was important to remind wives of such things from God's commands as would soften (*yaṣdaʿu*, lit. crack open) their hearts, but he also encouraged husbands to cause their wives to fear (*yukhīfahunna*) the majesty of God. Al-Biqāʿī (n 31) 5:271.

[45] Exegetes who interpreted *fa-ʿiẓūhunna* as at least partly a "reminder" include Ibn Abī Ḥātim (A14) 3:941; Ibn al-ʿArabī (n 7) 1:495; Ibn ʿAṭiyya (A13) 2:48; Ibn al-Jawzī (A13) 2:75; al-Qurṭubī (A13) 5:164–5; al-Suyūṭī (A14) 2:155; and al-Ṭabarī (n 6) 4:65.

[46] Al-Ṭabarī recorded Mujāhid as saying that when a husband fears *nushūz* from his wife, he should say to her, "Fear God (*ittaqī-llāh*)." He also cited al-Ḥasan as saying that a

cosmological order in which the marriage was ensconced, as well as the immediate and long-term consequences for wives who disrupt this divine order. Quoting Muḥammad ibn Idrīs al-Shāfiʿī (d. 204/820), al-Rāzī wrote that husbands should say to their wives, " 'Fear God (*ittaqī-llāh*), for I have rights over you, so return from whatever it is you are up to, and know that obedience to me is obligatory upon you', and so on."[47] Pre-colonial exegetes also encouraged husbands to remind their wives of God's preference of men over women, which granted husbands moral authority and disciplinary power in marriage. Abū Jaʿfar Muḥammad ibn Jarīr al-Ṭabarī (d. 311/923) reported from Ibn ʿAbbās that "When [a wife] commits *nushūz*, God has commanded [the husband] to admonish her, remind her of God and emphasize/aggrandize (*yuʿaẓẓim*) his rights over her."[48] Wives were required by God to be obedient to their husbands, and their marital shortcomings—through disobedience—indicated their religious failing.

If wives continued to disobey their husbands—and God—then they were subject to punishment at the hands of both. As deputies of God, it was the duty of husbands to discipline their wives when they committed *nushūz*, and since God was watching over them, wives ought also to be afraid of God's punishment in the Hereafter. For example, ʿAlī ibn Muḥammad al-Māwardī (d. 450/1058) wrote that when a wife is disobedient, a husband should "warn his wife (*yukhawwifahā*) of what will be due to her on the Day of Reckoning as a result of her disobeying him, and that God has permitted him to hit her when he is opposed [by her]."[49] The role of admonishment, then, was to make wives fearful of the punishment they faced at the hands of their husbands—as prescribed by God—if they rose out of their divinely ordained place in the marital hierarchy.

husband should "command his wife to fear God and obey him (*yaʾmuruhā bi-taqwā allāhi wa-ṭāʿatihi*)." Al-Ṭabarī (n 6) 4:65. Al-Samarqandī wrote that a husband should say, "Fear God, for the rights of the husband are obligatory upon you (*fa-ʿiẓūhunna bi-llāhi, ay yaqūlu lahā: ittaqīillāh, fa-ʾinna ḥaqq al-zawj ʿalayki wājib*)." Al-Samarqandī (n 6) 1:352. For a list of exegetes who used a conjugation of *kh-w-f* or *t-q-w* to interpret "*fa-ʿiẓūhunna,*" see Appendix 18 (A18).

[47] Al-Rāzī (n 14) 4:72. Al-Khāzin used the same quotation verbatim in his exegesis but did not attribute it to either al-Shāfiʿī or al-Rāzī. Al-Khāzin (A13) 1:374.

[48] Al-Ṭabarī (n 6) 4:65. Al-Jaṣṣāṣ wrote that admonishment was meant to remind wives of God in an effort "to attract them to the reward that resides with God, as well as make them fear His punishment. In addition, the consequence of this is that [a husband] should make her cognizant (*yuʿarrifuhā*) of the good etiquette required for creating beatific companionship as well as the fulfillment of marital responsibilities and meeting the claims of obedience to the husband, and recognizing his degree over her." Al-Jaṣṣāṣ (A14) 1:376 and 2:188–9. Al-Qurṭubī wrote that husbands were to remind their wives about "what God has made obligatory on [wives], of good companionship and beatific companionability (*jamīl al-ʿishra*) with the husband, and a recognition of his degree over her (*wa-l-iʿtirāf bi-l-daraja allatī lahu ʿalayhā*)". Al-Qurṭubī (A13) 5:164.

[49] "*wa-mā abāḥa allāhu taʿālā min ḍarbihā ʿinda mukhālifatihi.*" Al-Māwardī (n 6) 1:482.

It is significant that for pre-colonial exegetes, when a husband feared his wife's *nushūz,* he was instructed to instill fear of physical punishment in her.[50] Some exegetes recommended that husbands list abandonment in bed alongside beating as repercussions of wifely *nushūz*. These interpretations of admonishment turned the first disciplinary measure into a threat of the second and third disciplinary measures.[51] The fact that most pre-colonial exegetes identified physical violence as the main outcome of persistent wifely *nushūz* illustrates two related points. One, pre-colonial exegetes understood the right to hit wives to be a key tool available to husbands in order to enforce their marital authority; and, two, hitting wives was one of the main foci of Q. 4:34. This hitting was a husbandly duty, as it restored the divinely ordered hierarchy by returning wives to their correct place in marriage and was morally good for both wives and husbands. In the case of wives, it protected them from further divine punishment in the Hereafter, and in the case of husbands it secured them merit for discharging their husbandly duties by keeping their wives in line.

THE SECOND IMPERATIVE: "ABANDON THEM IN BEDS" (*WA-HJURŪHUNNA FĪ AL-MAḌĀJIʿ*)

The role of historical interpretive precedent is central to the exegesis of the second imperative in Q. 4:34. Scholarly precedent played an authoritative and authenticating role in pre-colonial Qur'anic commentaries. In order to garner legitimacy for their own positions, exegetes often tried to link their preferred interpretations to the positions of earlier scholars. Sometimes,

[50] Al-Shirbīnī wrote that a husband should say to his wife, " 'Fear God concerning the obligatory rights upon you and avoid the punishments (*al-ʿuqūba*)'. And he should explain to her (i.e. the wife) that *nushūz* cancels out maintenance (*nafaqa*) and allotment of nights (*qasm*)." Al-Shirbīnī (A13) 1:346. Loss of economic sustenance (*nafaqa*) and clothing (*kiswa*) was also mentioned in Ibn al-ʿArabī and al-Qurṭubī's discussion of the three disciplinary steps. However, they did not discuss loss of division of allotted nights. Ibn al-ʿArabī (n 7) 1:498; and al-Qurṭubī (A13) 5:166. While the issue of the maintenance of wives and what actions might result in its nullification was the subject of lively juridical debate, it was not popular in exegetical literature. For a greater juridical discussion of the issue of maintenance and when husbands must or may not maintain their wives, see Kecia Ali, *Marriage and Slavery in Early Islam* (Cambridge, Harvard University Press, 2010) ch 2.

[51] Eg, Abū Ḥayyān wrote that husbands ought to remind their wives of the disciplinary power their degree granted them. He interpreted *fa-ʿiẓūhunna* as "reminding [wives] of God's commands of obedience to the husband, and explaining to them that God has permitted hitting them when they are disobedient, as well as God's punishment for them when they are disobedient (*wa-taʿrīfuhunna anna-llāha abāḥa ḍarbahunna ʿinda ʿiṣyānihinna, wa ʿiqābu-llāhi la-hunna ʿalā-l-ʿiṣyān*)." Abū Ḥayyān (n 7) 3:251. Also, al-Sulamī wrote that admonishment consisted of ordering wives to be God-conscious (*bi-l-taqwā*) and further "warning (*al-takhwīf*) them of the hitting (*al-ḍarb*) that God has authorized (*adhina-llāh*)." Al-Sulamī (n 8) 1:321.

these reverse attributions accurately reflected the positions of earlier scholars, while at other times these attributions stretched and maybe even misrepresented earlier scholarly opinions. In a bid to gain authority and give their own positions authenticity, exegetes occasionally cited their forebears in a way that reflected what they wished their predecessors had said, rather than what they had actually said.

It was standard practice for exegetes to present several possible interpretations of a given verse or term that had been posited by previous authoritative scholars and then choose one of the foregoing positions as their own preferred interpretation. The ability of *tafsīr* to maintain a multiplicity of interpretations is considered a great strength of the genre, since Qur'anic interpretations did not restrict dialogue by demanding uniformity of opinion. However, the reliance on historical scholarly precedent in order to anchor any interpretation also potentially stifled creativity. Specifically, it was difficult to claim authority for an interpretation of the Qur'anic text that had no precedent in earlier scholarly opinions. Yet the interpretations surrounding the exhortation to abandon wives in bed illustrate that despite the centrality of historical precedent in Qur'anic commentaries, precedent did not restrict exegetes' creativity in either positing new interpretations or in rejecting the interpretations of previous authoritative scholars. Exegetes exercised a great deal of independence when evaluating the opinions of their predecessors for adherence or rejection, and as a result they were able to construct creative and innovative hermeneutical moves.

The central problem that preoccupied pre-colonial exegetes about the prescription to abandon wives in bed was the paradox that it created: if wifely *nushūz* was the disobedience of wives or their sexual refusal, or even hatred of their husbands, how did it make sense to abandon them in bed when they exhibited such behavior? Would not sexually disobedient wives welcome abandonment in bed? In this case, husbands would be giving their wives exactly what they wanted. Furthermore, if abandonment in bed meant that husbands could not have sex with their wives, then husbands—and perhaps only husbands—suffered from this disciplinary measure. How did this imperative discipline *nāshiza* wives?[52]

[52] Mahmoud has written, "The 'sexual deprivation' measure expressed by '*wa-hjurūhunna fī al-maḍāji*'' (and abandon them in bed) proved confusing to the exegetes. For one thing, if a woman's disobedience is motivated by her dislike or hatred of her husband, such an abstention on his part would be most desirable as far as she is concerned." Mohamed Mahmoud, "To Beat or Not to Beat: On the Exegetical Dilemmas over Qur'ān Q. 4:34," *Journal of the American Oriental Society*, 126(4) (2006) 543. Also see Bauer (n 2) 167, 180. For a list of exegetes who considered "avoiding sex" with one's wife as a possible interpretation of *wa-hjurūhunna fī al-maḍāji*', see Appendix 19 (A19).

Pre-colonial scholars responded to this paradox with several creative interpretations of the prescription to abandon wives in bed.[53] The plain-sense meaning of abandoning wives in bed is most likely sexual abandonment, since Q. 4:34 mentions the marital bed as the site of abandonment. Interpreted in this way, the second imperative functions in opposition to the first; the first requires husbands to command wives to return to the marital bed in admonition, whereas the second requires them to abandon wives in their beds.[54] There was disagreement about the exact meaning of "abandon them in beds." This prescription could mean that husbands ought to abandon both the marital bed and sex with their wives[55] or that they were required to remain in the marital bed while sexually abandoning their wives.[56] Exegetes who believed that husbands were required to abandon the marital bed alongside sexual abandonment may have worried about a husband's resolve in sexually abandoning a wife while remaining in bed with her.[57] In contrast, exegetes who argued that the bed was meant to be the site of abandonment insisted that husbands remain in the marital bed while sexually abandoning their wives.[58] This meaning was justified through a lexical argument. ʿAbd Allāh ibn Aḥmad al-Nasafī (d. 710/1310) reasoned that if husbands were meant to leave the marital bed, the prescription *wa-hjurūhunna fī al-maḍājiʿ* would have used the preposition "from" (ʿ*an*) rather than "in"

[53] Karen Bauer considers these discussions, with specific attention to their development over time, in her dissertation. Bauer (n 2) 162–80.

[54] The phrases "returning to bed," "abandoning in bed" must be understood somewhat euphemistically here. Taking these phrases literally poses many problems. Eg, if a wife has literally left the marital bed, then a husband leaving the same bed would simply leave the bed empty, and he would not actually be abandoning her. Al-Wāḥidī used another word, "separate" (*farriqū*), to suggest that husbands should separate from their wives in bed: "*farriqū baynakum wa-bayna[hunna] fī al-maḍājiʿ*". Al-Wāḥidī (n 23) 1:263. His wording did not specify if husbands and wives should "separate" in bed by being in separate beds altogether, or if they should remain in the same bed but avoid sex. For a list of exegetes who considered "leaving the bed" as an interpretive possibility of "abandon them in beds," see Appendix 20 (A20).

[55] Several exegetes mentioned that husbands could not have sex with their wives (*lā tubāshirūhunna*). Eg, see Abū al-Suʿūd (n 15) 1:339. Exegetes who considered the possibility of sexual abandonment as part and parcel of abandoning the marital bed included Abū Ḥayyān (n 7) 3:251; al-Ḥaddād (A13) 2:250; Ibn ʿAṭiyya (A13) 2:48; Ibn al-Jawzī (A13) 2:76; Ibn Wahb (A13) 1:146; al-Khāzin (A13) 1:375; al-Māwardī (n 6) 1:482; al-Shirbīnī (A13) 1:346; al-Suyūṭī (A14) 2:155; and al-Zamakhsharī (n 22) 1:496. For additional discussion on the exegetical opinions of al-Ṭabarī's contemporaries, see Bauer (n 2) 171–2.

[56] Exegetes who considered the hermeneutic option of sexual abandonment as meaning that husbands remain in the same bed as their wives while denying them sexual access include Ibn al-ʿArabī (n 7) 1:496–7; Ibn ʿAṭiyya (A13) 2:48; al-Māwardī (n 6) 1:482; al-Nasafī (n 22) 1:355; al-Sulamī (n 8) 1:321; and al-Suyūṭī (A14) 2:155.

[57] Al-Zajjāj interpreted abandonment as not "sleeping" with one's wife (*fī al-nawm maʿahunna*). Al-Zajjāj (n 27) 2:49.

[58] For a list of exegetes who mentioned that husbands should turn their backs to their wives, see Appendix 21 (A21).

(*fī*) before "beds" (*al-maḍājiʿ*).[59] Since the text of Q. 4:34 prescribes that wives are to be abandoned *in* bed, husbands must remain in the marital bed with their wives while avoiding sex by turning their backs to them (*yuwalliyahā al-ẓahr*).[60] In order to ensure that husbands remain in bed but sexually deny their wives (and themselves), some exegetes suggested that husbands should refrain from sharing the covers (*falā tudkhilūhunna taḥta al-luḥuf*) with their wives.[61]

There is a third way to think about the marital bed when interpreting "abandon them in beds." Some exegetes posited that the marital bed was not at all meant to be the site of abandonment but was rather simply the location where the "cause" (*sabab*) for the abandonment (ie, wifely *nushūz*) occurred.[62] According to this interpretation, the second imperative in Q. 4:34 would read "concerning those women from whom you fear *nushūz* in bed ... abandon them" rather than "concerning those women from whom you fear *nushūz* ... abandon them in beds."[63] Here, the meaning of wifely *nushūz* was restricted to sexual disobedience, while the meaning of abandonment was expanded so that husbands were permitted to abandon their wives in multiple settings. This interpretation is significant for three reasons. First, since it requires rearranging the order of words in the Qur'anic text, it demonstrates the interpretive flexibility available to scholars. Second, as a minority opinion, this interpretation exemplifies the ability of exegetes to devise new interpretations of the Qur'anic text without historical precedent. Third, it illustrates that despite the constraints of an idealized cosmology which upheld a vision of marriage that was asymmetrical, exegetes still had room to posit varying interpretations of Qur'anic texts on marriage. In other words, a shared idealized cosmology did not predetermine a flat and unimaginative interpretive tradition.

Exemplifying the fecund interpretive possibilities available to exegetes, some scholars interpreted the imperative to "abandon them in beds" as general abandonment—which included but was not limited to sexual abandonment. In this interpretation, "turning one's back on one's wife"

[59] Al-Nasafī (n 22) 1:355.

[60] Eg, al-Ṭabarī cited Ibn ʿAbbās as having restricted the site of abandonment to the marital bed. He wrote that "a man and his wife were to remain on the same bed and not have sex," and/or that the husband was to "turn his back (*yuwalliyahā al-ẓahr*)" to his wife. Al-Ṭabarī (n 6) 4:66.

[61] Abū al-Suʿūd (n 15) 1:339; al-Bayḍāwī (A14) 1:85; al-Nasafī (n 22) 1:355; and al-Zamakhsharī (n 22) 1:496. See also, Bauer (n 2) 173.

[62] Eg, al-Samīn (n 5) 3:672–3; and al-Thaʿālibī (A13) 2:230.

[63] Al-Samīn also cited al-Wāḥidī as connecting "*al-maḍājiʿ*" with "*nushūz*," such that the reworded portion of the verse reads "*wa-l-lātī takhāfūna nushūzahunna fī al-maḍājiʿi*." I did not find this in al-Wāḥidī's *al-Wajīz*. Al-Samīn (n 5) 3:673.

(*yuwallīhā ẓahrahu*)[64] was understood metaphorically rather than literally, and the consequence of this imperative was that wives were shunned through denial of intimacy, companionship, and even conversation.[65] While some exegetes believed that abandonment in bed included sexual abandonment, others argued that husbands were meant to ostracize their wives in bed, without forfeiting their own sexual rights. This meant that husbands were permitted to have sex with their wives while shunning them in other ways.[66]

As seen previously, exegetes understood "admonishment" to mean that husbands should verbally advise their wives to abandon their *nushūz* through persuasion and/or intimidation. When admonishment was ineffective, some exegetes advised husbands to shun their wives by refusing to speak to them (*lā yukallimahā* or *tark al-kalām*).[67] In this scenario, speech became a tool of power that was wielded against wives in multiple ways. Speech could be employed for disciplinary purposes—threatening wives with the impending physical chastisement if they persisted in their *nushūz*—and it could be used to shun wives by stonewalling them. Abandoning speech, like turning one's back on one's wife and avoiding sex, was a form of withholding intimacy.

How long were husbands supposed to spurn their wives? This is an important question, especially in cases where the three disciplinary prescriptions are interpreted to be applied sequentially, after each previous measure has been exhausted. Whether husbands exhaust this disciplinary measure by not speaking to their wives for an hour, week, month, or year has serious consequences for both spouses. Leaving the duration of abandonment unspecified or having husbands wait until wives obey them (*ḥattā yarjiʿna ilā mā yuḥibb*)[68] can lead to indefinite estrangement. Some exegetes chose this interpretation despite its indefinite nature,[69] while other scholars felt that husbands were permitted to speak to their wives during abandonment only in order to terminate the marriage.[70] Others

64 Bauer notes that this is the most widespread interpretation of abandonment as a disciplinary measure. Bauer (n 2) 180.

65 Eg, al-Qurṭubī (A13) 5:164; and Abū Ḥayyān (n 7) 3:252.

66 Eg, Al-Naḥḥās, citing Sufyān, "*wa-hjurūhunna fī al-maḍājiʿ, qāla Sufyān, min ghayr tark al-jimāʿ*." Al-Naḥḥās (A15) 2:79.

67 For a list of exegetes who mentioned abandonment of speech as a possible interpretation of *wa-hjurūhunna fī al-maḍājiʿ*, see Appendix 22 (A22).

68 Al-Ṭabarī offers this as a possibility. Al-Ṭabarī (n 6) 4:67.

69 Al-Thaʿālibī linked the duration of abandonment to its (in)effectiveness. He wrote that husbands should leave off speaking to their wives and turn away from them until "they returned" to obedience. Al-Thaʿālibī (A13) 2:230.

70 Al-Ṭabarī and Ibn Kathīr cited Ibn ʿAbbās as arguing for this position, mentioning that this would be difficult (*shadīd*) for a wife to bear (*lā yukallimuhā min ghayr an yadhara nikāḥahā, wa-dhālika ʿalayhā shadīd*). Al-Ṭabarī (n 6) 4:66; and Ibn Kathīr (n 23) 1:602.

still recommended that abandonment of speech be restricted to either three days or a month.[71] Prophetic practice was used to justify the time constraints on abandonment of speech. Muḥammad is reported to have advised believers not to cut off communications from another believer for longer than three days. Abū Ḥayyān argued that abandonment was meant to be sexual as well as verbal and could last up to a month. He was the only exegete who relied on Muḥammad's example to support this point; when Muḥammad was displeased with his wives, he expressed his displeasure by moving into a separate quarter for an entire month.[72]

If the purpose of admonishment is to persuade and/or intimidate wives into relinquishing their *nushūz*—partly through the threat of beating—then what is the desired end of abandonment in beds? While some exegetes felt that the purpose of abandonment was to anger, exasperate, or make things difficult for one's wife, other exegetes saw abandonment in beds as an intermediary step that tested the presence of wifely *nushūz* and thereby helped to clarify whether husbands could hit their wives.[73] These scholars argued that if a woman was actually guilty of wifely *nushūz*—whether this was general disobedience, sexual refusal, or hatred for her husband—she would be thrilled by abandonment, which in turn would provide evidence of her manifest *nushūz*.[74] Therefore, if a wife seemed content with being

[71] Abandonment of speech was al-Rāzī's preferred interpretation for abandonment as a disciplinary measure, although he acknowledged that sexual abandonment was also a possible interpretation of the phrase. He cited al-Shāfiʿī to argue that abandonment of speech should not exceed three days, alluding to the *ḥadīth* wherein Muḥammad is alleged to have advised believers to refrain from abandoning speech with other believers for more than three days. Al-Rāzī (n 14) 4:72. This *ḥadīth* figured largely in juridical discussions of husbands' disciplinary powers. Al-Suyūṭī cited opinions of predecessors that restricted abandonment to speech ("*lā yukallimhā*") and specified that abandonment was meant to be verbal and not sexual (*al-kalām wa-l-ḥadīth, wa-laysa bi-l-jamāʿ*). Al-Suyūṭī (A14) 2:155.

[72] Though Abū Ḥayyān used the prophetic example of leaving his wives' quarters to argue that abandonment was meant to be sexual as well as verbal, he argued also against this particular prophetic example by insisting that the abandonment was meant to be carried out in the home and not in public. Whereas Muḥammad had publicly shunned his wives, Abū Ḥayyān argued that the Qur'anic passage "in the beds" indicated that abandonment was meant to be a domestic affair in which the community was not to be involved. He interpreted "home" as a place where one sleeps, hence the connection between "beds" and "home." Abū Ḥayyān (n 7) 3:251–2. In line with Abū Ḥayyān's interpretation, Al-Huwwārī understood *wa-hjurūhunna* as "not going near" one's wife. Al-Huwwārī (A16) 1:378. Interestingly, modern Muslim feminists have used this story to argue the exact same point as Abū Ḥayyān—that the Qur'ān actually orders husbands to separate from their wives. However, a key difference is that they use this incident to encourage separation as an interpretation of *wa-ḍribūhunna* rather than of *wa-hjurūhunna fī al-maḍājiʿ*. Eg, see See Laleh Bakhtiar, *The Sublime Quran* (Chicago: Kazi Publications, 2007) Introduction, esp. p. xxvi.

[73] Exegetes who suggested that abandonment was meant to be a test to verify the presence of wifely *nushūz* include al-Ḥaddād (A13) 2:250; al-Qurṭubī (A13) 5:164; al-Rāzī (n 14) 4:72; al-Samarqandī (n 6) 1:352; al-Suyūṭī (A14) 2:155; and al-Zajjāj (n 27) 2:49.

[74] For example, al-Zajjāj wrote, "If they love their husbands, then the abandonment would be unbearable (*shaqq*) for them, but if they hate [their husbands] then they will find [the

abandoned, her husband would be authorized to exercise physical violence against her.[75] Abandonment was thereby a kind of test: when a husband suspected *nushūz*, the abandonment would show him if his suspicions were warranted. Just as a wife's happiness during the phase of abandonment would prove that she is a *nāshiza*, her unhappiness during this phase would prove that she is innocent of *nushūz*. Needless to say, this is not a very rigorous test; for instance, it does not account for various forms of (mis)communication. What if a wife is verbally abandoned by her husband based on an erroneous suspicion of wifely *nushūz*, and because her husband refuses to speak to her, he misinterprets her patience with his abandonment as happiness, concluding that he ought to hit her due to incontrovertible evidence of *nushūz*?

The command to "abandon" was interpreted in multiple ways, including "verbal abuse." Some exegetes interpreted abandonment in beds as speaking to wives harshly, using "ugly," "obscene," and/or "vile" speech.[76] As Bauer has pointed out, this interpretation was based on one of the lexical meanings of the verb *h-j-r* to mean "vile or offensive speech."[77] In this interpretation, abandonment in beds functioned as an intensified form of admonishment, whereby husbands ostracized their wives through verbal abuse.[78] As encountered in previous interpretations, exegetes debated whether this verbal abuse should be restricted to the marital bed or if it could be expanded to multiple settings.[79] They also offered varied

abandonment] agreeable and this is evidence of their *nushūz* (*fa-kāna dalīlan ʿalā al-nushūz min hunna*)". Al-Zajjāj (n 27) 2:49.

[75] For example, al-Rāzī argued that if wifely *nushūz* persisted after abandonment, then a husband could hit his wife (*in baqiyat ʿalā al-nushūz ḍarabahā*). Al-Rāzī (n 14) 4:72. See also Ibn al-Jawzī (A13) 2:76; and al-Ḥaddād (A13) 2:247–51.

[76] Al-Ḥaddād described this speech as "ugly." Al-Ḥaddād (A13) 2:250. See also, al-Sulamī (n 8) 1:321. Ibn ʿAṭiyya considered "harsh speech" to be a misinterpretation of abandonment, preferring instead sexual or verbal abandonment. Ibn ʿAṭiyya (A13) 2:48. Ibn al-ʿArabī also disparaged this interpretation of *wa-hjurūhunna*. Ibn al-ʿArabī (n 7) 1:496–8. For a list of exegetes who considered "harsh speech" as a possible interpretation of "abandonment in bed," see Appendix 23 (A23).

[77] Bauer writes, "The method of interpretation here is to change the form of the word. The verbal form *hajara* is changed to *ahjara*, rendering it as 'speak roughly/harshly' rather than 'avoid.'" Bauer (n 2) 164.

[78] Eg, Ibn Abī Ḥātim mentioned that abandonment could be in speech (*bi-l-manṭaq*), in that a husband would be rude or impolite to his wife (*yagluẓ lahā*). Ibn Abī Ḥātim (A14) 3:943. Al-Ḥaddād described the appropriate speech as obscene/vile (*al-kalām al-fāḥish*). Al-Ḥaddād (A13) 2:250. Al-Qurṭubī described the nature of speech to be used by husbands in this interpretation as "ugly words, meaning rough/coarse speech." Al-Qurṭubī (A13) 5:164.

[79] Al-Ṣanʿānī reported from Ibn ʿAbbās that abandonment in bed referred to speaking roughly (*yughliẓ la-hā bi-l-qawl*) to one's wife, not to avoiding sexual relations with her. Similarly, he reported from ʿIkrima (d. ca. 105/723) that abandonment meant speaking roughly to one's wife but did not mean the abandonment of sexual relations (*an yughliẓa la-hā wa-laysa bi-l-jimāʿ*). Al-Ṣanʿānī (n 13) 1:158. Al-Māwardī and Ibn al-Jawzī did not specify whether husbands were to use crude speech with their wives while they were avoiding

opinions about whether sexual abandonment was meant to accompany verbal abuse or if verbal abuse was the stand-alone meaning of "abandon them in beds."[80] Restricting verbal abuse to the marital bed is especially troubling, in part because some exegetes considered it acceptable for husbands to verbally abuse their wives while having sex with them. This interpretation solved the paradox of understanding "abandon them in beds" as sexual withdrawal from wives who were already sexually refusing their husbands. In this scenario, husbands could verbally discipline their wives while also enjoying their marital rights of sexual access.

Two interpretations of "abandon them in beds" are especially instructive in highlighting the capacity of exegetes to reject and selectively accept interpretations from authoritative predecessors. Both ʿAbd al-Razzāq al-Ṣanʿānī (d. 211/826) and al-Ṭabarī (d. 311/923) offered interpretations of "abandon them in beds" that were either largely ignored or rejected outright. Based on the authority of al-Kalbī, al-Ṣanʿānī proposed a meaning for "abandon them in beds" that was the opposite of its plain-sense meaning; instead of abandoning wives in bed, he argued that this prescription actually meant that husbands should call their wives to the marital bed.[81] Al-Ṣanʿānī's position did not gain currency in later works of exegesis, but it was not discredited either, illustrating that the genre of *tafsīr* allowed for a range of viable hermeneutic options, even when a proposed interpretation was the opposite of the plain-sense meaning of a text.[82]

In contrast to al-Ṣanʿānī, al-Ṭabarī considered the various lexical meanings of *h-j-r* and concluded that the most accurate interpretation of *wa-hjurūhunna* is not abandonment at all but rather "securing" or

sexual relations with them in bed or whether they were to use rough speech while having sex with their wives. Al-Māwardī (n 6) 1:482; and Ibn al-Jawzī (A13) 2:76. Others mentioned the possibility that husbands were to abandon speaking to their wives, and this ought to continue even during sexual congress. See, eg, Ibn al-ʿArabī (n 7) 1:498.

80 For more discussion on this see, Bauer (n 2) 164–5. She mentions that some exegetes argued for this recourse when husbands were motivated by a desire for sex.

81 On the authority of Hishām b. Muḥammad b. al-Sāʾib bin Bishr al-Kalbī (d. 146/763), al-Ṣanʿānī disagreed with the interpretation of abandonment as harsh speech. He wrote, "Al-Kalbī says, the *hajr* in the beds does not mean to speak roughly to wives (*yaqūl lahā hujran*). It is ordering them to come back, and return to their beds." Al-Ṣanʿānī (n 13) 1:158. Bauer finds this to be the "most arbitrary" of all the interpretations of this phrase, reflecting most clearly the "exegete's desired interpretation." Bauer (n 2) 164.

82 In the contemporary period, Ahmed Ali has translated *wa-ḍribūhunna* to mean "and have sex with them." Ahmed Ali, *Al-Qurʾan: A Contemporary Translation* (Princeton: Princeton University Press, 2004) Q. 4:34. More recently, Laleh Bakhtiar has translated *wa-ḍribūhunna* to mean "to walk away from them." In both instances, they have come under criticism for misinterpreting the prescription *wa-ḍribūhunna* to mean something other than its plain-sense meaning in favor of their own desired interpretations. Exegetes such as al-Ṣanʿānī demonstrate a historical precedent for such an approach in Qurʾanic exegesis. Al-Ṣanʿānī (n 13) 1:158.

"tethering" one's wife. Using the analogy of tethering a camel, al-Ṭabarī argued that in the event that admonishment failed, "*wa-hjurūhunna fī al-maḍājiʿi*" prescribed husbands to imprison their wives by tying them to their beds.[83] This interpretation was rejected by some later exegetes, who found it to be ethically abhorrent, but it was upheld by others.[84] Still, this interpretation did not compromise al-Ṭabarī's standing as an authoritative predecessor, since the same exegetes who denounced his stance on abandonment continued to rely on al-Ṭabarī's authoritativeness on other matters. Furthermore, centuries later, Abū Ḥayyān mentioned al-Tabarī's position authoritatively, even while acknowledging that later scholars, such as Maḥmūd ibn ʿUmar al-Zamakhsharī (d. 538/1143), had rejected this interpretation by calling it the "argument of the boors."[85] However, Abū Ḥayyān did not interpret the second imperative to mean that husbands ought to tie their wives in bed, arguing instead that if the three imperatives failed to work, then husbands could tie their wives in bed and force them to have sex with them, since this was their right.[86] By drawing on this particular interpretation, Abū Ḥayyān disregarded all the critiques of al-Ṭabarī's position and refashioned it to suit his own purposes. Al-Ṭabarī's example demonstrates that pre-colonial exegetes did not

[83] Al-Ṭabarī offered this interpretation as a way out of the paradox of giving disobedient wives exactly what they wanted by denying them sexually and verbally. He wrote, "The likeliest interpretation concerning His words *wa-hjurūhunna*, and that which comes closest to its intention, is securing with the *hijār*. According to [the sources] in which the Arabs say about the camel, when its owner has tied it up as we have described, that it has been 'tethered'... When this [is taken as] the meaning, then the interpretation of the verse is: those from whom you fear *nushūz*, admonish them concerning their rising up against you. And if they accede to the admonition, then you have no way against them. If they refuse to repent of their disobedience, then imprison them, tying them to their beds, meaning in their rooms or houses in which they sleep and in which their husbands lie with them." This translation is based on Bauer (n 2) 167. I replaced "ostracized" with "tethered" in the translation, since al-Ṭabarī is arguing not that people "ostracize" camels but that the verb in question can refer to "tethering" rather than to ostracism. Al-Ṭabarī (n 6) 4:69. See also al-Zajjāj (n 27) 2:49. For more discussion on this interpretation, see Bauer (n 2) 165–9 and 171–9; Manuela Marín, "Disciplining Wives: A Historical Reading of Qur'ān 4:34," *Studia Islamica* (2003) 24; and Mahmoud (n 52) 544.

[84] Although some exegetes rejected this interpretation, others, like al-Māwardī and al-Sulamī, cited al-Ṭabarī's interpretation as one of several legitimate interpretations of abandonment. Al-Māwardī wrote that *wa-hjurūhunna fī al-maḍājiʿi* could mean that a husband should "tie her with a *hijār*, which is the rope used to tie camels, to subdue her to have sex with him." Al-Māwardī (n 6) 1:482; and al-Sulamī (n 8) 1:321. Marín and Bauer show that exegetes such as Abū Bakr Ibn al-ʿArabī took great pains to discredit this interpretation. Marín (n 83) 24 and Bauer (n 2) 165. Azizah al-Hibri and Raja' M. El Habti also translate Abū Bakr Ibn al-ʿArabī's passage in refutation of al-Ṭabarī's interpretation of *wa-hjurūhunna fī al-maḍājiʿi* as "tying one's wife in bed." See Don S. Browning, M. Christian Green, and John Witt, Jr. (eds.), *Sex, Marriage and Family in World Religions* (New York: Columbia University Press, 2006) 195–6.

[85] Al-Zamakhsharī (n 22) 1:497.

[86] Abū Ḥayyān (n 7) 3:252.

consider themselves to be bound by the opinions of their predecessors; rather, they exercised choice with regard to which interpretations they adhered to, which ones they repudiated, and how they employed the interpretations of their predecessors.

THE THIRD IMPERATIVE: "HIT THEM" (*WA-ḌRIBŪHUNNA*)

Husbands are allowed to hit their wives in order to rectify their behavior. The command "*wa-ḍribūhunna*" appears in the imperative form of *ḍ-r-b* and was unanimously understood by pre-colonial exegetes to mean "to hit," "to strike," or "to beat."[87] Specifically, they understood *wa-ḍribūhunna* to mean "hit (masc. pl) them (fem. pl.)." The consistency of this interpretation is especially striking given the broad variance found in the interpretation of other terms in Q. 4:34, such as the imperative to "abandon them in beds," as seen in the previous section. The consistent interpretations of "beat them" (*wa-ḍribūhunna*) demonstrate that uniform interpretive choices were not the result of creativity-stifling scholarly precedent; rather, it was a reflection of interpretive choice.

Although pre-colonial exegetes invariably understood *wa-ḍribūhunna* as granting husbands the right to physically discipline wives, they disagreed with one another regarding the procedure and extent of permissible hitting. The exegesis surrounding the third imperative primarily revolved around ethical questions regarding procedure: when husbands can discipline wives; whether the three imperatives in Q. 4:34 are meant to be applied sequentially and exhaustively, or whether they can be applied simultaneously; what role a husband's discretion has in determining when to hit his wife; how hard a husband can hit his wife; where he can hit her; what objects he can hit her with; and whether a husband can be prosecuted for hitting his wife excessively.

None of the exegetes in this study questioned the right of husbands to physically discipline their wives as a basic marital right; the closest some of them came to struggling with physical discipline as an essential marital right was in their attempts to reconcile prophetic discomfort—as captured in some prophetic reports—with the Qurʾanic license to hit wives

[87] In the contemporary period, there has been a move to interpret *wa-ḍribūhunna* to mean something other than its more violent connotations. See Ahmed Ali (n 82) Q. 4:34 and Bakhtiar (n 72) Introduction and Q. 4:34. For more discussion of contemporary interpretations of *wa-ḍribūhunna*, see Ayesha S. Chaudhry, "The Problems of Conscience and Hermeneutics: A Few Contemporary Approaches," *Comparative Islamic Studies*, 2(2) (2006) 158; and Chapter 4 of this book.

as a disciplinary measure. The *ḥadīth* literature surrounding the issue of wife-beating illustrates some such discomfort.[88] Exegetes therefore had an important resource at their disposal to propose alternate, even opposing, interpretations of *wa-ḍribūhunna*. After all, if "abandon them in beds" could be interpreted to mean "call them to bed," then it should be possible to interpret *wa-ḍribūhunna* as something that did not involve physical violence. However, when exegetes drew on the *ḥadīth* literature, they did so only to reconcile the Qur'anic text permitting physical violence with prophetic discomfort of this permission. They did not explore alternative lexical interpretations of the third imperative.

By designating the right of husbands to physically discipline their wives a central focus of Q. 4:34, pre-colonial jurists and exegetes rendered their interpretations of each part of the verse—men's preference, the description of ideal women, the definition of *nushūz*, the first two imperatives—in service of justifying the right of husbands to hit wives for disciplinary purposes. But one should not assume that because scholars justified the right of husbands to hit their wives, that they found the prescription "to beat" to be unproblematic. Rather, exegetes found this command to be at least somewhat troublesome and therefore devoted a great deal of energy to making it sound reasonable. Examining their detailed discussions allows us to appreciate their moral compunctions and the thrust of their idealized cosmology.

Although the prescription to hit wives in the text of Q. 4:34 is left unqualified—the text does not describe how to hit one's wife—all exegetes qualified this imperative in one way or another. The most common qualifier was that husbands ought to hit their wives in a manner that was *ghayr mubarriḥ*.[89] Marín translates this as "non-violent hitting," but Bauer has made the compelling point that hitting is "intrinsically violent."[90] For the sake of conceptual clarity and convenience, I translate *ghayr mubarriḥ* as "non-extreme"; this is how I believe pre-colonial exegetes understood the term. The source of this ubiquitous qualifier was a *ḥadīth* recording Muḥammad's "farewell sermon" during his final pilgrimage, in which he dispensed general advice. Among other things, he advised believers about the rights of each spouse. In this sermon, Muḥammad instructed husbands to hit their wives in a non-extreme manner if wives either allowed those whom their husbands disliked into their beds and/or if they displayed openly lewd

[88] Ayesha S. Chaudhry, " 'I Wanted One Thing and God Wanted Another . . .': The Dilemma of the Prophetic Example and the Qur'anic Injunction on Wife-Beating," *Journal of Religious Ethics*, 39(3) (2011) 416–39.

[89] For a list of exegetes who used the qualifier *ghayr mubarriḥ* to limit the prescription of *wa-ḍribūhunna*, see Appendix 24 (A24).

[90] Marín (n 83) 22 and Bauer (n 2) 111 and 114.

behavior (*fāḥishatin mubayyina*).[91] The variations of this tradition offer two specific definitions of wifely *nushūz* (if *nushūz* is defined as wifely behavior that sanctions physical discipline); allowing those whom one's husband dislikes into bed and exhibiting openly lewd behavior both qualify as *nushūz*. The narrations further instruct husbands to hit their wives for such behavior; in some narrations hitting is prescribed without any intermediary steps, but in all cases the nature of the hitting is qualified as "non-extreme."

The incorporation of this *ḥadīth* into exegetical literature demonstrates the complexity of pre-colonial scholars' interpretive choice. On the one hand, the qualification of hitting one's wife in a non-extreme (*ghayr mubarriḥ*) manner achieved normative status in Qur'ān commentaries and legal texts; the qualification of "non-extreme" was applied as a limit on husbands who physically discipline their wives. On the other hand, the specification of wifely *nushūz* in this *ḥadīth* was not applied to the definition of wifely *nushūz*. As seen previously, most scholars preferred to define wifely *nushūz* in Q. 4:34 broadly as disobedience and did not limit this definition to wives who were openly lewd or allowed disliked persons into their beds. In fact, wifely *nushūz* was never described in this way. That the restriction on hitting but not the description of wifely *nushūz* in this *ḥadīth* became normative illustrates that, even within a single report, scholars could adhere to one part while ignoring another.

While pre-colonial scholars agreed that husbands could hit their wives only in a "non-extreme" (*ghayr mubarriḥ*) manner, this qualifier is ambiguous and lends itself to multiple interpretations. What does

91 The basic version of this report is cited by Al-Qurṭubī. "Fear God concerning women, you take them as a trust from God and make their private parts permissible for you with the word of God. Your rights over them are that they not give your beds (*furushakum*) to anyone whom you dislike. If they do this, hit them in a non-extreme (*ghayr mubarriḥ*) manner." Al-Qurṭubī commented on this report, writing "[Wives are] not to permit anyone you dislike from among relatives and foreign women into your homes (*manāzilakum*)." This *ḥadīth* is from *Ṣaḥīḥ Muslim* and cited by al-Qurṭubī. The wording of these reports, which restricts wives from allowing only those who are disliked by their husbands into their beds, is strange since it raises the question of whether those whom one's husband likes might be allowed into their beds. Some exegetes such as al-Qurṭubī interpreted the wording of "beds" away by substituting "beds" with "homes." However, al-Qurṭubī cited another version of this report, which states that wives are to be disciplined if they are openly lewd (*fāḥishatin mubayyina*). Read literally, these reports offer an alternative definition of wifely *nushūz*—unfaithfulness and open lewdness rather than disobedience. Although this interpretive move has become popular in the post-colonial period, it was discounted by al-Qurṭubī. He argued that openly lewd behavior could not mean adultery (*zinā*), since that required the application of the *ḥadd* penalty rather than husbandly discipline. Al-Qurṭubī (A13) 5:165–6. Exegetes who included some version of the portion of the Ḥajj sermon dealing with hitting wives in their exegesis include Ibn Abī Ḥātim (A14) 3:943; al-Jaṣṣāṣ (A14) 1:375 and 2:189; al-Māwardī (n 6) 1:483; Ibn al-ʿArabī (n 7) 1:498; al-Thaʿālibī (A13) 2:230; al-Khāzin (A13) 1:375; Ibn Kathīr (n 23) 1:602; and al-Suyūṭī (A14) 2:156.

it mean to hit someone in a non-extreme manner? The answer to this question varied drastically in the pre-colonial period, ranging from hitting one's wife symbolically with a folded handkerchief to lashing her with a whip.[92] The most commonly recommended tool for hitting one's wife was a toothbrush (*siwāk*),[93] although some also favored a shoelace (*shirāk*).[94] Some scholars recommended hitting one's wife with a handkerchief or headscarf (*mandīl*). At first glance, these recommendations to use a shoelace, toothbrush, or folded handkerchief might be seen as attempts to reduce the extent of potential physical injury by rendering the beating largely symbolic. However, this conclusion cannot be readily made, since scholars who recommended using a folded handkerchief also suggested that husbands hit their wives with their hands.[95] Hitting with one's hand would imply slapping or punching one's wife, which can be severe and injurious. For example, Muḥammad ibn Aḥmad al-Qurṭubī (d. 671/1273) held that husbands ought to hit their wives with a *siwāk* and that they

[92] Deliberation on the definition of *ghayr mubarriḥ* appeared in reports related to the punishment of lashing as a consequence for alcohol consumption. A man was ordered to be whipped in a *ghayr mubarriḥ* manner. The Companion and narrator of this report, Abū Mājid, asked, "What is *ghayr mubarriḥ*?" He was told that it was "a hitting that is neither severe/intense (*shadīd*) nor negligible/easy (*hayyin*)." It is significant that the descriptor *ghayr mubarriḥ* was used to characterize the lashing meted out to a drunkard and the physical discipline permitted for husbands to use upon their wives. Al-Bayhaqī, *Sunan al-kubrā* (Beirut: Dar al-Kutub al-ʿIlmīya, 1999) 8:326.

[93] In a commonly cited *ḥadīth*, Muḥammad is reported to have said, "Hit women in a non-extreme manner when they disobey you in what is appropriate (*maʿrūf*)." ʿAṭāʾ said, "I asked Ibn ʿAbbās, 'What is hitting in a non-extreme manner (*al-ḍarb ghayr mubarriḥ*)?' He replied, 'With a toothbrush (*siwāk*) or something similar.'" Al-Qurṭubī (A13) 5:166. See also al-Baghawī (A15) 5:423; Ibn Abī Ḥātim (A14) 3:944; al-Jaṣṣāṣ (A14) 2:189; al-Khāzin (A13) 1:375; al-Suyūṭī (A14) 2:155; and al-Ṭabarī (n 6) 4:69. For more discussion on *miswāk*, see A.J. Wensinck, "*Miswāk*" in *Encyclopaedia of Islam*, 2nd edn. (Leiden: Brill, 2009). Mahmoud translates *siwāk* as "toothpick." Mahmoud (n 52) 545. Marín mentions that according to Sufyan b. ʿUyayna (d. 196/811), the hitting was meant to be carried out with a *siwāk*. Marín (n 83) 22. Although most scholars understand the *siwāk* to be a toothbrush because it is a twig that was and continues to be used for cleaning one's teeth, the context suggests that "switch" is a more accurate rendering. In markets in the Middle East and South Asia, I have seen *siwāks* that are long curly branches, which are often cut into ten inch sticks and used for cleaning one's teeth, following the example of Muḥammad. If used for hitting someone, I imagine these branches could cause serious damage. The rereading of *siwāk* as a switch would be in line with interpretations that allow for hitting one's wife with a whip or a stick.

[94] Ibn ʿAṭiyya and al-Thaʿālibī reported the previously mentioned narration with a slight variation. When ʿAṭāʾ asked Ibn ʿAbbās what the meaning of non-extreme hitting was, he responded that it was hitting with a shoelace (*shirāk*), as opposed to a toothbrush (*siwāk*). In conversation, Dr. Everett Rowson pointed out, *siwāk* and *shirāk* appear almost identical when written without dots and diacritics, so it is difficult to confirm what a given author actually wrote. Ibn ʿAṭiyya (A13) 2:48; and al-Thaʿālibī (A13) 2:230.

[95] Eg, al-Rāzī and al-Khāzin both wrote that husbands could hit their wives with a folded handkerchief or with their hand (*yanbaghī an yakūna al-ḍarb bi-mandīl malfūf aw bi-yadihi*). Additionally, al-Rāzī permitted somewhere between twenty and forty blows as the upper limit of hitting one's wife and encouraged spreading the blows so that they did not all fall on the same body part. Al-Rāzī (n 14) 4:72; and al-Khāzin (A13) 1:375.

should not punch them. However, he also supported the right of husbands to physically discipline their wives by citing *aḥādīth* that permitted husbands to hit their wives and family members (*ahl*) with a whip (*sawṭ*) and a stick (*ʿaṣā*).[96]

Other exegetes were explicit about the fact that husbands could use more severe instruments for disciplining wives. Abū Bakr ibn ʿAlī al-Ḥaddād (d. 799/1397–8) directed husbands to hit their wives with a sandal (*naʿl*) or to slap (*laṭm*) them, but he limited the strikes to two or three times.[97] In contrast, al-Rāzī prohibited husbands from hitting their wives with a whip (*siyāṭ*) or rod (*ʿaṣā*), recommending a folded handkerchief or hand instead. However, he imagined the hitting to be severe enough that it needed to be distributed to several parts of the body rather than concentrating on just one in order to avoid serious damage, and he set the upper limit of strikes to either twenty or forty blows.[98] Although al-Khāzin al-Baghdādī (d. 741/1341) himself did not advocate hitting wives with a whip or a rod, he cited another scholarly opinion in which husbands could whip their wives as long as they restricted themselves to ten lashes (*wa-lā yablughu bi-l-ḍarb ʿashara aswāṭ*).[99] The discussion of whipping wives might have emerged from the prophetic tradition that advised believers to "Hang the whip where your family members can see it (*ʿalliq al-sawṭ ḥaythu yarāhu ahl al-bayt*)."[100] A few scholars cited—and did not object to—a prophetic report that described the Companion al-Zubayr excessively beating his wives with a rod/clothes rack (*ʿūd al-mishjab*).[101] ʿAbd al-Karīm ibn Hawāzin al-Qushayrī (d. 464/1072) acknowledged the potentially legitimate use of a rod (*ʿaṣā*) in the physical chastisement of wives when he nonetheless commanded husbands to avoid using the rod (*'aṣā*) in favor of milder punitive actions if the latter would be sufficient to correct a wife's behavior.[102] Although al-Qushayrī mentioned the use of the rod disapprovingly, he did not object to the use of the stick/rod itself; rather, he objected to the use of the rod as the first course of action for physically disciplining a wife.

[96] Al-Qurṭubī (A13) 5:167.

[97] Al-Ḥaddād (A13) 2:250.

[98] Al-Rāzī (n 14) 4:72.

[99] Al-Khāzin (A13) 1:375.

[100] Cited by al-Thaʿlabī (n 37) 3:303; al-Zamakhsharī (n 22) 1:497; and Abū Ḥayyān (n 7) 3:252.

[101] Eg, see al-Thaʿlabī (n 37) 3:303.

[102] He wrote, "And those from whom you fear *nushūz*, admonish them, leave them in the beds, and beat them i.e., increase the punishment gently, by degrees, and if the matter is fixed after the admonishment, then do not use the stick (*ʿaṣā*) to hit." Bauer's translation. Bauer (n 2) 158. ʿAbd al-Karīm ibn Hawāzin al-Qushayrī, *Laṭāʾif al-ishārāt: tafsīr Ṣūfī Kāmil li-l-Qurʾān al-Karīm* (Cairo: Dār al-Kātib al-ʿArabī, 1968) 2:330. This quote of al-Qushayrī's is the same al-ʿAyyāshī's, verbatim. See Muḥammad ibn Masʿūd Al-ʿAyyāshī, *Tafsīr* (Qom: Mu'assasat al-Baʿtha, 2000) 1:330.

Given the previous points, we can see that non-extreme (*ghayr mubarriḥ*) hitting can have varied interpretations. Pre-colonial exegetes might restrict the beating of wives using the exact same qualifying language but construe its meaning in entirely different ways. Aḥmad b. 'Alī al-Jaṣṣāṣ (d. 370/980–1) and Aḥmad ibn Muḥammad al-Thaʿlabī (d. 427/1035) present a good case study for this phenomenon. Both qualified a husband's disciplinary beating of his wife with the very same words—*ghayr mubarriḥ* (non-extreme) and *ghayr shā'in* (not indecent, or not disgraceful). Yet al-Jaṣṣāṣ used prophetic reports to emphasize the fragile nature of women, thus discouraging husbands from hitting wives unless it was absolutely necessary. For example, he mentioned the report wherein Muḥammad said "A woman is like a rib (*ḍilʿ*). If you try to straighten her she will break, but leave her [as she is] and you can enjoy (*tastamtiʿ*) her."[103] Al-Thaʿlabī's opinion stood in juxtaposition to that of al-Jaṣṣāṣ, since al-Thaʿlabī imagined women as capable of handling rather severe beatings. He maintained this position through the use of prophetic reports that hinted at the acceptability of severe beatings. Such reports included the one in which the Companion al-Zubayr beat his wives with a clothes rack severely enough to break it, and also wherein Muḥammad advised husbands to hang a whip in plain sight to keep wives in line.[104]

Apart from addressing ethical questions about how husbands should physically discipline their wives, pre-colonial exegetes also elaborated on the procedure and acceptable limits of hitting wives. This discussion was moral in nature. Delving further into the shades of meanings for *ghayr mubarriḥ*, exegetes stipulated that husbands should hit their wives without leaving any marks or impressions (*ghayr mu'aththir*) on the body,[105] that they should not hit their wives in a disgraceful (*ghayr shā'in*) manner,[106] and that they should avoid hitting them in the face.[107] They

[103] Al-Jaṣṣāṣ (A14) 2:189. Al-Khāzin also mentions this *ḥadīth*, but in his narration, women are made from a "crooked (*aʿwaj*) rib." Al-Khāzin (A13) 1:374.

[104] Al-Thaʿlabī (n 37) 3:303.

[105] See, eg, Ibn Abī Ḥātim (A14) 3:944; Ibn Kathīr (n 23) 1:602; al-Suyūṭī (A14) 2:155; and al-Thaʿālibī (A13) 2:231.

[106] For a list of exegetes who used *ghayr shā'in* as an interpretation of *ghayr mubarriḥ*, see Appendix 25 (A25).

[107] Al-Baghawī cited Muḥammad as saying, "The right of a woman is that you feed her as you feed yourself, and clothe her as you clothe yourself. Do not hit her face, do not revile her, and do not abandon her except in the house." Al-Baghawī (A15) 5:423. See also al-Khāzin (A13) 1:375. Al-Māwardī cited a similar report that tied husbands' sexual access and disciplinary rights together. His citation read, "[Your wife is] your tilth, so come to your tilth as you wish, do not hit her in the face and do not revile her except in the house. Feed her as you eat, clothe her as you clothe yourselves and indeed some of you have been preferred over others." Al-Māwardī (n 6) 1:483. The directive to avoid hitting wives in the face had theological underpinnings. Al-Biqāʿī wrote, "This is [hitting that] does not break bones or wound limbs. It [also] shifts [location] on the body and does not repeatedly [strike] one spot.

also stipulated that husbands should not hit the same part of the body repeatedly but rather that the blows should be distributed,[108] and further that a beating should not result in broken bones or wounds.[109] In general, disciplinary hitting was not supposed to compromise the soundness (*salāma*) of a wife's body or lead to death.[110]

Husbands were encouraged to keep in mind that hitting was meant to be disciplinary (*ḍarb al-adab*),[111] and the desired end of the hitting was to rectify a wife's behavior.[112] If the purpose of hitting wives was to stop wifely *nushūz*, then husbands were required to stop hitting their wives when the latter desisted from behavior that was classified as wifely *nushūz*.[113] This means that if wifely *nushūz* was defined as general disobedience, then husbands could not hit their wives after they returned to obedience. If wifely *nushūz* was defined as sexual disobedience, then husbands could

[Furthermore, this hitting] avoids the face because [the face] is the place where beautiful features are gathered (*majmaʿa al-maḥāsin*), and it should be fewer than forty [strikes]." Al-Biqāʿī (n 31) 5:271. For al-Biqāʿī, avoiding hitting a wife's face was not out of concern for her well-being; it would be difficult to make such an argument since he was comfortable with a husband striking his wife up to forty times. Rather, the concern was connected to the face as a symbol for the convergence of divine beauty. Hitting the face of another was seen as an affront to the divine. See also Abū al-Suʿūd (n 15) 1:339; al-Rāzī (n 14) 4:72; al-Shirbīnī (A13) 1:346; and al-Zamakhsharī (n 22) 1:497.

108 Eg, al-Khāzin (A13) 1:375 and al-Rāzī (n 14) 4:72.

109 Exegetes who stipulated that hitting should not result in broken bones or wounds include Ibn al-ʿArabī (n 7) 1:498; Ibn ʿAṭiyya (A13) 2:48; Ibn Kathīr (n 23) 1:602; al-Qurṭubī (A13) 5:165; al-Suyūṭī (A14) 2:155; al-Ṭabarī (n 6) 4:71; al-Thaʿālibī (A13) 2:230; and al-Zamakhsharī (n 22) 1:496–7.

110 Eg, al-Ḥaddād wrote, "The [extent of the beating] will be entrusted to the husband's reasoned opinion and his independent judgment (*ijtihād*), according to what he sees as being helpful (*maṣlaḥa*). Because of this, it is said that this blow is restricted by the condition that [the wife remains] sound [in body] (*muqayyad bi-sharṭ al-salāma*), and the best thing is to hit [recalcitrant wives] with a sandal or a slap, and [the blow] should be twice or three times." This translation is based on Bauer's translation of al-Ḥaddād, with some modifications. Bauer (n 2) 160–1. See also al-Ḥaddād (A13) 2:250 and al-Rāzī (n 14) 4:72.

111 Ibn ʿAṭiyya wrote, "The hitting in this verse is hitting for disciplinary purposes (*ḍarb al-adab*). It is the type of hitting that does not break bones or disfigure a limb (*yashīn jāriḥa*)." Ibn ʿAṭiyya (A13) 2:48. Al-Qurṭubī considered the various reasons for which a husband could hit his wife, such as her marital, religious (*dīniyya*), and service (*khidma*) obligations. Al-Qurṭubī (A13) 5:166–7.

112 Al-Qurṭubī wrote, "What is desired [from the hitting] is rectification (*ṣilāḥ*) [of wifely *nushūz*] and nothing else. So of course, if [the hitting] leads to death, [the husband] is liable. This is the same principle in case of the educator (*al-muʾaddib*) hitting his student in the teaching of the Qurʾān and literature (*al-adab*)." Al-Qurṭubī (A13) 5:165. The discussion of the teacher–student relationship as legally analogous to the husband–wife relationship was a prominent feature of Mālikī legal discussions on the question of liability. However, it was not restricted to Mālikī scholars. Al-Ḥaddād, a Ḥanafī, also compared a husband hitting his wife to a man hitting a child. Al-Ḥaddād (A13) 2:250.

113 Al-Māwardī wrote, "It is permitted for [a husband] to hit [his wife] for disciplinary purposes (*taʾdīb*) in order to prevent (*yazjurhā*) her from *nushūz*. The hitting should not be in an extreme or severe manner (*wa-lā munhik*)." Al-Māwardī (n 6) 1:483. See also al-Sulamī (n 8) 1:321.

not hit their wives once they agreed to sexual intercourse. Several scholars explicitly stated that husbands could hit their wives until they were willing to have sex with them.[114]

Yet another restriction on disciplinary beating was the matter of sequence. The three imperatives in Q. 4:34 are punctuated by *wa*, which linguistically can have three meanings: "and," "or," and "then." Depending on how one interprets "*wa*," the plain-sense meaning of Q. 4:34 could be understood as suggesting that husbands should apply the three prescriptions of admonishment, abandonment, and hitting sequentially, simultaneously, or in ad hoc manner. If *wa* is understood as meaning "and," the three steps might be applied simultaneously, whereas if it is interpreted to mean "or," then there is a case for arguing that husbands are to use their discretion in applying the most effective of the three prescriptions. Despite the ambiguity of the Qur'anic text on this point, most pre-colonial exegetes chose to interpret *wa* as "then," arguing that the three measures were meant to be applied sequentially.[115] However, there was disagreement regarding the exact sequence. Some argued that the three steps were meant to be applied sequentially and exhaustively. If a husband feared *nushūz* from his wife, he was required to admonish her verbally. If this failed, he could abandon her in the marital bed. If this also failed, he could hit her. Other exegetes believed that husbands were required to admonish their wives if they merely feared wifely *nushūz*; however, they were permitted to employ all three prescriptions when wifely *nushūz* became manifest. Yet others contended that both admonishment and abandonment could be enacted on the basis of the fear of *nushūz*, but hitting was authorized only after wifely *nushūz* became clear.[116]

Most Qur'ān commentators agreed though that physical discipline was to be undertaken only after admonishment and abandonment had proven ineffective in dissuading wives from their *nushūz*;[117] it could not be adopted as the first course of action.[118] This meant that if either

[114] Exegetes who thought that it was permissible to hit wives until they were willing to have sex with their husbands include al-Huwwārī (A16) 1:378; Ibn Abī Ḥātim (A14) 3:944; Ibn Abī Zamanīn (A14) 1:367; Ibn ʿAṭiyya (A13) 2:48; Ibn al-Jawzī (A13) 2:76; al-Jaṣṣāṣ (A14) 2:189; al-Māwardī (n 6) 1:483; Mujāhid (A17) 274; al-Suyūṭī (A14) 2:155; and al-Ṭabarī (n 6) 4:69.

[115] For a list of exegetes who argued that the three prescriptions in Q. 4:34 were to be followed sequentially, see Appendix 26 (A26).

[116] See, eg, al-Māwardī (n 6) 1:483 and al-Rāzī (n 14) 4:72.

[117] Eg, al-Nasafī wrote, "[God] commanded [husbands] to first admonish [their wives], then (*thumma*) abandon them in the beds, then hit them if [the previous two measures of] admonishment and abandonment were ineffective." Al-Nasafī (n 22) 1:355. See also al-Khāzin (A13) 1:375.

[118] Ibn al-Jawzī wrote, "And a group of scholars have said: the verse [promotes] sequence (*al-tartīb*). Admonish [your wives] when you fear *nushūz*. Abandon them when *nushūz*

admonishment or abandonment yielded the desired result—a return to wifely obedience—then husbands were to avoid hitting wives.[119] A few exegetes argued that once wifely *nushūz* became manifest, then husbands were permitted to apply any of the three steps, including hitting, as their first course of disciplinary action.[120] If all of the three imperatives in Q. 4:34 were ineffective in motivating wives to abandon their *nushūz*, then the matter was considered to be irreconcilable in the private domain. At this point, Q. 4:35 became operative and external arbitrators were assigned to each spouse to help the couple to reconcile or facilitate a divorce.[121]

becomes manifest (*ẓuhūr*) and hit them when they repeat (*takarrar*) [their *nushūz*] and continue (*lajāj*) in it. It is not permissible to hit at the beginning (*ibtidāʿ*) of *nushūz*." Ibn al-Jawzī (A13) 2:76.

[119] Ibn ʿAṭiyya argued for following each of the three prescriptions in sequence and further stipulated that "if obedience occurs (*waqaʿat*) in any of these stages [the husband] should not proceed to the rest of [the prescriptions]." Ibn ʿAṭiyya (A13) 2:48.

[120] Al-Baghawī mentioned both interpretive possibilities, applying the three disciplinary steps either simultaneously or sequentially. He argued that the more "obvious" (*ẓāhir*) reading of the verse is that a husband can join the three steps. In the end he argued that the prescriptions were meant to be applied according to the "order of crimes" (*tartīb al-jarāʾim*). Al-Baghawī (A15) 5:423. Al-Khāzin argued that once *nushūz* was established, husbands could combine all three disciplinary steps. Al-Khāzin (A13) 1:375. Similarly, according to al-Rāzī, once wifely *nushūz* was established, the Shāfiʿī juridical school allowed husbands to decide which disciplinary action was the most effective means of persuading their wives to abandon their *nushūz*. Al-Rāzī wrote, "And I say: What indicates this is [ie the point he just made] that God [intended a progression] beginning with admonition, then proceeded to abandonment in bed, and then proceeding to hitting/beating. This hint serves as an explicit statement that whenever the objective is obtained by the lighter method one must be satisfied with that, and it is impermissible to embark upon a more severe method, and God knows best. The third problem: our contemporaries disagree amongst themselves as to whether the injunctions in the verse must be carried out sequentially. Some say yes, arguing that although the apparent reading of the verse indicates simultaneity, the holistic message of the verse indicates [that they should be carried out] sequentially. The Chief of the Believers, ʿAlī b. Abī Ṭālib (d. 40/660), may God be pleased with him, said: [a husband] should admonish [his wife] with speech, and if she stops then there is no path for him against her. If she [continues to] disobey, then abandon her in her bed, and if she [further] disobeys then strike her. And then if she [still] does not heed the hitting, he should appoint two arbiters [to adjudicate between them]. And others say: the sequence is only relevant when there is fear of *nushūz*, meaning that when there is certainty of *nushūz*, there is no harm in combining all [three prescriptions]. And some of our contemporaries say: There is agreement in our [Shāfiʿī] school of law that [a husband] may admonish [his wife] when he fears *nushūz*, but may he also abandon her? When there is the possibility [of *nushūz*], that is with the nascence of *nushūz* it is for [the husband to decide] whether to admonish, abandon, or strike [his wife]." Al-Rāzī (n 14) 4:70.

[121] Eg, Al-Wāḥidī wrote, "If she still refuses to be admonished with hitting, then appoint two adjudicators." Al-Wāḥidī (n 23) 1:263. Abū Ḥayyān suggested that if the imperatives in Q. 4:34 did not work, then husbands ought to tie their wives in bed and rape them (force them to have sex), because sexual access was a husband's right over his wives. Abū Ḥayyān provided a wildly inaccurate summary of al-Rāzī's position on Q. 4:34. He wrote, "The apparent (*ẓāhir*) [meaning] of the verse indicates (*yadullu*) that [a husband can] admonish, abandon in bed and hit [his wife when] he fears her *nushūz*. He can combine (*yajmaʿu*) [the three prescriptions] and begin with [whichever measure] he wishes, because the *waw* [in this verse] is not a *waw* of sequence (*tarattub*). While some people say this, the general

A few exegetes paused to consider whether husbands might be prosecuted for exceeding the recommended limits of physical discipline. What if a husband hit his wife in such a way that the beating left an impression, broke bones, caused wounds and/or death? According to exegetes, husbands were not legally accountable for hitting their wives in a non-extreme (*ghayr mubarriḥ*) manner unless a beating resulted in broken bones, caused wounds or death. In the case of broken bones and wounds, husbands were liable for some sort of monetary compensation but not retaliation in kind (*qiṣāṣ*).[122] They relied on the legal maxim "there is no retaliation (*qiṣāṣ*) in marriage" to make this point.[123] In the case of a wife's death, however, a husband was subject to retribution in kind (*qiṣāṣ*).

A final issue that exegetes tackled was the prophetic discomfort with the right of husbands to hit wives. The closest that Qur'ān commentators came to questioning the right of husbands to hit wives as a basic marital right was their discussion of a prophetic report in which Muḥammad morally censured husbands for hitting wives. In their deliberations on this

opinion is that [a husband is to] admonish [his wife] when he fears *nushūz* from her, and hit her when her *nushūz* manifests itself. Ibn ʿAṭiyya said that the admonishment, abandonment and hitting is sequential. If obedience occurs at any of these stages then [the husband] should not advance to the remaining [steps]. Al-Zamakhsharī said: [God] commanded admonishment [for wives] first, then abandonment in their beds and then hitting, if admonishment and abandonment were ineffective. And al-Rāzī said, in summary: Begin with pliable speech in admonishment, but if this does not work, then [admonish] her with rough (*fa bi-khashinihi*) [speech]. [If this is ineffective] then abandon her sexually. [If this is still ineffective], then avoid her altogether (*bi iʿrāḍ ʿanhā kulliyya*). Then hit her lightly, such as slapping and punching/kicking her (*lakza*) and such things that make known (*yushʿir*) his contempt (*iḥtiqār*) [for her] and how she forfeited her inviolability (*wa-isqāṭ al-ḥurma*). Then, [if she is still not persuaded], hit [her with] a whip (*sawṭ*) and a soft switch/stick (*al-qaḍīb al-layyin*) or something similar, that results in pain (*alam*) and scrapes (*wa-l-inkā'*). [However, the hitting] should not result in destroying/shattering (*hashama*) [bones] and should not lead to bleeding. If none of these measures are effective, then [the husband] should tie [his wife] with a rope and force her to have sexual intercourse (*al-waṭ'*) [with him], because this is his right [upon her]. If any [of the above mentioned measures] that we have sequenced brings [the wife] back from her *nushūz*, then it is impermissible for [the husband] to move to the next [measure], because 'if they obey you, do not find a means against them' (Q. 4:34)." Abū Ḥayyān (n 7) 3:252.

[122] Al-Ṭabarī wrote on the authority of al-Zuhrī (d. 124/742) that "Even if a man fractures [his wife's skull] (*shajjahā*) or wounds her (*jaraḥahā*), there is no retaliation (*qawad*) on him for this, but he is responsible for monetary compensation (*al-ʿaql*). Except [in the case] that he transgresses against her and kills her, and so is killed because of her." Al-Ṭabarī (n 6) 4:61. Al-Zamakhsharī wrote, "And [the scholars] disagreed in this [matter]: some said there is no retaliation (*qiṣāṣ*) between a man and his wife in matters other than [taking] a life (*al-nafs*), even if he wounds her. If he wounds her, he is only responsible for monetary compensation. Others have said, there is no retaliation [between a married couple] except in the case of a wound (*jarḥ*) or death (*qatl*)." Al-Zamakhsharī (n 22) 1:496. See also Ibn ʿAṭiyya (A13) 2:48; al-Huwwārī (A16) 1:377; al-Māwardī (n 6) 1:481; Muqātil (n 6) 1:235; and al-Thaʿlabī (n 37) 3:302.

[123] Eg, Ibn ʿAṭiyya (A13) 2:48; Muqātil (n 6) 1:235; al-Sulamī (n 8) 1:320; al-Suyūṭī (A14) 2:151; al-Ṭabarī (n 6) 4:61; al-Thaʿlabī (n 37) 3:302; and al-Zamakhsharī (n 22) 1:496.

topic, exegetical scholars were less concerned with the ethical problems associated with the husbandly prerogative to physically discipline wives and more interested in addressing the theological issues that emerged from a conflicting prophetic impulse and the Qur'anic text. How might the unqualified prescription to hit wives in Q. 4:34 be understood in light of Muḥammad's expressed moral censure of men who hit their wives? The two major approaches to resolving this tension are highlighted in the examples of al-Rāzī and Abū Bakr Ibn al-ʿArabī (d. 543/1148). Both exegetes used different hermeneutical strategies to mitigate the problem; neither scholar denied husbands their disciplinary privilege, but they did argue that exercising the right to physically discipline wives was not the preferred course of action.[124]

Al-Rāzī based his exegetical argument on al-Shāfiʿī's legal approach.[125] Al-Shāfiʿī's ruling on physical discipline was that while hitting wives was permitted (*mubāḥ*), avoiding it was preferred. The prophetic report in which Muḥammad first allowed men to hit their wives and then rebuked them for doing so played a central role in problematizing the prescription to physically discipline wives in Q. 4:34. In al-Rāzī's narration of this report, ʿUmar approached Muḥammad and complained about the threatening/frightening (*dhaʾara*)[126] behavior of Meccan women after moving to Medina. Meccan women had begun to pick up social cues from their more independent Medinan counterparts, resulting in behavior that, according to the report, amounted to wifely *nushūz*. ʿUmar asked Muḥammad for permission to hit them.[127] Muḥammad granted Meccan men permission to hit their wives, but this response is only implied in al-Rāzī's narration of this story. In response to this permission, women surrounded the house of Muḥammad, complaining about the beatings and holding Muḥammad accountable for his permission. Muḥammad responded by saying, "The family of Muḥammad was surrounded tonight by seventy women, all

[124] Al-Shirbīnī mentioned specifically that "it is preferable (*awlā*) for him (i.e. the husband) to be forgiving." See also Ibn al-ʿArabī (n 7) 1:500; al-Khāzin (A13) 1:375; al-Rāzī (n 14) 4:72; and al-Shirbīnī (A13) 1:346.

[125] Marín (n 83) 20. For a thorough discussion of al-Shāfiʿī's approach to hitting wives, see Kecia Ali, " 'The Best of You Will Not Strike': Al-Shāfiʿī on Qur'an, *Sunnah*, and Wife-Beating," *Comparative Islamic Studies*, 2(2) (2006) 143–55.

[126] This translation is based on Ibn Manẓūr, *Lisān al-ʿArab* (Beirut: Dār al-Kutub al-ʿIlmiyya, 2003). Marín notes that this narration is included in Ibn Saʿd's *Ṭabaqāt*. Her analysis of this report is that "the conflict here arises, thus, from the difficulties in assimilating two different family structures within the same religious community during its formative years." Marín (n 83) 19.

[127] In Ibn Kathīr's narration of this *ḥadīth*, the report begins with Muḥammad actively prohibiting men from hitting their wives: "Do not hit the slave women of God." ʿUmar resisted this prohibition, asking for permission to hit them. Ibn Kathīr's version of the *ḥadīth* was related by Abū Dāwūd, al-Nasāʾi, and Ibn Mājah. Ibn Kathīr (n 23) 1:602. See also al-Khāzin (A13) 1:375.

of them complaining about their husbands, and you will not find [those husbands who hit their wives] to be the best of you."[128]

This prophetic report raised a theological problem: how could Muḥammad criticize husbands for an action that was divinely prescribed in the Qur'ān? According to pre-colonial scholars, husbands were responsible for correcting their wives' behavior if they committed *nushūz*, and in order to do this, they were licensed to engage in physical violence. When applied correctly, this physical violence represented a husband's fulfillment of his religious duties. Yet this prophetic report complicates the picture by censuring husbands who hit their wives, even if it is to rectify behavior that constitutes *nushūz*. Al-Rāzī offered a compromise to reduce the contradiction between the divine text and prophetic report. He read the imperative to hit wives in Q. 4:34 as a permission rather than command and interpreted Muḥammad's rebuke of husbands who hit their wives as a recommendation. Muḥammad was merely counseling Muslim men to avoid exercising their divinely sanctioned privilege to physically discipline wives. For those who chose to utilize their privilege to physically discipline wives, al-Rāzī encouraged moderation.

Abū Bakr Ibn al-ʿArabī used a different hermeneutical strategy in order to dissuade husbands from exercising their husbandly right to physically discipline their wives. He privileged prophetic practice over divine text and made a case for avoiding hitting wives—not out of concern for the

[128] Al-Suyūṭī reported another version of this *ḥadīth*, which was narrated by Umm Kulthūm. In this report, Muḥammad told husbands that "the best of you will never hit," even as he granted husbands permission to hit their wives. Al-Suyūṭī (A14) 2:155. The full text from al-Rāzī reads, "Al-Shāfiʿī said: Hitting is permissible (*mubāḥ*) and leaving it is better/preferred. It has been related that ʿUmar b. al-Khaṭṭāb said: [When] we were in the society of the Quraysh, our men owned (*tamlik*) our women, but when we came to Medina we found their women owned their men. Then our women mingled with their women and they became frightening/threatening (*dhaʾara*) to their husbands, meaning they committed *nushūz* and became audacious. So I went to the Prophet and said: the women are quarreling with their husbands, so permit us to strike them. Thereafter the apartments of the wives of the Prophet were surrounded by a gathering of women complaining about their husbands. So [the Prophet] said: 'The family of Muḥammad was surrounded tonight by seventy women, all of them complaining about their husbands, and you will not find [those husbands] to be the best of you.' And the meaning [of this *ḥadīth*] is that those people who struck their wives are not better than those who did not strike them. Al-Shāfiʿī said, 'This *ḥadith* indicates that it is more fitting that one leave off hitting. Though if [a husband] does strike [his wife], it is absolutely obligatory that the striking not be carried out with in such a way as to lead to [her] death; [so] the blows should be distributed by him (*mufarraqan*) to different parts of her body, and he should not strike one place consecutively, and he should avoid the face—because it is the consummate place of beauty—and [the striking] should be less than forty [overall strikes]. And from amongst our contemporaries are those who say: do not reach twenty [strikes] because the rights of a slave prescribe [twenty strikes] as the utmost limit [when beating a slave]. And from amongst them are those who say: It is desirable that the striking be [carried out] with the use of a folded handkerchief/headscarf (*mandīl*) or with his hand. And he should not hit her with a whip or a stick. In sum, the preponderant view is that one should try to be light/moderate [in hitting].'" Al-Rāzī (n 14) 4:70. See also Al-Biqāʿī (n 31) 5:271.

welfare of wives but for the spiritual well-being of husbands. He based his own position on that of the Successor 'Aṭā', whom Ibn al-'Arabī cited as explicitly stating that "the command [for a husband] to hit [his wife] is [merely] a command of permission (*amr ibāḥa*)."[129] In his opinion, although it is permissible for a husband to hit a disobedient wife, it is preferable for him to be angry (*yaghḍabu*) with her instead. Abū Bakr Ibn al-'Arabī's exegesis of Q. 4:34 suggests that he understood "anger" as admonishment and abandonment, rather than beating. He used several prophetic reports to buttress his case, including the previously mentioned report, which morally censured husbands who hit their wives, though he cited only a portion of this report, which reads, "The Prophet of God was asked permission to hit women and he said, 'Hit, and the best of you will not hit (*aḍribū wa-lan yaḍriba khiyārukum*)'." This particular wording seems to make the case for al-Rāzī's interpretation by placing both the permission to hit as well as the recommendation to avoid hitting in Muḥammad's mouth. Ultimately, Abū Bakr Ibn al-'Arabī argued for a paradox; on the one hand, men were religiously responsible for rectifying the behavior or their charges (their wives, children, and slaves), while on the other hand, by doing so, men lost something of their own religiosity. He wrote, "When God does not grant a man a righteous wife and an upright slave, [the man] does not straighten his affair with the two of them except by losing (*bi-dhahāb*) a part (*juz'*) from his [own] religion (*dīn*). And this is well known with experience."[130] The ambiguous nature of this

[129] Ibn al-'Arabī (n 7) 1:499–500

[130] The full text from Ibn al-'Arabī reads, " 'Aṭā' said: 'If [a husband] commands [his wife] (*amarahā*) and prohibits her (*nahāhā*) and she does not obey him, he should not hit her but rather be angry with her (*yaghḍabu 'alayhā*).' Al-Qādī [Abū Bakr Ibn al-'Arabī] said that this was the jurisprudence (*fiqh*) of 'Aṭā' based on his understanding of the *sharī'a*. His position was an indication of his independent legal reasoning [*ijtihād*], [whereby] he argued that the command [for a husband] to hit [his wife] is [merely] a command of permission (*amr ibāḥa*). In one sense, he was arguing for the reprehensibility (*al-karāhiya*) [of hitting], based on Muḥammad's saying in the *ḥadīth* of 'Abdallāh b. Zam'a (d.): 'I dislike that a man hit his slave-woman in anger, and then bed her on the same day.' It is also narrated by... Yaḥyā b. Sa 'īd [al-Qaṭṭān, d.198/813–14] that 'The Prophet of God was asked permission to hit women and he said, "Hit, and the best of you will not hit" (*aḍribū wa-lan yaḍriba khiyārukum*).' So [Muḥammad] permitted [hitting] but encouraged refraining from it (*fa-abāḥa wa-nadaba ilā al-tark*). The extreme limit (*ghāya*) of discipline (*al-adab*) is in abandonment (*al-hajr*). In my opinion men and women are not the same (*yastawūn*) in this; for the slave is [in need of] of being struck (*yuqra'u*) with a rod (*'aṣā*) while a symbolic gesture (*ishāra*) is sufficient for the free man. As for women, and even for some men, they are not rectified except with discipline. So when a man knows [of his wife's *nushūz*] he [should] discipline (*yu'addib*) her, but if he leaves it then it is better (*wa-in taraka fa-huwa afḍal*). And someone said that when he was asked 'What is the worst *adab* (*aswa'u al-adab*)?' He replied, 'I do not like it when my child/son persists in the corruption (*fasād*) of my religion (*dīn*).' And it is said, 'The good character of the master (*al-sayyid*) is the bad etiquette of his slave (*min ḥusni khuluq al-sayyid sū'u adabi 'abdihi*).' And when God does not grant a man a righteous wife and an upright slave, [the man] does not straighten his affair with the two of

loss made the threat of it all the more sinister. It should be noted that Abū Bakr Ibn ʿArabī's position stands in stark contrast to that of the majority of exegetes, who agreed that husbands were religiously responsible for the moral probity of their wives but saw husbands' right to physically discipline as instrumental for enforcing that religious duty.[131]

CONCLUSION

It is useful to place the ethical discussions found in pre-colonial Qur'anic commentaries in the context of the idealized cosmologies of pre-colonial exegetes. The idealized cosmology that framed discussions of the disciplinary rights of husbands assumed that God prefers men over women, which results in husbands having moral authority over their wives. Within this scheme, husbands mediate the relationship of their wives with God; "good" wives are obedient and seek to please their husbands; and "bad" wives resist their placement in the marital hierarchy by being disobedient to their husbands. Since husbands have a higher placement in the marital ranking, God has equipped husbands with the necessary disciplinary tools to return wives to their appropriate place in the marital hierarchy when they rise (*nashaza*) from their lower ranking. Physical discipline is one of the tools available to husbands in "returning" wives from their rebellion to their proper place of obedience.

Due to this idealized cosmology, no pre-colonial exegete questioned the right of husbands to hit their wives as a fundamental husbandly privilege. Nevertheless, the disciplinary privilege of husbands sometimes raised moral concerns. Since the procedure for disciplining a wife was enacted entirely in the private sphere and therefore relied on the husband's discretion, husbands were accorded the power of judge, jury, and executioner when it came to disciplining wives. Husbands determined if and when their wives committed *nushūz* and were responsible for disciplining them, verbally and/or physically, in order to rectify their behavior. This unbridled power brings with it the spectre of abuse, and pre-colonial exegetes were acutely aware of this problem. As a result, their exegesis of Q. 4:34 revolved around two points.

them except by losing (*bi-dhahāb*) a part (*juz'*) from his [own] religion (*dīn*). And this is well known with experience." Ibn al-ʿArabī (n 7) 1:499–500.

[131] It is important to emphasize that Abū Bakr Ibn al-ʿArabī's position here is unique. Al-Hibri and El-Habti present the previous passage as representative of the Islamic tradition rather than as a unique position. Al-Hibri (n 84) 195–6. Furthermore, it is important to remember that Ibn al-ʿArabī's moral qualms with the right of husbands to hit their wives was not motivated by an egalitarian impulse, since he fully supported a patriarchal view. In fact, he was one of a few exegetes who mentioned the prophetic report about women being deficient in intellect and religion to support marital hierarchy. Ibn al-ʿArabī (n 7) 1:494 and 499.

First, they emphasized that husbands did in fact have disciplinary power over their wives; and, second, they restricted this disciplinary privilege based on moral and ethical grounds. Due to the opposing thrust of these two movements—simultaneously affirming and restricting a husband's disciplinary rights—pre-colonial exegetes were able to offer primarily moral exhortations and some compensatory liability for husbands to use their power judiciously. Hence, the discussions surrounding the right of husbands to hit wives were procedural in nature, and exegetes examined the moral contours of when and how husbands could use physical violence as a disciplinary measure rather than questioning whether husbands had the right to hit their wives at all. These scholars could not imagine husbands being prosecuted for their use of excessive violence against their wives without restricting their divinely endowed disciplinary privileges. Prosecution was therefore restricted to cases of severe injury or death, when marital disputes leave the private domestic sphere and enter into the public domain.

Exegetical discussions surrounding the possible meanings of *khawf* and *nushūz* as well as the three prescriptions in Q. 4:34 of admonishment, abandonment in bed, and beating, highlight the interpretive flexibility available to pre-colonial exegetes. Exegesis of these terms and imperatives illustrates that pre-colonial exegetes were comfortable with multiple interpretations of a given term or phrase and sometimes even posited meanings that stood in opposition to the plain-sense meaning of a given text. At times they designed new and creative exegesis while criticizing the earlier opinions of major Qur'ān commentators, and at other times, they chose to follow and reaffirm scholarly precedent. Given the interpretive flexibility available to pre-colonial exegetes, it is significant that they uniformly interpreted the command of *wa-ḍribūhunna* to mean "hit them," especially since prophetic discomfort—as recorded in *aḥādīth*—provided them with legitimate grounds for interpreting this command differently.[132] In the post-colonial period, Muslim scholars have availed themselves of this opportunity, arguing for *wa-ḍribūhunna* to have non-violent connotations. The difference in the approaches to this prescription, between pre- and post-colonial, is therefore not one of methodology. Rather, the difference can be attributed to the divergent idealized cosmologies of scholars in the pre- and post-colonial periods. Before putting the opposing cosmologies into conversation, it is useful first to explore the impact of Q. 4:34 on pre-colonial Islamic legal texts, which we will do in the next chapter.

[132] Marín asserts that "male superiority and the necessity to discipline wives are assumptions common to all the texts consulted." Marín (n 83) 39.

3

The Legal Boundaries of Marital Discipline

Far from being hermetically sealed genres, pre-colonial Qur'anic commentary and Islamic jurisprudence greatly influenced one another. Exegetical works were often written by scholars who were also trained in jurisprudence; as a result, the exegesis of Q. 4:34 was informed by the legal framework of a given exegete. While Chapter 2 focused on the interpretive choices of pre-colonial Qur'ān commentators in the exegesis of Q. 4:34, this chapter investigates the treatment of wife-beating in pre-colonial jurisprudence (*fiqh*).[1] An examination of the ways that the two genres treat the issue of wife-beating raises some fascinating questions. What are the similarities and differences between Qur'anic commentary and Islamic jurisprudence with regard to wife-beating, and what do those similarities and differences tell us about the relationship between the two genres? Does one have more egalitarian potential than the other? What is the benefit of looking at these genres side by side? Is it important to do so, and do we miss out by looking at the treatment of a particular issue in only one genre?

Certainly, contemporary scholars have grappled with these questions in the intersecting fields of gender and Islamic studies. In her book *Women and Gender in Islam*, Leila Ahmed argues that historical Islam offered the potential of both egalitarian understandings of women's roles and patriarchal manifestations, but because patriarchal Islam coincided with the social mores of early and medieval Islamic societies, it ultimately came to define the legal and exegetical corpora of orthodox Islam.[2] The scholarship of Asma Barlas, Hadia Mubarak, Sa'diyya Shaikh, and Amina Wadud, particularly their study of exegetical works, reinforces this idea.[3]

[1] As with works of *tafsīr*, this study only looks at *fiqh* works from the Sunnī jurisprudential schools. A study of Shi'ī pre- and post-colonial legal and exegetical works would be very interesting and most welcome.

[2] Leila Ahmed, *Women and Gender in Islam: Historical Roots of a Modern Debate* (New Haven: Yale University Press, 1992) 65–6.

[3] Asma Barlas, *Believing Women: Unreading Patriarchal Interpretations of the Qur'an* (Austin: University of Texas Press, 2002); Fatima Mernissi, *The Veil and the Male*

These scholars have argued that while there is an undeniable egalitarian vision to be found in the Qur'anic text, this vision was lost in the works of exegesis in which the subjective views of individual exegetes—based on their social, cultural, and historic milieus—erased the egalitarian vision of Islam in favor of a patriarchal, perhaps even misogynistic vision. Still, contemporary scholars are divided as to whether pre-colonial scholarship was uniformly patriarchal.

Mohammad Fadel has taken issue with Ahmed's portrayal of the triumph of a patriarchal Islam over an egalitarian one, arguing that while there have been two opposing voices in Islam, one did not undeniably dominate the other. Based on his study of women's testimony in the Islamic legal tradition, Fadel sees the patriarchal and egalitarian voices of Islam in constant tension with each other.[4] Fadel has posited that in contrast to the field of Qur'anic exegesis, Islamic jurisprudence provided greater space for the emergence of an ethical, perhaps even egalitarian, voice of Islam. While Qur'anic exegesis was "dominated by the atomistic methodology of verse-by-verse interpretation [which] allowed the misogynistic assumptions of the reader to dominate the text,"[5] Islamic jurisprudence dictated that jurists take into account a much wider set of data when deriving rulings.[6] As a result, Fadel finds the Sunnī legal tradition to "exist in tension with popular notions of gender roles" in the pre-colonial period.[7] According to Fadel, legal—and, by extension, systematic—thinking placed in doubt discriminatory inferences (such as women's lesser capacity for credible testimony) that conflicted with other known rules (such as the fact that women could unrestrictedly transmit *ḥadīth* with the same credibility as men). This meant that jurists were less likely to "impeach the probative value of women's statements based on their gender."[8] Fadel has proposed that the case study of female witnesses might shed light on the general character of the legal genre as opposed to the field of Qur'anic exegesis.

Kecia Ali's work on the relationship between conceptions of marriage and concubinage in foundational juridical texts challenges Fadel's claims

Elite (Cambridge: Perseus Books, 1991); Hadia Mubarak, "Breaking the Interpretive Monopoly: Re-Examination of Verse 4:34," *Hawwa*, 2(3) (2005) 261–98; Sa'diyya Shaikh, "Exegetical Violence: *Nushuz* in Qur'anic Gender Ideology," *Journal for Islamic Studies*, 17 (1997) 49–73; and Amina Wadud, *Qur'ān and Woman* (New York: Oxford University Press, 1999).

4 Mohammad Fadel, "Two Women, One Man: Knowledge, Power, and Gender in Medieval Sunni Legal Thought," *International Journal of Middle East Studies*, 29 (1997) 200.

5 Fadel (n 4) 186.

6 Fadel (n 4) 200.

7 Fadel (n 4) 186.

8 Fadel (n 4) 200.

that Islamic legal works were likely to defy existing gender norms as a result of the juristic process. While it may have been the case that jurisprudence concerning female witnesses upended patriarchal gender norms, Ali has illustrated that this was not the governing principle in the jurisprudence of marriage, where jurists institutionalized existing gender norms. A husband's ownership (*milk*) of his wife, expressed through the right of husbands to have sexual access to their wives, formed the structural foundation for the conception of marriage in the Ḥanafī, Mālikī, and Shāfiʿī legal schools.[9] Ali's findings bolster Ahmed's claims regarding the patriarchal voice of Islam as having triumphed in the juridical tradition, at least with regard to the conception of marriage in the major legal schools.

This project further underscores the triumph of the patriarchal voice in pre-colonial Islamic jurisprudence. In addition to the social and historic context of Muslim jurists, a shared idealized cosmology motivated jurists to rank men above women in a gendered hierarchy. Juridical discussions of the marital relationship reflected the exegetical discourse; jurists were ethically untroubled by the right of husbands to physically discipline wives. Jurists granted husbands moral authority over their wives and upheld the disciplinary privileges of husbands, while morally exhorting them to hit in a non-extreme (*ghayr mubarriḥ*) fashion. Husbands who hit their wives excessively, causing severe injuries such as broken bones, loss of limbs, disfigurement, or death, were legally liable for compensation. Echoing the concerns of Qur'anic exegesis, jurisprudential works addressed only the ramifications of extreme hitting, not the underlying right of husbands to physically discipline their wives. As a result of this narrow focus, jurists did not legislate for the intermediary levels of violence between extreme and non-extreme. This left wives vulnerable and unprotected, because husbands could not be sued for beating their wives unless they beat them in an extreme manner, either injuring them severely or killing them.

The exegetical discussions surrounding Q. 4:34 were theoretical in nature: exegetes speculated about God's rationale for preferring men over women, and for husbands' resulting disciplinary privilege over wives. If Qur'ān commentators theorized an idealized cosmology in their exegesis, Muslim jurists institutionalized this cosmology in Islamic jurisprudence. Jurists used Q. 4:34 as a proof text for supporting the right of husbands to physically hit their wives, but they emphasized the procedural aspect of this permission/prescription, considering the

[9] Kecia Ali, *Marriage and Slavery in Early Islam* (Cambridge, MA: Harvard University Press, 2010) Introduction.

liability of husbands in the case of severe hitting. The attention to detail regarding both the nature of husbandly authority in marriage, as well as their accountability to both wives and the state, allowed jurisprudential texts to offer a fuller picture of how this prescription was institutionalized and insights into the social reality of pre-colonial jurists. Although these scholars shared an ideal cosmology wherein men ranked above women and were responsible for disciplining them, they differed with regard to the understanding of the human proclivity to err and the level of social and state oversight needed to ensure justice in the domestic sphere. The varied positions of the four Sunnī legal schools illustrate that the patriarchy inherent in the ideal shared cosmology was complex and nuanced rather than flat and uniform. Ḥanafī jurists safeguarded the authority of husbands in marriage by shielding them from legal accountability in cases of excessive violence, whereas Mālikī scholars endeavored to protect wives from abuse by instituting social and judicial supervision over husbands. Shāfiʿī jurists struggled with the theological predicament created by the contradictory nature of the divine imperative to hit recalcitrant wives in Q. 4:34 and the prophetic censure against hitting wives. Ḥanbalī jurists extended the definition of *nushūz* and further protected husbands from liability in cases of excessive violence by denying wives clear legal recourse.

The systematic method of juridical thinking, which follows a different logic than hermeneutical reasoning, shows how an alternative use of foundational sources—specifically, the Qur'ān and *ḥadīth*—can lead to similar conclusions. Contrary to claims made about the atomistic nature of Qur'anic exegesis preventing it from addressing the Qur'ān holistically, the previous chapters demonstrate that exegetes did in fact think systematically about the Qur'ān. The ideal cosmology that underpinned their interpretive choices was informed by the Qur'ān itself and also informed their reading of the text. That they chose to interpret the Qur'ān word by word and verse by verse did not mean that they lost sight of each verse's connection to the rest of the Qur'ān. This point is underscored by the fact that Muslim jurists, who also applied systematic thinking to their reading of the Qur'anic text, arrived at conclusions regarding the marital hierarchy that were similar to the conclusions of exegetes. It cannot be argued that either Qur'anic exegesis or Islamic jurisprudence were more egalitarian than the other; both endorsed a marital hierarchy in which husbands rank above women, wielding disciplinary privilege over them. However, the distinct discussions in Qur'anic exegesis and Islamic jurisprudence are worth reading side by side, as they shed light on each other. The justifications of husbandly disciplinary power in Qur'anic exegesis illuminated the idealized cosmology of pre-colonial

Muslim jurists, who placed the marital relationship in an intricate legal and doctrinal web of many other relationships—with God, children, and slaves.[10]

THE ḤANAFĪS: PROTECTING A HUSBAND'S AUTHORITY

In Ḥanafī jurisprudence, the discussion of the husbandly privilege to physically discipline wives was characterized by three salient features: their understanding of marital *nushūz*, the conception of husbandly discipline, and the notion of discretionary punishment (*taʿzīr*). Ḥanafī jurists understood marital *nushūz* as having three types: reciprocal *nushūz*, husbandly *nushūz*, and wifely *nushūz*. This typology was based on the two references to marital *nushūz*, wifely and husbandly, in Chapter 4 of the Qur'ān (Q. 4:34 and 4:128 respectively). Contemporary scholars find it perplexing that pre-colonial exegetes rarely referred to husbandly *nushūz* or Q. 4:128 in their discussions of wifely *nushūz* in Q. 4:34.[11] To explain this phenomenon, they often blame the atomistic nature of Qur'anic commentaries, which prevented pre-colonial scholars from seeing the two verses as connected—basically, for missing the forest for the trees. According to these scholars, placing wifely *nushūz* (Q. 4:34) in conversation with husbandly *nushūz* (Q. 4:128) permits the reconceptualization of marital *nushūz* as a reciprocal and egalitarian concept. However, the Ḥanafī treatment of husbandly and wifely *nushūz*, and their direct references to Q. 4:34 and 4:128, illustrate that the atomistic nature of Qur'anic exegesis was not responsible for the patriarchal bent of the exegesis of Q. 4:34. It is perfectly possible to take both Q. 4:34 and Q. 4:128 into account and still come to a patriarchal understanding of husbandly and wifely *nushūz*. It is more likely that pre-colonial exegetes did not refer to husbandly *nushūz* in their discussion of wifely *nushūz* because they saw the two as discrete behaviors that were irrelevant to each other. Ḥanafī jurists, many of whom were also exegetes, were fully aware of the separate types of *nushūz* of husbands and wives but saw the two as wholly incommensurate.

Ḥanafī jurists defined reciprocal *nushūz* as the hatred of one spouse for the other; this *nushūz* could be exhibited by either spouse. For all practical purposes, Ḥanafīs understood a spouse's hatred to manifest itself with the

[10] Kecia Ali (n 9) 6.

[11] A few exegetes, such as al-Zajjāj, offered a gender-neutral interpretation of *nushūz* as the repugnance of one spouse for the other (*al-nushūz karāhiya aḥadihimā li-ṣāḥibihi*). Abū Isḥāq Ibrāhīm ibn al-Sarī al-Zajjāj, *Maʿānī al-Qur'ān wa-iʿrābuhu* (Beirut: al-Maktaba al-ʿAṣriyya, 1973) 2:48.

initiation of divorce proceedings. Hence, if one spouse initiated divorce proceedings against the other, the initiating spouse was guilty of *nushūz*. Since both spouses could initiate divorce proceedings, I refer to this as reciprocal *nushūz*.[12] Ḥanafīs had a particular animus towards divorce, generally viewing it as a legally permissible but nevertheless abhorrent (*makrūh*) act.[13] Muḥammad ibn Aḥmad al-Sarakhsī (d. 483/1090), for example, described divorce as "ingratitude of [God's] blessings (*kufrān al-niʿma*)."[14] The Ḥanafī abhorrence for divorce was captured in a ruling whereby the party initiating divorce was penalized for doing so: a husband divorcing his wife could not demand return on the dower (*mahr*), and a wife who sought divorce from her husband had to forgo her *mahr*.[15] Despite the reciprocal nature of this penalty—both parties sacrificed the *mahr*—a patriarchal social structure determined that a greater economic disincentive was levied against wives seeking divorce from their husbands.

[12] Although both spouses can initiate a divorce, only husbands can divorce their wives, while wives must persuade a third party to petition for her divorce. In his tenth/sixteenth-century commentary on al-Nasafī's legal work, Ibn Nujaym (d. 970/1563) cited al-Zajjāj's opinion on *nushūz* as the "hatred of one spouse for the other." Zayn al-Dīn ibn Ibrāhīm Ibn Nujaym, *al-Baḥr al-Rāʾiq, Sharḥ Kanz al-Daqāʾiq* (Quetta: al-Maktaba al-Mājidīya, 1983) 4:76, 179. Al-Kāsānī described the initiation of divorce (*khulʿ*), which could be launched by either spouse, as a type of *nushūz*. Abū Bakr ibn Masʿūd al-Kāsānī, *Badāʾiʿ al-ṣanāʾiʿ fī tartīb al-sharāʾiʿ* (Beirut: Dār al-Kutub al-ʿArabī, 1974) 3:150. Al-Bābartī characterized divorce as an expression of reciprocal *nushūz*. Muḥammad ibn Maḥmūd Akmal al-Dīn Al-Bābartī, *al-ʿInāya sharḥ al-Hidāya* in *Sharḥ fatḥ al-qadīr li-l-ʿājiz al-faqīr* (Cairo: Muṣṭafā al-Bābī al-Ḥalabī, 1970) 4:210. See also Muḥammad ibn Aḥmad Al-Sarakhsī, *Kitāb al-Mabsūṭ* (Beirut: Dār al-Maʿrifa, 1972) 6:3.

[13] The fifth/eleventh-century Ḥanafī jurist al-Sarakhsī noted that both the wife and the husband could seek divorce from the other as a function of their respective *nushūz*. Drawing on *aḥādīth* that comment on the moral reprehensibility of divorce, he argued that divorce was not permitted (*lā yaḥill*) except in cases of necessity (*ḍarūra*). This is because divorce constitutes "ingratitude for [God's] blessings (*kufrān al-niʿma*)." Al-Sarakhsī mentioned several *aḥādīth* to prove his point. After citing the *ḥadīth* that stated "God curses the one who enjoys (*dhawwāq*) divorce," al-Sarakhsī mentioned two *aḥādīth* regarding divorce initiated by a wife or husband. As for a divorce initiated by a woman, the *ḥadīth* read, "The curse of God, the angels, and all the people are on the woman who seeks divorce from her husband out of *nushūz*." It was narrated about men who sought divorce from their wives that "a man who seeks divorce (*yakhlaʿu*) from his wife [demonstrates] his ungratefulness (*kufrān*) of [God's] blessings, since [marriage] is from amongst the blessings of God upon His servants." Al-Sarakhsī (n 12) 6:3. Many Ḥanafī jurists included *aḥādīth* that described divorce as something that is permissible but repugnant. Ibn al-Humām cited Ibn Mājah and Abū Dāwūd as recording the prophetic report, "To God, the most hated amongst the permissible things is divorce." Muḥammad ibn ʿAbd al-Wāḥid Ibn al-Humām, *Sharḥ fatḥ al-qadīr li-l-ʿājiz al-faqīr* (Cairo: Muṣṭafā al-Bābī al-Ḥalabī, 1970) 3:464. See also ʿAbd al-Raḥmān ibn Muḥammad al-Ḥalabī, *Majmaʿ al-anhur* (Beirut: Dār Iḥyāʾ al-turāth al- ʿArabī, 1980) 1:381–2.

[14] Al-Sarakhsī (n 12) 3:2.

[15] To support his point, al-Kāsānī cited Q. 4: 20, which states "But if ye decide to take one wife in place of another, even if ye had given the latter a whole treasure for dower, take not the least bit of it back: would ye take it by slander and a manifest wrong?" Abdullah Yusuf Ali, *The Meaning of the Holy Quran* (Beltsville: Amana Publications, 1997) Q. 4:20. Al-Kāsānī (n 12) 3:150.

The practical result of this ruling was that husbands who divorced their wives could not make financial claims on their wives, but wives appealing for divorce had to make a financial sacrifice to do so. To complicate matters further, Ḥanafī jurists waived the economic penalty against husbands who divorced their wives on the ground of wifely *nushūz*, such as open lewdness (*fāḥisha mubayyina*). In this case, divorce was not an instance of reciprocal *nushūz* but rather the result of wifely *nushūz*, which meant that husbands would not be penalized for seeking divorce. In this scenario, a husband could divorce his wife and demand to be financially compensated for it by stipulating a return of the *mahr*.[16] The penalty for divorce initiation in the Ḥanafī school underscores an important legal attitude; Ḥanafī jurists were comfortable with authorizing morally reprehensible acts.

The descriptions of husbandly and wifely *nushūz* were imbedded within a patriarchal vision of the marital relationship. Husbandly *nushūz* was mentioned briefly in discussions of wifely *nushūz*. It was described as a husband abandoning his wife (*tarakahā*), shunning her, or treating her with cruelty (*jafāhā*).[17] While husbandly *nushūz* was characterized primarily as a husband's neglect of his marital duties, wifely *nushūz* was portrayed as disobedient and belligerent behavior. Wifely *nushūz* was a wife's sexual refusal, general disobedience, her leaving the house without her husband's permission, not beautifying herself (*tark al-zīna*), not bathing or purifying (*ghusl*) herself, possibly for abandoning her daily prayers, failing to submit (*tusallim*) herself to her husband, and/or struggling against (*al-ʿiṣāba ʿalā*) him.[18]

[16] Here, al-Kāsānī referred to Q. 4:14, which states "O ye who believe! Ye are forbidden to inherit women against their will. Nor should ye treat them with harshness, that ye may take away part of the dower ye have given them—except where they have been guilty of open lewdness; on the contrary live with them on a footing of kindness and equity. If ye take a dislike to them, it may be that ye dislike a thing and Allah brings about through it a great deal of good." Yusuf Ali (n 15) Q. 4:14 and Al-Kāsānī (n 12) 3:150. See also Ibn Nujaym (n 12) 4:128, 303.

[17] Ibn Nujaym (n 12) 4:76.

[18] According to al-Zaylaʿī there was some debate about whether a husband could hit his wife for not praying. He came down on the side of those who say that, unlike in the case of a child (who should be hit for not praying), a wife should not be hit for failing to pray. He also mentioned that husbands were required to stop their wives from visiting churches. ʿUthmān ibn ʿAlī al-Zaylaʿī, *Tabyīn al-ḥaqāʾiq sharḥ kanz al-daqāʾiq* (Beirut: Dār al-Kutub al-ʿIlmiyya, 2000) 3:640–1. See also al-Nasafī in al-Zaylaʿī's commentary and Ibn Nujaym (n 12) 5:81–2. Ibn ʿĀbidīn added that a man could not hit his wife for abandoning prayer, and further he could not hit his wife's younger sister after she reached the age of ten for abandoning prayer. Additional characteristics for which wives could be disciplined included a wife uncovering her face for a non-*mahram*, talking to a stranger, and calling her husband names. Al-Haskafī in Ibn ʿĀbidīn. Muḥammad Amīn ibn ʿUmar Ibn ʿĀbidīn, *Radd al-muḥtār ʿalā al-Durr al-mukhtār sharḥ Tanwīr al-abṣār* (Beirut: Dār al-Kutub al-ʿIlmiyya, 1994) 6:128–9. Concerning the restriction on a wife's mobility, Marín mentions that al-Suyūṭī cited a *ḥadīth* in which "a woman was forbidden by her husband to leave

According to Ḥanafī jurists, wives owe their husbands obedience and are to guard themselves in their husbands' absence in exchange for the bride-price (*mahr*) they receive at the time of marriage and the maintenance (*nafaqa*) they receive from their husbands throughout their marriage.[19] Abū Bakr ibn Masʿūd al-Kāsānī (d. 587/1191) cited Q. 2:228—a verse that refers to the similar rights of husbands and wives over each other—to argue that a husband's economic obligation to support his wife is balanced out by her duty to obey him.[20] Although this verse is used by modern scholars to support an egalitarian vision of marriage, it was used by al-Kāsānī to support a patriarchal marital structure. He made this argument by reading Q. 2:228 in light of Q. 4:34; the "similar rights" mentioned in Q. 2:228 were properly understood in the context of the marital hierarchy outlined in Q. 4:34. In general, Ḥanafī jurists used Q. 4:34 as a source text to ground the disciplinary rights of husbands over wives. They saw this Qur'anic passage as mandating (*mashrūʿ*) the discipline of recalcitrant wives; they portrayed the imperative statements in Q. 4:34 as commands rather than mere permission.[21] As a result, Ḥanafī legal discussion of a husband's disciplinary duties followed the three prescriptions in Q. 4:34—admonishment, abandonment, and hitting.[22]

their home while he was away on a military expedition. The woman, learning that her father was gravely ill, asked the Prophet's permission to attend to him. The Prophet's answer was to recommend that she obey her husband, even when the father finally died. This is how, said the Prophet, the dead man was forgiven by God, thanks to his daughter's faithful obedience to her husband." Manuela Marín, "Disciplining Wives: A Historical Reading of Qur'ān 4:34," *Studia Islamica* (2003) 37–8. Also see Jalāl al-Dīn ʿAbd al-Raḥmān al-Suyūṭī, *al-Durr al-manthūr fī al-tafsīr al-maʾthūr* (Beirut: Dār al-Maʿrifa, 1970) 2:154.

[19] Al-Kāsānī used Q. 4:34 to explain that ownership associated with marriage (*milk al-nikāḥ*) and the *qiwāma* of husbands over wives obligated husbands to support their wives through maintenance. He understood Q. 4:34 to mean that "maintenance was made obligatory [on husbands] because they are *qawwāmūn* [over their wives]." Al-Kāsānī (n 12) 4:416. See also Ibn Nujaym (n 12) 4:305.

[20] Q. 2:228 reads "... And women shall have rights similar to the rights against them, according to what is equitable; but men have a degree (of advantage) over them and Allah is Exalted in Power, Wise." Yusuf Ali (n 15) Q. 2:228. The full text of al-Kāsānī reads: "It is obligatory for her to be obedient to her husband when he calls her to bed. God said, 'And [wives] have rights similar [to the rights] against them, according to what is equitable (*maʿrūf*).' It is said that she is entitled to the *mahr* and *nafaqa* in exchange for obedience to him with regard to herself and protecting [herself] in his absence. [And this is evident in] God's order to discipline them (fem. pl.) with abandonment and hitting when they disobey. [God] also prohibited [husbands from] the obedience [of their wives] by saying, 'And if/when they obey you [husbands], do not seek a means against them.' This proves that discipline is required." Al-Kāsānī (n 12) 2:334 and 4:15. See also Ibn Nujaym (n 12) 3:385.

[21] Ibn al-Humām (n 13) 5:345–6.

[22] Al-Kāsānī saw the Ḥajj sermon as an exposition of Q. 4:34. He wrote that the sermon "clarifies what is already in the [Qur'ān]." He cited the following portion of the sermon to support the right of husbands to hit their wives for disciplinary purposes in a non-extreme manner: "Fear God concerning women, for they are your prisoners. They do not have ownership over themselves. You take them as a trust from God and make their private parts permissible for yourselves with the word of God. Your right over them is that they not give your

According to Ḥanafī jurists, husbands were required to discipline wifely *nushūz*; they could discipline their wives physically, and there was a great deal of leeway in the extent and severity of hitting permissible to them. Though they offered moral exhortations to husbands to live with their wives in kindness and equity,[23] Ḥanafī jurists maintained the principle set out by Aḥmad b. ʿAlī al-Jaṣṣāṣ (d. 370/980–1) that there is no retaliation (*qiṣāṣ*) in marriage, except in the case of death.[24] A husband was permitted to hit his wife without any liability, even if the beating resulted in wounds or broken bones, as long as he did not kill her. Within these parameters, Ḥanafī jurists emphasized the importance of following the three prescriptions of admonishment, abandonment, and hitting sequentially, interpreting the "and" (*wa*) between each prescription as sequential rather than conjunctive.[25] Al-Kāsānī added a step to the process by stipulating that husbands were required to admonish their wives first gently[26] and then harshly,[27] before proceeding to abandonment. If at any

bed to anyone and not permit anyone you dislike into your homes. If you fear *nushūz* from them, then admonish them, abandon them in their beds, and hit them in a non-extreme (*ghayr mubarriḥ*) manner. And their rights over you are that you clothe them and provide for them equitably…" Al-Kāsānī relied on the following *ḥadīth* to emphasize the intertwined nature of the financial and disciplinary obligations of husbands over wives in marriage: "A man came to the Prophet of God, may peace and blessings be upon him, and said, 'What are the rights of a woman over her husband?' He replied, 'That he feed her as he eats and clothe her as he clothes himself, and that he does not abandon her except in the house, and does not hit or revile her.' " It is interesting that although he cited this report, which prohibits husbands from hitting their wives altogether ("does not hit her"), he ignored this prohibition. Privileging the Qur'anic text on this point, he did not incorporate this prohibition into his legal reasoning on wife-beating. Al-Kāsānī (n 12) 4:15.

[23] Here, al-Kāsānī drew on Q. 4:19, which reads, "On the contrary, live with them on a footing of kindness and equity (*bi-l-maʿrūf*)…" in order to exhort husbands to live with their wives "with graciousness (*faḍl*) and excellence (*iḥsān*) in speech, actions and character." He also referenced the *ḥadīth* in which Muḥammad said, "The best of you is the one who is the best to his wife, and I am the best of you to my wives." In this *ḥadīth*, Muḥammad granted men permission to hit their wives and then morally censured them for hitting them. As discussed in Chapter 2, this report created theological problems for Shāfiʿī scholars in particular. However, this report did not create similar problems for the Ḥanafīs, who were more comfortable with morally reprehensible but legally legitimate acts. Al-Kāsānī (n 12) 2:334 and Yusuf Ali (n 15) Q. 4:19. Ibn Nujaym made a similar appeal to live with equity and kindness, using Q. 4:19 in his commentary on al-Nasafī's *Kanz al-Daqāʾiq*. Ibn Nujaym (n 12) 3:385.

[24] Aḥmad b. ʿAlī al-Jaṣṣāṣ, *Aḥkām al-Qurʾān* (Beirut: Dār al-Kitāb al-ʿArabī, 1971) 2:188.

[25] See, eg, Al-Kāsānī (n 12) 2:334 and Ibn Nujaym (n 12) 3:385. For a discussion on the significance of the sequential/simultaneous debate in Q. 4:34, see Chapter 2 of this book.

[26] When confronted with wifely *nushūz*, a husband was first required to admonish his wife with gentleness (*rifq*) and compassion (*līn*), encouraging her to "be from amongst the righteous (*ṣāliḥāt*), obedient (*qānitāt*), and protectors in [her husband's] absence (*ḥāfiẓāt li-l-ghayb*)." Al-Kāsānī (n 12) 2:334.

[27] Positive exhortation was to be followed by threatening speech, whereby a husband was to "warn (*yukhawwif*) [his wife] of abandonment" before actually abandoning her. Al-Kāsānī (n 12) 2:334.

stage a disciplinary action was effective in rectifying a wife's behavior, then husbands were to cease disciplining their wives and refrain from proceeding to the next step.

The prescription for abandonment resulted in the same paradox for Ḥanafī jurists as it did for several exegetes: sexual abandonment caused husbands to suffer unjustly, since they did not deserve to lose their sexual rights because of their wives' *nushūz*. Al-Kāsānī offered three solutions to this problem: a husband could abandon his wife verbally rather than sexually; or he could bed another woman (wife or concubine) during the nights allotted to his recalcitrant wife; or he could abandon the marital bed but nevertheless have sex with his wife when he desired her, rather than when she desired him. This ensured that the husband would continue to enjoy his sexual rights while denying a woman her rights; after all, disciplinary action was meant to discipline a wife and not deny a husband his sexual rights.[28] The last solution offered by Al-Kāsānī is especially disturbing, since it forces a wife to engage in non-consensual sex. If a wife's *nushūz* consisted of her sexual refusal, then her husband could have sex with her against her will. According to al-Kāsānī, marital rape was legally permissible.[29]

[28] Al-Kāsānī wrote, "There is disagreement about the nature of abandonment. It is said, 'Abandon her by not having intercourse with her, and do not sleep with her in the marital bed.' And it is said, 'Abandon her by not speaking to her during intercourse with her, and it does not mean abandoning sex and sleeping with her.' This is so because this [sexual intimacy] is a shared right between them (*ḥaqqun mushtarakun baynahumā*), and in this [abandoning of sex and the bed] there is some harm/disadvantage (*al-ḍarar*) for [the husband] as there is for [the wife]. [The husband] is not to discipline [his wife] in a manner whereby he hurts/damages himself and nullifies his own rights (*ḥaqqahu*). Some say, 'Abandon her by separating from her in bed, and instead bedding another on her rightful night.' [This is a possible reading] because he is obligated to fulfill her rights in division [of nights] and protect the boundaries of God only in a state of agreement, and not in a state where she forfeits her rights, and there is fear of *nushūz* and strife (*al-tanāzuʿ*). And it is said, 'He should abandon her by leaving her bed (*muḍājiʿatihā*) but he should have sex with her when he is overcome with desire for her (*li-waqt ghalabat shahwatihā*), and not at the time that she needs him.' This is so because this discipline (*al-taʾdīb*) and rectification (*al-zajr*) are meant to discipline her (*yuʾaddibhā*) and not [the husband] by preventing him from having intercourse when he needs her." Al-Kāsānī (n 12) 2:334.

[29] Kecia Ali notes that "marital rape is an oxymoron; rape (*ightiṣāb*) is a property crime that by definition cannot be committed by the husband. Still, they do make a distinction between forced and consensual sex within marriage." Kecia Ali (n 9) 120. She is correct in her assessment, but given that in modern parlance, forced sex in marriage is referred to as "marital rape," I have decided to use this term to describe the type of behavior that jurists permitted for husbands. I believe this is necessary to emphasize what Lisa Hajjar calls the "uncriminizable" nature of this act. She writes, "Under shariʿa, there is no harm—and thus no crime—in acts of sex between people who are married. Thus, marital rape is literally 'uncriminalizable' under dominant interpretations of shariʿa. For example, Sura 2, Verse 223, provides a Qurʾanic basis for men's unabridged sexual access to their wives." This is important because "In contexts where shariʿa is interpreted to permit violence against women by family members, the harms women suffer not only go unpunished but

Marital rape was also regarded as acceptable husbandly conduct by others in the Ḥanafī legal school.[30] For example, Zayn al-Dīn ibn Ibrāhīm Ibn Nujaym (d. 970/1563) argued that as long as a wife remains in her husband's house, she is owed maintenance, even if she is disobedient and withholds sex. This is because as long as she remains in his house, a husband can dominate her (*yaghlibu ʿalayhā*), forcing her to have sex with him.[31] Like al-Kāsānī, Ibn Nujaym was comfortable with marital rape, seeing it as a natural consequence of a wife's sexual disobedience. ʿAbd Allāh ibn Aḥmad al-Nasafī (d. 710/1310) added an undeniable shade of violence to his discussion of marital rape. While he argued that a necessary condition of hitting one's wife is to leave her intact or sound (*bi-sharṭ al-salāma*), soundness is not a condition for sex, so if a wife dies while her husband is having sex with her, he is not liable. Al-Nasafī understood this to be Abu Ḥanīfa's position, who argued that sexual intercourse—unlike disciplinary beating—was not restricted by the condition of soundness (*salāma*).[32]

Ḥanafī jurists used general qualifiers to describe the type of hitting a husband might undertake when disciplining his wife: the hitting ought to be non-extreme (*ghayr mubarriḥ*), and it should not cause disfigurement. As seen in the exegetical literature, non-extreme hitting is a vague qualifier, and the actual definitions of non-extreme hitting can include surprisingly severe actions. Ḥanafī jurists often compared the disciplinary beating of a wife with the disciplinary beating of a child or a slave.[33] Muḥammad ibn ʿAbd al-Wāḥid Ibn al-Humām (d. 861/1457) thought that as in the case of hitting a child, a husband can whip his wife as long as he restricts himself to ten lashes. He based this opinion

also unrecognized as harms." Lisa Hajjar, "Religion, State Power, and Domestic Violence in Muslim Societies: A Framework for Comparative Analysis," *Law & Social Inquiry*, 29(1) (2004) 11–12.

[30] Kecia Ali writes about the Ḥanafīs, "a wife's sexual refusal is irrelevant if not accompanied by her departure from the conjugal home, because her husband is permitted to have sex with her without her consent." Kecia Ali (n 9) 120.

[31] Ibn Nujaym wrote, "even if it were seen that [the wife] was sexually disobedient to her husband, she is owed maintenance; even when she is disobedient to him, she is still in the house. Thus, the maintenance is not cancelled because the husband can prevail upon her (*yaghlibu ʿalayhā*)." Ibn Nujaym (n 12) 4:180.

[32] Al-Nasafī in al-Zaylaʿī (n 18) 3:640. See also Ibn ʿĀbidīn (n 18) 6:131.

[33] In the case of the child, a father's hitting was obligatory and considered to be in the interest of a child's well-being (*maṣlaḥa*). Furthermore, a father could permit a teacher to physically discipline his child when teaching the child, by transferring his ownership rights to the teacher. Here, the teacher hitting the child would be like the father hitting his child. In contrast, the benefit of hitting a wife—like hitting a slave—was for the good of the husband/master. Ibn Nujaym (n 12) 5:49, 83. Al-Haskafī wrote that husbands were required to discipline their wives, as masters (*mawlā*) were responsible for their slaves. Al-Haskafī in Ibn ʿĀbidīn (n 18) 6:128. See also Ibn ʿĀbidīn (n 18) 6:129–30.

on several prophetic reports, including two that tells believers to "Hang the whip where your household can see it" and "Do not lash more than ten times except in the case of corporal (*ḥadd*) punishment."[34] Lashing a wife or child for more than ten strikes transformed the punishment from a legitimate discretionary (*taʿzīr*) punishment to a *ḥadd* penalty, which was meant to be applied by a court, not by individuals.[35] In contrast, al-Nasafī argued that the *taʿzīr* punishment was restricted to thirty-nine, seventy-five, or seventy-nine lashes; in general he argued that the upper limit of *taʿzīr* punishment was a hundred lashes, and the minimum limit was three lashes (*thalāth jaldāt*).[36]

Ḥanafī jurists understood the right of husbands to physically discipline their wives as an essential husbandly right and compared the husband–wife relationship in this regard to a master–slave relationship.[37] The analogy between the husband–wife relationship and the master–slave relationship is not coincidental; it is one that persisted in both exegetical

[34] Ibn al-Humām (n 13) 5:345. The first *ḥadīth* was also mentioned by al-Nasafī but interpreted very differently. Al-Zaylaʿī (commentary on al-Nasafī) (n 18) 3:633. See also Ibn Nujaym (n 12) 5:81.

[35] Al-Nasafī defined *taʿzīr* as "the non-specified (*ghayr muqaddara*) chastisement (*al-zawājir*) [applied] when necessary in order to remove corruption (*fasād*) . . . [It] requires a disciplinary action (*taʾdīb*) other than the application of the *ḥadd* penalty." Al-Zaylaʿī (commentary on al-Nasafī) (n 18) 3:633. See also Ibn ʿĀbidīn (n 18) 6:103. Dien describes *taʿzīr* as "a term of Islamic law meaning discretionary punishment, e.g. by the *kāḍī*, for the offenses for which no *ḥadd* [q.v.] punishment is laid down." Although the term *taʿzīr* itself cannot be found in the Qurʾān and *aḥādīth*, both "contain practical examples of *taʿzīr*." In its practical application, Dien mentions that "the amount of *taʿzīr* should be lower than the lowest *ḥadd*" and often involves instruments such as "the hand, whip, stick, and *dirra*, which is a whip of ox-hide, or made of strips of hide on which date-stones have been stitched." According to Muḥammad b. ʿIwaḍ al-Sunāmī (d. 734/1333), "*Ḥadd* is specified by the text, unlike *taʿzīr* which is at the discretion of the Imām; *ḥadd* lapses if based on suspicion (*s̲h̲ubha*), whereas *taʿzīr* is obligatory if there are grounds for suspicion. *Ḥadd* is not applicable to a minor (*ṣabī*), while *taʿzīr* can be applied to minors." M. Izzi Dien. "Taʿzīr (a.)" in P. Bearman, Th. Bianquis, C.E. Bosworth, E. van Donzel, and W.P. Heinrichs (eds.), *Encyclopaedia of Islam*, 2nd edn. (Leiden: Brill, 2009). See also Ibn al-Humām (n 13) 5:344–5.

[36] Al-Zaylaʿī supported and explained al-Nasafī's opinion here (n 18) 3:634 and 637–8. See also Ibn Nujaym (n 12) 5:68 and 79–80. See also al-Haskafī and Ibn ʿĀbidīn in Ibn ʿĀbidīn (n 18) 6:103–4.

[37] Regarding the analogy between the master–slave relationship and the husband–wife relationship, al-Kāsānī wrote, "[Discipline] begins with kind and gentle exhortation without harshness (*al-taghlīẓ*) in speech. If she accepts this [the matter is settled] but if she does not [accept this] then [the husband] is to use harsh/coarse speech (*ghallaẓa al-qawl*). If she accepts [then the matter is settled], but if she does not, then [the husband's] power is extended (*basaṭa*). And similarly, if she engages in something that is worthy of censure (*maḥẓūran*) other than *nushūz* that transgresses clearly demarcated boundaries, it is the [responsibility] of the husband to discipline her (*yuʾaddibuhā*) through discretionary punishment (*taʿzīr*). It is the right of the husband to chastise his wife just as it is the right of the master (*mawlā*) to chastise his property/slave (*mamlūkahu*)." Al-Kāsānī (n 12) 2:334. Ibn ʿAbidīn explained that "*taʿzīr* is carried out by a husband, master or anyone who [is charged with] overseeing a disobedient person." See also Ibn ʿĀbidīn (n 18) 6:103 and 131. For more on the obligation on husbands to rectify a wife's behavior, see Ibn al-Humām (n 13) 5:345.

literature and legal sources.[38] Thinking of marriage as analogous to the master–slave relationship helps to explain the inherent hierarchy in marriage, the right and duty of husbands to discipline their wives, and the discussion surrounding liability if a husband killed his wife while disciplining her. If the wife is seen as property—alongside a slave—then the absence of legal repercussion for a husband who injures his wife (unless he kills her) begins to make sense.[39] While Ḥanafī legal scholars encouraged husbands to hit their wives in a moderate manner, most held fast to the rule that there was no retaliation in marriage, except in the case of a wife's death at the hands of her husband.[40]

In the case of a wife's death, there was debate regarding the nature of a husband's liability. If a husband killed his wife while disciplining her, was he liable? If so, in what way—could he be killed for killing his wife, or was his liability only monetary? Al-Nasafī argued that if a wife dies as a result of her husband's disciplinary beating, which did not exceed a hundred strikes, then the husband was not liable for her death.[41] Al-Nasafī defended his position by arguing that if a husband were financially liable for killing his wife while disciplining her in a reasonable manner (striking her less than a hundred times), then he would be unfairly financially penalized twice: once for paying the bride-price (*mahr*) at the time of marriage and then again for killing her while fulfilling his husbandly disciplinary duties. However, if he exceeded a hundred strikes, then he crossed the boundary of disciplinary beating into abusive hitting and was then liable to pay the treasury (*bayt*

[38] Kecia Ali (n 9) especially Introduction.

[39] For Ibn Nujaym, the husband–wife relationship was analogous to the master–slave one in many ways. Eg, he wrote that a husband was required to discipline his wife the way a master (*sayyid*) was required to discipline his slave (*'abd*). Ibn Nujaym (n 12) 5:82.

[40] As seen in Chapter 1, al-Jaṣṣāṣ used the *sabab al-nuzūl* of Q. 4:34 to support this legal position. He narrated a version of the *sabab* wherein Ḥabība complained to Muḥammad after being wounded (*jaraḥa*) by her husband. In this context, Q. 4:34 voided Muḥammad's pronouncement for retaliation, protecting the right of husbands to hit their wives even past the point of wounding them. Al-Jaṣṣāṣ (n 24) 2:188. Al-Haskafī and Ibn 'Ābidīn argued that a husband could be held liable for *ta'zīr* punishment if he hit his wife excessively (*ḍarb al-fāḥisha*), but they did not discuss what would constitute proof for such hitting or what this punishment would look like. Al-Haskafī and Ibn 'Ābidīn in Ibn 'Ābidīn (n 18) 6:131.

[41] Al-Nasafī in Al-Zayla'ī (n 18) 3:641. Al-Zayla'ī also considered the punitive possibilities of *ta'zīr* to extend beyond merely hitting one's wife and killing her accidentally. He argued that a husband could intentionally kill an unfaithful wife, along with her lover, if her husband found them together. Such killing fell under "rectifying an abomination (*munkar*) with one's hands" based on the *ḥadīth* in which Muḥammad advised his companions, "Whosoever sees an abomination should change it with his hands. If he is not able to, then he should speak out against it. If he is not able to do this, then he ought to hate it in his heart—and this is the weakest of faith." Al-Zayla'ī (n 18) 3:634. See also Ibn 'Ābidīn and al-Haskafī in Ibn 'Ābidīn (n 18) 6:107–8 and 130; Ibn al-Humām (n 13) 5:346.

al-māl) half the monetary compensation (*diya*) of a free man. In the end, al-Nasafī pleaded with the judiciary to show mercy to the husband who killed his wife, since he might have children and other dependents for whom he was responsible.[42] Ibn Nujaym and ʿAlāʾ al-Dīn al-Haskafī (d. 1088/1677) agreed that a husband owed monetary compensation—not his life—if he killed his wife while disciplining her.[43]

In general, the Ḥanafī scholars under study imagined a limited role for the court in domestic affairs. Most of their legal efforts in their discussions of husbands' disciplinary privileges were aimed at protecting a husband from the court in the case of a wife's death at the hands of her husband. Al-Kāsānī made brief reference to external adjudication; if a husband found that hitting his wife was ineffective, then he could refer the matter to a judge.[44] Ibn al-Humām believed that a husband could seek a judge's opinion when applying discretionary punishment, since the different temperaments of people require varied responses, ranging from yelling and hitting to imprisonment. Judicial intervention was not envisioned as an oversight of a husband's judicious execution of his disciplinary authority; rather, it was offered to husbands as a resource upon which they could rely for external support. This underscores the weight granted to a husband's discretion in applying discretionary punishment (*taʿzīr*) to his wife.[45]

The value of a husband's discretion in the Ḥanafī school is further emphasized by the fact that Ḥanafī scholars discouraged public inquiries into men's domestic affairs. Ibn Nujaym cited two prophetic reports to this end. The first states, "Do not ask a man why he hit his wife"; the second reports that Muḥammad "forbade a woman from complaining against her husband."[46] Both of these prophetic reports limited a wife's ability to seek legal redress if she was beaten by her husband, adding a level of moral and social taboo against speaking about domestic matters in public. The Ḥanafī legal position was a logical extension of their reading of Q. 4:34 as instituting a husband's disciplinary power over his wife with minimal legal accountability.

[42] Al-Nasafī in Al-Zaylaʿī (n 18) 3:640. See also Ibn ʿĀbidīn (n 18) 6:132.

[43] Al-Haskafī and Ibn ʿĀbidīn in Ibn ʿĀbidīn (n 18) 6:131–2 and Ibn Nujaym (n 12) 5:82.

[44] Al-Kāsānī (n 12) 2:334.

[45] Ibn Humām considered it a husband's right to kill both his wife and her adulterating partner, if he felt that yelling and hitting them would not deter them from adultery (*zīna*). The discussion of domestic violence and honor killings falls under the subheading of discretionary punishment (*taʿzīr*) for several Ḥanafī jurists. Ibn Humām (n 13) 5:345–6. Ibn Nujaym held that the same rule applied to a thief. There was no *qiṣāṣ* if a man killed his unfaithful wife, her adulterating partner, or a thief. Ibn Nujaym (n 12) 5:69–70.

[46] Ibn Nujaym (n 12) 3:237.

THE MĀLIKĪS: SUSPECTING POWER

The most distinctive feature of Mālikī jurisprudence was a suspicion that husbandly disciplinary privileges might slip easily into abusive behavior. Ḥanafī jurists devoted their energies to protecting the disciplinary privileges of husbands and thereby limiting legal oversight, in order to avoid litigation for abuse. In contrast, Mālikī jurists created judicial and extra-judicial mechanisms for supervising the disciplinary privileges of husbands. The Mālikīs are often held up as a counterexample to the Ḥanafīs for their position that wives might be entitled to retaliation in marriage for extreme injuries short of death, even if that retaliation is reduced on account of gender.[47] Although the Ḥanafīs and Mālikīs agreed that husbands were entitled to physically discipline their wives based on Q. 4:34—which was used as a proof text to establish this point in both schools—they interpreted this right as having varied consequences.

Mālikī jurists did not dwell extensively on the meaning of wifely *nushūz*, which they discussed entirely in isolation from husbandly *nushūz*. In general, they understood wifely *nushūz* as a wife sexually refusing her husband, being disobedient to him such that he no longer had control over her, behaving in a blameworthy manner by leaving his house without his permission, and/or refusing to fulfill her divinely ordained obligations to him.[48] They also promoted a sequential and exhaustive application of the three prescriptions in Q. 4:34. Muḥammad Ibn Muḥammad al-Ḥaṭṭāb (d. 954/1547) followed Khalīl b. Isḥāq al-Jundī's approach of replacing the conjunctive "and" (*wa*) in the text of Q. 4:34 with the adverbial "then" (*thumma*) to describe the temporal relationship between each disciplinary action.[49] Muḥammad ibn ʿAbd Allāh al-Khurashī

[47] "The *diyāt* vary in accordance with the status of the victim. The factors effective in the reduction of *diya* are the feminine gender, *kufr* and bondage." Ibn Rushd, *The Distinguished Jurist's Primer* (trans. Imran Ahsan Khan Nyazee) (Reading, UK: Ithaca Press, 2000) 500. There is a Qur'anic precedent for differentiating punishment based on social class in Q. 2:178, which reads, "O ye who believe! The law of equality is prescribed to you in cases of murder; the free for the free the slave for the slave the woman for the woman. But if any remission is made by the brother of the slain then grant any reasonable demand, and compensate him with handsome gratitude, This is a concession and a Mercy from your Lord. After this whoever exceeds the limits shall be in grave penalty." Yusuf Ali (n 15) Q. 2:178.

[48] Muḥammad Ibn Muḥammad al-Ḥaṭṭāb (d. 954/1547) wrote a commentary on al-Khalīl's *Mukhtasar.* Muḥammad ibn Muḥammad al-Ḥaṭṭāb, *Mawāhib al-Jalīl li-sharḥ Mukhtaṣar Khalīl* (Ṭarabulus: Maktaba al-Najāḥ, 1972) 4:187. See also al-Mawwāq's (d. 897/1492) commentary in the margins of this manuscript. For more discussion on the connection between sexual disobedience and *nushūz* in foundational legal Sunnī texts, see Kecia Ali (n 9) chs 2 and 3.

[49] Al-Khalīl originally wrote in his *Mukhtasar*, "admonish the one who commits *nushūz*, then (*thumma*) abandon her, then hit her if [the husband] thinks (*ẓanna*) it will be beneficial (*ifādatahu*)." Al-Ḥaṭṭāb (n 48) 4:15–16.

(d. 1101/1690) proposed that the first two imperatives, admonishment and abandonment, were different in nature from hitting. He classified the first two as "a person's removing harm from himself," while hitting was catalogued under "the commanding of good and forbidding of evil." As such, he believed that a husband could admonish and abandon his wife based on the suspicion (*shakk*) of wifely *nushūz*—thereby limiting the applicability of "fear" (*khawf*) in Q. 4:34 to the first two prescriptions—but he required a husband to have knowledge of wifely *nushūz* before he could proceed to hit his wife.[50]

A unique feature of Mālikī jurisprudence is the prominent role of external authorities, such as judges and local leaders, in mediating marital conflict. The obtrusive role of the external authority meddling in domestic disputes obscured the line between the public and private spheres. For example, in his discussion of admonishment, al-Ḥaṭṭāb assumed the involvement of an external authority from the outset. The admonishment of a husband could be carried out in three ways. A husband was responsible for restraining (*zajr*) his wife when he knew (*ʿalima*) of her *nushūz*, "if the matter had not already been referred to the local leader (*imām*)."[51] Al-Ḥaṭṭāb did not clarify who exactly would refer the matter to a local leader, whether this was the husband or some family or community member. If the matter was referred to an *imām*, then the *imām* could ask the husband to restrain his wife, or he himself could assume responsibility for restraining/rebuking the wife (*zajrahā*).[52] Despite the intrusion of the *imām* into admonishment, Mālikīs understood the command to admonish in the same way as encountered in the exegetical texts. Admonishment was meant to remind a wife of her obligation to obey her husband and threaten her with abandonment and hitting if she did not rectify her behavior.

If admonishment was ineffective in persuading a wife to return to obedience, then husbands could abandon their wives in the marital bed. In contrast to the Ḥanafīs, Mālikī jurists were not concerned with the paradox of how sexual abandonment denied a husband access to a sexually

[50] He read the relevant portion of Q. 4:34 as "if you fear harm of [wifely] *nushūz* (*takhāfūna ḍarara nushūzahunna*)." Muḥammad ibn ʿAbd Allāh al-Khurashī wrote a commentary on al-Khalīl's *Mukhtasar* and used al-Ḥaṭṭāb's commentary on al-Khalīl's *Mukhtasar* in order to supplement his own. Muḥammad ibn ʿAbd Allāh Al-Khurashī, *al-Khurashī ʿalā mukhtaṣar Sīdī Khalīl wa-bi-hāmishihi Ḥāshiyat al-Shaykh ʿAlī al-ʿAdawī* (Beirut: Dār Ṣādir, 1975) 4:191.

[51] I translate *imām* as a local leader because in this text he mentions both religious and communal authority. Al-Khalīl's (d. 767/1365) legal manual, *Mukhtasar al-Khalīl*, formed an important basis for discussions of the disciplinary power of husbands over wives. Al-Ḥaṭṭāb (n 48) 4:15. See also al-Khurashī (n 50) 4:191.

[52] Al-Ḥaṭṭāb (n 48) 4:15.

dismissive wife. Instead, they reflected on the question of how long a husband was required to abandon his wife, proposing one to four months as a reasonable range.[53] This time frame was considerably lengthier than all other schools, where three days was the standard. Through their lengthening of the period of abandonment and their insistence on following the three imperative sequentially and exhaustively, Mālikī jurists effectively delayed the application of hitting.

If there was one overriding feature of Mālikī jurisprudence on the husbandly right to physically discipline wives, it is constraint. Mālikī jurists upheld the physical discipline of wives as a husbandly privilege yet simultaneously sought to reduce and restrict the use of this right without making it meaningless. The extensive discussion surrounding the restrictions on when and how husbands could physically discipline their wives is especially significant in contrast to the lack of such discussion among the Ḥanafīs, who only mentioned that hitting ought to be non-extreme (*ghayr mubarriḥ*). Citing al-Qurṭubī's exegesis of Q. 4:34 and moving beyond him with additional restrictions, subsequent Mālikī jurists considered in great detail the type of hitting that was permissible and prohibited. A husband could hit his wife only for disciplinary purposes (*ḍarb al-adab*), with the desired end of rectification. The hitting was to be non-extreme (*ghayr mubarriḥ*), non-severe (*ghayr shadīd*), and only mildly violent. It could not leave impressions (*ghayr muʾaththir*), be fearsome (*ghayr makhūf*), cause fractures (*wa-lā shāqqin*), break bones, or cause disfiguring wounds (*yashīnu jāriḥatan*). Punching (*al-lakza*) in general and punching someone in the chest in particular were unacceptable.[54] The hitting could not harm a wife (*taḍrīruhā*), and if it led to death, the husband was legally liable. A husband was prohibited from hitting his wife, even for disciplinary reasons, if he did not think that it would be beneficial (*yufīdu*) or if he thought (*ghalaba ʿalā ẓannihi*) that she would not abandon her *nushūz* except by more threatening and

[53] Al-Qurṭubī, whose *tafsīr* was regularly cited by late Mālikī jurists, suggested that a husband ought to abandon his wife for four months before proceeding to hitting. Muḥammad ibn Aḥmad al-Qurṭubī, *al-Jāmiʿ li-aḥkām al-Qurʾān: tafsīr al-Qurṭubī* (Beirut: Dār al-Kitāb al-ʿArabī, 1997) 5:165. Al-Ḥaṭṭāb conceded al-Qurṭubī's position as the upper limit on abandonment, though he considered a month to be a more reasonable time frame for abandonment. Al-Ḥaṭṭāb (n 48) 4:15.

[54] Al-Khurashī mentions this specifically, and the specificity of his position here is somewhat strange considering the *ḥadīth* in which ʿĀʾisha reported that Muḥammad once hit her on her chest in such a manner that caused her pain. According to al-Khurashī, who makes no mention of this report, this would have been unacceptable. It is worth mentioning here how infrequently the Mālikī scholars in this study refer to prophetic reports. Al-Khurashī (n 50) 4:19. For a lengthier discussion on this report, see Laury Silvers, "'In the Book We have Left out Nothing': The Ethical Problem of the Existence of Verse 4:34 in the Qur'an," *Comparative Islamic Studies*, 2(2) (2006) 171–80.

severe hitting. Hitting with greater intensity than these restrictions was impermissible.[55] It is important to note, however, that in placing extensive restrictions on the physical discipline of wives, Mālikī jurists were not motivated by an egalitarian impulse. Despite these restrictions, they viewed the marital relationship as essentially a hierarchal one in which husbands are obligated to restrain their wives from committing *nushūz*.[56] Furthermore, by trusting a husband's judgment regarding the kind of

[55] A-Ḥaṭṭāb wrote, "In his exegesis of God's speech, 'And concerning those women from whom you fear *nushūz*', al-Qurṭubī said that the hitting in this verse is disciplinary hitting (*ḍarb al-adab*), in a non-extreme (*ghayr mubarriḥ*) manner. [The hitting] should not break bones or cause a disfiguring wound (*yashīnu jāriḥatan*), as would be the case with punching (*al-lakza*), etc. This is because the desired end [of the hitting] is rectification and nothing else. If the [hitting] advances to death, then [the husband] is liable. Al-Abīyun related on the authority of ʿIyāḍ in his commentary on the *ḥadīth* of Jābir in the Book of the pilgrimage (*Ḥajj*): what is meant by *ghayr mubarriḥ* (non-extreme) is *ghayr shadīd* (non-severe/intense). In chapter ten of *al-Qurbā,* in his description of the prophet's Pilgrimage, al-Muḥibb al-Ṭabarī stated that when [the prophet] said, 'and hit them in a non-extreme (*ghayr mubarriḥ*) manner', he meant in a manner that does not leave impressions (*ghayr mu'aththir*) and does not cause a fracture (*wa-lā shāqqin*). Some say that [the hitting] may be in a mildly violent manner, meaning that the disciplinary hitting [of wives] is such that it does not leave apparent impressions... [Jamāl al-Dīn] Ibn al-Ḥājib (d. 646/1248) restricted hitting by saying that the hitting should not cause fear [of injury or death] (*ghayr makhūf*). [Khalīl b. Isḥāq al-Jundī (d. 749/1348 or 767/1365)] said in *al-Tawḍīḥ*: the hitting should be corrective and should not be threatening. If [the husband] thinks that the hitting is not beneficial (*yufīdu*) then it is impermissible for him to hit her. It is stated in *al-Jawāhir* [probably the *al-Jawāhir al-thamīna fī madhhab ʿālim al-madīna* of the Mālikī Jalāl al-Dīn b. Shās (d. 616/1219)] that if he thinks (*ghalaba ʿalā ẓannihi*) that she will not abandon her *nushūz* except by means of threatening hitting then it is completely impermissible for him to use a discretionary punishment (*taʿzīruhā*)." Al-Ḥaṭṭāb (n 48) 4:15–16. Also, al-Khurashī wrote, "If it becomes clear to [a husband] that [his wife] will not abandon her *nushūz* except by means of fearsome (*makhūf*) hitting, then it is impermissible for him to harm her (*taḍrīruhā*). If [the wife] claims aggression (*al-ʿadā'*) and the husband claims discipline, then she has the final say. It is similar in the case of the slave and the master when they disagree with each other. [The husband] is not to proceed from one [disciplinary] step to the next until it is clear to him that the previous step was insufficient for reining her in. He should do everything except hitting. If he thinks that [hitting] will not be beneficial, perhaps something other than hitting [will be beneficial]. He should not [hit] except when he knows that intensifying [the discipline] will be beneficial for him." Al-Khurashī (n 50) 4:192.

[56] If a wife persisted in *nushūz* even after her husband exhausted the three prescriptions in Q. 4:34, and he found that neither he himself nor a judge (*ḥākim*) was capable of returning her to a state of obedience, then a wife was guilty of the most extreme *nushūz* (*ashadda al-nushūz*). At this point she ought to be offered the choice of adjudication or loss of maintenance. Once again, al-Khurashī compared her case to that of a slave, writing, "When [a woman] leaves the place of [her husband's] obedience without his permission, and he is not capable of bringing her back (*ʿawdihā*) either by himself or with the judge (*ḥākim*), then this is the most intense *nushūz* (*ashadda al-nushūz*), and the maintenance (*nafaqa*) is dropped. At that point she becomes deserving (*tastaḥiqqun*) of *taʿzīr* for [this behavior]... He should say to her, 'You can either return to your house or seek adjudication with your husband and see that justice is done. If [you do not do either of these things], then you are not owed maintenance.' This is a form of chastisement of the judge (*ḥākim*) and justice... [Her husband] or the judge should discipline her. And the case of the runaway/fugitive (*al-hāriba*) is similar to the case of the recalcitrant wife." Al-Khurashī (n 50) 4:191–2.

beating that would be effective in restraining a wife, Mālikī jurists granted husbands a great deal of discretionary power.

The complexity of the Mālikī position on hitting wives is demonstrated well in the event of a court case in which a wife accuses her husband of aggression (*al-ʿadāʾ*), and her husband defends himself on grounds of his license to discipline. Mālikī jurists disagreed about the correct course of action in this situation. Al-Ḥaṭṭāb believed that the wife's claims should take precedence over her husband's (*fa-l-qawl qawluhā*), because her claim is similar to that of a slave against his master. In both of these cases the claim of the wife/slave takes precedence over that of the husband/master.[57] However, Al-Khurashī relied on al-Qurṭubī's authority to argue the opposite case—that a husband's claim ought to settle the matter. The master–slave relationship was used as a model to justify this legal position as well: just as a master's claims would settle the matter with regard to his charge, this rule ought to be applied to husbands as well.[58]

Ibrāhīm Shams al-Dīn Muḥammad b. Farḥūn (d. 799/1396) offered a third alternative, proposing that when a wife complained of harm (*al-ḍarar*) from her husband, she is required to bring forth clear proof of such harm in order to verify her claim. Although Ibn Farḥūn did not specify what such "clear proof" would look like, we can presume that it is either a mark of the beating or a witness. The purpose of the proof for Ibn Farḥūn was to confirm that the wife actually had a case, because it was entirely possible that what she considered "harm" was in fact a husband exercising his rights over her by "preventing her from going to the bathhouse or disciplining her for abandoning prayer."[59] If the court found that she was indeed being harmed, and her husband confessed, then he was to be confronted. However, if the husband denied her claims of

[57] This Mālikī position might be justified through three *aḥādīth*. The first is found in the context of the revelation of Q. 4:34, when Ḥabība bt. Zayd approached Muḥammad regarding her husband's slapping/hitting her, and Muḥammad simply accepted her claim, granting her retaliation. Similarly, when Jamīla bt. ʿAbdullāh's brother complained to Muḥammad about her husband, Qays b. Thābit, hitting his sister and breaking her hand, Muḥammad accepted her claim against her husband's without considering Qays' side of the story. Finally, when Walīd b. ʿUqba's wife complained to Muḥammad about her husband beating her, Muḥammad urged Walīd to refrain from beating her and eventually cursed him. He did this without investigating her claim or ascertaining if the motivation for Walīd's beating was disciplinary. For a detailed discussion of prophetic reports on wife-beating, see Ayesha S. Chaudhry, " 'I Wanted One Thing and God Wanted Another . . .': The Dilemma of the Prophetic Example and the Qur'anic Injunction on Wife-Beating," *Journal of Religious Ethics*, 39:3 (2011) 416–39.

[58] However, al-Khurashī conceded that despite the preference of a husband's claim over his wife's, his claim could not overrule his wife's with regard to voiding maintenance (*nafaqa*). Al-Khurashī (n 50) 4:191.

[59] Ibrāhīm ibn ʿAlī Ibn Farḥūn, *Tabṣirat al-ḥukkām fī uṣūl al-aqḍiya wa-manāhij al-aḥkām* (Cairo: Maktaba al-Kullīyāt al-Azhariyya, 1986) 1:170.

abuse, and she persisted in those claims without clear evidence, the judge was to involve the neighbors in the affair, seeking a trustworthy witness to shed light on the matter. If no trustworthy person was found, then the judge was to have his own wife live with the couple and see for herself if the wife's claims were verifiable. Supposing the judge's wife verified that the husband was hitting without proper cause, then it was the judge's responsibility to discipline the husband and prevent him from returning to abusive behavior.[60]

The case of the quarreling couple highlights several important characteristics of Mālikī jurisprudence regarding marital conflict. First, there was no stigma attached to a woman complaining about her ill-treatment by her husband. A wife's claims were taken seriously and were to be investigated, even if she made them without clear evidence. Second, the line between the public and private spheres was blurred through the assumed involvement of the following characters in domestic affairs: the local leader (*imām*), the court (*qāḍī*), a judge's wife, and the couple's neighbors. Together, these judicial and extra-judicial actors formed several levels of social oversight into a couple's domestic affairs, which constitutes the third distinctive feature of Mālikī jurisprudence—namely, a degree of social responsibility in regulating a husband's authority. This meant that an abused wife, at least theoretically, had judicial and extra-judicial recourse against her husband. These three features of Mālikī jurisprudence do not indicate a discomfort with the patriarchal marital structure. This is underlined in the fourth characteristic of Mālikī jurisprudence, which is the belief that the slave–master relationship was a blueprint for the marital one and that the reasoning regarding slaves was applicable to wives. Husbands were in charge of the moral well-being of their wives, just as masters were responsible for their slaves; however, this responsibility came with a requirement for judicious conduct.

What happens if husbands abuse their authority? What if they hit their wives severely, punch them, cause disfiguring wounds, fracture or break bones? As with Ḥanafī jurists, there was a spectrum of hitting between

[60] Ibn Farḥūn (n 59) 1:170. See also Al-Ḥaṭṭāb and al-Mawwāq in al-Ḥaṭṭāb (n 48) 4:16. This examination of three Mālikī positions on the correct legal procedure in the case of contesting spousal claims of abuse calls into question M. Fadel's monolithic presentation of the Mālikī position (and Islamic law) in this case. In fact, we see here that Mālikī jurists disagreed on this issue; they did not uniformly privilege a wife's claims over her husband's. Fadel writes, "Islamic law also reduced the evidentiary burden of a wife claiming spousal abuse by admitting hearsay evidence in such cases and by permitting witnesses to testify based on circumstantial evidence of abuse." Mohammad Fadel, "Public Reason as a Strategy for Principled Reconciliation: The Case of Islamic Law and International Human Rights." *Chicago Journal of International Law*, 8(1) (2008), <http://papers.ssrn.com/sol3/papers.cfm?abstract_id=981777> (last accessed Dec. 12, 2012).

non-extreme and extreme beating that was left unaccounted for by Mālikī jurists. Hitting that does not reach the level of "extreme" was morally reprehensible in both legal schools, but there was no penalty associated with such beating. Still, whereas the Ḥanafīs did not hold husbands legally liable unless they killed their wives, and even then in a limited manner, Mālikīs held husbands legally accountable for hitting their wives in a severe manner when it resulted in certain injuries. Abū al-Walīd al-Bājī (d. 474/1081) referenced three source texts—two Qur'anic verses and one prophetic report—to ground his legal position that wives deserve retaliation from their husbands for excessive beating.[61] The permission to physically discipline wives in Q. 4:34 was restricted by Q. 5:45, which advocates the principle of retaliation. Q 5:45 reads, "Life for life, eye for eye, nose for nose, ear for ear, tooth for tooth, and wounds equal for equal."[62] Additionally, Muḥammad is reported to have said that "for everything, there is retaliation."

If a husband harmed his wife irreparably, his intention was decisive for Mālikī jurists in determining his liability. Assuming that a husband hit his wife with the intention of disciplining her (*adabihā*) with a whip (*sawṭ*) or a rope (*ḥabl*) and accidentally damaged her eye or some other body part, then he was responsible for compensating her monetarily (*diya*)[63] but was not subject to retaliation (*qiṣāṣ*).[64] However, supposing a husband had

[61] Al-Bājī wrote a commentary on Mālik b. Anas (d. 179/795) *al-Muwaṭṭa'*. Sulaymān ibn Khalaf Al-Bājī, *al-Muntaqā: sharḥ Muwaṭṭa' Mālik* (Cairo: Dār al-Fikr al-ʿArabī, 1982) 7:79.

[62] "We ordained therein for them: 'Life for life, eye for eye, nose for nose, ear for ear, tooth for tooth, and wounds equal for equal.' But if any one remits the retaliation by way of charity, it is an act of atonement for himself. And if any fail to judge by (the light of) what Allah hath revealed, they are (No better than) wrong-doers." Yusuf Ali (n 15) Q. 5:45.

[63] Tyan describes *diya* as "a specified amount of money or goods due in cases of homicide or other injuries to physical health unjustly committed upon the person of another. It is a substitute for the law of private vengeance. Accordingly it corresponds exactly to the compensation or *wergeld* of the ancient Roman and Germanic laws. Etymologically the term signifies that which is given in payment. The *diya* is also called, though very much more rarely, *ʿaḳl*. In a restricted sense—the sense which is most usual in law— *diya* means the compensation which is payable in cases of homicide, the compensation payable in the case of other offences against the body being termed more particularly *ars̲h̲*." For more on *diya*, see E. Tyan, "Diya" in *Encyclopaedia of Islam* (n 35).

[64] Schacht writes about *qiṣāṣ* that it is "synonymous with *ḳawad*, retaliation ('settlement', not 'cutting off' or 'prosecution'), according to Muslim law is applied in cases of killing, and of wounding which do not prove fatal, called in the former case *ḳiṣāṣ fi 'l-nafs* (blood-vengeance) and in the latter *ḳiṣāṣ fī mā dūn al-nafs*." Here, Mālik discussed *qiṣāṣ* in matters other than death. Schacht writes the following about this type of *qiṣāṣ*: "*Ḳiṣāṣ fī-mā dūn al-nafs* according to the S̲h̲arīʿa. If anyone deliberately (with *ʿamd*, opposite of *k̲h̲aṭ'*; cf. ḳatl, i, 5) and illegally (this excludes the wounding of one who tries to murder or injure or rob a fellowman, if it is not possible to repel him otherwise; it is for example permitted to strike someone in the eyes or throw something in the eyes of a man who forces his way into another's house without permission) has inflicted an injury, not fatal, which could be inflicted on the doer's person in an exactly similar way (what is meant by this is very fully discussed in the *Fiḳh* books), he is liable to *ḳiṣāṣ* on the part of the wounded man, (except

intended to harm his wife by "gouging out her eye or cutting her hand," then he was liable for retaliation without any restrictions.[65] With regard to compensation, al-Bājī referenced Mālik's discussion of the subject in his *Muwaṭṭa'*. A wife was owed twenty camels if her husband cut off four of her fingers, but if he cut off only her index finger, then scholars disagreed whether she ought to receive five camels (a fourth of the compensation for four fingers) or ten camels, given the importance of the index finger.[66]

The position of Mālik and al-Bājī on compensation illustrates the intricacy of their position on the right of husbands to physically discipline wives. They were concerned with justice, safeguarding wives against abusive husbands, and regulating the power of husbands. At the same time, they protected the right of husbands to physically discipline wives and permitted husbands to use weapons such as whips and ropes when disciplining their wives, as long as they did not damage a wife's body parts. In this instance, their position seems to differ from that of al-Ḥaṭṭāb and al-Khurashī, who stipulated that a husband's hitting should be neither fearsome nor extreme. The variance within the same legal school on this point showcases the flexibility available to jurists in deriving legal injunctions from the Qur'anic text.

THE SHĀFIʿĪS: RECONCILING THE PROPHET WITH GOD

Shāfiʿī jurists understood the weight of the imperative "hit them" (*wa-ḍribūhunna*) in Q. 4:34 as a permission rather than a command. Husbands are permitted to hit their wives as a disciplinary measure;

that Mālik makes it be inflicted by an expert), if the conditions necessary for carrying out the *ḳiṣāṣ fī 'l-nafs* are present with the following modifications: according to Abū Ḥanīfa, *ḳiṣāṣ fī-mā dūn al-nafs* is not carried out between man and woman or slaves among themselves, but it is according to Mālik, al-S̲h̲āfiʿī and Aḥmad b. Ḥanbal; Abū Ḥanīfa and Mālik further allow no *ḳiṣāṣ fī-mā dūn al-nafs* between free men and slaves. According to Mālik, al-S̲h̲āfiʿī and Aḥmad b. Ḥanbal, this *ḳiṣāṣ* is inflicted for one on several, but not according to Abū Ḥanīfa. A sound limb may not be amputated for an unsound one; if the guilty person has lost the limb, there can of course be no *ḳiṣāṣ*. In the case where he loses it after committing the deed, there is a corresponding difference of opinion, as in the case of his death before the execution of *ḳiṣāṣ fī 'l-nafs*." For more on *qiṣāṣ*, see J. Schacht, "*Ḳiṣāṣ*" in *Encyclopaedia of Islam* (n 35).

[65] Al-Bājī (n 61) 7:77–9 and 131.

[66] Ibn Rushd explained how Mālikī jurists calculated a woman's *diya* for loss of limbs: "The majority of jurists of Medina said that a woman is equal to a man in the case of compensation for *shijāj* and limbs, when the amount is up to one-third *diya*, but when it exceeds this, her *diya* reverts to the rule of one half that of a man, I mean, the *diya* for his various limbs. An example of this is that each of her fingers is a *diya* of ten camels, for two it is twenty camels, for three thirty, but for four it is twenty." Ibn Rushd (n 47) 513.

although they are allowed choice in the matter, it is preferable for them to abstain from exercising this right. At first glance, this position appears more progressive than that of the previous two juridical schools. However, a critical analysis reveals that the Shāfiʿī approach was a mix of the Ḥanafī and Mālikī positions. The Shāfiʿī preference to avoid hitting wives was not driven by an impulse to protect women; rather, it was motivated by their theological discomfort with a textual contradiction between the Qurʾanic text of Q. 4:34, which prescribed the hitting of wives as an imperative, and variations of a prophetic report in which Muḥammad either prohibited or morally censured men who hit their wives. This concern was not shared by jurists from other legal schools who were comfortable privileging the Qurʾanic imperative over prophetic censure. Despite the Shāfiʿī stance that it was preferable for a husband to avoid hitting his wife, Shāfiʿī scholars expanded the definition of wifely *nushūz* to permit the disciplining of wives for a greater range of behaviors. They were also willing to combine the application of all three prescriptions at once, without sequence, and they protected husbands from legal accountability when they beat their wives excessively.

Like the Ḥanafīs, Shāfiʿī jurists touched on the topic of reciprocal and husbandly *nushūz* in their discussion of wifely *nushūz*. In both cases, legal discussions reflected the differences in the Qurʾanic texts of Q. 4:34 and Q. 4:128, which define husbandly and wifely *nushūz* distinctively, with varied consequences.[67] Shāfiʿī jurists conceded that discord (*shiqāq*) and estrangement (*waḥsha*) in a marriage could be caused by the *nushūz* or transgression (*yataʿaddī*) of either spouse against the other. Husbandly *nushūz* was seen as a husband's neglect of or aversion toward his wife resulting from the diminishing attractiveness of a wife, such as illness or advanced age. In light of God's disdain for divorce, Shāfiʿī jurists encouraged wives to give up some of their rights in exchange for remaining married to their husbands. The model of Muḥammad's wives was used to illustrate this legal ruling. Muḥammad's wife Sawdāʾ offered up her nights to ʿĀʾisha in order to remain married to Muḥammad. She was held as an exemplar for believing women who were encouraged to find ways to remain married to their husbands, even if this meant forgoing some of their marital rights.[68]

[67] Q. 4:128 reads, "If a wife fears cruelty or desertion on her husband's part, there is no blame on them if they arrange an amicable settlement between themselves; and such settlement is best; even though men's souls are swayed by greed. But if ye do good and practice self-restraint, Allah is well-acquainted with all that ye do." Yusuf Ali (n 15) Q. 4:128.

[68] Kecia Ali (n 9) 127–8. Also see Abū Zakarīyā Yaḥyā ibn Sharaf Al-Nawawī, *Rawḍat al-ṭālibīn* (Beirut: Dār al-Kutub al-ʿIlmiyya, 1992) 5:674 and Abū Isḥāq Ibrāhīm b. ʿAlī b. Yūsuf al-Fīrūzābādī al-Shīrāzī, *Al-Muhadhdhab fī fiqh al-Imām al-Shāfiʿī* (Beirut: Dār al-Kutub al-ʿIlmiyya, 1995) 2:487.

In contrast to husbandly *nushūz*, Shāfiʿī jurists interpreted wifely *nushūz* expansively to include the signs and symptoms of *nushūz*, as well as *nushūz* proper, deeming them all to be worthy of discipline. "Signs" of wifely *nushūz* include behaviors that might lead to a reprehensible act (*fiʿl al-makrūh*) and are expressed through a wife's disagreeable behavior.[69] Such behaviors include alteration of speech and/or actions. The jurists under study provided the following examples of such behaviors: if a wife habitually converses with her husband in a gentle and kind manner (*layyin*) but then begins speaking to him crudely/roughly (*khaṣim/khashin*); if she initially hurries to answer his call and expresses her gratitude but then stops; and if she habitually treats her husband with kindness (*luṭf*) and then begins shunning (*iʿrāḍan*) him and acting annoyed (*ʿabūsan*) by him.[70] If a wife exhibits these signs, her husband can begin the progressive disciplinary process, starting with admonishment. However, he is not permitted to use physical violence at this stage; physical discipline is only permissible once wifely *nushūz* is verified. Wifely *nushūz* is a wife's disobedience, her sexual refusal, leaving the marital home without her husband's permission, and not opening the door for him.[71] According to Muḥammad b. Muḥammad al-Ghazālī (d. 505/1111), a wife's abusive and reviling speech (*al-shatm wa-l-badhāʾ*) does not constitute *nushūz* proper but still requires a husband's discipline because of its offensive nature.[72] This indicates that, according to Abū Zakarīyā Yaḥyā ibn Sharaf al-Nawawī (d. 676/1278), wives stand to be disciplined for actions apart from actual wifely *nushūz*. By expanding the definition of wifely *nushūz* and designating actions that do not constitute *nushūz* proper as discipline-worthy, Shāfiʿī jurists considerably expanded the disciplinary purview of husbands.

Shāfiʿī jurists differed in their opinions regarding the application of the three prescriptions in Q. 4:34. They offered at least five perspectives

[69] Muḥammad ibn Idrīs al-Shāfiʿī, *Aḥkām al-Qurʾān* (Beirut: Dār al-Kutub al-ʿIlmiyya, 1975) 1:208. See also Kecia Ali, "The Best of You Will Not Strike," *Comparative Islamic Studies*, 2(2) (2006) 146. She describes al-Shāfiʿī's approach to wife-beating in the *al-Umm* in the following manner, "Throughout this discussion, Shafiʿī attempts to restrict the circumstances under which husbands may resort to physical chastisement without ever questioning its basic lawfulness." See also al-Shīrāzī (n 68) 2:486.

[70] We encountered these examples in the previous chapter in al-Rāzī's exegesis. See also Zakarīyā ibn Muḥammad Al-Anṣārī, *Fatḥ al-Wahhāb bi-sharḥ Manhaj al-ṭullāb* (Beirut: Dār al-Kutub al-ʿIlmiyya, 1998) 2:110; ʿAlī Ibn Muḥammad al-Māwardī, *al-Ḥāwī al-kabīr fī fiqh madhhab al-Imām al-Shāfiʿī* (Beirut: Dār al-Kutub al-ʿIlmiyya, 1994) 9:597; al-Nawawī (n 68) 5:676; Shams al-Dīn Muḥammad ibn al-Khaṭīb al-Shirbīnī, *Mughnī al-Muḥtāj fī sharḥ al-Mināj* (Beirut: Dār al-Maʿrifa, 1997) 3:342; and Shams al-Dīn Abū ʿAbdullah Muḥammad b. ʿAbdullah al-Zarkashī, *Sharḥ al-Zarkashī ʿalā matn al-Kiraqī* (Mecca: Maktaba al-Asadī, 2009) 3:325.

[71] Al-Anṣārī (n 70) 2:107; al-Nawawī (n 68) 5:676; and al-Shirbīnī (n 70) 3:342–3.

[72] Muḥammad b. Muḥammad Al-Ghazālī, *Al-Wasīṭ fī al-Madhhab* (Beirut: Dār al-Kutub al-ʿIlmiyya, 2001) 3:234. See also Al-Nawawī (n 68) 5:677.

on this point. One, a husband was required to apply each prescription—admonishment, abandonment, and hitting—sequentially and exhaustively.[73] Two, he could select whichever of the three imperatives he thought was most likely to be effective in correcting his wife's behavior and apply them out of order.[74] Three, all three prescriptions could be applied simultaneously.[75] Four, a husband should admonish and abandon his wife based on feared *nushūz* but hit her only when she manifests clear *nushūz*.[76] Five, a husband should admonish his wife when he suspects wifely *nushūz*, abandon her when she begins *nushūz*, and combine all three measures when she persists in *nushūz*.[77]

For the most part, Shāfiʿī jurists supported a sequential approach, with the caveat that in the event of manifest wifely *nushūz* a husband was permitted to combine all three disciplinary measures simultaneously.[78] The progressive approach to discipline was defended by reference to Q. 5:33, which reads, "The punishment of those who wage war against Allah and His Messenger, and strive with might and main for mischief through the land is: execution, or crucifixion or the cutting off of hands and feet from opposite sides, or exile from the land . . ."[79] ʿAlī ibn Muḥammad

[73] Al-Nawawī (n 68) 5:676–7. Al-Zarkashī wrote that the *waw* between each imperative indicated temporal sequence (*tartib*), and the goal (*maqṣūd*) of discipline is to eliminate corruption (*zawāl al-mufsida*), so a husband should begin with lighter (*ashal*) punishment. However, he also noted that a husband is permitted to hit for wifely disobedience. Al-Zarkashī (n 70) 3:325.

[74] Al-Ghazālī cited two opinions; one is to follow the three steps in sequence, and the other is to combine all three at once. He believed that if a husband thinks that his wife would be restrained by admonishment and abandonment then he is not permitted to hit her, but if he thinks that admonishment and abandonment would not restrain her, then hitting is permitted. However, in contrast to the *walī* who should hit a child, it is preferable for the husband to avoid hitting his wife. This is because hitting the child is for the correction/*iṣlāḥ*/rectification of the child, whereas the rectification of the wife is for the benefit of the husband; as a result the hitting of the wife is restricted by the condition of soundness (*salāma*). Al-Ghazālī (n 72) 3:234–5.

[75] Al-Nawawī (n 68) 5:676–7.

[76] There was an additional question here about the placement of abandonment—should it be combined with admonishment when a husband fears his wife's *nushūz*, or should it be used after a wife had committed *nushūz*? Al-Māwardī cited the position of the people of Basra as preferring the first (joining abandonment with admonishment) because both of these were warnings of the punishment that might come, which was hitting; however, the people of Baghdād preferred the second, since they saw abandonment and hitting as punishments that should only be applied with the beginning of sin and not before it. In this way, the punishment of a wife was similar to the application of the *ḥadd* penalty, which should only be applied once the sin had occurred. Al-Māwardī (n 70) 9:597–8. See also al-Shīrāzī (n 68) 2:487.

[77] Al-Shāfiʿī (n 69) 1:208 and 210. See also al-Māwardī (n 70) 9:598 and al-Shīrāzī (n 68) 2:487.

[78] Al-Anṣārī (n 70) 2:107.

[79] Yusuf Ali (n 15) Q. 5:33. Al-Māwardī (n 70) 9:597 and al-Zarkashī (n 70) 3:324. This verse was also referenced by the Ḥanbalī jurist to make the same point about matching

al-Māwardī (d. 450/1058) explained the relevance of this verse by comparing the three disciplinary actions in Q. 4:34 with the punishments outlined in Q. 5:33. In both these verses, varied sins (*dhunūb*)[80] had corresponding penalties (*al-ʿuqūbāt*) so that major punishments were reserved for major sins while minor punishments were reserved for minor sins.[81] By introducing the language of sin and punishment in their interpretations of wifely *nushūz* and husbandly discipline, while expanding the definition of wifely *nushūz*, al-Māwardī turned a wife's disagreeable behavior into sinful conduct.

When a husband fears his wife's *nushūz*, he is expected by Shāfiʿīs to admonish her. This reminds her of her wifely responsibilities and warns her (*yukhawwifhā*) of the punishments that await her if she persists in her *nushūz*. Such punishments include beatings and loss of maintenance and allotted nights. Admonishment might also help to clarify whether or not a wife is actually committing *nushūz*, and in case she is, it might cause her to repent.[82] If it turns out that the husband's fear was misplaced, then admonishment was still not a wasted endeavor since "it could not hurt [a wife]" (*lam yuḍirruhā*) to be reminded of God's commands with respect to her obligations to her husband.[83] If, on the other hand, a husband's fears are confirmed (*yataḥaqqaq*), then he is to abandon his wife. Shāfiʿī jurists, like the Ḥanafīs, believed that abandonment is meant to be sexual. Unlike the Ḥanafīs, though, they were not troubled by the fact that a husband's lack of sexual access to his wife compromised his own sexual rights. They addressed this problem by having the husband spend the nights apart from the disobedient wife with one of his other wives or concubines. Abandonment could also be verbal, unless it is accompanied by admonishment. In the case of verbal abandonment, Shāfiʿī jurists agreed that a husband is not permitted to abandon his wife for more than three days, on account of the prophetic report that forbade believers from not speaking to one another for longer than three days.[84]

An interesting consequence of treating wifely *nushūz* as a sin was that it allowed Shāfiʿī jurists to inject the language of forgiveness into

punishments to crime/sin. Muwaffaq al-Dīn ʿAbd Allāh ibn Aḥmad Ibn Qudāma, *al-Mughnī li Ibn Qudāma* (Cairo: Hajr, 1986) 7:46.

[80] Al-Shirāzī makes a similar point but describes a wife's *nushūz* as "crimes" (*jarāʾim*) rather than "sins" (*dhunūb*). Al-Shīrāzī (n 68) 2:487.

[81] Al-Māwardī (n 70) 9:597.

[82] Al-Anṣārī (n 70) 2:110.

[83] Al-Nawawī (n 68) 5:675. Al-Māwardī wrote that a husband should say to his wife, "God has mandated my rights upon you, if you refuse them, I am allowed to hit you (*abāḥanī ḍarbaki*)." Al-Māwardī (n 70) 9:598.

[84] Al-Anṣārī (n 70) 2:110; al-Māwardī (n 70) 9:598; al-Shāfiʿī (n 69) 1:209; al-Shīrāzī (n 68) 2:487; and al-Zarkashī (n 70) 3:324.

their discussions of disciplining wives.[85] As mentioned earlier, the Shāfiʿī approach to the physical discipline of wives was unique in that it emphasized the permissive rather than obligatory nature of the command to hit wives in Q. 4:34. As a corollary, husbands were granted the choice to hit or not hit their wives.[86] So while Shāfiʿīs were comfortable with the admonishment and abandonment of wives, their position on hitting was more complex. They underscored the permissibility of physically disciplining wives if they persist in their *nushūz* and also the preferability to avoid hitting whenever possible.[87] Shāfiʿī jurists used the management of children as a useful counterpoint for discussing the handling of wives. The treatment of wives by husbands was different than that of children by their fathers or teachers; while it was preferable to forgive (*ʿafw*) a wife and avoid hitting her for misbehavior, it was better to hit a child than forgive him/her. This is because hitting a child was for his/her own betterment (*maṣlaḥa*), whereas hitting a wife was advantageous for the husband. In this way, hitting a wife was construed as a selfish act while hitting a child was seen as a selfless act.[88]

Supposing a husband chooses to utilize the permission to hit his wife granted by Q. 4:34—for which he had "supremacy" (*tasalluṭ*)[89]—Shāfiʿī jurists provided the usual restrictions: a husband should only hit his wife if he thinks it will be effective in deterring her from her *nushūz*; he should hit her in a non-extreme (*ghayr mubarriḥ*) manner; he should avoid hitting her face, sensitive places, and places of beauty and not hit her in a manner that causes disfiguration, bleeding, loss of limbs, or death.[90] A husband's hitting should not cross over from a discretionary (*taʿzīr*) punishment to a *ḥadd* penalty, so the beating cannot exceed between thirty-nine strikes or seventy-nine strikes, depending on whether the *ḥadd* penalty is set

[85] Al-Nawawī (n 68) 5:676 and al-Shirbīnī (n 70) 3:343.

[86] Al-Shafiʿī (n 69) 11:165–6.

[87] Al-Ghazālī (n 72) 3:234–5.

[88] Al-Nawawī (n 68) 5:676 and al-Shirbīnī (n 70) 3:343. This position was not uniquely Shāfiʿī; it was shared by some Ḥanafī scholars. See, eg, Ibn Nujaym (n 12) 5:83.

[89] Al-Ghazālī (n 72) 3:234–5.

[90] Some combination of these qualities were mentioned by al-Shāfiʿī, *Mawsūʾat al-Imām al-Shāfiʿī al-kitāb al-Umm* (Beirut: Dār Qutayba, 1996) 11:166. See also al-Nawawī (n 68) 5:676; al-Shīrāzī (n 68) 2:487; and al-Shirbīnī (n 70) 3:343. Al-Anṣārī wrote, "And hitting (*al-ḍarb*) is restricted (*taqayyad*) by its benefit... [A husband] should not hit when it is not beneficial, just as he should not hit in an extreme (*mubarriḥ*) manner, not [hit her] face, or cause death. And it is preferable to forgive, leave the bed and abandon speech." Al-Anṣārī (n 70) 2:110. Al-Māwardī cited a *ḥadīth* in which Muḥammad was asked, "'Our women, what should we take from them and what should give them (*mā naʾtī minhā wa-mā nadhar*)?' He replied, 'They are your tilth (*ḥarth*), go unto your tilth however and whenever you desire but do not hit them in the face, do not make them ugly, do not abandon them except in the house, and feed them when you eat and clothe them as you clothe yourselves.'" Al-Māwardī (n 70) 9:598–9.

at forty or eighty strikes.[91] A husband is permitted to hit his wife with a cloth (*thawb*), sandal (*naʿl*), and a stick (*ʿaṣā*), but not with a whip (*sawṭ*), because using a whip was not customary and crossed into *ḥadd* territory.[92]

As with Ḥanafīs and Mālikīs, these moral exhortations did not translate into legal repercussions for a husband who beat his wife in what Shāfiʿīs termed an "extreme" fashion. Shāfiʿī jurists rarely discussed the legal accountability of husbands in cases other than when they killed their wives. Al-Nawawī briefly mentioned that if a husband's hitting exceeded the customary norm and harmed his wife's body, then he was financially liable. This is because a husband's physical discipline of his wife was meant to correct her behavior while maintaining the soundness of her body (*baqāʾ al-nafs*).[93] Al-Nawawī did not say how much a husband must compensate his wife, and most Shāfiʿīs did not mention compensation at all. In this respect, the Shāfiʿī stance appears to be similar to the Ḥanafī position, although Shāfiʿī jurists never asserted the Ḥanafī principle that there is no retaliation in marriage.

Shāfiʿī scholars maintained a role for judicial and extra-judicial actors in marriage, even if that role was limited and exhortative in nature. In the event that a husband killed his wife while beating her, Shāfiʿīs instructed the judge to determine whether or not the killing was premeditated. If it was premeditated, then the husband was liable for retribution (*qawad*) and so could be killed himself. If it was determined that he killed her by accident (*khaṭaʾ shubh al-ʿamad*), then he was liable for monetary compensation (*diya*).[94] In the case of a wife who claimed abuse by her husband, citing excessive beating, or loss of maintenance and allotted nights without cause, it was the judge's responsibility to forbid the husband from such behavior.[95] A trustworthy neighbor could help to enforce the judge's prohibition; the judge could have this neighbor live with the couple to observe the husband's behavior and to stop him from transgressing against his wife.[96] The relatives of the couple were also expected to stop a husband from transgression. If both spouses claimed that the other was transgressive, and the testimony from the trustworthy neighbor did not settle the case, then either the judge (*ḥākim*) himself could live with the couple and observe them in order to determine which party was at fault, or he could divorce them.[97] Finally, if a wife complained of abuse and her

[91] Al-Shāfiʿī (n 90) 12:508.
[92] Al-Shāfiʿī (n 90) 11:166 and 12:506.
[93] Al-Nawawī (n 68) 676–7. See also al-Ghazālī (n 72) 3:234–5.
[94] This same liability is applied to the case of a teacher hitting a child. Al-Māwardī (n 70) 9:599.
[95] Al-Nawawī (n 68) 5:677.
[96] Al-Nawawī (n 68) 5:677.
[97] Al-Nawawī (n 68) 5:678–9. See also al-Māwardī (n 70) 9:596.

husband defended himself on grounds of discipline for *nushūz*, then his claim superseded hers, since he was her guardian (*walī*).[98]

Despite tolerating social intrusion into the domestic life of a couple—with the judge or trustworthy neighbor residing in domestic space with a couple—Shāfiʿī jurists limited the role of public actors in the private sphere. Perhaps in response to the Mālikī position of involving local leaders or judges at the very beginning of the disciplinary process with admonishment, al-Nawawī encouraged husbands to discipline their wives themselves. It was preferable to handle the matter domestically rather than referring it to a judge, which might lead to difficulty (*mashaqqa*) and disgrace (*ʿār*) for the husband.[99] In general, Shāfiʿī jurists discouraged husbands from hitting their wives and promoted a limited sense of social oversight for abusive husbands, all the while increasing the disciplinary purview of husbands, protecting their right to hit wives, and shielding husbands from liability in the case of excessive hitting.

This somewhat convoluted Shāfiʿī position was based on jurists' attempts to reconcile the command to hit wives in Q. 4:34 with the moral censure against hitting wives in prophetic reports (*aḥādīth*). In the prophetic report mentioned earlier, Muḥammad first permitted and then morally censured men for hitting their wives. To quickly review, in this report Muḥammad prohibited husbands from hitting wives, but the Companion ʿUmar asked for permission for Muslim men to hit their wives due to their contemptuous and insolent speech. He was granted permission, and the men in Medina hit their wives, only to then be censured by Muḥammad, who stated, "The best of you will not strike."[100] Muḥammad's initial prohibition against hitting wives directly

[98] Al-Anṣārī (n 70) 2:111. *Wilāya* is an important concept in legal discussions in the marital relationship and deserves further study. Dien describes it as the following: "Technically, *wilāya* can be either optional (*ikhtiyāriyya*), when entered into by personal choice, such as *wakāla* [q.v.], or compulsory (*idjbāriyya*). However, in practice *wilāya* is a term used only to describe the latter, namely, *idjbāriyya*, which is determined by legal rule or judicial order. This can be divided into the following categories: the custody of infants (*haḍānat al-ṣaghīr*) and the custody of a person (*wilāyat al-nafs*) requiring care for a child who has passed the age of infancy or for an insane person. It also includes the marriage custody of a virgin girl. Financial custody may cover all young persons, the insane, and those with proven impediments to the exercise of normal free will." Mawil Y. Izzi Dien and P.E. Walker, "Wilāya (a.)" in *Encyclopaedia of Islam* (n 35).

[99] Al-Nawawī (n 68) 5:677 and al-Shirbīnī (n 70) 3:343.

[100] Al-Shāfiʿī (n 90) 11:165. In al-Māwardī's narration of this report, "Muḥammad said, 'Do not hit the maidservants of Allah', so 'Umar came to him and explained that, 'In the society of the Quraysh, our men dominated (*yaghlibu*) our women, and a man from amongst us in Mecca used to carry cudgel/cane (*hirāra*) with him, if his wife crossed (*tarmarrat*) him, he would hit her with it. Then we came to the Aws and Khazraj and found the men like sheep (*maghānim*) to their women, their women dominate their men, so our women mingled with their women and became audacious (*dha'ira*), so I said to the Prophet, the women have become audacious over their husbands, permit us to hit them.' " According to al-Māwardī,

contradicted the instruction to hit them in Q. 4:34. Since the Qur'ān could not be abrogated by prophetic practice according to Shāfiʿīs, Shāfiʿī jurists had to find a way to reconcile this initial prophetic prohibition with the Qur'anic permission to hit wives. There were three possibilities for arranging the Qur'anic text and prophetic report in relation to each other so that the integrity of both was maintained. The first possibility was to make wifely *nushūz* the determining factor for the correct course of action; Q 4:34 permitted husbands to hit their wives when their wives committed *nushūz*, whereas the report of ʿUmar prohibited husbands from hitting wives when they did not commit *nushūz*. The second possibility was to change the force of the command in Q. 4:34 to a permission (*idhn*) and the prohibition in the *ḥadīth* to a matter of choice (*ikhtiyār*).[101] In this arrangement, jurists avoided the problem of abrogation and could adopt the ruling that while hitting wives was permissible (*mubāḥ*), avoiding it was preferable. The third option was that Muḥammad's permission to hit wives and moral censure in the *ḥadīth* of ʿUmar abrogated his initial prohibition. In this case Muḥammad's practice, or *sunna*, was abrogated by another *sunna*; there was no contradiction between prophetic practice and the Qur'anic text.[102]

Most Shāfiʿī jurists considered in this study followed the example of al-Shāfiʿī himself and opted for the second interpretation, which maintained the relevance of both Q. 4:34 and the *ḥadīth* under discussion. By altering the meaning of the imperative in Q. 4:34 from an injunction to a permission and the meaning of the initial prohibition in the *ḥadīth* to a recommendation, al-Shāfiʿī reconciled the Qur'anic text with prophetic practice without worrying about abrogation. As a result, the physical discipline of wives took on an intermediary status between command and prohibition; it was designated as discouraged (*makrūh*). In this framework, a husband who hits his wife for *nushūz* avails himself of his God-given right, but the one who avoids hitting his wife follows the higher path and example of Muḥammad. Thus, the official Shāfiʿī position on hitting wives was that following the prophetic example was preferred to exercising one's rights.[103]

dha'ira can mean two things: arrogance/insolence or contemptuous/obscene behavior. Al-Māwardī (n 70) 9:599.

101 J.L. Austin, *How to Do Things with Words* (Oxford: Oxford University Press, 1962).

102 Al-Māwardī has an excellent exposition of this Shāfiʿī problem. Al-Māwardī (n 70) 9:598–9. See also al-Nawawī (n 68) 5:676 and al-Shāfiʿī (n 90) 11:165–6. For a more extensive discussion on this issue, see Kecia Ali (n 69) 143–55.

103 "In his saying 'The best of you will not hit' is evidence that hitting is permitted but not obligatory. We choose what the Prophet chose, so we prefer for a man to not hit his wife for her sharp tongue or other similar things." Al-Shāfiʿī (n 90) 11:165–6. It is interesting that al-Shāfiʿī restricted his recommendation to hitting wives for a sharp tongue and

THE ḤANBALĪS: AN ARGUMENT FROM SILENCE

The Ḥanbalī position on the right of husbands to physically discipline wives was an amalgamation of the positions of earlier schools. In general, they encouraged husbands to follow a sequential approach to disciplining wives, beginning with lighter punishments before hitting their wives for disciplinary purposes. They differentiated between signs of wifely *nushūz* and *nushūz* proper, which expanded the types of behavior for which a wife could be disciplined. They also permitted husbands to hit their wives with whips and imagined judges residing in the domestic space of a couple if each claimed transgression from the other. As a rule, Ḥanbalīs protected husbands from liability if they used excessive violence when disciplining their wives. In comparison to other schools, Ḥanbalī jurists spent the least amount of time considering a husband's liability for hitting his wife excessively. Apart from this difference, Ḥanbalī jurisprudence on marital discipline followed the patterns of the other three schools.

Like the Ḥanafīs, Ḥanbalī scholars discussed husbandly and wifely *nushūz* side by side but differed on their legal implications. Husbandly *nushūz* was defined as a husband's antipathy toward and aversion of his wife, or his beating her without just cause;[104] it was presumed that this aversion was caused by some unattractive feature of the wife, and wives were urged to forfeit some of their marital rights in order to please their husbands. The example of Muḥammad's wife Sawdāʿ giving up her nights to ʿĀ'isha in exchange for remaining married was treated as a normative model. Muwaffaq al-Dīn ʿAbd Allāh ibn Aḥmad Ibn Qudāma (d. 620/1223) wrote, "If a woman fears her husband's lack of attraction because of her sickness, old age or ugliness, there is no harm in her giving up some of her rights to please him."[105] Whereas wives were burdened with rectifying husbandly *nushūz* through appeasement, husbands were responsible for removing wifely *nushūz* through disciplinary measures.

Like the Shāfiʿī jurists, Ḥanbalī scholars distinguished the signs/indications (*amārāt*) of *nushūz* from *nushūz* proper, clarifying that while husbands were permitted to hit their wives for the latter, they could not hit

not wifely *nushūz* more generally. This is so especially in light of al-Ghazālī's clarification that a sharp tongue does not constitute wifely *nushūz* but is still discipline-worthy. It is important to emphasize that al-Shāfiʿī himself was quite comfortable with the physical discipline of wives as long as it was non-extreme and did not exceed the *ḥadd* penalty. In setting these limits, he permitted husbands to lash their wives between thirty-nine to seventy-nine strikes. Al-Shāfiʿī (n 90) 12:507–8 and al-Ghazālī (n 72) 3:234. See also al-Nawawī (n 68) 5:677.

[104] Abī Isḥāq Burhān al-Dīn Ibrāhīm b. Muḥammad b. ʿAbdullah b. Muḥammad Ibn Mufliḥ al-Ḥanbalī, *Al-Mubdaʿ Sharḥ al-Muqniʿ* (Beirut: Dār al-Kutub al- ʿIlmiyya, 1997) 6:263.

[105] Ibn Qudāma (n 79) 10: 262–3.

them for signs of *nushūz*.[106] Indications of wifely *nushūz* included behavior such as sluggishness, withholding, grudging, and grumbling. A wife exhibited *nushūz* proper if she disobeyed her husband, sexually refused him, left the house without his permission, opposed him, lacked etiquette, aggrandized herself over him, or angered him.[107] Importantly, for the Ḥanbalīs, husbands could hit their wives for abandoning religious obligations (*tark al-farā'iḍ*) such as prayer, based on Q. 66:6, which instructs believers to "save yourselves and your families from the Fire."[108] Ibn Qudāma cited Aḥmad Ibn Ḥanbal (d. 241/855) as saying, "I fear it is not permissible (*ḥalāl*) for a man to remain with a woman who does not pray, not ritually purify herself or study the Qur'ān."[109] Husbands were viewed as the moral overseers of their wives; they ensured that wives fulfilled their mandatory religious obligations but could also prevent wives from performing supererogatory devotions such as praying or fasting outside the prescribed times.[110]

Ḥanbalī jurists advocated that the disciplinary process be applied sequentially rather than simultaneously.[111] Admonishment was described

[106] Ibn Qudāma wrote, "The punishment should correspond to the [level] of fear of *nushūz*; and there can be no debate that it is impermissible to hit her for [mere] fear of *nushūz*, without its manifestation." Ibn Qudāma (n 79) 10:260. See also Ibn Mufliḥ (n 104) 6:263; and 'Alā' al-Dīn Abī al-Ḥasan 'Alī b. Sulaymān al-Mardāwī, *Al-inṣāf fī ma'rifa al-rājiḥ min al-khilāf 'alā madhhab al-īmām Aḥmad Ibn Ḥanbal* (Beirut: Dār Iḥyā' al-turāth al-'Arabī, 1956) 8:376.

[107] Ibn Qudāma wrote, "The literal meaning of *nushūz* is rising (*al-irtifā'*) [of a wife over her husband] because she raises herself and aggrandizes herself over and above the God-given obligation to obey her husband," and "So when signs of *nushūz* become manifest in her—for example, if she is sluggish (*tatathāqal*) or withholding (*tudāfi'*) when he calls her and she only complies grudgingly (*bi-takarruhin*), grumbling (*damdamatin*) the whole time—then he should admonish her." Ibn Qudāma (n 79)10:259. See also Ibn Mufliḥ (n 104) 6:263; Mar'ī ibn Yūsuf al-Karmī, *Ghāyat al-muntahā fī al-jam' bayna al-Iqnā' wa-al-Muntahā* (Riyaḍh: al-Mu'assasa al-Sa'īdīyya, 1981) 2:91; al-Mardāwī (n 106) 8:376; and Aḥmad b. 'Abd al-Ḥalīm Ibn Taymiyya, *Majmū' fatāwā Shaykh al-Islām Aḥmad Ibn Taymiyya* (Riyadh: Dār 'Ālim al-Kutub, 1991) 30:38, 32:174–5 and 277–8.

[108] "O ye who believe! Ward off from yourselves and your families a Fire whereof the fuel is men and stones, over which are set angels strong, severe, who resist not Allah in that which He commandeth them, but do that which they are commanded." Yusuf Ali (n 15) Q. 66:6. Al-Karmī (n 107) 2:92; and Ibn Qudāma (n 79) 10:261–2.

[109] Ibn Qudāma (n 79) 10:262. See also al-Karmī (n 107) 2:92 and al-Mardāwī (n 106) 8:378.

[110] Al-Karmī (n 107) 2:91. Ibn Taymiyya explained that obedience to a husband was obligatory on a wife, whereas supererogatory devotions were optional; so if a husband forbade her from performing supererogatory devotions, then "how could a believing woman prioritize the optional (*al-nāfila*) over the mandatory (*al-farīḍa*)?" To this end, he cited several *aḥādīth*: "It is not permitted for a woman whose husband is present to fast without his permission, except in the month of Ramadān"; and "The rights of husbands over wives are so great that if I had ordered a person to prostrate to another, I would have ordered the woman to prostrate to her husband." Ibn Taymiyya (n 107) 32:274–5.

[111] In his *Fatāwā*, Ibn Taymiyya mentions hitting without any of the preceding steps, but given the lack of detail in the passage, it is not clear that he was advocating a sequential approach. He wrote, "When [the wife] refuses to answer his call to bed, she is disobedient ('āṣiya) and *nāshiza*, and it is permissible to hit her, as God said, 'As for those from whom

as both a reminder and a threat. A husband was first required to admonish his wife, reminding her of her place and her duty to obey her husband, and warning (*yukhawwifhā*) her of impending abandonment and hitting, as well as loss of maintenance (*nafaqa*) and clothing, if she persisted in her *nushūz*.[112] Abandonment was meant to be primarily sexual, based on the reference to "beds" in the text of Q. 4:34. However, it could include abandonment of speech as long as it did not exceed three days.[113]

In case neither admonishment nor abandonment succeeded in persuading a wife to return to obedience, husbands could hit their wives. Again, the text of Q. 4:34 was used as a proof text to justify this point.[114] Muḥammad's farewell sermon was referenced to stipulate that the hitting ought to be non-extreme (*ghayr mubarriḥ*). Though some versions of this sermon mention hitting without the preceding steps of admonishment and abandonment, Ḥanbalī jurists treated only parts of the sermon as carrying legal weight. Beating out of sequence was ignored, while the restriction of hitting in a non-extreme (*ghayr mubarriḥ*) manner was used as a legally relevant constraint.[115]

There was disagreement among Ḥanbalī jurists about whether a husband could hit his wife the first time she committed *nushūz* or if physical violence could be employed only in response to recurrent *nushūz*. Aḥmad Ibn Ḥanbal and Ibn Qudāma agreed that a husband could hit his wife in the first instance of *nushūz*. In this respect, they compared the physical discipline for *nushūz* with a *ḥadd* penalty for a crime. While these two punishments were distinct from each other, they were similar in that they were applicable regardless of the number of times a crime was committed; they were not contingent on the recurring nature of a crime. Manṣūr ibn Yūnus al-Buhūtī (d. 1052/1641–2) and ʿUmar ibn al-Ḥusayn al-Khiraqī (d. 334/945–6) disagreed, arguing that it was impermissible to

you fear *nushūz* ... (to the end of the verse).'" He followed this with a prophetic report in which Muḥammad stated that if he had ordered anyone to prostrate themselves to another person, he would have ordered a woman to prostrate to her husband. Ibn Taymiyya (n 107) 32:275. See also Ibn Qudāma (n 79) 10:259 and al-Mardāwī (n 106) 8:377.

[112] Ibn Qudāma wrote, "This means he should frighten her (*yukhawwifhā*) from God, most Glorious, remind her that he has divinely-mandated rights over her [that include] obedience, and [remind her] that she gains sin by opposing him (*bi mukhālafatihi*) and by disobedience (*al-maʿṣiya*). Further, [he should remind her] of what she will lose as a result of her behavior—namely, maintenance (*al-nafaqa*) and clothing (*al-kiswa*)—and that he is allowed to abandon and beat her." Ibn Qudāma (n 79) 10:259. The additional threat of loss of clothing is a bit strange, given that it could be subsumed under loss of maintenance.

[113] Ibn Mufliḥ (n 104) 6:263; Ibn Qudāma (n 79) 10:259; al-Karmī (n 107) 2:92; and al-Mardāwī (n 106) 8:376.

[114] Eg, see Ibn Qudāma (n 79) 10:259–60.

[115] Ibn Qudāma cited this report: "It is your right that [your wives] not let anyone into your bed/home whom you dislike, and if they do so then beat them in a non-extreme manner." Ibn Qudāma (n 79) 10:260.

hit a wife at the first instance of *nushūz*; rather, husbands should wait for persistent *nushūz* before applying physical discipline.[116]

Though neither the *ḥadd* penalty nor the physical disciplining of wives were contingent on the recurrent nature of a crime, they were different from each other in terms of the punishment itself. Ḥanbalī jurists, like the jurists encountered earlier, restricted husbandly disciplinary privileges as falling short of a *ḥadd* penalty; a husband's beating of his wife could not mimic the punishment of the state. Consequently, jurists' understanding of the *ḥadd* penalty influenced the degree of violence acceptable in the domestic realm. Whereas Shāfiʿī jurists believed that since a whip was used in implementing *ḥadd* penalties, it could not be used by a husband disciplining his wife, some Mālikī jurists and Ḥanbalī jurists relied on prophetic reports to argue that a husband could hit his wife with a whip as long as he did not exceed ten lashes (*aswāṭ*).[117]

Hitting a wife was further restricted by standard guidelines encountered earlier: the beating should be non-severe (*ghayr shadīd*) and not lead to death; it should avoid the face, places of beauty (*mustaḥsina*), perilous parts of the body (*al-mawāḍiʿ al-makhūfa*), and not be applied repeatedly to the same part of the body. The purpose of beating was discipline (*al-taʾdīb*), not injury or death (*al-itlāf*).[118] Some Ḥanbalī jurists mentioned that if both spouses accused each other of transgression (*ẓulm*), then a judge (*ḥākim*) was required to live with the couple to determine the transgressing party and set them straight.[119] They did not discuss what constituted transgression (*ẓulm*), how the judge would determine the offending party (since they would both presumably be on their best behavior), or how the court would rectify the behavior of each spouse.

[116] Al-Buhūtī argued that husbands should hit their wives only after admonishing and abandoning them. Manṣūr ibn Yūnus Al-Buhūtī, *Irshād ulī al-nuhā li-daqāʾiq al-Muntahā: ḥāshiya ʿalā Muntahā al-irādāt* (Mecca: Dār Khiḍr, 2000) 2:1133. Ibn Qudāma made the case of pairing lighter punishments with lighter crimes and heavier punishments with graver crimes. Like the Shāfiʿīs, he cited Q. 5:33 to support this point. Ibn Qudāma (n 79) 10:260.

[117] Ibn Qudāma mentioned three prophetic reports to support this point: "None of you should hit your women like you hit a slave and then sleep with her at the end of the day"; "You should not lash with a whip more than ten times except in *ḥadd* penalty"; and "God has mercy on His servant (*ʿabd*) who hangs the whip (*sawṭ*) in his house to discipline his household (*ahlihī*)." Ibn Qudāma (n 79) 10:261–2. See also al-Buhūtī (n 116) 2:1133; Ibn Mufliḥ (n 104) 6:264; and al-Karmī (n 107) 2:92.

[118] Al-Khallāl asked Ibn Yaḥyā what was meant by "non-extreme" (*ghayr mubarriḥ*) hitting. Ibn Yaḥyā replied that it meant [something] other than severe/intense (*ghayr shadīd*). The "Ibn Yaḥyā" referenced here is likely the Baghdādī grammarian Abu al-ʿAbbās Aḥmad b. Yaḥyā al-Thaʿlab (d. 291/903). See also Ibn Mufliḥ (n 104) 6:263; Ibn Qudāma (n 79) 10:260; and al-Karmī (n 107) 2:91.

[119] Eg, see Ibn Mufliḥ (n 104) 6:264 and al-Mardāwī (n 106) 8:378.

Still, Ḥanbalī jurists did not specifically discuss a husband's liability if he exceeded the recommendation of non-extreme hitting and injured his wife, though al-Karmī stated that if a wife died (*talafat*), there was no liability (*ḍamān*) on the husband.[120] On the basis of this brief note in al-Karmī in conjunction with the predominant Ḥanbalī silence on the liability of husbands, it can be argued that Ḥanbalī jurists did not hold husbands liable for excessive violence. Such an argument is further supported by the Ḥanbalī emphasis on not interfering with the domestic affairs of men, especially in the case of wife-beating. For example, al-Buhūtī wrote that "No one, not even [a woman's] father, should ask a man why he beat his wife."[121] The absence of discussion on the topic of excessive violence in the Ḥanbalī school when discussing marital violence is remarkable.

Overall, the Ḥanbalī scholars under study offered a jurisprudence for disciplining wives that was an amalgamation of the preceding three schools. Like the Shāfiʿīs, they expanded the definition of wifely *nushūz*; like the Mālikīs, they considered it permissible to hit with a whip; and like the Ḥanafīs, they protected husbands from liability if they used excessive violence when disciplining their wives. However, there was an important difference between the Ḥanbalīs and the other three schools regarding excessive beating. Whereas scholars from the other schools took time to consider a husband's liability in the case of excessive beating, Ḥanbalīs were notably silent on the issue. This silence left wives without clear legal recourse against abusive husbands, effectively protecting husbands against litigation.

CONCLUSION

This study of the four Sunnī legal schools in the pre-colonial period illustrates the range of legal opinions in the application of Q. 4:34, as well as the connections and overlap between the genres of Qurʾān commentaries (*tafsīr*) and Islamic jurisprudence (*fiqh*). If Qurʾanic exegesis offered cosmological justifications for the prescription to hit wives in Q. 4:34, then Islamic jurisprudence institutionalized this imperative in multiple ways. The two genres fit together in a complementary way, with the same

[120] Al-Karmī (n 107) 2:91–2.

[121] Al-Buhūtī (n 116) 2:1133. Like al-Buhūṭī, Ibn Qudāma believed that no one, not even the wife's father, should ask a man why he beat his wife. According to Ibn Qudāma, this might be embarrassing for the husband, who may not want to tell his father-in-law about his sexual troubles with this wife. This in turn might lead him to lie unnecessarily. Ibn Qudāma (n 79) 10:262. Al-Karmī also insisted that a man should not be questioned as to why he hit his wife. Al-Karmī (n 107) 2:92.

scholars often writing works in both disciplines. Al-Qurṭubī's exegetical work was referenced in Mālikī jurisprudence, where it had a great deal of influence; al-Rāzī's Qur'ān commentary relied on Shāfiʿī jurisprudence for its stance on the physical discipline of wives.

Despite the overlap between the two genres, each genre maintained distinctive features. Qur'ān commentaries sought to justify the right of husbands to hit wives in a variety of ways that drew on a shared cosmology in which husbands were mandated to oversee the moral, social, and financial well-being of their wives. In doing so, they provided a framework on which works of jurisprudence relied—but did not expound—in institutionalizing this prescription. The exegetical discussions surrounding the issue of wife-beating provide insights into the assumptions of Muslim jurists. It would be difficult to make sense of the easy correlations drawn between hitting a wife, slave, or child in jurisprudence without a sense of the underpinning cosmology that justified this social hierarchy.[122]

Additionally, exegetes and jurists emphasized the polyvalence of the Qur'anic text in different ways. For example, pre-colonial Qur'ān commentators offered a greater range of interpretations for the imperative to abandon wives in bed than was incorporated into works of jurisprudence. On the whole, jurists treated the command to abandon wives in bed in a straightforward manner as sexual abandonment with the possibility of verbal abandonment. The question of the length of this abandonment invited speculation, which ranged from three days to four months. However, jurists considered a much wider range of interpretations with regard to the command "to hit" than their exegetical counterparts. While exegetes dwelled briefly on the nature of hitting and questions of retribution, jurists devoted considerable energy to outlining the amount of hitting permissible, along with the conditions under which a husband might be liable for excessive violence. They also reflected on the role of judges and the community in regulating the private affairs of couples; this discussion was absent in exegetical works.

The four schools of jurisprudence brought various concerns to bear in their discussions of wife-beating. The Ḥanafīs were concerned with offering husbands maximal authority in marriage without oversight and with protecting them against legal action for disciplining their wives. The Mālikīs had the opposite concern, as they introduced judicial and extra-judicial oversight into marriage, with another person often sharing the domestic space. Shāfiʿī jurists were most troubled by the possible

[122] Vardit Rispler-Chaim, "Nušūz between Medieval and Contemporary Islamic Law: The Human Rights Aspect," *Arabica*, 39(3) (1992) 315.

contradiction between the Qur'anic text and prophetic practice, which they resolved by expanding the definition of wifely *nushūz*, thereby increasing the authoritative purview of husbands. They also altered the meaning of "to hit" from a command to a permission, and recommended abstinence from hitting. Finally, the Ḥanbalīs reflected some of the trends in the earlier schools. They were most distinct amongst jurists in their lack of attention to husbands' liability in the case of excessive violence: thus they safeguarded husbands from legal action initiated by their wives and left wives without legal recourse from abusive husbands.

Despite the disparate motivations and concerns of the four schools, it is noteworthy that in the end their stances on the right of husbands to physically discipline wives shared essential similarities. The pre-colonial Sunnī jurists under study were in agreement that husbands had a right to hit their wives if they committed *nushūz* and that the beating ought to be non-extreme. There was also consensus among the jurists that the span between non-extreme and extreme hitting was legally ambiguous; no jurist discussed the legal recourse available to a wife whose husband hit her in a severe manner, but without breaking bones or causing wounds. In the case of extreme hitting, jurists were mostly reluctant to hold husbands liable for excessive violence. While most jurists agreed that a husband was liable for retribution (*qiṣāṣ*) in the case of a wife's death, only the Mālikīs and Shāfiʿīs conceded that a husband was financially liable for using excessive violence against a wife that resulted in serious injuries. Although Fadel has argued that some of the most interesting discussions of gender in medieval Islam can be found in Islamic jurisprudence, where the two voices of Islam—the patriarchal and ethical—are in "battle" with one another, this study does not support his claim.[123]

It is helpful to look at works of jurisprudence and exegesis side by side, as they help us to gain a greater understanding of the various perspectives as well as of shared assumptions and cosmologies of pre-colonial scholars. This is especially useful when we contrast the treatment of wife-beating in pre-colonial scholarly discourse with modern discussions on the same topic. It gives us the ability to separate the pre-colonial threads from modern ones in contemporary discourse. It also helps to de-mythologize the tradition, enabling us to look at the Islamic tradition with a clear and

[123] Fadel (n 4) 200–1. This study of juristic texts bears out Ziba Mir-Hosseini's assertion that "Juristic disagreements were not, as now, about the legitimacy or legality of a husband's right to beat his wife if she defies his authority; they were about the extent and harshness of the beating he should administer." Ziba Mir-Hosseini, "Justice, Equality and Muslim Family Laws: New Ideas, New Prospects" in Ziba Mir-Hosseini, Kari Vogt, Lena Larsen, and Christian Moe (eds.), *Gender and Equality in Muslim Family Law: Justice and Ethics in the Islamic Legal Tradition* (London: I.B. Taurus, 2013).

steady gaze. This is crucial for contemporary scholars, particularly if we are to differentiate between those issues of modern conversations to which pre-colonial Islamic scholarship is valuable and, on the other hand, those arenas where the influence of pre-colonial Islamic scholarship is counterproductive. As we will see, pre-colonial scholarship is often detrimental to substantive discussions of gender in the present day.

Part II

Restoring Authority in the Living Community

Meaning is bent by expectation.
Jack Hitt, "Words on Trial"[1]

[1] The *New Yorker* (July 23, 2012).

4

Asserting Authority, Enriching Tradition

The post-colonial period (specifically the twentieth and twenty-first centuries) has brought with it a transformed discourse regarding wife-beating in Q. 4:34. This transformation has not resulted from a changed Qur'anic text but rather from a re-fashioned idealized cosmology in which interpretations of Q. 4:34 hinge on an imagined, perfect relationship between God, men, and women. In this new cosmology, men no longer mediate women's relationships with God; rather, men and women possess equal human worth, and every individual has an independent relationship to the divine. When the lexical meanings of a divine text clash with expectations of believers, a crisis arises that must be resolved through hermeneutic negotiations.

In the twentieth and twenty-first centuries, the prescription to hit wives—even read as mere permission—has become increasingly controversial. Many contemporary Muslims abhor the pre-colonial plain-sense meaning of Q. 4:34, which instructs husbands to hit their wives if the latter commit *nushūz*, and they are ill at ease with pre-colonial legal and exegetical scholarly interpretations of this verse. As adherents of the Muslim faith who believe in the sacredness of the Qur'anic text, they exert a great deal of effort to re-imagine the meanings of this verse so that it aligns with their expectations of a just God's revelation for ethical marital conduct. In this re-imagination of the Qur'anic text, the literal wording of the divine text matters less than a believer's expectation of the text. As demonstrated in previous chapters, the Qur'anic text can be interpreted to have multiple meanings, including meanings that contradict the lexical wording of the text. Post-colonial Muslim scholars and activists have proposed disparate approaches to resolve the larger problem of marital hierarchy in Q. 4:34, as well as the specific issue of divine consent (if not command) for the physical disciplining of wives. In this process, the inherited tradition plays a central role: it can aid or obstruct the new innovative legal interpretations of Qur'anic texts that have emerged in response to the needs of contemporary Muslim communities.

The main problem faced by Muslim scholars when balancing traditional concerns with contemporary ones is the fundamentally incompatible nature of patriarchal and egalitarian cosmologies. Since these two idealized cosmologies cannot be maintained simultaneously with integrity, present-day scholars face an egalitarian–authoritative dilemma. In communities where authority is rooted in a deeply patriarchal Islamic tradition, how can Muslim scholars produce interpretations of Q. 4:34 that are at once egalitarian and authoritative? Offering gender-egalitarian interpretations necessarily means breaking from the patriarchal tradition. But breaking from tradition results in a loss of authority in the eyes of their communities. The flipside of this dilemma is that if scholars rely on the patriarchal tradition in order to maintain authority and legitimacy, then they must compromise their commitment to gender egalitarianism.

The way that post-colonial scholars choose to reconcile these two cosmologies determines the role that the pre-colonial tradition plays in their interpretations of Q. 4:34 as well as the traction that their explanations might have in various Muslim communities. The most significant differentiator between pre- and post-colonial discussions of wife-beating is that modern scholars are *always* juggling competing cosmologies. In contrast, pre-colonial scholars had the luxury of writing and speaking in a context where a patriarchal idealized cosmology enjoyed hegemony. As a result, whereas pre-colonial legal and exegetical scholars had a largely monolithic approach to the right of husbands to hit wives, the perspectives of post-colonial scholars are much more diverse, ranging from unapologetically permitting husbands to hit wives to categorically forbidding the beating of wives under any and all circumstances. Contemporary interpretations of Q. 4:34 display a great deal of creativity and hermeneutical ingenuity, as some scholars propose entirely new interpretations of the prescription "hit them," including "have sexual intercourse with them," "leave the marriage," and "travel."

Before we more closely examine these post-colonial approaches to Q. 4:34, a few general remarks are in order. First, as opposed to the critical survey of pre-colonial approaches to Q. 4:34 in the previous chapters, which was based on the genres of Qur'anic exegesis and Islamic law, post-colonial sources will be classified by approach rather than genre. This is because post-colonial sources have developed in such a manner that the categories of genre have become largely irrelevant. In the pre-colonial period, scholars undertook multi-volume works that fit neatly into the categories of Qur'anic commentaries or legal works, despite the overlap between the genres, wherein exegetes considered legal questions and legal scholars offered interpretations of Qur'anic verses. In the post-colonial period, many Muslim scholars have addressed the question of wife-beating in works that cannot be assigned to the genre of either Islamic law or Qur'ān commentary in a straightforward manner. This development is in part the result of a change in the production and dissemination of religious knowledge. In a post-colonial and globalized world, the production and distribution of knowledge has become increasingly democratized. Whereas in the pre-colonial period, only an elite class of highly educated scholars spoke for Islam and wrote texts that were preserved for the reading pleasure of their colleagues, multiple media outlets have made it possible for many more voices to speak about Islam to a broader audience. The voices that speak for Islam now include Muslims from various educational and vocational backgrounds, and different cultural and national histories. For the first time in Muslim history, both men and women are actively engaged in the creation and dissemination of knowledge about Islam, and the receiving audience is considered to include women alongside men.

Second, in the previous three chapters only Arabic sources were surveyed, but in the post-colonial period approaches to Q. 4:34 in English, Arabic, and Urdu will be examined. In the pre-colonial period, Arabic was the preferred language of the scholarly elite, who wrote in Arabic even if they were not Arabs themselves. This means that a survey of Arabic sources spanning several centuries and geographic regions, and encompassing various theological and juridical schools, provides a good sense of pre-colonial positions on the question of wife-beating in scholarly discourse. However, as a result of the developments in the post-colonial period, it is no longer sufficient to consider only Arabic written sources. Hence, this study scrutinizes sources in multiple mediums (written, electronic, audio, and video), in three languages (English, Arabic, and Urdu) to get a representative sample of post-colonial approaches to Q. 4:34. English is the new global language spoken by Muslims around the world. Proficiency in Arabic continues to be expected of the scholarly elite, and Urdu is, in one form or another, understood by approximately 500 million people, making it the most commonly understood Islamicate language in the world today. By considering non-Arabic sources, this study also challenges the prevailing bias in favor of Arabic sources as representative of global Muslim attitudes.

Third, an important point to keep in mind is that both the voices that speak authoritatively about Islam as well as the desired audiences of those voices have changed significantly. Pre-colonial scholars were part of an educated elite who wrote for the scholarly Muslim class. They did not expect the popular masses to have access to their writings. By comparison, a much greater number of people in the post-colonial period write authoritatively about Islam without formal training in Islamic studies. As a result, there is much greater representation of accessible Muslim voices in the post-colonial period, spanning different religious perspectives, genders, classes, cultural backgrounds, and scholarly levels. Furthermore, the expected audience has shifted to include the popular masses, who are expected to interact with the message of a given scholar in several mediums, including print, electronic, audio, and video. An added dimension is that the audience is not only Muslim but also non-Muslim. Many of the post-colonial scholars in this study engage a theoretical interlocutor who is not Muslim and thus ignorant—whether innocently or belligerently—of Islam's "true" position on the "status of women." Sometimes the tone of these writings is polemical, while at other times it is earnest, and yet other times it is defensive.

Post-colonial Muslim scholars who offer innovative and unprecedented interpretations of Q. 4:34 in which the hitting of wives in all circumstances is unjust, immoral, and unethical must privilege an egalitarian cosmology over a patriarchal one without equivocation. In spurning the pre-colonial, patriarchal cosmology, these scholars must discard the Islamic tradition; that is, they must reject all pre-colonial understandings of the right of husbands to hit their wives as outlined in Q. 4:34. As can be imagined, positing new, alternative meanings for Q. 4:34 that do not sanction marital violence is a daunting prospect because it necessitates rejecting the position of the entire Islamic tradition on wife-beating, as well as undermining the pre-colonial cosmology. This move is intimidating because in addition to compromising the authority of the new interpretation, it also threatens the authenticity and "Islamic-ness" of the scholar him or herself.

Muslim scholars employ various methods in response to the egalitarian–authoritative dilemma. Their various strategies fall into four broad categories: traditionalist, neo-traditionalist, progressive, and reformist. These categories are a heuristic device and not meant to be hard and fast. Still, they are useful for organizing Muslim perspectives on various issues.[1] These divisions are based on how Muslim scholars answer three related questions: (1) which idealized cosmology—patriarchal or

[1] Eg, these categories translate well to the various approaches Muslims have to women's covering. Bear in mind this chapter does not consider perspectives on wife-beating as codified in the legislative structure of Muslim-majority nation states. Judith Tucker provides an initial treatment of this subject in her book *Women, Family and Gender in Islamic Law*. Her work illustrates that modern religious discussions on wife-beating have tangible effects on women's lives. Eg, definitions for wifely *nushūz* are codified in many Muslim-majority countries from Morocco to Jordan, and its definitions range from general disobedience to leaving the house without a husband's permission. In countries such as Egypt, a husband can appeal to the police to assist him in returning his wife to his house. Judith E. Tucker. *Women, Family and Gender in Islamic Law* (Cambridge: Cambridge University Press, 2008) 74, 77, and 80–1.

egalitarian—is ultimately privileged over the other; (2) is the pre-colonial Islamic tradition appealed to for authority, or is it rejected; and (3) in the end, is there any circumstance in which a husband can hit his wife? The answers to these three questions determine the approach of modern Muslim scholars to Q. 4:34.

The "traditionalist" approach unambiguously privileges a patriarchal idealized cosmology over an egalitarian one and thus maintains the right of husbands to physically discipline their wives. In doing so, traditionalist scholars adhere to the "Islamic tradition," defined here as the pre-colonial legal and exegetical traditions. The "neo-traditionalist" strategy also favors a patriarchal idealized cosmology over an egalitarian one, allowing husbands to hit their wives in increasingly restricted circumstances. All the while, neo-traditionalist scholars seek to portray the patriarchal Islamic tradition as just, equitable, and mostly harmonious with an egalitarian idealized cosmology. "Progressive" scholars ultimately prefer an egalitarian idealized cosmology over a patriarchal one, denying husbands the right to hit their wives in any circumstance. However, they seek to portray both their position and the larger egalitarian idealized cosmology as compatible with traditional views, even if they rest their authority upon minority or even singular pre-colonial opinions. By anchoring their own perspectives in the inherited tradition—even if in minority or imagined opinions—progressive scholars hope to retain authority in mainstream religious communities. The "reformist" approach opts for an egalitarian idealized cosmology over a patriarchal one and categorically forbids husbands from ever hitting their wives. Reformist scholars are willing to sacrifice any authority that might be garnered through an association with a patriarchal tradition in order to maintain the integrity of their egalitarian idealized cosmology.

In the first three of four approaches, the inherited "Islamic tradition" functions as an obstacle to a truly gender-egalitarian vision of marriage. In all three of these approaches, the clashing patriarchal and egalitarian cosmologies create a crisis for Muslim scholars, who must necessarily retain inconsistencies in the logic of their arguments in order to anchor their positions in both cosmologies. Therefore, scholars who root their authority in the pre-colonial tradition—to any degree—must also save this tradition. Since pre-colonial scholars did not think that hitting one's wife for disciplinary purposes was either morally or ethically problematic, contemporary scholars who want to anchor their egalitarian positions in this tradition must find a way to locate their own ethical concerns with hitting wives in the positions of scholars who were themselves entirely unperturbed by this license. Neo-traditionalists and progressive scholars especially devote a great deal of energy to minimizing the differences between the idealized patriarchal cosmology espoused by pre-colonial scholars and the gender-egalitarianism advocated by contemporary scholars. However, the uniformly patriarchal nature of the Islamic tradition necessitates that post-colonial scholars seeking to root egalitarian positions in this tradition either misrepresent the tradition in order to reconcile it with egalitarian values or compromise their commitment to gender-egalitarian values. As a result, neo-traditionalist and progressive scholars in particular, who are attempting to uphold patriarchal and egalitarian idealized cosmologies at once, engage in intricate hermeneutical acrobatics to maintain these opposing idealized cosmologies.

TRADITIONALISTS: DEFENDING TRADITION FROM MODERN HERESIES

In the tussle between the patriarchal and egalitarian idealized cosmologies, traditionalist scholars side with the patriarchal. However, this choice is not as straightforward in the post-colonial period as it was in the pre-colonial period, when the patriarchal idealized cosmology was unquestionably dominant. Although this choice may grant scholars authority within some Muslim communities, it must also be defended against the competing claims of an egalitarian idealized cosmology that is not prevalent in larger society. Whereas pre-colonial scholars did not have to explain their idealized vision of a gendered marital hierarchy, post-colonial traditionalist scholars expend a great deal of energy defending this perspective. Holding onto a patriarchal idealized cosmology in the post-colonial period requires scholars to be somewhat divorced from their own social and historical reality, where scientific and social advances have demonstrated that men are not physically and intellectually superior to women. The defensive stance of traditionalist scholars is most clearly obvious in their lengthy tracts that justify a divinely sanctioned patriarchal cosmology, which they argue is wise and judicious, even if it might initially appear to be unfair.

Responding to potential criticism, traditionalist scholars defend the right of husbands to physically discipline their wives through an elaborate explanation of the ideal hierarchical relationship between the genders.[2] Though their basic conclusions are the same as those of pre-colonial

[2] Dr. Israr Ahmed (d. 2010), a Pakistani cleric, foregrounds his discussion of this verse by describing it as "thorny" and as a verse that "women have trouble swallowing." Israr Ahmed, *Dawra Tarjuma Qur'ān* (audio) (Lahore: Markazi Anjuman Khuddam-ul-Qur'an, 2008).

scholars, their justifications vary significantly. Traditionalist scholars agree with pre-colonial scholars that God favors men over women, resulting in husbandly responsibility for the moral, religious, and social oversight of wives. Dutiful wives are obedient to their husbands, and when they are disobedient—to their husbands or to God—it is the duty of husbands to return them to an obedient state. Husbands may discipline their wives by means of admonishment, abandonment in bed, and physical violence.

However, traditionalist scholars frame their arguments in particularly modern ways. One example of this is that they describe the marital relationship as one in which both spouses are valuable and contribute to the happiness of the couple; marriage is meant to be based on mutual love, affection, and understanding between the spouses. The UK-based jurist Muhammad ibn Adam al-Kawthari argues that "bilateral co-operation" in marriage is meant to create tranquility, love, and mercy, and fulfill the emotional, spiritual, and physical needs of each spouse.[3] Muhammad Shafi (d. 1976), a Grand Mufti of Pakistan and founder of Dār-ul-Ulūm Karachi, cited Qur'anic verses to argue for the complementarity of each spouse and their respective responsibilities in marriage.[4] He described marriage as the foundation of society and believed that it was designed to bring each spouse closer to God. Pre-colonial scholars never mentioned the reciprocal nature of the marital relationship when discussing the husbandly privilege to physically discipline wives, and they certainly never considered mutuality in the emotional and physical needs of spouses.

[3] Mufti Muhammad ibn Adam al-Kawthari is the Director and a researcher at the Institute of Islamic Jurisprudence. Ibn Adam, Question # 07275472, <http://www.daruliftaa.com/question?txt_QuestionID=q-07275472> (last accessed Jan. 15, 2013). See also Sayyid Qutb, *In the Shade of the Qur'ān* (Rajshahi: Islamic Cultural Centre, 1981) 3:108–10; Dr. Sano Koutoub Moustapha, Professor of Comparative Jurisprudence and Islamic Finance at the International Islamic University of Malaysia, "Rebuttal to James Arlandson: Domestic Violence in Islam and Qur'an on Beating Wives," <http://www.answering-christianity.com/umar/beating_rebuttal.htm> (last accessed Jan. 15, 2013); and Ahmad Shafaat, Part-Time Lecturer, Decision Sciences and Management Information Systems, University of Concordia, Montreal, "Tafseer of Surah *an-Nisa*, Ayah 34," <http://www.islamicperspectives.com/quran-4-34.htm> (last accessed Jan. 15, 2013).

[4] These verses include Q. 30:21 and Q. 4:19. In his exegesis of the Qur'ān, Shafi discussed Q. 2:228 extensively to argue that spousal rights are reciprocal, but they need not be the same. He wrote, "Despite having equal rights in many thing, men have the favor (u. *fazīlat*) of rulership (u. *hākamiyyat*) over women, and women are ruled (u. *mahkūm*) and obedient (u. *tābiʿ*)." Here he advanced a theory of gender complementarity rather than equality. Muhammad Shafi, *Maʿārif al-Qur'ān* (Karachi: Maktaba-e-Darul-Uloom, 1996) 2:395 and 401. Israr Ahmed also saw Q. 2:228 as establishing the degree of men over women, and he further asserted that the exhortation not to covet the favor of others in Q. 4:32 is meant to "mentally prepare women" for the assertion of men's favor over women in Q. 4:34. Israr Ahmed (n 2).

Despite the emphasis on the complementary nature of an ideal marriage, traditionalist scholars are quick to point out that there are natural distinctions between men and women which make each gender more suitable for different roles.[5] These scholars frame the natural differences between the genders in the larger context of other differences that are not, they are quick to point out, designed to be oppressive. Syed Qutb (d. 1966), a leading member of the Egyptian Muslim Brotherhood, wrote that since God created both men and women, the differences between them are not an expression of injustice.[6] Abul ala Maududi (d. 1979), the founder of the Islamic revivalist party of Pakistan, Jamaat-e-Islami, wrote an exegesis of the Qur'ān in which he explained that humans are simply not all made the same (u.[7] *yaksān*): some are beautiful, while others are ugly; some are powerful, while others are weak; some are able-bodied, while others are disabled; some are intelligent, while others have been gifted with other strengths; and some are wealthy, while others are poor.[8] All of these variations reflect God's favor (*faḍl*) upon each human being, and this in turn reflects God's mysterious wisdom.[9] God's favor over his creation is meant to be entirely innocuous and not degrading for anyone. For example, His favor of the Kaʿba over other mosques does not diminish the sacredness of mosques in general.[10] When humans endeavor to overcome their natural and divinely designed limitations, they cause corruption (u. *fasād*) by waging war (u. *jang*) with their own natures (u. *fiṭrat*). Such corruption leads to social problems like jealousy, enmity, rivalry (u. *raqābat*), struggle (u. *kashākash*), and opposition (u. *muzāhamat*). Here, Maududi made an allusion to women who might object to their lower ranking in the divine order; he warned them that by challenging—and therefore rebelling—against their divinely assigned position, they become agents of corruption (u. *fasād*).[11]

[5] For more on this, see Mahmoud's discussion of the Egyptian scholar and Islamic modernist Muḥammad ʿAbduh (1905) in Mohamed Mahmoud, "To Beat or Not to Beat: On the Exegetical Dilemmas over Qur'ān Q. 4:34," *Journal of the American Oriental Society*, 126(4) (2006) 545. See also Rashid Rida, *Ḥuqūq al-nisā' fī al-Islām: nidā' li-l-jins al-laṭā'if* (Beirut: Maktab al-Islāmī, 1975) 54.

[6] Qutb (n 3) 3:109–10.

[7] Since I am transliterating Arabic and Urdu terms in this chapter, Urdu words and phrases are differentiated with a "u." before the transliteration to indicate that the following word is in Urdu.

[8] Abul ala Maududi, *Tafhīm al-Qur'ān* (Lahore: Islamic Publications, 1962) 1:348. This list includes natural and social limitations, but he did not differentiate between the two.

[9] Maududi (n 8) 1:348. See also Rida (n 5) 52.

[10] Shafi (n 4) 2:395–6.

[11] Maududi (n 8) 1:348. Qutb wrote that when men and women deny their essential natures, this leads to the "decline of human life," "serious danger," "confusion," "serious repercussions." Furthermore, assuming the responsibilities and authority of men makes women "dissatisfied and unhappy," which they "readily admit." Children also "suffer" from

Traditionalist scholars stress that as with the differentiation of genders, ranking husbands above wives in marriage in no way diminishes the status of women, whose contribution to marriage continues to be invaluable. Through this argument, they dissociate God's favor for men from the dishonor of women; men are favored by God, but women are not dishonored by this favor. Men are placed in authority over women only because it is necessary for someone to assume the headship of every institution and organizational structure, and men happen to be better suited for this position than women. According to Shafi, Q. 2:228 makes it clear that "despite having equal rights in many things, men have the privilege (u. *fazīlat*) of rulership (u. *ḥākamiyyat*) over women, and women are [required to be] subordinate (u. *maḥkūm*) and obedient (u. *tābiʿ*)."[12] Maududi analogized the role of men and women in marriage to the role of various body parts, all of which are integral to the body. The superiority (u. *fazīlat*) of the head over the hand or the heart over the stomach does not diminish the status (u. *maqām*) and importance (u. *ahmiyyat*) of the hand or stomach; rather, the preference of some body parts over others is for the benefit of the entire body.[13] Similarly, men's dominance[14] in marriage by being the head of the household does not reduce, dishonor, or harm (u. *nuqṣān, darar*) a women's status (u. *darja*) in marriage.[15] Shafi believed that by assigning each gender a role appropriate to its attributes, a "division"[16] of labor was created: men are financially responsible for women, and women must give birth and oversee their households.[17] Just like men cannot bear children—that would be unnatural!—it is in the interest of women to avoid working in the marketplace or in offices. Rather, their interests are better served when they are dependent (u. *muhtāj*) on men.[18]

"mental perversion and behavioral deviation" if their parents' behavior does not fit their traditional gender roles. Qutb (n 3) 3:112.

[12] The relevant portion of Q. 2: 228 reads, "And women shall have rights similar to the rights against them, according to what is equitable; but men have a degree (of advantage) over them and Allah is Exalted in Power, Wise." Abdullah Yusuf Ali, *The Meaning of the Holy Quran* (Beltsville: Amana Publications, 1997) Q. 2:228. Rida (n 5) 51; and Shafi (n 4) 2:395 and 401. Rida and Shafi used this verse to make the opposite point that is made by progressive and reformist scholars; rather than emphasizing the similarity of spousal rights, they highlighted the status of men over women.

[13] The specific examples of the preference, favor, or superiority (u. *fazīlat*) of the head over the hand and heart over the stomach were mentioned by Shafi (n 4) 2:397. See also Rida (n 5) 54.

[14] Qadi Sanaullah Panipati, *al-Tafsīr al-Mazharī* (Quetta: Baluchistan Book Depot, 1983) 2:343.

[15] Maududi (n 8) 1:349; Qutb (n 3) 3:112–3; Rida (n 5) 52; and Shafi (n 4) 2:397.

[16] Shafi actually used this English word by transliterating it into Urdu. Shafi (n 4) 2:398.

[17] Shafi argued that the greater inheritance assigned to men actually comes back to women. Shafi (n 4) 2:398–9.

[18] Shafi commented on the paradox that though women are naturally weaker than men, it appears that men have a greater propensity to be embroiled in sins that display their

Rashid Rida (d. 1935), the Cairo-based Islamic reformer and jurist, went as far as to say that in being entrusted with a role that corresponds to their nature, women are actually "honored".[19]

Political and maritime analogies are especially common among traditionalist scholars, who often describe men's rank above women in marriage as similar to the authority of a ruler over his people or a captain over his ship. Yusuf al-Qaradawi, president of the International Association of Muslim Scholars and the head of the European Council for Fatwā and Research, has said that without a captain, a ship would "flounder and sink."[20] Amin Ahsan Islahi (d. 1997), a Pakistani scholar famous for his Qur'anic exegesis focusing on the thematic structure and coherence of the Qur'ān, compared the household to a small polity (u. *waḥdat*) or government (*riyāsat*),[21] which, like any other social unit, requires a leader or manager (u. *sarbarāh*, u. *sar parast*, *amīr*, or *ḥākim*).[22]

weakness, such as sexual sins. He explained this by saying, "The machinations of the self (u. *nafs*) and Satan always surround humans, men and women, and although women especially are weaker in their strengths of intellect and action, despite this, they appear stronger than men with regard to these responsibilities. This is because God the Great aids (u. *imdād*) them with his grace (u. *tawfīq*); this is why women are entangled (u. *mubtalā*) in sins of shame (u. *bay hayā'ī*) less than men." Shafi (n 4) 2:399.

[19] Rida (n 5) 50–1. Rida also cited the example of "women in some countries who give their husbands *mahr* and still remain under the supervision of men." Although he did not mention which countries this practice is common in, he held up this vague example to illustrate the point that the Islamic religion treats women more equitably.

[20] Yusuf al-Qaradawi, *The Lawful and Prohibited in Islam* (Indianapolis: American Trust Publications, 1984) 205–6. See Maududi (n 8) 1:349. Rida used the shepherd analogy, citing a prophetic report in which Muḥammad stated, "The man is the shepherd of his household, and he is responsible (*mas'ūl*) for his flock. And the woman is the shepherd in her husband's household, and she is responsible for her flock." Rida (n 5) 42.

[21] Islahi used the Urdu term "u. *riyāsat*" here, but Rida used the Arabic version of this word to describe marriage (*'aqd al-zawjiyya*) as a woman's entering into the supervision of her husband (*riyāsat al-rijāl*). Amin Ahsan Islahi, *Tadabbur-e-qur'ān* (Lahore: Faran Foundation, 2000–4) 2:291; and Rida (n 5) 50.

[22] Israr Ahmed saw this status as basically guaranteeing that husbands have the final say in family matters. Wives can advocate for their own opinions with supporting evidence, but if a couple cannot reach an agreement, then the husband should make the final call. Israr Ahmed (n 2); Qutb (n 3) 3:110; and Shafi (n 4) 2:396. By arguing that the family is the foundation of society, these scholars were following the "functionalist paradigm" famous among Western sociologists in the 1950s and 60s. "Functionalists described society as a system of interdependent parts—the family, the economy, the political system, the educational system—that worked together to meet the system's 'functional needs' and keep it stable." Aulette and Wittner explain further that according to the "Functionalist" model, each individual had a particular "role" that they were required to play for the larger good. The genders were seen as "complementary"; men were the "single breadwinners" who supported their families and women were required to remain in the domestic sphere and care for their children and make a home for their husbands. When men or women deviated from this model, they created a "deviant family" and also "undermine[d] the social system." Judy Root Aulette and Judith Wittner, *Gendered Worlds*, 2nd edn. (New York: Oxford University Press, 2012) 68–71.

The question for traditionalist scholars is not whether the marital relationship should be hierarchical—it must necessarily be so—but rather which spouse should manage the other. The unsurprising answer to this question is that men ought to rank above women. To justify this conclusion, traditionalist scholars provide their own take on the arguments of pre-colonial scholars. Men are essentially (u. *ghayr ikhtiyārī*) and naturally (u. *qudratī*) better suited to have authority over women because they have greater physical strength and intellectual capacity.[23] They are also more deserving of authority in marriage for acquired (u. *ikhtiyārī* and *kasbī*) reasons; in particular, husbands are financially responsible for wives, providing both dower (*mahr*) and maintenance (*nafaqa*).[24] According to Islahi, this entitles them to their wives' obedience and cooperation, given the rule that "the one who spends is superior."[25]

Qadi Sanaullah Panipati (d. 1810), a student of Shah Walīullah and an eminent legal scholar from the Subcontinent, offered a list of reasons for why men are superior to women.[26] This list brings to mind the lists offered by al-Zamakhsharī and al-Rāzī.[27] He wrote that evidence of the fact that men have been created superior to women can be found in the general characteristics of men, who as a gender, possess sound intellect (u. *kāmil-e-ʿaql*), good reasoning (u. *husn-e-tadbīr*), and excellence in knowledge (*ʿilm*) and body (u. *jism*). As a result of their greater abilities (u. *salahiyyat*), men are chosen for roles such as prophethood (u. *nabuwwat*), leadership (u. *imāmat*), guardianship (u. *wilāyat*), and judgment (*qaḍā'*), and are qualified to bear witness in cases of corporal (*ḥudūd*) punishment and retaliation (*qiṣāṣ*). Men are charged with the duty of *jihād*, delivering sermons, and leading prayer, and are obligated to attend the Friday

[23] Islahi (n 21) 2:291–2; Maududi (n 8) 1:349; and Shafi (n 4) 2:394–8.

[24] Islahi (n 21) 2:292; Panipati (n 14) 2:343; and Shafi (n 4) 2:394 and 401. Panipati used the words "u. *iṭāʿī*" and "u. *kasbī*" to differentiate between innate and acquired characteristics. Islahi said that men's capacity to provide for their wives financially is not coincidental (*ittifāqī*); only men are capable of doing this. Al-Qaradawi (n 20) 203 and 205.

[25] Shafi (n 4) 2:394. For Qutb the pivotal factor for deciding the correct role of men and women was children. He wrote, "What is even more important is that the child should receive the type of care which enables him or her to fulfill their social function in order to contribute to the betterment of human society, so as to leave it in a better state than they receive it. All this is particularly significant in explaining the importance of the family and the great care Islam takes to ensure its protection. With this in mind, the next verse makes it clear that the man is in charge of the family institution, as God has given him the necessary qualities and training to undertake this task and assigned to him the duty of meeting the family's living expenses. It also outlines man's additional task to protect the family against collapse as a result of fleeting whims, delineating the way to deal with these, should they occur." Qutb (n 3) 3:109–10. See also Israr Ahmed (n 2) and Maududi (n 8) 1:349.

[26] Islahi used the specific term "*bā-lā-tar*." Islahi (n 21) 2:291. See also Panipati (n 14) 2:343.

[27] Fakhr al-Dīn al-Rāzī, *al-Tafsīr al-kabīr* (Beirut: Dār Iḥyā' al-Turāth al-ʿArabī, 1997) 4:70 and Maḥmūd ibn ʿUmar al-Zamakhsharī, *al-Kashshāf ʿan ḥaqāʾiq ghawāmiḍ al-tanzīl wa-ʿuyūn al-aqāwīl fī wujūh al-taʾwīl* (Beirut: Dār al-Kutub al-ʿIlmiyya, 2003) 1:495.

(*jumūʿa*) and ʿĪd prayers. Men are also endowed with a privileged legal status, as they are allotted a greater portion in inheritance, are the master (u. *mālik*) in marriage, can have multiple wives, and have the unilateral option (u. *ikhtiyār*) to divorce. Their religious superiority is demonstrated by the basic fact that men can complete all prayers and fasting without interruption (u. *inqiṭāʿ*) due to menstruation or childbirth.[28]

Although this list sounds similar to those provided by pre-colonial scholars, it is not asserted with the same self-evident conviction in the post-colonial period. Traditionalist scholars such as Islahi, Maududi, Rida, and Shafi, acknowledge that though their comments about the superiority of men are generally applicable to the male gender, there are of course exceptions to this rule. An individual woman might be more intelligent than an individual man, for instance, but these exceptions are merely coincidental and do not significantly challenge the general observations about men and women. Furthermore, there are other variances between men and women in which women are superior, such as running a household and raising children. However, men excel over women in the characteristics that are relevant to leadership (*qiwāma*) over the household.[29]

Just as traditionalist scholars justify the preference (*faḍl*) of men through modern argumentation, their interpretations of the *qiwāma* of husbands over wives are likewise in line with the pre-colonial tradition, but their rationale continues to differ significantly.[30] Traditionalist scholars stress the principle of justice surrounding the "dual" roles of men and women,[31] expand the economic responsibilities of husbands, and

[28] Panipati (n 14) 2:343. Qutb and Rida offered their own lists of reasons for why men are ranked above women. Qutb mentioned that men are "tough" and make considered decisions, based on "proper thought and reflection." "These attributes are hard-wired in the constitution of men from the days of hunting and gathering, when men developed the skills of hunters, which make them perfect for earning their livelihoods and protecting women and children." Qutb (n 3) 3:111. Rida's list includes men's responsibility of *jihād*, maintenance, *mahr*, their legal rights to greater inheritance, and their natural (*aṣl al-khilqa*) superiority in physical strength (*quwwa*). Rida (n 5) 50.

[29] Islahi (n 21) 2:291; Maududi (n 8) 1:349; Rida (n 5) 52; and Shafi (n 4) 2:397.

[30] Shafaat has written, "From the statement that God has favoured men more than women in some ways we should not conclude, as many careless readers of the Qur'an do, that Islam views men superior to women. For this statement does not exclude the possibility that in some other ways women may be favoured more than men. Indeed observation shows that women are in general more patient, caring and have a more developed intuition than men." Shafaat (n 3). See also Qutb (n 3) 3:102–18.

[31] Qutb wrote, "God has created human beings as males and females, following the 'dual' rule which is central to the system of creation. He has given the woman the great tasks of childbearing, breast-feeding and looking after her children. These are not tasks which can be fulfilled without careful preparation, physically, psychologically, and mentally. It is only just, therefore, that the other part, i.e. the man, should be assigned the task of providing the essential needs and the protection required for the woman to fulfill her highly important duties. She could not be given all those tasks and still be required to work in order to earn her living. It is only fair as well that the man be given the physical, mental and psychological qualities

emphasize the weightiness of the economic burden carried by husbands.[32] Traditionalist scholars also counsel husbands to avoid oppressing their wives. Panipati wrote that men are the protectors (u. *muḥāfaz*), overseers (u. *nigrān*), and guardians of their wives, and thus they are required to help and support them.[33] As a result, he and Shafi believed that husbands must attend to the well-being (u. *maṣāliḥ*), education (u. *tadbīr*), and disciplining of their wives (u. *ta'dīb*). They are to provide for all of their wives' necessities (u. *dharūrat*) as well as comfort (u. *arām*). They may not use their authority to create sorrow for their wives, but rather they ought to seek their wives' counsel and follow religious laws (u. *qānūn shar'ī*) when making decisions for their households.[34] In exchange, righteous wives should accept (u. *taslīm*) their husbands' authority (u. *ḥākimiyyat*), be extremely (u. *nahāyat*) and "willingly"[35] obedient (u. *farmān bardār*), protect their chastity (u. *sharam ghāh*, lit. trans. "places of shame") and innocence (u. *'iṣmat*), avoid what their husbands dislike, and keep their husbands' secrets.[36] Farhat Hashmi, the conservative Pakistani Islamic

which enable him to fulfill his duties in the same way as the woman is given the abilities to fulfill hers. All this is clearly seen in real human life, because God maintains absolute justice among all." He went on to say that women's tenderness is not a "superficial" attribute but is "implanted in the woman's physical, mental and psychological constitution. Some leading scientists believe that they are present in each cell in the woman's constitution, because they are rooted in the first cell that multiplies to form the fetus and the child." Qutb (n 3) 3:110–11.

[32] Islahi described a man's guardianship and responsibility to provide for his wife and children as falling entirely on the husband's "head." Islahi (n 21) 2:292. See also Shafi (n 4) 2:397.

[33] Panipati (n 14) 2:342; Islamweb team, "Explanation of Surah al-Nisa': 4:34," <http://www.islamweb.net/emainpage/index.php?page=showfatwa&Option=FatwaId&Id=84120> (last accessed Jan. 25, 2013); and Shafaat (n 3).

[34] Panipati (n 14) 2:342 and Shafi (n 4) 2:397.

[35] Qutb wrote, "It is, then, in the nature of the righteous, believing woman and part of her essential characteristics to be devoted and obedient. Devotion means willing obedience, motivated by love, not the sort of obedience enforced against one's will. Hence, the Qur'ān uses the term 'devout', or *qānitāt* to stress its pleasant psychological connotations, which fit perfectly with the sort of affectionate and compassionate relationship which exists between man and woman, the two parts of the single soul from which all mankind descend. Islam stresses that this relationship is essential in the family home where young ones are reared." Qutb (n 3) 3:112–13.

[36] Israr Ahmed, in an especially modern and misogynistic move, acknowledged that women's inferior status might cause them suffering (u. *ṣadma*). However, he claimed that for this very reason, God created women with a material that makes them forgetful (u. *nisyān ka madda*) so they will not suffer as a result of their lower status. For Israr Ahmed, this explained why the witness of two women is the equivalent of one man. He also stated that a wife must protect three things in her husband's absence: her husband's wealth, his secrets, and her chastity, because the chastity (u. *'izzat*) of a wife belongs to her husband. Israr Ahmed (n 2). See also Islahi (n 21) 2:292; Maududi (n 8) 1:349; Rida (n 5) 53; and Shafi (n 4) 2:398–9. Shafi cited a unique *ḥadīth* to emphasize this point. The *ḥadīth* states, "The Prophet, may God be pleased with him, said that a woman who is obedient and submissive to her husband, receives the prayers of the birds in the air, fish in the sea, angels in the heavens, and beasts in the jungle."

scholar and preacher, teaches women to be "humble" and submissive (u. *ājzī ikhtiyār karayn*) to their husbands.[37]

When describing the appropriate role of wives, traditionalist scholars repeat pre-colonial views, but once again, they situate these positions in the modern world. Although all traditionalist scholars maintain that it is the duty of wives to obey their husbands, they restrict the acquiescence of wives to what is right and proper. Maududi wrote that wives must disobey their husbands if they are asked to break God's laws or to undertake any action that is "un-Islamic."[38] When the decrees of husbands and God diverge, obedience to God takes precedence over obedience to husbands.[39] By trusting wives with the ability to discern when they should (dis) obey their husbands, traditionalist scholars break from the position of pre-colonial scholars, who did not dwell extensively on the possibility of a wife disobeying her husband in order to obey God. This departure from the pre-colonial Islamic tradition is important because it reduces the role of husbands as mediators of their wives' relationships with God, though it does not eliminate that role altogether. The relationship of a wife with God continues to be mediated by her husband, because she is still not authorized to undertake any supererogatory devotional act without her husband's permission. A wife's obedience to her husband is still seen as an act of worship (u.*ʿibādat*), while displeasing him constitutes a major sin.[40]

In this framework, as in the pre-colonial explications of the patriarchal idealized cosmology, wives who resist, oppose (u. *mukhālifat*), challenge,[41] or disobey (u. *nā farmānī, ʿiṣyān*) their husbands are charged with wifely *nushūz*.[42] Wifely *nushūz* is described as a wife's carelessness

[37] Farhat Hashmi, "Tafseer: Surah Nisāʾ 33–35" (audio), <http://www.farhathashmi.com/quran/tafsir/> (last accessed Jan. 25, 2013).

[38] Maududi (n 8) 1:349. Ibn Adam has added that a wife does not have to obey her husband if she is harmed by obeying him or if her own rights are violated. Interestingly, in his *fatwās*, he insists that a wife should obey her husband in all the matters that were considered by pre-colonial scholars—ie, sexual intimacy, supererogatory devotions, leaving the house without his permission, and letting those whom he dislikes into their home. However, he does not uphold the obedience of a wife in other examples that were not considered by pre-colonial scholars; eg, a wife does not have to obey her husband in buying a more expensive soap or cooking a particular dish. Ibn Adam, Question # 07275472 (n 3). See also Islam Q &A Team, "His Wife is Not Very Interested in Intercourse...," <http://islamonline.com/news/articles/3/His_wife_is_not_very_interested_in_intercourse_so_.html> (last accessed Dec. 21, 2012); and Shafaat (n 3).

[39] Maududi (n 8) 1:349.

[40] Maududi (n 8) 1:349 and Ashraf Ali Thanvi, *Bayān al-Qurʾān* (Multan: Idara ta'lifāt Ashrafiyya, n.d.) 173–4.

[41] Islahi used the Urdu transliteration of the English word "challenge." Islahi (n 21) 2:293.

[42] Eg, see Islahi (n 21) 2:292–3; Shafi (n 4) 2:399; and Islam Q & A, "Husband Forcing His Wife to Have Intercourse," <http://islamqa.info/en/ref/33597/> (last accessed Jan. 16, 2013).

(u. *lā-parwāhi*) in her husband's absence, dishonesty, obstinacy (u. *haṭ-darmī*), rudeness (u. *bad-tamīzī*), disrespectful behavior, persistence in bad habits, contemptuous behavior, disregard for marital obligations, sexual lewdness, extreme refractoriness, rejection of reasonable requests, threat to the peace of the house, and endangerment of family life.[43] A *nāshiza* disrupts the governance of the house, is rebellious and arrogant, makes married life difficult, engages in deliberate ill-conduct, is willfully defiant and sexually disobedient, and in general displays bad attitude (*bad-damāghī*, lit. bad-brain).[44] She engages in supererogatory devotional acts and leaves her house without her husband's permission. A *nāshiza* wife also abandons her religious obligations, such as her daily prayers and fasting in the month of Ramadan, and refuses to purify herself after sex and/or menstruation—if she is Muslim.[45] Islahi expanded the political undertones of the marital relationship by describing wifely *nushūz* as rebelliousness (u. *sarkashī* and u. *sartābī*) and mutiny (u. *baghāwat*).[46] A *nāshiza* is sometimes portrayed with pre-colonial descriptors as someone who raises herself (*tastaʿlī, irtifāʿ*) over her husband or, as in Qutb's case, with new characterizations, such as someone who accentuates herself (*tabarraz*) or revolts (*tamarrud*) against her husband.[47]

Although many of the descriptors of wifely *nushūz* replicate pre-colonial renditions of such behavior, post-colonial portrayals of wifely *nushūz* are informed by and respond to the discourse of feminism. For example, Islahi wrote,

> the [women] who are lobbying that they will not be women but rather men in every aspect of life, they are not righteous (u. *ṣāliḥāt*), but rather transgressors (u. *fāsiqāt*). They seek to overturn the [divine] order (u. *niẓām*) on which the blessings and happiness of a family life depends.[48]

[43] Israr Ahmed (n 2); Islahi (n 21) 2:292; Qutb (n 3) 3:113–14; and Shafi (n 4) 2:398.

[44] Abdul Qadir Awda, *al-Tashrīʿ al-Jināʾī al-Islāmī* (Cairo: Dār al-turāth, 1985) 1:157; Panipati (n 14) 2:344; al-Qaradawi (n 20) 204–5; Shafaat (n 3); Shafi (n 4) 2:394; and Thanvi (n 40) 174.

[45] Awda restricted this definition of wifely *nushūz* to a Muslim wife. Awda (n 44) 2:67–8. See also al-Qaradawi (n 20) 206.

[46] Islahi (n 21) 2:292.

[47] Hashmi describes wifely *nushūz* as a wife raising her head or herself (u. *ūpar uṭhnā*). Hashmi (n 37). *Tamarrud* can mean "refractoriness, recalcitrance and disobedience," but these carry political undertones, since other translations of *tamarrud* are "uprising, insurrection, mutiny, revolt and rebellion." Hans Wehr, *The Hans Wehr Dictionary of Modern Written Arabic* (ed. J. M. Cowan) (Ithaca: Spoken Languages Services Inc., 1994). Syed Qutb, *Fī Ẓilāl al-Qurʾān*, 4:24–34, <http://altafsir.com/Tafasir.asp?tMadhNo=0&tTafsirNo=53&tSoraNo=4&tAyahNo=34&tDisplay=yes&UserProfile=0&LanguageId=1> (last accessed Jan. 25, 2013).

[48] Islahi (n 21) 2:292. Rida also mentioned "women these days," who do not keep their husbands' secrets and do not protect the unseen. Rida (n 5) 54.

Islahi explicitly acknowledged what many traditionalist scholars imply: that Muslim women who challenge a patriarchal arrangement in marriage or society at large are actually questioning God's social ordering, and in doing so, they herald social chaos.

Breaking from pre-colonial scholars, traditionalist scholars add two dimensions to their discussions of wifely *nushūz*. They describe wifely behavior that does *not* qualify as *nushūz*; and they outline behavior that is forbidden to husbands. Islahi, for example, wrote that wifely *nushūz* is not a wife's "every laziness, carelessness, irresponsibility, and expression of her opinion or taste."[49] Also, husbands are not allowed to behave like petty tyrants and abuse their authority over their wives. In a legal exchange concerning the rights of an incompetent husband over his skillful wife, Ibn Adam has argued that a wife's obedience to her husband does not encompass small matters, such as the color of socks she wears, the kind of soap she buys, or the food she cooks. A husband ought to appreciate his wife's work at home and seek to be a means of comfort for her. And although wifely *nushūz* includes a wife's sexual refusal of her husband, this is only the case if she refuses him without a good excuse. However, if she is sick, cannot "bear" having sex, is harmed by intercourse, or is menstruating, then she is permitted to refuse her husband. Husbands should understand that their wives are not "machines" and are prohibited from demanding "too much sex" from their wives such that it becomes harmful for them. However, since it is also prohibited for husbands to masturbate, wives must permit their husbands to enjoy them from over their clothing.[50]

Like pre-colonial scholars, traditionalist scholars understand the *qiwāma* of men over women as translating into disciplinary privilege for husbands over wives. The disciplinary tools or "treatments"[51] available to husbands are admonishment, abandonment, and physical violence.[52] Panipati described admonishment as husbands reminding their wives of their own rights over them and frightening (u. *ḍaraw*) them of God's reach

[49] Islahi (n 21) 2:292–3.

[50] Ibn Adam has said that wives can orally relieve their husbands; however, they are not permitted to swallow "the filth," unless it affects their marriage, in which case they may swallow the fluid. While some traditionalist scholars categorically prohibit marital rape, others leave some room for its possibility, even while voicing strong discouragement. Ibn Adam has written that a husband cannot force himself on his wife if she has a legitimate reason for not having sex, which leaves open the possibility of raping a woman if she refuses her husband without reasonable cause. He makes interesting use of a prophetic report to discourage husbands from raping their wives. In this report, the angels are said to curse the woman whose husband is displeased with her. Ibn Adam points out that if husbands were permitted to rape their wives, then there would be no reason for a husband to spend the night in a sexually frustrated state. Ibn Adam, Question # 07335282 (n 3).

[51] Qutb (n 3) 3:113.

[52] Panipati (n 14) 2:344–5 and Rida (n 5) 55.

(u. *pakaṛ*).[53] Hashmi has characterized admonishment as gentle and loving persuasion,[54] while Islahi portrayed it as advice (u. *nasihat, mawʿiẓa*) or reasoning, and threatening or accusatory (u. *malāmat*) speech.[55] The traditionalist interpretation of admonishment is distinctly post-colonial in two ways. First, traditionalists like Ahmad Shafaat, a lecturer at Concordia University, emphasize that in order for husbands to be able to admonish their wives effectively, husbands must first cultivate a strong moral character themselves. Otherwise, a wife might use her husband's immoral behavior as an excuse for disobedience.[56] Second, traditionalist scholars interpret admonishment at least partially as "reasoning." Wives are not simply to be reminded or warned but reasoned with (u. *samjhao*).[57] Examples of such reasoning include inviting wives to think about their children, who might be harmed by disharmony between the spouses.[58] Shafi wrote that the desired outcome of admonishment is a wife's mental rectification, which will save wives from sin (u. *gunā*), men from heartache (u. *qalbī aziyyat*) and pain, and further, both spouses will be spared sorrow and unhappiness (u. *ranj-o-gham*).[59] Thus admonishment is obligatory (*wājib*) on the husband, who is the "lord of the family" (*rabb l-usra*).[60]

As with admonishment, abandonment is interpreted by traditionalist scholars in a manner that upholds the historical interpretations of this imperative and supplement it with modern meanings. Historically, abandonment could be sexual, verbal, or both.[61] In traditionalist writings, there is a marked emphasis on the location of a wife's abandonment. Traditionalist scholars stress that wives are to be abandoned only in their homes, which according to Shafi, will increase their sorrow and reduce the danger (u. *andaysha*) of corruption (u. *fasād*).[62] The emphasis on abandoning wives in the homes creates an image of women as endlessly in danger of committing adultery, since it generates the expectation that if wives were abandoned outside the home, they might be sexually

[53] Maududi (n 8) 1:349; Panipati (n 14) 2:344; Qutb (n 3) 3:114; Shafaat (n 3); Al-Qaradawi (n 20) 205–6.

[54] Hashmi (n 37). [55] Islahi (n 21) 2:293.

[56] Shafaat has written, "Such admonition however, will be effective only if the husband has a good character, at least in comparison with the wife. Otherwise, the wife can say to him, either in her heart or aloud, 'Look who is talking'." Shafaat (n 3).

[57] Hashmi (n 37); Maududi (n 8) 1:349; Panipati (n 14) 2:342; al-Qaradawi (n 20) 205; Shafaat (n 3); and Shafi (n 4) 2:399.

[58] Shafaat (n 3). [59] Shafi (n 4) 2:402. [60] Qutb (n 47).

[61] Hashmi has actually referred to this as "u. *kuṭṭī*," emphasizing the verbal nature of abandonment, especially in contrast to the loving advice prescribed in admonishment. She has also said that husbands can leave the room, in addition to the marital bed during abandonment. Hashmi (n 37). See also Islahi (n 21) 2:293; Panipati (n 14) 2:344–5; al-Qaradawi (n 20) 205; Qutb (n 3) 3:114; Shafaat (n 3); and Shafi (n 4) 2:399–400.

[62] Shafi (n 4) 2:399.

disloyal. Panipati and Qutb additionally limited abandonment to beds and places of intimacy (u. *khawāb gāhon*,[63] *makān al-khalwa*[64]) and specified that abandonment should not be carried out in front of strangers or one's children.[65] The desired outcome of abandonment is the expression of a husband's displeasure (u. *nā rāzgī*)[66] with his wife, an awakening of her "agreeable feminine nature" so that serenity might be restored to the house,[67] and to help her understand that if she does not change her behavior she will face grave consequences.[68] Abdul Qadir Awda (d. 1956), a famous Egyptian jurist, argued that abandonment is meant to be punitive,[69] while Qutb insisted that abandonment should not be humiliating for a wife, since what is intended is a cure for *nushūz*.[70] An interesting difference between pre- and post-colonial discussions of abandonment is that traditionalist scholars do not assume husbands to be polygamous. As such, they underline the importance of a husband's control over his own sexual desires in order to effectively abandon his wife.[71] If a husband is sexually weak, he will not be able to follow through with sexual abandonment; instead, he will either capitulate to his wife or commit a sin, such as masturbation or adultery. Unlike pre-colonial scholars, none of the traditionalist scholars examined for this study consider the possibility of a husband simply bedding a concubine or another wife while abandoning a *nāshiza* wife.

Traditionalist discussions concerning the right of husbands to hit their wives are complex and intriguing. In the end, however, traditionalist scholars uphold the pre-colonial position that husbands are permitted to hit their wives.[72] Hashmi has interpreted the imperative form of "hit them" as permissive in case of a necessity (u. *ḍarūrat*),[73] while Panipati insisted

[63] Literally, "places of dreams." Panipati (n 14) 2:342. [64] Qutb (n 47).

[65] Qutb wrote, "It is in bed that a woman's temptation is most effective. A rebellious, self-conscious woman exercises her true power. When a man is able to overcome this temptation, he deprives the woman of her most effective weapon. In the majority of cases, a woman becomes more ready to give way when the man demonstrates a good measure of will-power in the most difficult of situations." Qutb (n 3) 3:115.

[66] Shafi (n 4) 2:399. [67] Al-Qaradawi (n 20) 205. [68] Islahi (n 21) 2:293.

[69] Awda (n 44) 1:157. To this end, he cited Q. 10:118, which describes the three companions who did not participate in battle and for whom the Earth became constricted. "And to the three also (did He turn in mercy) who were left behind, when the earth, vast as it is, become straitened for them, and their own souls were straitened for them till they bethought them that there is no refuge from Allah save toward Him. Then turned He unto them in mercy that they (too) might turn (repentant unto Him). Lo! Allah! He is the Relenting, the Merciful." Yusuf Ali (n 12) Q. 9:118.

[70] Qutb (n 3) 3:115. [71] Shafaat (n 3).

[72] Awda said that husbands are obligated or mandated to execute their disciplinary duties. Awda (n 44) 1:157.

[73] Hashmi underscores the optional nature of hitting and takes up Qutb's description of the disciplining of wives as a cure. She has described hitting as a medicine for a disease. Since hitting is a dispensation (u. *rukhsat*), not an order (u. *ḥukm*), it is only meant to be

that it is a command.[74] Traditionalist discussions reproduce pre-colonial readings of "hit them" yet argue for novel ways to understand and apply the phrase. Panipati, for instance, relied on the pre-colonial Islamic tradition for authority in his interpretation of Q. 4:34 but broke from pre-colonial interpretations of *wa-ḍribūhunna* to expand its meaning. He suggested that a husband's beating of his wife cannot and should not be restricted by any qualification. He contended that pre-colonial scholars who restricted the physical discipline of husbands to *ghayr mubarriḥ*, which he translated as "without causing too much pain," violated the intended meaning of the divine text. He acknowledged that all or most pre-colonial scholars restricted the right of husbands to hit wives to *ghayr mubarriḥ* hitting, but this did not deter him from disagreeing with the tradition. Since the Qur'anic text does not restrict the right of husbands to hit their wives by qualifying the imperative "hit them" in any way, Panipati felt that a scholar would need a great deal of evidence to restrict the meaning of this imperative. According to Panipati, pre-colonial scholars restricted the hitting of wives to non-extreme hitting based on the farewell sermon, which Panipati classified as having a weak transmission (*isnād*). Since a weak transmission cannot amend the meaning of the Qur'anic text, he insisted that a husband is required to beat his wife in a manner that is commensurate with her disobedience or crime (u. *jurm*).[75] Panipati's treatment of *wa-ḍribūhunna* brings into sharp relief a hermeneutical strategy that is common amongst traditionalist scholars: his reliance on the Islamic tradition did not prevent him from presenting an innovative interpretation of the Qur'anic text as being more authoritative than the pre-colonial tradition on which he based his own authority.

Other traditionalist scholars agree that husbands are permitted to hit (u. *mār pīṭ*,[76] u. *jismānī sazā*[77]) their wives if necessary (u. *majbūrī*) to deter them from *nushūz*. Islahi, like pre-colonial scholars, believed that the analogy of a husband hitting his wife with a teacher hitting a student was particularly relevant.[78] If light or honorable (u. *sharīfāna*) hitting is effective, then husbands should avoid harsh beating.[79] Traditionalist

used in small "doses," as a light "shock" administered to save a marriage. Hashmi (n 37). See also Rida (n 5) 57.

[74] "Beating is among the requirements of being a protector and maintainer of the wife." Islamweb team (n 33). Hashmi has insisted that the three steps must be followed sequentially and argues that various people respond differently to each step. Some women will correct their behavior based on loving advice, while others require more firm measures, such as abandonment and hitting. Hashmi (n 37).

[75] Panipati (n 14) 2:345. [76] Shafi (n 4) 2:400 and 402. [77] Islahi (n 21) 2:293.

[78] Islahi (n 21) 2:293.

[79] Shafi (n 4) 2:402. He described the optimal physical violence as "u. *ma'mūlī*," meaning "customary," describing its limits as a beating that does not leave a mark (u. *athar*) or wound (u. *zakham*).

scholars offer varied interpretations regarding the amount of hitting permissible. While scholars like Panipati hold that the hitting should be unrestricted, other scholars allow for moderate or extremely restricted hitting. Scholars such as Israr Ahmed, Hashmi, and al-Qaradawi insist that hitting is always meant to be non-extreme and ought not to leave physical marks. Husbands are not permitted to hit their wives in the face, cause bodily harm, hit sensitive parts, or batter their wives.[80] The non-extreme (*ghayr mubarriḥ*) nature of hitting means that the hitting should be carried out with a "folded handkerchief" or with a *miswāk*, which husbands can use to "gently tap their wives."[81] While some traditionalist scholars stipulate that husbands can hit their wives with a stick, whip, board, or any other instrument that would cause injury, a minority of scholars, including Awda, have been comfortable with a greater degree of hitting, allowing husbands to beat their wives with sticks (*ʿasā*), whips (*jald*), or switches (*sawṭ*).[82] Still, most of the scholars in this study agree that a husband's hitting cannot result in broken bones, wounds, or bruises; hitting is not meant to seriously hurt wives, and it should not be without compassion (u. *bay rahmī*).[83]

In general, beating is seen by traditionalists as a last-ditch effort to save a marriage, so it is not meant to be continual or regular. Hitting one's wife to save a marriage might seem paradoxical, but none of the scholars who have made this point recognize this as a paradox. For example, Hashmi accepts as fact that hitting can be an effective tool for creating marital harmony and, based on this fact, asserts that if beating does not save a marriage, then that is a clear indication that a wife is no longer under her husband's control, and at this point, external help must be brought in through the process of arbitration.[84] Traditionalists also disagree about whether hitting is meant to be symbolic or punitive. Those who argue that a husband's beating of his wife is meant to be symbolic rather than punitive make a distinction between hitting and violence. They see Q. 4:34 as allowing husbands to hit their wives in a moderate manner, but not as condoning violence.[85] In contrast, scholars who argue that the hitting should be punitive

[80] Israr Ahmed (n 2); Hashmi (n 37); and al-Qaradawi (n 20) 205.

[81] See Umar, "Rebuttal to Qur'an on Beating Wives," <http://www.answering-christianity.com/umar/beating_rebuttal.htm> (last accessed July 12, 2013).

[82] Awda (n 44) 1:157.

[83] Islahi (n 21) 2:293; Maududi (n 8) 1:350; Shafaat (n 3); al-Qaradawi (n 20) 205–6; and Thanvi (n 40).

[84] Hashmi (n 37). Shafaat also misrepresents the pre-colonial tradition, arguing that wives were under no obligation to "take" the beating and could divorce their husbands at any point. Hence, he implies that if a wife tolerates her husband's beating then it is consensual. Shafaat (n 3). See also Islahi (n 21) 2:293.

[85] See Umar (n 81).

contend that the hitting should be proportional to the desired punishment, and reducing it to a set of symbolic measures renders it meaningless.[86] For these scholars, the harm of moderate hitting is negligible in comparison to the social trauma of divorce.

Traditionalists sometimes consider the case of an abusive husband who hits his wife excessively or for unwarranted reasons. In such circumstances, Ibn Baaz (d. 1999), the Grand Mufti of Saudi Arabia, encouraged a wife to choose one of two options. The first is to use her wealth to ransom herself from her husband and seek divorce. However, this might be harmful for their children, so it is preferable that she choose the second option: to be patient and remain with her husband, pray for his guidance, and repent for any sin she might have committed that resulted in her being married to an abusive man. Wives are promised greater reward for following this avenue. However, if a husband abandons prayer or curses the religion of Islam, then he is considered an apostate, and his wife is required to divorce him.[87] The logic of these opinions suggests that it is better for wives to remain married to physically and emotionally abusive husbands than for them to be married to husbands who hold incorrect religious beliefs.

Finally, in a squarely post-colonial move, traditionalists grapple with an interlocutor who might judge them for adhering to a religion that permits husbands to hit their wives. This interlocutor is personified either as a Christian missionary or an enemy of Islam who is trying to make Muslims lose confidence in their own religion. They defend Q. 4:34—and Islam—against this antagonistic interlocutor by pointing out that the hitting permitted in the verse is not meant to be torturous or humiliating. There are clear guidelines about how a husband might hit his wife, and in general, hitting is discouraged. However, some, such as Israr Ahmed, are also uncomfortable overemphasizing the restrictions on hitting, since this may indicate that they are ashamed of the Qur'anic text.[88]

Traditionalists use two strategies to both assert and defend the right of husbands to physically discipline their wives. One strategy is to produce statistics or make claims about the widespread phenomenon of domestic

[86] Shafaat (n 3).

[87] Eg, see Ibn Baaz, "My husband does not treat me in a good and proper fashion," <http://www.fatwa-online.com/fataawa/marriage/maritalrelations/0000206_5.htm> (last accessed Jan. 25, 2013) and Ibn Baaz, "My husband curses and abuses me," <http://www.fatwa-nline.com/fataawa/marriage/maritalrelations/0000206_6.htm> (last accessed Jan. 25, 2013).

[88] Israr Ahmed asserted that "these are God's words, we are not embarrassed by them." Israr Ahmed (n 2) and Shafaat (n 3). Hashmi offers a unique twist on the occasion of revelation surrounding Q. 4:34. She has said that Ḥabība was denied retribution by this verse because if she had hit her husband, she would have been abused further (u. *awrat mār kar ziyāda mār khai gī*). Hashmi (n 37).

violence in liberal democracies.[89] By showing that wife battering, family violence, and the physical abuse of wives is commonplace in "Western society,"[90] they seek to delegitimize the moral high ground of their Western interlocutor and demonstrate that this problem is Western rather than Islamic.[91] In this strategy, the primary concern of scholars is to protect and save Islam from being sullied rather than to protect and save Muslim women from marital violence. A second maneuver is to make claims about women's "nature" that justify the right of husbands to hit their wives. Al-Qaradawi has argued that some women—though not all women—enjoy and/or need (*yaḥtāj*) to be hit.[92] These women need to see a display of their husbands' physical strength in order to mend their ways. Maududi and Qutb cited practical and psychological reasons for why a wife might need beating in order to be brought back in line.[93] Shafaat has written that seeing an

[89] "The religious permission for a husband to beat his wife is conditioned upon strict rules and permitted on a very limited scale. Therefore, it is very rare for a husband to beat his wife. The evidence about this is that according to reliable and trustworthy statistics published by the west, women in western societies are physically abused in large numbers compared to Muslim societies." Islamweb team, "Explanation of Surah al-Nisa': 4:34" (n 33).

[90] In traditionalist texts, "Western society" is spoken of as a simple, undifferentiated, monolithic category, in much the same way as "Muslims" or the "Muslim world" are portrayed in neo-conservative political circles in Western countries. For an excellent example of this, listen to Hashmi (n 37). After briefly interpreting Q. 4:34, Hashmi and another (unidentified) woman list detailed statistics about domestic violence as reported by the U.S. Department of Justice. They enumerate these statistics at length, discussing them for a longer period of time than Hashmi's exegesis of Q. 4:34.

[91] Badawi has written, "This makes it clear that even this extreme, last resort, and 'lesser of the two evils' measure that may save a marriage does not meet the definitions of 'physical abuse', 'family violence', or 'wife battering' in the 20th century law in liberal democracies, where such extremes are so commonplace that they are seen as national concerns." Jamal Badawi, "Wife Beating?," <http://islamic-world.net/sister/wife_beating.htm> (last accessed Jan. 16, 2013).

[92] On his highly rated television show, *Sharīʿa and Life*, al-Qaradawi said, "Beating is not suitable for every wife; it is suitable for certain wives and for other wives it is not. There is a woman who cannot agree to being beaten, and sees this as humiliation, while some women enjoy the beating and for them, only beating to cause them sorrow is suitable." (Oct. 15, 1997)

[93] Maududi wrote, "Some women are not corrected without beating." Maududi (n 8) 1:350. Qutb wrote, "Practical and psychological indications suggest that in certain situations this measure [ie beating] may be the appropriate one to remedy a certain perversion and to bring about satisfaction. Even when such a pathological perversion exists, a woman may not sufficiently feel the man's strength for her to accept his authority within the family, at least not unless he overcomes her physically. This is by no means applicable to all women. What we are saying is that such women do exist and that Islam considers this measure a last resort used necessarily to safeguard the family. We have to remember here that these measures are stipulated by the Creator, who knows His creation. No counter argument is valid against what the One who knows all and is aware of all things says. Indeed to stand against what God legislates may lead to a rejection of the faith altogether. What we have to understand is that God has laid down these measures within a context that describes, in absolute clarity, their nature and aim and the intention behind them." Qutb (n 3) 3:115–16. See also Shafaat (n 3).

"energetic demonstration" of her husband's "anger, frustration, or love" can help return such a woman to her husband's obedience. He uses movies as evidence of this point, declaring that as long as there is an "undercurrent of love," no harm will be done to women through such beating.[94] Further, although he admits to having no statistics to back up his claim, Shafaat is confident that Muslim men hit their wives much less than non-Muslim men.[95]

In summary, traditionalists uphold the pre-colonial permission for husbands to hit their wives for disciplinary purposes, albeit through different arguments. Most scholars restrict the kind of beating that is available to husbands, though some scholars oppose any restriction on the potential for marital violence outlined in Q. 4:34. Although the arguments they use reflect post-colonial concerns and methodologies, ultimately they support a patriarchal cosmology. Traditionalists expend great effort in defending this cosmology against the anticipated criticisms of an egalitarian cosmology, thereby preserving the pre-colonial plain-sense reading of the Qur'anic text in which they ground their own authority.

NEO-TRADITIONALISTS: CLINGING TO PRE-COLONIAL PLAIN-SENSE INTERPRETATIONS

Neo-traditionalist scholars are in the unenviable position of trying to balance the authority of a patriarchal tradition while appealing to communities whose members espouse gender-egalitarian values. However, since the patriarchal and egalitarian cosmologies are fundamentally irreconcilable, one must supersede the other. For neo-traditionalist scholars, the scales ultimately tip in the favor of the former, and in the end, they carve out a space in which husbands can ethically hit their wives. One of

[94] Shafaat writes, "To be effective in its purpose of shaking the wife out of her nasty mood it is important that [the beating] should provide an energetic demonstration of the anger, frustration and love of the husband. In other words, [the beating] should neither seriously hurt the wife nor reduce it to a set of meaningless motions devoid of emotions." In footnote 5 he writes, "In movies, for example, one often sees the following type of scene: a man and a woman love each other but in some matter the woman simply does not want to listen to the man even though she realizes deep down that he is thinking for the good of both of them. The man tries all the tender ways to bring the woman around to his point of view without any success. Frustrated, the man at last bursts into anger and gives the woman a slap. This shakes the woman out of her mood and she falls on his shoulders, with both happier than before. Of course, movies are no guide for us but sometimes they do represent human nature and life as it is." Shafaat (n 3).

[95] Shafaat writes, "No statistics exist, but I feel confident that if we research the behavior of men in different religious groups over a long enough period and a vast enough area of the globe, we will find that the incidents of cases of wife battering and other forms of cruelty to women have been less, both in terms of numbers and seriousness, among Muslims than in other groups." Shafaat (n 3).

the ways that they soften the rough edges of a patriarchal cosmology is by promoting a model of gender complementarity rather than gender equality. Neo-traditionalist scholars reformulate pre-colonial and traditionalist discourses of the superior qualities of men over women by advancing the view that men and women are special in their own ways, and while men might appear to have advantage in the social realm, women are spiritually ascendant.[96] It is of no use for the genders to compete for authority or importance, because each has his/her own place in society, which has been appointed by God. In this way, although a patriarchal cosmology is maintained, its logic is significantly altered, since the worth of each human being, regardless of gender, is valued.

To briefly review, the pre-colonial patriarchal cosmology influences the Islamic legal and exegetical discourse of Q. 4:34 in two important ways: it determines the plain-sense meaning of the imperative *wa-ḍribūhunna* as "hit them [wives]," and it also affects the legal and ethical discussions surrounding the application and procedure of hitting wives for disciplinary purposes. Neo-traditionalist scholars, for whom a patriarchal cosmology is an uncomfortable fit, are willing to ignore or abandon the surrounding legal and ethical considerations of the Islamic tradition regarding the right of husbands to hit wives. They disregard the discussions of retaliation for excessive marital violence, and they seek to restrict the hitting of wives to a purely symbolic act. Although they are willing to diverge from the Islamic tradition's legal conclusions surrounding wife-beating, they accept the Islamic tradition's plain-sense meaning of the Qur'anic text, where *wa-ḍribūhunna* is interpreted as "hit them [wives]." They cannot imagine the text of Q. 4:34 to have any meaning other than sanctioning husbands to hit their wives, even if this is permitted only in extremely restricted circumstances and only in a symbolic manner. Hence, adherence to the pre-colonial Islamic tradition's interpretation of *wa-ḍribūhunna* as "hit them [wives]" is the most emblematic position of neo-traditionalist scholars, who may lean heavily toward an egalitarian cosmology but still manage to create an ethical space for husbands to hit wives. They are forced to do this because they take the Islamic tradition's interpretation of *wa-ḍribūhunna* as representative of divine intent, and at times, they appear trapped by this

[96] Abdullah Adhami has pointed out that "The word *shams* (sun) is feminine, and *qamar* (moon) is masculine. The sun burns itself out to give light and life to everything around, and the *moon* is *muneer*, meaning it reflects the light. Within itself it has no light; it radiates the brilliance of the sun. So when we shine as men, the implication is that we are reflecting the glorious light of our women..." Abdullah Adhami, "Shams (sun) and Qamar (moon)," <http://healing-hearts-blog.com/category/shaykh-abdullah-adhami/> (last accessed Jan. 16, 2013).

interpretation, and though they display overt discomfort with this meaning, it ultimately leads them to conclude that husbands may hit wives.

Although neo-traditionalist scholars maintain the pre-colonial patriarchal cosmology, their attempt to balance this cosmology with an egalitarian one means that they engage in intricate hermeneutic acrobatics to uphold both at the same time. This is illustrated through their description of an ideal marital relationship, the degree of men over women in Q. 2:228, their interpretation of *qawwāmūn* husbands and obedient wives, their definition of wifely *nushūz*, and their understanding of the three disciplinary measures in Q. 4:34. At times, this balancing act leads neo-traditionalist scholars to misrepresent the "Islamic" tradition, claiming it to say things it does not say or softening the patriarchy of pre-colonial scholars.[97]

Neo-traditionalist scholars describe an ideal marriage as one that is premised on love and harmony, positing Q. 30:21 as the necessary context for understanding Q. 4:34. Q. 30:21 reads, "And among His Signs is this, that He created for you mates from among yourselves, that ye may dwell in tranquility with them, and He has put love and mercy between your (hearts); verily in that are Signs for those who reflect."[98] Faraz Rabbani, the Toronto-based Islamic scholar and educational director of the online forum SeekersGuidance, has further claimed (without reference) that the Qur'ān encourages spouses to "communicate," "consult in positive ways," and have "reciprocal sexual rights" that fulfill each other's "spiritual, emotional, and physical" needs.[99] It is not readily apparent which verses in particular he is referencing here, since no Qur'anic verse actually says these things outright. Rabbani attributes these ideas to the Qur'ān itself because he aims to portray the Qur'ān and Western ideals of marriage as somewhat harmonious. This reasoning is supported by the fact that he asserts that "Western sources" confirm the vision of a mutually beneficial marriage

[97] Hamza Yusuf illustrates this point well. Regarding the meaning of wifely *nushūz*, he has stated that all the "exegetes (*mufassirūn*)" agree that wifely *nushūz* is a woman's "gross disobedience" to Allah and not her disobedience to her husband. However, as we saw in Chapter 2, most exegetes define wifely *nushūz* as her disobedience to her husband and God. Hamza Yusuf cites Ibn ʿĀshūr's *tafsīr*, using it to buttress his own claims; however, Ibn ʿĀshūr's *tafsīr* states that "Most jurists (*fuqahā*) said that *nushūz* is a woman's disobedience (*ʿiṣyān*) of her husband." Ibn ʿĀshūr, *al-taḥrīr wa-l-tanwīr* (Tunis: Dār al-Tūnisiyya li-nashaz, 1984) 5:41. See Hamza Yusuf, "Sermon: Removing the Silence on Domestic Violence," (Feb. 21, 2009), video available at <http://www.youtube.com/watch?v=BDEKJDgXOU> (last accessed Sept. 5, 2013).

[98] Yusuf Ali (n 12) Q. 30:21.

[99] Faraz Rabbani, "Is It Not a Form of Sexual Abuse for a Husband to be Able to Force His Wife to Have Sex?," <http://spa.qibla.com/issue_view.asp?HD=11&ID=1830&CATE=117> (last accessed Jan. 17, 2013). See also Zaynab Ansari, a.k.a. Umm Salah, "Is It a Distortion to Say that Wife-Beating Is Allowed in Islam?," <http://www.ummah.com/forum/archive/index.php/t-51317.html> (last accessed Jan. 17, 2013).

that he sees as endemic to the Qur'ān. This vision of a perfect marriage represents a departure from pre-colonial Islamic scholarship, in which reciprocity of any kind between the spouses, as well as women's needs—emotional, physical, and/or spiritual—was never considered. Pre-colonial scholars understood marriage—at least in the context of Q. 4:34—as serving divine intent and the needs of men. Happiness, for men or women, did not figure in their discussions, except for the observation that righteous wives make husbands happy, and *nāshiza* wives make husbands unhappy. Neo-traditionalist scholars thus diverge from the Islamic tradition by considering the happiness of women, even if they connect it to the happiness of men, and they further recognize that the happiness of men is at least somewhat contingent on the happiness of women.

Rabbani's treatment of sexual rights in marriage demonstrates the balancing act in which neo-traditionalists must engage. Although he asserts that each spouse has sexual rights that ought to be fulfilled, he nevertheless distinguishes between sexual rights and sexual needs. For him, the difference pivots on which party may demand sex, even against the wishes of the other spouse; and he concludes that husbands may demand sex, while wives may not. He refers to the traditionalist distinction between the "nature" of the sexual desire of men and women, in that women may *desire* sex, while men *need* it. A disturbing corollary to this line of thinking is that since masturbation is "unlawful," husbands may force their wives to have sex with them in order to avoid sin.[100] Despite the fact that this position tacitly upholds the pre-colonial Ḥanafī position that permits marital rape, it also represents a shift in Rabbani's cosmology, since he does not assume that husbands can sexually fulfill themselves through other wives or concubines. Rabbani's justification is modern; he does not see himself as advocating marital rape so much as marital happiness. A healthy sex life leads to a happy marriage and vice versa, and therefore spouses must do whatever they can to ensure the happiness of the marriage. He characterizes the pre-colonial tradition as being intimately concerned with the happiness of both spouses, arguing that pre-colonial regulations were geared toward promoting marital bliss, as opposed to ensuring that a husband's—and, by extension, God's—rights were fulfilled.

Rabbani's approach illustrates one of two common approaches that neo-traditionalists take when describing the Islamic position on marital relations. In the first, like Rabbani, they re-imagine the Islamic tradition

[100] Rabbani (n 99). As mentioned earlier (n 50), Ibn Adam has stated that marital rape is not permissible, even though it is a sin for a wife to refuse her husband sexually. Ibn Adam, "Can a Wife Refuse the Husband's Call to Bed?," <http://spa.qibla.com/issue_view.asp?HD=11&ID=2360&CATE=117> (last accessed Jan. 25, 2013).

or the Qur'ān in order to locate contemporary conceptions of an ideal marriage in pre-colonial texts. In the second, they take the reverse approach, dressing up present-day ideas in traditional garb. The South African legal scholar Mufti Ebrahim Desai and his student, the jurist Luqman Hansrot, provide excellent examples of this strategy.

A man wrote in to the online forum "Ask Imam" requesting help with a problem: in a fit of anger he hit his wife, who hit him right back, and now he finds himself full of guilt for having hit her.[101] Hansrot counseled the man never to beat his wife again and then provided him with a list of ten strategies for a good marriage. Each rule was accompanied by a relevant supporting Qur'anic verse, a prophetic report, or a report about one of Muḥammad's Companions (*ṣaḥāba*). The ten rules are: 1. fear Allah; 2. never be angry at the same time (*ḥadīth*, "control your anger"); 3. let the other person win arguments (*ḥadīth*, "Whoever discards an argument despite being correct shall earn a place in the center of paradise"); 4. never yell (Q. 31:19, "And lower your voice for verily the most disliked voice is that of a donkey"); 5. criticize lovingly (*ḥadīth*, "A *Mu'min* is a mirror for a *Mu'min*"); 6. do not bring up past mistakes (*ḥadīth*, "Whoever conceals the faults of others, Allah shall conceal his faults on the day of *Qiyamah*[Judgement]"); 7. do not neglect your spouse (*ḥadīth*, "Verily there is a right of your wife over you"); 8. never sleep on an unsettled argument (report about Companion, "Hadhrat Abu Bakr (*Radhiyallahu Anhu*) resolved his dispute with his wife over feeding the guest before going to bed"); 9. express gratitude to your spouse at least once a day (*ḥadīth*, "Whoever does not show gratitude to the people has not shown gratitude to Allah"); and, finally, 10. be ready to admit your mistake (*ḥadīth*, "All the sons of Adam commit error, and the best of those who err are those who seek forgiveness"). In binding each of the ten rules to a prophetic report, Qur'anic verse, or report about a Companion, Hansrot attributed an Islamic basis for these rules, making them religiously authoritative. However, nine of the ten rules were taken—verbatim—from a list of "Tried and True Rules for a Happy Marriage" that was submitted to "Dear Abby."[102] The legal opinion (*fatwā*) issued by Hansrot, which was "checked

[101] Luqman Hansrot and Ebrahim Desai, Answer to question posted on August 21, 2009, <http://www.askimam.org/public/question_detail/18235> (last accessed Jan. 17, 2013).

[102] Hansrot replaced the tenth rule, "Remember it takes two to make a quarrel," with his first rule, "Fear Allah." "Tried and True Rules for a Happy Marriage" were submitted to "Dear Abby" and published in the *Chicago Tribune* on Feb. 1, 1996. They read, "1. Never both be angry at the same time; 2. Never yell at each other unless the house is on fire; 3. If one of you has to win an argument, let it be your mate; 4. If you must criticize, do it lovingly; 5. Never bring up mistakes of the past; 6. Neglect the whole world rather than each other; 7. Never go to sleep with an argument unsettled; 8. At least once every day say a kind or complimentary word to your life partner; 9. When you have done something wrong, admit it and ask for

and approved" by Mufti Ebrahim Desai, did not make any reference to "Dear Abby" or this submission. A reference to a non-Muslim source for guidance on a happy marriage might have compromised the authority of this *fatwā*, which was instead attributed to Islamic source texts.

This recasting of the tradition while upholding its dictates is seen throughout neo-traditionalist works on Q. 4:34, from notions of *qiwāma* and righteousness of wives, to hitting. Neo-traditionalists re-interpret the *qiwāma* of husbands over wives, shifting the emphasis from authority to responsibility. The most important responsibility that husbands have over their wives is their financial obligation to provide for their wives. Muhammad Asad (d. 1992), for example, translated "men are *qawwāmun* over women" as "men shall take full care of women." In the footnote to this translation, Asad explained that he meant this to include the "the physical maintenance and protection" as well as "moral responsibility" of men over women.[103] Although neo-traditionalist scholars continue to understand husbands to be the leaders (*amīr*) of their wives,[104] they ameliorate this stance by re-interpreting prophetic reports that were used in the pre-colonial period to express the dominance of husbands over their wives. One such *ḥadīth* records Muḥammad as saying that if he had ordered one human to prostrate to another, it would have been a wife to her husband.[105] G.F. Haddad, a Lebanese-American convert to Islam and member of Haqqani-Naqshbandi Sufi order, argues that this prophetic report was obviously meant to be figurative and is hyperbolic in nature. In fact, it must be read against "counter-balancing" prophetic reports that describe the rights of wives over their husbands, as well as Muḥammad's personal conjugal example.[106]

forgiveness; 10. Remember it takes two to make a quarrel." <http://articles.chicagotribune.com/1996-02-01/features/9602010300_1_dear-abby-dear-readers-name-calling> (last accessed Jan. 26, 2013).

[103] "Men shall take full care of women, with the bounties which God has bestowed more abundantly on the former than on the latter." Muhammad Asad, *The Message of the Qur'an* (Watsonville: The Book Foundation, 2003) Q. 4:34. Asad's footnote on the last phrase reads, "Lit., 'more on some of them than on the others'. The expression *qawwam* is an intensive form of *qa'im* ('one who is responsible for' or 'takes care of' a thing or a person). Thus, *qama 'ala l-mar'ah* signifies 'he undertook the maintenance of the woman' or 'he maintained her' (see Lane VIII, 2995). The grammatical form *qawwam* is more comprehensive than *qa'im*, and combines the concepts of physical maintenance and protection as well as of moral responsibility: and it is because of the last-named factor that I have rendered this phrase as 'men shall take full care of women'."

[104] Rabbani, "Marriage: 'Demanding Sex' as Abuse or Rape," <http://spa.qibla.com/issue_view.asp?HD=11&ID=4087&CATE=117> (last accessed Jan. 17, 2013).

[105] This *ḥadīth* was discussed previously in Chapter 1.

[106] Gibril F. Haddad, "Marriage and Men's Cruelty," <http://spa.qibla.com/issue_view.asp?HD=7&ID=3438&CATE=1> (last accessed Jan. 17, 2012).

Neo-traditionalists believe that when men are financially and morally responsible for their wives, righteous wives should respond with obedience. However, they are in disagreement as to whom righteous wives should obey. Although most follow the pre-colonial precedent, arguing that righteous women are obedient to both God and their husbands, others break from this precedent, interpreting a righteous wife's obedience as belonging solely to God. Asad avoided the word "obedience" entirely in his translation of *qānitāt*, translating it instead as "devout."[107] The object of a righteous wife's obedience has significant implications; if a righteous wife is required to be obedient to her husband, then her *nushūz* is interpreted expansively to include disobedience to her husband. However, if a righteous wife must obey God alone, then wifely *nushūz* might be interpreted more restrictively to acts that do not necessarily include disobedience of husbands.

The primary definitions of wifely *nushūz* offered by neo-traditionalists include only the intentionally destructive behaviors offered by pre-colonial exegetes and jurists. Wifely *nushūz* is no longer represented as general disobedience, undesirable, displeasing, or annoying actions. Neo-traditionalists define wifely *nushūz* as either manifest indecency (*fāḥisha mubayyina*)—implying sexual disloyalty—or a wife's ill-will. Additional interpretations include a wife's rebelliousness, desertion, recalcitrance, lewd behavior, adultery, disloyalty, violation of marital duties, and deliberate disobedience or bad behavior that results in "mental cruelty."[108] Although most of the descriptors of wifely *nushūz* are quite vague, Zaynab Ansari, a SunniPath and SeekersGuidance teacher, has insisted that only "very specific" behaviors can be characterized as wifely *nushūz*. Even though Ansari has characterized this position as being in line with the pre-colonial tradition, these definitions of wifely *nushūz* break significantly from pre-colonial interpretations of wifely *nushūz*.[109]

[107] In reference to Q. 4:34, Asad's translation reads, "And the righteous women are the truly devout ones, who guard the intimacy which God has [ordained to be] guarded." Asad (n 103) Q. 4:34. Asad's footnote on the last phrase reads, "Lit., 'who guard that which cannot be perceived (*al-ghayb*) because God has [willed it to be] guarded.' "

[108] Asad wrote, "And as for those women whose ill-will you have reason to fear . . ." His footnote reads, "The term *nushuz* (lit., 'rebellion' here rendered as 'ill-will') comprises every kind of deliberate bad behaviour of a wife towards her husband or of a husband towards his wife, including what is nowadays described as 'mental cruelty'; with reference to the husband, it also denotes 'ill-treatment', in the physical sense, of his wife (cf. verse 128 of this *surah*). In this context, a wife's 'ill-will' implies a deliberate, persistent breach of her marital obligations." Asad (n 103) Q. 4:34. G.F. Haddad has described wifely *nushūz* as a "euphemism for adultery." G.F. Haddad, "Wife Beating," <http://www.livingislam.org/fiqhi/fiqha_e32.html> (last accessed Jan. 20, 2013). Yusuf Ali has translated wifely *nushūz* as "disloyalty and ill-conduct" (n 12); Mohsin as "ill-conduct"; and Pickthall as "rebellion." See also Zaynab Ansari (n 99).

[109] "I have found that the majority of scholars have interpreted this as permission for men to discipline their wives who have become '*nashiz*', which means rebellious, recalcitrant, or

A wife's disobedience to her husband, sexual or otherwise, is no longer a dominant interpretation of wifely *nushūz*. Rather, it is her sexual disloyalty and any behavior that "threatens the harmony of marriage" constitutes *nushūz*. This vague but nevertheless restrictive definition of wifely *nushūz*, especially in comparison to pre-colonial interpretations, is the result of neo-traditionalist scholars balancing competing cosmologies. By restricting the definition of wifely *nushūz*, they limit the circumstances in which a husband might discipline his wife, while increasing the enormity of acts that might necessitate physical discipline.

Interestingly, while pre-colonial exegetes and jurists devoted a great deal of energy expounding the meanings of "admonishment" and "abandonment," virtually passing over physical discipline as a given, this trend is reversed in neo-traditionalist writings. Neo-traditionalist scholars do not worry about "admonishment" or "abandonment," which they perceive as innocuous and uncontroversial, and instead focus their attention on the right of husbands to physically discipline their wives. If wives commit *nushūz*, then husbands should first admonish them. Admonishment is interpreted as using kind, wise words to reason with wives. There is no mention of warning wives of upcoming punishments if they persisted in their *nushūz*. If admonishment fails, then husbands can abandon their wives by forsaking marital intimacy, which includes verbal and sexual abandonment.[110]

The most intriguing conversation in the neo-traditionalist model appears in discussions of wife-beating. All neo-traditionalist scholars agree that husbands are permitted to hit their wives, although they increasingly restrict the ethical parameters in which this hitting is acceptable.[111] Like traditionalist scholars, the tone of their discussion is defensive, and they engage a hostile and disingenuous interlocutor. Neo-traditionalist scholars believe that non-Muslims, Christian missionaries, and feminists

lewd. This permission is not a general permission to discipline the wife whenever the husband feels like it, but rather is meant for women who act out in very specific circumstances and threaten the harmony of the marriage." Zaynab Ansari (n 99).

110 "Note how the Qur'an commands men to first talk to their wives and persuade them with kind, wise words. Then if that fails, he is allowed to forsake marital intimacy, that is, sexual intercourse, as a way to make the wife understand the seriousness of her actions." Zaynab Ansari (n 99).

111 Qur'ān translators interpret *wa-ḍribūhunna* differently. Yusuf Ali has translated it as "beat them (lightly)," Khan as "beat them (lightly, if it is useful)," M. Pickthall as "scourge them," and Shakir as "beat them." Yusuf Ali (n 12); Mohsin Khan, *The Noble Qur'an: Interpretation of the Meanings of the Noble Qur'an in the English Language* (Riyadh: Dar-us-Salam Publications, 1999) Q. 4:34; Marmaduke William Pickthall and Arafat Kamil 'Ashi, *The Meaning of the Glorious Qur'an: Text and Explanatory Translation* (Beltsville: Amana Publications, 1994) Q. 4:34; M. H. Shakir, *The Qur'an* (Elmhurst, NY: Tahrike Tarsile Qur'an, 1990) Q. 4:34.

misunderstand and misrepresent the Islamic position on the right of husbands to hit their wives—a right that is not as bad as it sounds when placed in the proper context.[112] Whereas only some traditionalist scholars distinguish between, on the one hand, the symbolic physical discipline that they believe is prescribed in Q. 4:34 and, on the other hand, injurious, abusive, and violent hitting, all neo-traditionalist scholars make this distinction. Separating violence from physical discipline is important, because it enables neo-traditionalists to condemn domestic violence while also preserving the right of husbands to physically discipline their wives. Thus, they are able to uphold both their understanding of the Qur'anic ethos and the pre-colonial plain-sense reading of Q. 4:34.[113] Neo-traditionalist scholars never explain the exact difference between violent hitting and physical discipline, which is notable especially since it is difficult to cognize how someone can hit without violence. Rabbani has come close by asserting that hitting is only conditionally permissible in situations where its benefit is greater than its harm, but he has not specified the benefits of hitting or why the benefits are better than the potential harm.[114]

Neo-traditionalists cannot break from the pre-colonial plain-sense reading of Q. 4:34, but they nevertheless try to present wife-beating as anti-Islamic in most cases. Ansari, for instance, has made two claims that allow for wife-beating while at the same time decrying it. Her first claim is that hitting wives is "strictly prohibited" in Islam, and she has declared that anyone who says that a husband can hit his wife in Islam is "mistranslating" the Qur'ān and misunderstanding its message due to a deficiency of their grasp of the Arabic language.[115] Her second claim contradicts her first by conceding that husbands can actually hit their wives if wives commit *nushūz*. Relying on the opinion of Fakhr al-Dīn al-Rāzī, she argues that the imperative *wa-ḍribūhunna*in Q. 4:34 is actually meant to be understood as

[112] G.F. Haddad writes, "Some people who were influenced by feminism until they forgot the Adab of Islam, tend to badmouth Sayyidina 'Umar for what they term his mistreatment of women. While it is true that the Arabs in general and Sayyidina 'Umar in particular had a very high sense of self-respect (*ghira*) as attested by no less than the Prophet (in the hadith where he mentions seeing 'Umar's palace in Paradise), nevertheless we should observe Adab so as not to commit a sin whenever mentioning the Prophet, his Family, and His Companions, indeed all Muslims as Allah (SWT) made the honor of a Muslim as sacrosanct as his life and property." G.F. Haddad (n 108). See also Hamza Yusuf (n 97).

[113] G.F. Haddad (n 108); Rabbani, "What Does It Mean to Hit the Wife Lightly?," <http://spa.qibla.com/issue_view.asp?HD=11&ID=4758&CATE=121> (last accessed Jan. 20, 2013); Zaynab Ansari (n 99); and Hamza Yusuf (n 97).

[114] Rabbani (n 113).

[115] Zaynab Ansari (n 99). Hamza Yusuf has made a similar move, discrediting the opinion, translation, or interpretation of any Qur'anic verse from anyone who has studied Islam for "less than 20 years" or has not mastered "twelve" (unnamed) sciences related to Qur'ān interpretation. Hamza Yusuf (n 97).

a permission rather than a command, and furthermore, husbands can only hit their wives with a *miswāk*. Husbands cannot hit their wives with their hands, they must avoid the face and other delicate body parts, and their beatings cannot leave bruises. She adds contemporary restrictions on the hitting of wives, stipulating that husbands cannot hit their wives in a state of anger, and their beatings should not cause their wives "emotional harm." Hitting is meant to be symbolic rather than punitive, and both parties—husbands and wives—ought to behave like "adults."[116] In a quintessentially modern move, she has stated that neither spouse can hit the other without cause. No pre-colonial scholar considered the possibility of a wife hitting her husband; since they believed men to have superior physical strength, it made little sense to imagine a wife overpowering her husband physically.

Despite the fact that Ansari adds several innovative restrictions and stipulations on marital violence, she nonetheless claims authority by rooting these limits in the pre-colonial Islamic tradition. However, since these positions are entirely modern, Ansari cannot marshal pre-colonial sources to buttress her claims. Instead, she locates a significant portion of her authority in her claims to mastery of the Arabic language, and she links that mastery to the pre-colonial tradition. Anyone who disagrees with her is portrayed as misunderstanding the true message of the Qur'ān because of an imperfect grasp of the Arabic language. Arabic language is also key to learning what pre-colonial scholars of Islam have to say about this topic. The implication is that knowledge of the Arabic language vindicates Ansari's reading of the Qur'ān, which would have been upheld by pre-colonial scholars, who were themselves masters of Arabic. This maneuver deflects

[116] Asad wrote, "Then beat them . . ." His footnote reads, "It is evident from many authentic Traditions that the Prophet himself intensely detested the idea of beating one's wife and said on more than one occasion, 'Could any of you beat his wife as he would beat a slave, and then lie with her in the evening?' (Bukhari and Muslim). According to another Tradition, he forbade the beating of any woman with the words, 'Never beat God's handmaidens' (Abu Da'ud, Nasa'i, Ibn Majah, Ahmad ibn Hanbal, Ibn Hibban and Hakim, on the authority of Iyas ibn 'Abd Allah; Ibn Hibban, on the authority of 'Abd Allah ibn 'Abbas; and Bayhaqi, on the authority of Umm Kulthum). When the above Qur'an-verse authorizing the beating of a refractory wife was revealed, the Prophet is reported to have said: 'I wanted one thing, but God has willed another thing—and what God has willed must be best' (see Manar V, 74). With all this, he stipulated in his sermon on the occasion of the Farewell Pilgrimage, shortly before his death, that beating should be resorted to only if the wife 'has become guilty, in an obvious manner, of immoral conduct' and that it should be done 'in such a way as not to cause pain (*ghayr mubarrih*)'; authentic Traditions to this effect are found in Muslim, Tirmidhi, Abu Da'ud, Nasa'i and Ibn Majah. On the basis of these Traditions, all the authorities stress that this 'beating', if resorted to at all, should be more or less symbolic—'with a toothbrush or some such thing' (Tabari, quoting the views of scholars of the earliest times), or even 'with a folded handkerchief' (Razi); and some of the greatest Muslim scholars (e.g., Ash-Shafi'i) are of the opinion that it is just barely permissible, and should preferably be avoided: and they justify this opinion by the Prophet's personal feelings with regard to this problem." Asad (n 103) Q. 4:34. See also G.F. Haddad (n 108).

criticism but also misrepresents the tradition, which does not uphold Ansari's reading of the Qur'anic text.

Ansari is not alone in drawing on the pre-colonial Islamic tradition for authority while misrepresenting the same tradition. G.F. Haddad has claimed that in all four Sunnī legal schools a husband cannot hit his wife with a whip, stick, or even a slap, and he is liable for retaliation (*qawad*) or monetary compensation (*diya*) if he does. However, as we saw in Chapter 3, this is mostly untrue, since husbands were held financially responsible only if they seriously injured their wives or killed them.[117] Similarly, Hamza Yusuf, an American convert to Islam and a co-founder of Zaytuna College, calls upon his personal mastery of the Arabic language to refute understandings of the Qur'ān that translate *wa-ḍribūhunna* as "hit them."[118] He portrays the pre-colonial tradition as prohibiting domestic violence by insisting on the sequential application of the three prescriptions in Q. 4:34. According to Yusuf, anyone who follows the three prescriptions in sequence will not abuse his wife; stopping to think about the procedure will eliminate domestic violence. Still, in a twenty-six-minute video on the topic he does not provide an alternative translation for *wa-ḍribūhunna*. He does describe the hitting permitted in Q. 4:34 as a tap similar to the way Muslims strike the earth when performing the ablution before prayer if they do not have water (*tayammum*). By interpreting *wa-ḍribūhunna* as a "light tap" and separating this from violence proper, he is able to carve out a space for husbands to physically discipline their wives "nonviolently". In an especially bold move, he declares that "anybody that tells you that violence against your own spouse is justifiable is not only a liar, but he is absolutely disparaging of the Messenger of Allah, who was sent as a mercy to all the worlds, and certainly a mercy to women."[119] In this way, Hamza Yusuf is able to break from the Islamic tradition by condemning "domestic violence", permit symbolic hitting, and present this position as traditionally Islamic at the same time.

117 G.F. Haddad (n 108). See also Chapter 3.

118 He has stated that because he "spent a lot of time in the Arab world," he knows that most Arabs do not know Qur'anic Arabic. Hamza Yusuf (n 97).

119 Yusuf has also said that describing a husband as a "metaphorical God (u. *majāzī khudā*)" is "not Islam"; it is "patriarchal ignorance (*jāhiliyya*)." Hamza Yusuf (n 97). As we saw in Chapter 1, however, the concept of husbands as shadow-deities played an important role in pre-colonial Islamic conceptions of an ideal marriage. Further, as Lisa Hajjar points out, by distinguishing "domestic violence" from "hitting," neo-traditionalist scholars such as Yusuf, obfuscate the harm inflicted on women though a semantic twist. She writes, "By imagining and referring to beatings, confinement, intimidation, and insults as 'discipline' or 'punishment' rather than 'battery' or 'abuse,' the nature of harm is obfuscated. Moreover, if prevailing social beliefs about family relations include the idea that men have a right or obligation to punish and discipline female family members, then the tactics used to do so can be seen–and even lauded–as necessary to maintain order at home and in society at large." Lisa Hajjar, "Religion, State Power, and Domestic Violence in Muslim Societies: A Framework for Comparative Analysis," *Law & Social Inquiry*, 29(1) (2004) 3.

Neo-traditionalist scholars find themselves in a seemingly painful predicament as they try to argue against a patriarchal Islamic tradition while also upholding the authority of the tradition by following its precedent. This is manifested in the contradictory claims of individual scholars who deny and accept the right of husbands to hit their wives at the same time. Two neo-traditionalists whose work embodies this conflicting approach are Kamran Memon and Rashad Khalifa (d. 1990). Memon is a Chicago-based civil rights attorney and activist, and Khalifa was the Qur'ān-only numerologist who was assassinated after the Islamic Legal Council of Saudi Arabia issued a *fatwā* declaring him a heretic. Both Memon and Khilafa desperately want to deny that husbands might be permitted to hit their wives, and yet both of them ultimately find a space, albeit restricted, in which husbands can ethically hit their wives.

Memon has addressed the Muslim community in a treatise designed to tackle what he sees as a very real problem of domestic violence.[120] This is a courageous act in that it pushes back against Muslim voices that insist that domestic violence is a Western, not Muslim, problem. Memon breaks from the pre-colonial Islamic legal tradition by stipulating five steps a husband should undertake if his wife commits wifely *nushūz*, which he interprets as action taken by a wife that will result in a "serious problem" for the marriage. These steps are meant to be followed sequentially. First, a husband must admonish his wife with peaceful discussion that is meant to soften her heart and eliminate misunderstanding. Second, he should outline his expectations in a firm and decisive manner. Here, the definition of "warning" that some pre-colonial scholars offered for "admonition" is replaced with firmly setting expectations.[121] Third, a husband must leave the marital bed, which Memon suggests is meant to be a punishment for both spouses for not resolving their differences.[122] Fourth, he moves to Q. 4:35 and stipulates external arbitration for the couple.

Since Memon skips over the hitting in Q. 4:34 by moving directly to the arbitration in Q. 4:35, he could have left the procedure at this, arguing for arbitration as the final step. Yet he returns to Q. 4:34 to allow husbands to hit their wives if external arbitration fails. If adjudication is unsuccessful, then as a fifth step, a husband can hit his wife. However, the hitting should be no more than a light slap on the hand or shoulder; he cannot hit any other part of the body or leave a mark. A husband can do this only if he is innocent, compassionate, and well behaved. For Memon, it goes without saying that if a

[120] Kamran Memon, "Wife Abuse in the Muslim Community," <http://www.zawaj.com/articles/abuse_memon.html> (last accessed Jan. 20, 2013).

[121] See Chapters 2 and 3.

[122] Note how this position is different from the pre-colonial Ḥanbalī concern to safeguard a husband's right to sexual access while punishing a *nashiza* wife.

husband is the cause of the problem, then he cannot hit his wife. He suggests further that before husbands hit their wives, they should ensure that they are of exemplary character and that they follow Muḥammad's conjugal example of kindness, mercy, compassion, forgiveness, and gentleness. This is a rather strange move, not least because Memon seems to suggest that hitting might succeed in resolving a marital problem when arbitration fails. Despite the restricted definition of wifely *nushūz* and the additional steps before husbands are permitted to hit, Memon preserves husbands' disciplinary authority in marriage, as well as their right to hit their wives. That Memon in the end carves out an acceptable space, however restricted, for a husband to hit his wife in a treatise that seeks to combat domestic violence speaks to the authority and weight of the pre-colonial tradition. In Memon's case, the pre-colonial Islamic tradition prevents him from interpreting Q. 4:34 in a manner that categorically prohibits husbands from hitting their wives.[123]

Memon's ethical struggle is reproduced, though in a slightly different form, in Rashad Khalifa's interpretation of Q.4:34. Neither Memon nor Khalifa cite pre-colonial scholars explicitly, yet both find themselves restricted by the pre-colonial plain-sense meaning of *wa-ḍribūhunna* as "hit them." Khalifa maintained the hierarchy of men over women more overtly than Memon and described the marital relationship as analogous to a ship: every ship needs a captain, and husbands have been divinely chosen for this role. This role appears to be incidental rather than a reflection of any essentially superior characteristics of men over women. Wives ought "cheerfully" to accept their husband's position "without mutiny." Despite upholding a patriarchal marital structure as ideal, Khalifa placed Q. 4:34 under the heading "Do not beat your wives." However, in his translation of Q. 4:34, he maintained that if wives persist in rebellion against their husbands, even after admonishment and desertion in bed, then husbands can beat them. In a footnote, he explained that admonishment and abandonment are meant as alternatives to hitting. Like Yusuf, he argued that by stipulating that they be exhausted before hitting, Q. 4:34 actually eliminates the possibility of husbands hitting their wives.[124] Thus,

[123] Memon (n 120).

[124] "4:34 God prohibits wife-beating by using the best psychological approach. For example, if I don't want you to shop at Market X, I will ask you to shop at Market Y, then at Market Z, then, as a last resort, at Market X. This will effectively stop you from shopping at Market X, without insulting you. Similarly, God provides alternatives to wife-beating; reasoning with her first, then employing certain negative incentives. Remember that the theme of this sura is defending the women's rights and countering the prevalent oppression of women. Any interpretation of the verses of this sura must be in favor of the women. This sura's theme is 'protection of women'." Rashad Khalifa, *Quran: The Final Testament* (Fremont: Universal Unity, 2001). Yusuf has similarly argued that by telling husbands to "think" and to follow a three-step procedure to disciplining wives, the Qur'ān basically aims to eliminate

Khalifa confirmed that husbands have divine sanction to hit their wives, but the sequence in the verse practically bars them from ever doing so. Here again, we see that Khalifa wanted to categorically prohibit husbands from hitting their wives but found himself constricted by the pre-colonial interpretation of *wa-ḍribūhunna*as "hit them." That is, he was forced to affirm the pre-colonial plain-sense reading of the verse while trying to explain away the implications of that very reading. He did not consider alternative meanings for the imperative and instead offered an argument for abandoning the hitting of wives that stretched his own translation of the verse in a manner that strains credulity.

What is immediately apparent in the neo-traditionalist interpretations of Q. 4:34 is the challenge of speaking to the mores of contemporary Muslim communities while rooting authority in the pre-colonial tradition. We observed no such hermeneutic effort in pre-colonial texts, which is unsurprising because the patriarchal cosmology of pre-colonial scholars influenced their designation of the plain-sense meaning of *wa-ḍribūhunna* in Q. 4:34 as well as their legal and ethical discussions surrounding this prescription. With the introduction of a new egalitarian cosmology, the patriarchal cosmology has lost its undisputed hegemony, and neo-traditionalist scholars are forced to abandon many of the pre-colonial exegetical and legal conclusions surrounding wife-beating, such as analogizing the marital relationship with the master–slave relationship, permitting husbands to hit their wives for general disobedience or using instruments such as whips or sandals.

In the neo-traditionalist framework, the influence of the Islamic tradition is most clearly represented through its monolithic reading of *wa-ḍribūunna* as "hit them." Despite their many ethical concerns surrounding this prescription, the creative impulse of neo-traditionalists is hamstrung by adherence to pre-colonial readings of *wa-ḍribūhunna* such that they are unable to re-imagine this prescription to have alternative meanings. For neo-traditionalist scholars, the authority of the Islamic tradition is captured in the plain-sense meaning of Q. 4:34, which they see as representing divine intent rather than simply an interpretive choice of pre-colonial scholars. There is a latent anxiety in neo-traditionalist writings that forces them to accept the pre-colonial reading of Q. 4:34, which was agreed upon by great scholars and masters of the Arabic language, as a product of divine will. If the pre-colonial scholars were all wrong, then that suggests that God allowed the Muslim community to agree upon error for many centuries, bringing the rest of

domestic violence. He says, "The Qur'ān is telling you to stop and think, which in itself will stop domestic violence." Hamza Yusuf (n 97).

the tradition under suspicion. Thus, if present-day scholars disagree or object to the plain-sense meaning of the Qur'anic text as agreed upon by pre-colonial scholars, then they might be seen as challenging God himself in addition to the Islamic tradition. Challenging what they consider to be the plain-sense meaning of the divine text poses an existential problem for neo-traditionalist scholars; what is at stake is their very belief in the Qur'ān as a divine text and their authority, if not membership, in the Muslim community.

PROGRESSIVES: ENTERTAINING NEW PLAIN-SENSE MEANINGS

Like the neo-traditionalists, progressive scholars try to balance the pre-colonial Islamic tradition with modern gender-egalitarian values. In doing so, they run into the same problem as neo-traditionalists: the contradictory natures of the underpinning patriarchal and egalitarian cosmologies necessitate that progressives choose one paradigm over the other. Faced with the same conundrum as neo-traditionalists, progressives make the opposite choice. For them, the scale tips in favor of an egalitarian cosmology, whereby gender-egalitarian values are privileged whenever they come into conflict with the patriarchy of the pre-colonial Islamic tradition. This means that progressives do not follow the "Islamic tradition" wholesale; they are willing to weigh its merits and, if necessary, speak about it critically. This allows them to acknowledge the limits of using a patriarchal tradition to address gender-egalitarian concerns. However, there are pragmatic reasons that keep them from rejecting the Islamic tradition out of hand. One reason is the egalitarian–authoritative dilemma. Progressives must find a way to speak authoritatively in the very communities into which they hope to bring gender reform. After all, what is the point of positing a gender-egalitarian vision of Islam if this vision lacks authority? Hence, progressives desire to maintain a constructive relationship with the pre-colonial Islamic tradition. One of the ways that they do this is to recuperate minority opinions in traditional sources that might support their own gender-egalitarian visions of Islam and present them as representative of the dominant position in the "Islamic tradition."[125] However, as seen in the previous chapter, when it comes to

[125] A good example of this is Leila Ahmed's treatment of the Qaramatians and Kharijites. Leila Ahmed, *Women and Gender in Islam: Historical Roots of a Modern Debate* (New Haven: Yale University Press, 1992) 66 and 95–8.

questions of gender-egalitarianism, the pre-colonial Islamic tradition offers few supporting voices.

Therefore a necessary corollary to recuperating elements of the pre-colonial Islamic tradition in order to articulate a gender-egalitarian vision of Islam is that the pre-colonial Islamic tradition must be misrepresented in order to be saved. Both neo-traditionalists and progressives manipulate the pre-colonial tradition in one way or the other in order to garner various degrees of authority from this tradition.[126] However, the conclusions that result from such manipulations are different: while neo-traditionalists allow for at least the symbolic hitting of wives, progressive scholars prohibit husbands from hitting their wives in any and all circumstances. By recognizing the humiliating implications of beating one's wife, even symbolically, they reject "hit them" as a possible meaning of *wa-ḍribūhunna* in Q. 4:34. For example, Hadia Mubarak, a Washington, DC-based Muslim activist, has written, "Any reading of the Qurʾān that promotes or sanctions domestic abuse would violate the Qurʾānic paradigm of marital relations."[127] Instead, progressive scholars move beyond the interpretive constraints of the pre-colonial Islamic tradition and offer alternative meanings of *wa-ḍribūhunna* that do not endorse spousal violence.[128] Nevertheless, progressive scholars are acutely aware of the power of the pre-colonial plain-sense meaning given to *wa-ḍribūhunna*, and they attempt to ameliorate and/or defend the Qurʾanic text just in case *wa-ḍribūhunna* does actually mean "hit them." For example, Mubarak and Asma Barlas, the Program Director of the Center for the Study of Culture, Race, and Ethnicity at Ithaca College, have argued that even if *wa-ḍribūhunna* is read as "hit them," this prescription is restrictive rather than permissive.[129]

[126] Eg, Hadia Mubarak has represented the Shāfiʿī position on hitting wives as "barely permissible" and ʿAṭā as classifying wife-beating as "*makrūh*," but she does not provide the citations for the scholarly works where they make these arguments. Hadia Mubarak, "Breaking the Interpretive Monopoly: A Re-Examination of Verse 4:34," *Hawwa*, 2(3) (2005) 278. For an in-depth analysis of the Shāfiʿī position on hitting wives, see Kecia Ali, "The Best of You Will Not Strike," *Comparative Islamic Studies*, 2(2) (2006) 143–55. Also, Mahmoud has claimed that "the beating measure has been met with moral unease and resistance by many authorities both past and present." Mahmoud (n 5) 537. As seen in the first three chapters of this book, this claim is difficult to support with regard to past authorities.

[127] Mubarak (n 126) 275.

[128] Khaled M. Abou El Fadl, *Conference of the Books. The Search for Beauty in Islam* (Lanham: University Press of America, 2001) 181.

[129] Mubarak has relied on *ḥadīth* literature to argue that even if Q. 4:34 intends to allow husbands to hit their wives, the "striking must not be injurious or inflict any real harm (*ghayr mubariḥ*) and it must avoid the face." She has also defended the revelation of Q. 4:34 in the context of revelation literature, where Q. 4:34 nullified Muḥammad's ruling for retaliation for Ḥabība bt. Zayd. Mubarak has argued that the "retaliation" that Muḥammad had granted Ḥabība was physical, so she was permitted to hit her husband as he had slapped her. In this re-imagining of the *sabab*, the purpose of Q. 4:34 is less to deny Ḥabība juridical recourse against an abusive husband and more to end the cycle of violence between

In offering new, innovative, and unprecedented meanings for *wa-ḍribūhunna*, progressive scholars walk on potentially dangerous ground. If they are seen as challenging the Qur'anic text, their standing with the Muslim community might be called into question. Progressive scholars walk this fine line by differentiating between the Qur'anic text as the literal, unadulterated, verbatim expression of God's word on the one hand and fallible, human interpretations of this divine text on the other hand. Whereas the wording of the Qur'anic text cannot be disputed, historical interpretations can. By historicizing the interpretive Islamic tradition, progressive scholars can reject particular interpretations as misogynistic and patriarchal, while recuperating others as just and equitable.[130] While the Qur'anic text, as the literal word of God, is eternal and unchanging, interpretations of God's words can and must "adapt to changing societal circumstances and norms."[131] In addition to fallible exegesis, imperfect translations of the Qur'ān might also introduce erroneous understandings of God's word. If Muslims have ethical qualms with what appears to be the Qur'anic text, this might be the result of an incorrect or mistaken translation of the Qur'anic text rather than the divine text itself. In separating the Arabic Qur'ān from its translations,

spouses. Mubarak cites Hamza Yusuf's defense for the revelation of Q. 4:34 in the context of the *sabab*. He has stated, "In other words, [God was saying] don't humiliate these men because they have already done so much to transform themselves; don't forget they're Arabs ... They're proud and if you humiliate them in this way, you're going to lose them. This was God understanding the psychology of the people that this message was given to as the first people." Mubarak (n 126) 276, 280, and 285–6; and Hamza Yusuf, *Men and Women*(CD) (Hayward: Alhambra Productions, 2003). See also, Hajjar (n 119) 10–11 and Sisters in Islam and Yasmin Masidi, *Are Muslim Men Allowed to Beat their Wives?* (Selangor: Sisters in Islam, 1991 and 2009) 2, 13–15.

[130] Asma Barlas, *"Believing Women" in Islam: Unreading Patriarchal Interpretations of the Qur'an* (Austin: University of Texas Press, 2002) 188; and Mubarak (n 126) 262. Conceding the patriarchal nature of the Islamic tradition, Sa'diyya Shaikh nevertheless has endeavored to recover elements of the tradition. Eg, she writes that al-Ṭabarī "conceptualized the relationship of *qiwāma* as contingent on a socio-economic phenomenon rather than some inherent quality of man or woman *per se*." Sa'diyya Shaikh, "Exegetical Violence: *Nushūz* in Qur'ānic Gender Ideology," *Journal for Islamic Studies*, 17 (1997) 57. In fact, al-Ṭabarī saw men as ontologically superior to women, writing that God had preferred men over women generally. Abū Ja'far Muḥammad ibn Jarīr al-Ṭabarī, *Tafsīr al-Ṭabarī: al-musammā Jāmi' al-bayān fī ta'wīl al-Qur'ān* (Beirut: Dār al-Kutub al-'Ilmiyya, 1999) 4:59–60.

[131] Shaykh M. Hisham Kabbani and Homayra Ziad, *The Prohibition of Domestic Violence in Islam* (Washington, DC: World Organization for Resource Development and Education (WORDE), 2011), available at <http://www.worde.org/wp-content/uploads/2011/09/DV-Fatwa-Online-Version.pdf> (last accessed Jan. 22, 2013). Aysha Hidayatullah has extensively studied modern feminist hermeneutical strategies, including their selective approaches for reading Qur'anic and *ḥadīth* texts. Aysha Hidayatullah, "Women Trustees of Allah: Methods, Limits, and Possibilities of 'Feminist Theology' in Islam," Ph.D. diss. (University of California, Santa Barbara, 2009), forthcoming 2014 as *Feminist Edges of the Qur'ān*, Oxford University Press.

progressive scholars create space for challenging interpretations of the Qur'ān rather than the Qur'ān itself.[132]

Since progressive Muslims posit alternative unprecedented meanings of the Qur'anic text that break from the Islamic tradition, they must find a way to seek authority from the Islamic tradition without adhering to its conclusions. Progressive scholars adopt three main strategies in order to maintain a positive relationship with the pre-colonial Islamic tradition. First, they characterize marginal voices from the pre-colonial Islamic tradition as central. Second, they speak extensively yet vaguely about the diversity and plurality of voices in the Islamic tradition, usually without mentioning specific examples of such multiplicity. In doing so, they are able to imply that their own position must have some precedent in the Islamic tradition, whether in content or methodology, since there was such a wide range of acceptable opinions in pre-colonial Islamic scholarship.[133] Alongside the claim about the plurality of perspectives in Islamic scholarship, some progressive scholars also contend that rigorous and extensive training is required in order to grasp the vastness and depth of the Islamic tradition.[134] The practical result of this move is that the authority of progressive scholars is bolstered, and the credentials of anyone who objects to their views are challenged. Third, progressive scholars invert Fazlur Rahman's double movement theory.[135] Rahman

[132] Kabbani and Ziad (n 131). Barlas and Mubarak have made a similar move by differentiating the Qur'ān from the "classical, exegetical tradition." Mubarak agrees with Barlas that "It was the secondary religious texts, not the Qur'ān that enabled the textualization of misogyny in Islam." Moreover, "It is the interpretive process, not the Revelation itself, that is open to critique and historicization." Mubarak (n 126) 262 and 266. See also Barlas (n 130) 9 and 51.

[133] Eg, Kabbani and Ziad project back a diversity of opinions of *wa-ḍribūhunna* onto the pre-colonial tradition, portraying al-Zamakhsharī as interpreting *wa-ḍribūhunna* to meaning "have sex with them." They have further claimed that al-Suyūṭī prohibited husbands from hitting their wives. As we saw earlier, al-Suyūṭī did not prohibit husbands from hitting their wives and rather was very comfortable with marital discipline. Jalāl al-Dīn 'Abd al-Raḥmān al-Suyūṭī, *al-Durr al-manthūr fī al-tafsīr al-ma'thūr* (Beirut: Dār al-Ma'rifa, 1970) 2:155; and Maḥmūd ibn 'Umar al-Zamakhsharī, *al-Kashshāf 'an ḥaqā'iq ghawāmiḍ al-tanzīl wa-'uyūn al-aqāwīl fī wujūh al-ta'wīl* (Beirut: Dār al-Kutub al-'Ilmiyya, 2003) 1:496–9.

[134] Regarding "deep scholarship," see Kabbani and Ziad (n 131) and also n 141 following. Sa'diyya Shaikh has offered a compelling alternative to this approach. In her article "A Tafsir of Praxis," she advocated "challenging dominant perspectives that limit the creation of religious meaning and knowledge production to a scholarly elite... Qur'anic *tafsir*, as an embodied praxis, is engaged in by women in their private and domestic spaces." Sa'diyya Shaikh, "A Tafsir of Praxis: Gender, Marital Violence, and Resistance in a South African Muslim Community" in Dan Maguire and Sa'diyya Shaikh (eds.), *Violence against Women in Contemporary World Religions: Roots and Cures* (Cleveland: Pilgrim Press, 2007) 89.

[135] Ziba Mir-Hosseini describes the Fazlur Rahman's "double movement" theory lucidly. She writes, "The interpretative process that Rahman proposes for this revival is a 'double movement', that is, a movement 'from the present situation to Qur'anic times, then back to the present'. In the first movement 'general principles, values and long-range objectives' of the Qur'an are elicited and separated from the socio-historical context of the revelation.

proposed that Muslim scholars ought to interpret the Qur'anic text in its own seventh-century background and then apply its message and ethos to the current circumstance, without feeling restricted by the historical specificity of the pre-colonial context. In comparison, progressive scholars interpret the Qur'anic text in the contemporary egalitarian cosmological context first and then justify their interpretation through an appeal to the vastness of the content and/or methodology of the pre-colonial Islamic tradition. In this way, they are able to anchor themselves in the pre-colonial Islamic tradition without being restricted by it.[136] Although this move delegitimizes their authority with some Muslims, others are comforted by their connection to the Islamic tradition.

Progressive Muslim scholars primarily address Muslim audiences, but like traditionalists and neo-traditionalists, they also address "non-Muslims." However, these non-Muslims are not antagonistic Christian missionaries and feminists; rather, they are characterized as people who, perhaps due to their unfamiliarity with Islam, misunderstand Islam to be violent. Progressives are sympathetic to this perception of Islam, given

In the second, these principles are applied to issues at hand, taking into consideration the current context and its imperatives." Ziba Mir-Hosseini, "Justice, Equality and Muslim Family Laws: New Ideas, New Prospects" in Ziba Mir-Hosseini, Kari Vogt, Lena Larsen, and Christian Moe (eds.), *Gender and Equality in Muslim Family Law: Justice and Ethics in the Islamic Legal Tradition* (London: I.B. Taurus, 2013) 21. In Rahman's own words, this theory "requires the careful study of the present situation and the analysis of its various component elements so we can assess the current situation and change the present to whatever extent necessary, and so we can determine priorities afresh in order to implement the Qur'anic values afresh. To the extent that we achieve both moments of this double movement successfully, the Qur'an's imperatives will become alive and effective once again. While the first task is primarily the work of the historian, in the performance of the second the instrumentality of the social scientist is obviously indispensable, but the actual 'effective orientation' and 'ethical engineering' are the work of the ethicist." Fazlur Rahman, *Islam and Modernity: Transformation of an Intellectual Tradition* (Chicago: University of Chicago Press, 1984) 5.

[136] Eg, Laury Silvers accepts that while Q. 4:34 might be read as permitting physical violence against wives: "Muḥammad's example demonstrates that cultivating that balance requires resisting divine prescriptions that are ultimately not worthy of us as children of Adam." Even though the "primary meaning" of *wa-ḍribūhunna* is "beat them," and "God may intend all meanings... it does not follow that He *approves* of all meanings." As such, based on Ibn ʿArabī's teachings, she has argued that "the purpose of the existence of the verse [is] to remind human beings of the extraordinary burden of freedom." I classify Silvers' approach as progressive for two reasons. First, although like both progressive and reformist scholars, she rejects the right of husbands to hit their wives, she secures authority for her position by appealing to the pre-colonial figure of Ibn al-ʿArabī. Second, she concedes that one of the many intended meanings of Q. 4:34 is a prescription of violence, even though humans are ethically challenged to resist this meaning. Still, unlike many of the scholars in this study, she manages to hold in dynamic equilibrium the multiple voices with which the Qur'anic text speaks. As such, her approach resists easy categorization. Laury Silvers. "'In the Book We have Left Out Nothing': The Ethical Problem of the Existence of Verse 4:34 in the Qur'ān," *Journal of Comparative Islamic Studies*, 2(2) (2006) 171–2.

the increasingly political relationship between Islam and violence in the modern world, and they tend to see themselves as educating rather than debating. They also speak to Muslims who may misunderstand their own Islamic tradition due to the widespread perception about Muslims being violent. Furthermore, in an unprecedented move, progressive scholars acknowledge the role and responsibility of Muslims themselves in portraying a problematic image of Islam.[137] They concede that Muslim extremists are responsible for eroding the "values of mercy, compassion and love" in family affairs that are enshrined by Islam.[138]

Progressive scholars represent a new breed of Islamic scholarship, by combining traditionalist scholarship with Western academic training in an attempt to bring out the best of both. Shaykh M. Hisham Kabbani and Homayra Ziad embody this phenomenon. Kabbani is the Lebanese-American deputy leader of the Naqshbandi-Haqqani Sufi Order, and Ziad is an Assistant Professor of Religion at Trinity College.[139] Together they published a *fatwā* that prohibits domestic violence based on a re-interpretation of Q. 4:34. But before offering their "alternative and linguistically valid"[140] interpretation of Q. 4:34, they established their authority by outlining the incredibly high standards of excellence that one must attain before making claims about the Qur'ān, implying that they themselves have achieved these high standards. Thus, they not only establish their own authority but also aimed to destabilize traditionalist and neo-traditionalist interpretations of Q. 4:34 and to silence lay critics.[141]

[137] This is done by pointing out pre- and post-colonial Muslim perspectives on Q. 4:34. Eg, Mubarak has challenged al-Ṭabarī's understanding of Q. 4:34 based on his sources. The fact that the majority of prophetic reports that al-Ṭabarī cites in order to argue his case can only be traced back to a Companion (*ṣaḥāba*) or Successor (*tābiʿīn*) weakens the authority of his position for Mubarak. Mubarak (n 126) 268.

[138] Kabbani and Ziad (n 131).

[139] Their educational pedigrees precede the *fatwā*. Kabbani and Ziad (n 131). Other examples of scholars who have mastery of Islamic studies through traditional and Western models are Farid Esack, Khaled Abou El Fadl, Hossein Moderrissi, Ebrahim Moosa, Seyyed Hossein Nasr, and Abdulaziz Sachedina. There are no women in this list, largely because gender segregation norms in traditional settings make it extremely difficult if not impossible for women to have access to the highest echelons of Islamic religious authority.

[140] Kabbani and Ziad (n 131).

[141] Kabbani and Ziad write, "A comprehensive approach to understanding problematic Qur'anic verses requires deep scholarship, seeking not only the reason a verse was revealed and what events transpired in connection with its revelation, but a genuine understanding of the intent behind that revelation, command of the classical Arabic language of the Qur'an and often a knowledge of the various dialects used in the different areas in which the Qur'an was revealed (for each tribe's usage of a word might have differed from that of others). One must also consider how the Prophet and his Companions often explained a verse of the Qur'an in a manner quite different from the apparent meaning of the text. It takes an expert in linguistics to understand all the meanings in a verse, both explicit and inferred. Moreover, the Qur'an frequently uses allegories suited to all readers: young and old, male

Progressive scholars display a greater ease with their own subjectivity than traditionalist and neo-traditionalist scholars. In fact, progressive scholars see their subjectivity playing a key role in their interpretation of Q. 4:34. In this regard, they understand their own approach as methodologically consistent with that of pre-colonial scholars, who also brought their subjectivities to bear on their particular interpretations of Qur'anic verses. Kabbani and Ziad have argued that though pre-colonial scholars emphasized prophetic reports that supported a patriarchal marital structure, they could just as easily have selected *aḥādīth* that support a vision of marriage that is predicated on love and mercy, a concept that is drawn from the Qur'anic text itself.[142] The fact that pre-colonial scholars did not do so suggests that they used their context and subjective opinions to determine their selection of sources and subsequent interpretations. In that spirit, Khaled Abou El Fadl, the al-Azhar-educated professor of law at UCLA, has put his subjective opinion of what is beautiful and ugly at the center of his Qur'ān interpretation. He argues that the Qur'ān can say only beautiful things, and as such it cannot possibly allow husbands to hit their wives. After all, how could an idea that makes any conscientious person cringe possibly be good?[143]

Progressive scholars are keenly interested in re-interpreting wife-beating out of the Qur'anic text, and they make it the focus of their interpretations of Q. 4:34. They do not, for instance, devote a great deal of energy to explaining the *qiwāma* of men over women. When they do, they discuss it as a descriptive statement about social conditions in seventh-century Arabia and do not see it as relevant for contemporary Muslims. Most scholars focus on the latter portion of Q. 4:34, addressing the contested nature of *wa-ḍribūhunna* head-on. For progressive scholars, the obedience of women outlined in Q. 4:34 is due solely to God. This is necessarily so because in an egalitarian cosmology a woman has direct, unfettered, and unmediated access to God. Kabbani and Ziad argue that the Qur'ān puts men and women on equal footing before God.[144]

and female. The Qur'an can be deliberately broad, using allusive rather than direct language when discussing issues that may need to be accessed at several different levels of understanding, consonant with the preparedness and receptivity of the reader. It is for precisely this reason that classical scholars insist that the deeper meanings of the Holy Qur'an can only be accessed through a knowledgeable scholar, well-versed in such subtleties." Kabbani and Ziad (n 131). Khaled Abou El Fadl has made a similar move by writing, "Further, do the people you consulted know what the previous generation of scholars have said? Most of the books of law are not even published yet." Abou El Fadl (n 128) 181.

142 Kabbani and Ziad (n 131) Q. 30:21.

143 "Is beating your spouse a part of superior character? Is it a virtue? Is it something beautiful and good?" Abou El Fadl (n 128) 180–1.

144 Kabbani and Ziad make this argument using Q. 2:187, which reads, "Permitted to you on the night of the fasts, is the approach to your wives. They are your garments. And ye are

A husband has his own relationship that is independent and does not encroach upon the relationship that his wife has to God. In support of their position, progressive scholars cite many Qur'anic verses that state that God alone should be the object of obedience for believers, whether male or female.[145] Sa'diyya Shaikh, Associate Professor of Islamic Studies at the University of Cape Town, has warned against the theological implications of propping up husbands as demigods who regulate their wives' religious devotions and otherwise intervene in women's relationship with God. Such a scheme would compromise the radical monotheism of Islam, which demands that each individual worship God directly without diluting this devotion in any way.[146] Instituting this cosmological backdrop enables progressive scholars to limit the definition of wifely *nushūz*.

Progressives break from the pre-colonial Islamic legal and exegetical traditions by interpreting wifely *nushūz* away from disobedience. Citing the references to both wifely and husbandly *nushūz* in Q. 4:34 and Q. 4:128 respectively, Kabbani and Ziad argue for a definition of *nushūz* that can be equally applied to both spouses.[147] These criteria rule out "disobedience" as a potential definition of *nushūz*, since obedience necessitates a hierarchy; one can disobey only a superior, not an inferior. Since both husbands and wives cannot be disobedient to each other, yet both can commit *nushūz*, it follows that *nushūz* cannot mean disobedience. Rather, progressive scholars interpret *nushūz* to mean "sexual infidelity and disloyalty," which

their garments. Allah knoweth what ye used to do secretly among yourselves; but He turned to you and forgave you; so now associate with them, and seek what Allah hath ordained for you and eat and drink, until the white thread of dawn appear to you distinct from its black thread; then complete your fast till the night appears; but do not associate with your wives while ye are in retreat in the mosques. Those are limits (set by) Allah; approach not nigh thereto. Thus doth Allah make clear His signs to men that they may learn self-restraint." Yusuf Ali (n 12) Q. 2:187. Kabbani and Ziad write, "The balanced wording of the verse [2:187] also demonstrates women's rights as equal with men. In this way, the Qur'an establishes the structure of the marital relationship by putting each individual on an equal footing. As they share one original soul, it only follows that they must dwell together in tranquility, love and mercy. A true family institution can only exist when each side complements and completes the other, just as a lamp without electricity will not give light any more than will electricity without a lamp. The two halves, male and female, need each other. Thus, God describes spouses as garments for one another." Kabbani and Ziad (n 131). Mubarak writes, "In terms of gender equality, over ten unambiguous verses from the Qur'ān establish that the male and female sexes are created from a single pair, denoting that they are related to each other onto logically, not merely sociologically." The verses she references are Q. 4:1, 6:98, 7:189, 16:72, 30:21, 49:13, 53:45, 75:39, 78:8, 50:7, and 51:49. Mubarak (n 126) 275.

[145] Such verses include Q. 3:17, 33:35, 399, 2:117, and 4:59.

[146] Shaikh (130) 61–2.

[147] Kabbani and Ziad (n 131). See also Abou El Fadl (n 128) 171. For a lengthier discussion of the pre-colonial exegetical treatment of husbandly and wifely *nushūz*, see Ayesha S. Chaudhry, "Marital Discord in Qur'anic Exegesis: A Lexical Analysis of Husbandly and Wifely *Nushūz* in Q. 4:34 and Q. 4:128" in S.R. Burge (ed.), *The Meaning of the Word: Lexciology and Tafsīr* (forthcoming).

is behavior that can be exhibited by both husbands and wives. Although the hermeneutical strategy of interpreting wifely and husbandly *nushūz* as "sexual infidelity" is uniquely modern, progressive scholars seek to portray it as squarely in line with the pre-colonial tradition. Kabbani and Ziad have written, "Therefore, in verse 4:34, some classical scholars have understood 'disloyalty and ill conduct (*nushūz*)' on the part of the wife to refer not to mere disobedience, but to sexual infidelity."[148] It is significant that Kabbani and Ziad have not offered the names of "classical scholars" who held this opinion. As demonstrated in earlier chapters, pre-colonial scholars such as al-Qurṭubī discounted "sexual disloyalty or infidelity" as possible definitions for wifely *nushūz* because, in his opinion, illicit sex necessitated corporal (*ḥadd*) punishment enforced by the state rather than mere discretionary (*taʿzīr*) punishment at the hands of a husband.[149]

Still, progressive scholars use various sources to support their interpretation of spousal *nushūz* as sexual disloyalty. Kabbani and Ziad cite an excerpt of the farewell sermon, in which Muḥammad informed men that their husbandly rights include that their wives "not allow those whom you dislike into your beds."[150] Kabbani and Ziad have translated this phrase as "never commit adultery." By referencing only a small excerpt of this prophetic report, Kabbani and Ziad hope to grant authority to their interpretation of *nushūz* while avoiding the other thorny issues raised by this *ḥadīth*. However, as seen earlier in Chapter 2, the farewell sermon was used to justify the right of husbands to hit their wives, since it advises husbands to hit their wives in a non-extreme (*ghayr mubarriḥ*) manner. Pre-colonial scholars interpreted the reference to "beds" in this *ḥadīth* to mean "homes," since translating the report literally would imply that wives could allow those whom their husbands liked into their beds. However, in

[148] The full quote reads, "Sexually promiscuous behavior was also commonplace. The Qur'an sought to restrict the expression of sexuality within the bounds of marriage and prevent all the concomitant dangers of adultery, such as disease and unwanted pregnancy. Therefore, in verse 4:34, some classical scholars have understood 'disloyalty and ill conduct (*nushūz*)' on the part of the wife to refer not to mere disobedience, but to sexual infidelity." Kabbani and Ziad (n 131). It is important that the exact positions of "classical scholars" who hold this position are not referenced.

[149] See, eg, Muḥammad ibn Aḥmad al-Qurṭubī, *al-Jāmiʿ li-aḥkām al-Qurʾān: tafsīr al-Qurṭubī* (Beirut: Dār al-Kitāb al-ʿArabī, 1997) 5:165–6.

[150] Al-Qurṭubī's narration of this *ḥadīth* reads, "Fear God concerning women, you take them as a trust from God and make their private parts permissible for you with the word of God. Your rights over them are that they not give your beds (*furushakum*) to anyone whom you dislike. If they do this, hit them in a non-extreme (*ghayr mubarriḥ*) manner." For more discussion on this *ḥadīth*, see Chapter 2. Interestingly, it is in his commentary on this very *ḥadīth* that al-Qurṭubī discounts adultery or unfaithfulness as a potential definition of wifely *nushūz*. But he does accept that openly lewd (*fāḥisha mubayyina*) behavior that falls short of fornication counts as wifely *nushūz*. Al-Qurṭubī (n 149) 5:165–6.

the case of Kabbani and Ziad, understanding beds literally allows them to support their interpretation of spousal *nushūz* as sexual infidelity.

Abou El Fadl has used a different version of the farewell sermon to interpret spousal *nushūz* as a "grave and known sin" (*fāḥisha mubayyina*) or "sexual lewdness."[151] He is incensed by the gender discrimination of pre-colonial jurists who defined wifely *nushūz* as "disobedience," "aloofness," or "arrogance" but husbandly *nushūz* as a "grave and known sin" (*fāḥishat mubayyina*),[152] which Abou El Fadl interprets as "sexual lewdness." He argues instead that a more balanced and honest approach would be to define *nushūz*, whether committed by a husband or wife, to be the sexual lewdness. As seen in Chapter 3, pre-colonial jurists did not interpret husbandly *nushūz* as "sexual lewdness" but rather "sexual apathy and withdrawal" from their wives. By (mis)representing the pre-colonial tradition, Abou El Fadl demonstrates his familiarity with it, which grants his words an authoritative status; by criticizing the tradition, he displays that his ethical standards do not bow even to the greatest authorities of Islam. In the end, Abou El Fadl offers a new interpretation of spousal *nushūz* based on egalitarian expectations of the Qur'ān as promoting contemporary notions of justice. This new perspective is hegemonic, since Abou El Fadl denounces competing interpretations as "disturbing" and "absurd."[153]

Interpreting spousal *nushūz* as sexual disloyalty is predicated on an egalitarian marital structure in which spouses are on an equal footing with each other. Thus, the methods of addressing *nushūz* are no longer disciplinary and hierarchical but consultative. According to progressive scholars, neither spouse has disciplinary authority over the other; rather, the couple is a team that must address their marital problems together. Couples should first communicate with each other and then try separation. However, if consultation and separation fail, then progressive scholars offer various subsequent steps for marital reconciliation. While some progressive scholars

151 "The jurists, may God bless and forgive them, troubled by this tension, said that *nushuz*, in the case of a wife, means disobedience or aloofness, arrogance, and the case of a husband, means a grave and known sin (*fahisha mubina*)." Abou El Fadl (n 128) 171 and 174.

152 Abou El Fadl does not tell his readers which scholars in particular hold this view.

153 Abou El Fadl (n 128) 179. Mubarak has made a similar point about the necessity of belief in God's and therefore the Qur'ān's justness: "As Gods' justness is unarguably a basic principle in Islamic theology, then God would not permit or promote acts that inflict *zulm* (injustice) upon any human being... More importantly, giving one spouse a level of supremacy over the other and an exclusive right to violently impose such supremacy not only violates God's commandment to ordain justice, but also violates Qur'ānic edicts of gender relations as well as the practice and teachings of Prophet Muhammad (pbuh) himself." Mubarak (n 126) 263–4. See also Barlas (n 130) 14. Shaikh has cited Q. 4:135 ("O ye who believe, stand out firmly for justice, as witnesses to Allah, even as against yourselves...") and Q. 16:90 ("Indeed Allah commands justice and the actualization of goodness, the realization of beauty") to argue for the centrality of justice in deriving meanings from the Qur'anic text. Shaikh (n 134) 66.

offer alternative meanings for the third imperative in Q. 4:34, translating *wa-ḍribūhunna* as "to have sex with," "to walk away from," or "to make an impression upon," others hint at possible meanings or emphasize instead the role of arbitration outlined in Q. 4:35.[154] Kabbani and Ziad have rejected all interpretations that permit husbands to hit their wives, labeling them "extremist." Despite the overwhelming consensus of pre-colonial scholars permitting husbands to hit their wives, Kabbani and Ziad contend that the primary historical interpretation of *wa-ḍribūhunna* was that a husband could "tap" his wife symbolically with a *miswāk*. Although tapping one's wife symbolically is actually a post-colonial, neo-traditionalist interpretation of *wa-ḍribūhunna*, it is useful for them to think of it as a pre-colonial interpretation since it makes responding to the authority of the pre-colonial Islamic tradition itself unnecessary. Kabbani and Ziad add that although tapping one's wife might have been considered "just" and "gentle" in a historical context where harsh violence against women was the norm, in the contemporary context any violence against women is unacceptable.[155] Through this claim, Kabbani and Ziad aim to preserve the authoritative status of the pre-colonial tradition—by portraying it as progressive for its historical context—and present their own interpretation as the logical culmination of the progressive trajectory of the Islamic tradition.

Due to altered cultural norms, then, progressives must re-imagine the meanings of *wa-ḍribūunna* so that Q. 4:34 does not sanction domestic violence. To do so, Kabbani and Ziad have enlisted the support of several Qur'anic verses that challenge the interpretations of Q. 4:34 that authorize

[154] Some of the meanings of *wa-ḍribūhunna* offered by post-colonial scholars include "to confine" women if they collectively refuse to bear children (Riffat Hassan); "to have intercourse" (Ahmed Ali); "to leave" (Abdulhamid Abusulayman); "to rescue or remove from danger" (Abdullah Adhami); and "to make an impression" (Mubarak). These positions are described in Mubarak (n 126) 282–4. See also, Riffat Hassan, *Women's Rights and Islam: From the I.C.P.D. to Beijing* (Louisville: NISA Publications, 1995) and Sisters in Islam (n 129) 12. Mahmoud has argued that the restricted and symbolic nature of hitting prescribed in Q. 4:34 is meant to be a "virtual abrogation" of the prescription. He insists that this hermeneutical strategy is not modern but rooted in the Islamic tradition. In his opinion, Muḥammad desired to prohibit wife-beating but was unable to because of the practice's social entrenchment, and so he instead resorted to discouraging his followers from hitting their wives, saying that "not beating one's wife carries a higher moral worth." Hence, instead of "editing out" the prescription from the Qur'anic text, Mahmoud seeks to "bracket" it so that it is effectively "abrogated." Mahmoud (n 5) 545–6 and 549–50. Silvers advocates for a prohibition of the imperative "to hit" while admitting to its existence: "*We may not deny the existence of the prescription or any aspect of God's intent,* but we may limit its practice to the point of complete prohibition in law and in our own ethical confrontation with the comprehensive possibilities of the Book, the world and ourselves." (Emphasis in the original.) Silvers (n 136) 177.

[155] "While tapping a wife with a *miswak* may have been just and gentle in a context where harsh violence against women had previously been culturally acceptable, in our contemporary context there is no place for physical punishment, however gentle, of a wife." Kabbani and Ziad (n 131).

violence against wives. For instance, Q. 30:21 states that an ideal marriage is founded on "love" and "mercy." How can such a marriage include any sort of violence against a wife? Q. 2:187 speaks about spouses as raiment for one another; how can spouses, understood as protective coverings, behave violently toward each other? Q. 4:19 instructs couples to live in kindness; how can kindness include violence? The first half of Q 2:228 stipulates similar rights for each spouse; how can a husband have exclusive authority to hit his wife if spouses have similar rights? Q 2:237 orders believers to remember the kindness between themselves; again, how does hitting fit into the message of this verse?

Highlighting the multiple meanings of the consonantal root *ḍ-r-b* in the Qur'ān, progressives hint that *wa-ḍribūhunna* might mean either "and have sex with them," "and mingle with them," or "and turn away from them."[156] It is conceivable that *wa-ḍribūhunna* means "and have sex with them" or "and mingle with them" after a period of separation. It is also plausible to interpret *wa-ḍribūhunna* as meaning "and turn away from them," in which case Q. 4:34 would naturally segue into Q. 4:35, which advocates arbitration. After all, it makes more sense to seek arbitration after a period of separation than after hitting one's wife. However, for any of these meanings to be grammatically sound, the phrase "*wa-ḍribūhunna*" requires additional modifiers. Kabbani and Ziad have recognized this point, but they argue that the meanings of Qur'anic phrases do not always follow the rules of grammar. In particular, they have noted that in Yusuf Ali's translation of the Qur'ān, he broke from Arabic grammar by translating the "and" (*wa*) that connects the three prescriptions in Q. 4:34 as "then." Since no one has criticized this translation, Kabbani and Ziad suggest that when understanding the Qur'ān, "scholars invoke the need for linguistic and semantic accuracy, as well as reasonableness."[157]

[156] Kabbani and Ziad (n 131). This point further highlights the differing interpretive consequences of patriarchal and egalitarian cosmologies. While Kabbani and Ziad use the multiple conjugations of *ḍ-r-b* in the Qur'ān to argue for a nonviolent interpretation of *wa-ḍribūhunna*, Hārūn b. Musā al-A'war (d. 170–80/786–96) used the same strategy to interpret this term in a way that confirms a violent reading. In his *Al-Wujūh wa-l-naẓā'ir fī al-Qur'ān al-karīm*, he cited the various uses of *ḍ-r-b* in the Qur'ān but differentiated the use of *ḍ-r-b* in phrases such as "and when you walk about the Earth" (*wa idhā ḍarabtum fī al-arḍ*, Q. 4:101) and "God presents the simile" (*ḍaraba allāhu mathalan*, Q. 14:24) from phrases such as "Hit them on their necks" (*fa-ḍribū fawqa al-a'nāq*, Q. 8:12) and "smite their necks" (*fa-ḍaraba al-riqāb*, Q. 47:4). In the latter two cases, he explained that the hitting is meant to be carried out with hands (*bi-l-yadayn*) and weapons (*bi-l-silāḥ*). Similarly, he understood *wa-ḍribūhunna* in Q. 4:34 as instructing hitting with one's hands (*bi-l-yadayn*), in a non-extreme (*ghayr mubarriḥ*) fashion. Hārūn b. Musā al-A'war, *Al-Wujūh wa-l-naẓā'ir fī al-Qur'ān al-karīm* (Amman: Dār al-Bashīr, 2002) 153.

[157] "In fact, nearly all scholars commonly infer words into this verse: for example, 'As to those women . . . admonish them (first), (Next), refuse to share their beds, (And last) beat them (lightly).' Here, each of the words in parentheses is inferred. They do not exist in the

Abou El Fadl has taken a different tactical approach than Kabbani and Ziad. In his ruminations in the *Conference of the Books*, he recounts a visit from a woman whose husband used Q. 4:34 to justify slapping her. This anecdote brings to mind the account of Ḥabība, who sought retaliation from Muḥammad against her husband for slapping her. Unlike Ḥabība, the unnamed woman who visited Abou El Fadl did not have a mark on her face from her husband's slap. Like Muḥammad himself, Abou El Fadl was moved by the woman's plight and troubled by the apparent permission that Q. 4:34 grants husbands to hit their wives. In Muḥammad's case, the discomfort manifested itself after the fact of revelation, whereas in Abou El Fadl's case, the preexistence of the verse is the cause of distress. Unlike Muḥammad, who in the narration bowed to the pre-colonial plain-sense meaning of Q. 4:34, which permits husbands to their wives, Abou El Fadl was compelled to think of this verse in a new light. Highlighting the very problematic result of the pre-colonial plain-sense meaning of Q. 4:34, in which the husband is "accuser, judge and enforcer" and where a trial is called only after "assigning the penalty first," Abou El Fadl asked the woman before him to reconsider her abusive husband's—and the pre-colonial Islamic tradition's—claims about Q. 4:34.[158] When wifely *nushūz* is interpreted as a "grave and known sin (*fāḥisha mubayyina*)," which he understands as sexual disloyalty,[159] then how is it possible for a husband to allege, investigate, and act as the penalizing commission for such a sin? It became clear to Abou El Fadl that a claim about sexual infidelity must be proven in court, after which the state may order either separation or corporal punishment. This, of course, opens another can of worms that Abou El Fadl has not addressed—namely, a state's regulation of the private sexual choices of individuals, as well as state-imposed corporal punishment for moral and sexual sins. That problem aside, he

Arabic text. In doing this, scholars invoke the need for linguistic and semantic accuracy, as well as reasonableness. All of this is due to the extremely concise wording of the Qur'an. That is why the Qur'an must not always be taken literally, but must be interpreted linguistically, juristically and culturally. If this is not done, the verse reads: 'admonish them, separate from them in bed, and beat them (lightly),' eliminating the stages of rectification, and rather applying them all at once. This interpretation would contradict the Qur'anic tradition of moderation in all affairs, and as a result is rarely supported by scholars." Kabbani and Ziad (n 131). For a detailed description of the pre-colonial disagreement about whether the three imperatives in Q. 4:34 were meant to be applied simultaneously or sequentially, see Chapter 2.

[158] Abou El Fadl (n 128) 169–70.

[159] Here, Abou El Fadl disagrees with al-Qurṭubī, who ruled out sexual infidelity as a possible meaning for wifely *nushūz* because this would lead to a *ḥadd* penalty that could only be applied by the state. However, since Q. 4:34 speaks of a husband punishing his wife, al-Qurṭubī believed that wifely *nushūz* was sexual lewdness short of sexual infidelity, and that it was inclusive of general disobedience. Abou El Fadl (n 128) 175; and al-Qurṭubī (n 149) 5:165–6.

proclaims that hitting one's family members is a "foul and revolting act" that can squarely be described as "ugly." Hence, there is no way that it could be sanctioned by the divine Qur'anic text.[160]

The driving force behind these interpretations is the egalitarian cosmology that progressive Muslim scholars favor over a patriarchal one. For them, humans were created by God to worship Him, and every human being, regardless of race, gender, or class, has direct and unfettered access to God. This unmediated access to God is an important aspect of their theology, according to which any encroachment on an individual's relationship to God represents a form of polytheism (*shirk*). In this scheme, marriage is a vehicle to come closer to God, and husbands and wives must aid each other in their journey to the divine. Neither spouse has authority or disciplinary privilege over the other; there is no place for this in a cosmology wherein humans distinguish themselves through piety, which intrinsically defies quantification and comparison.[161] As such, there is no room for husbands to hit their wives; in fact, any hierarchy is theologically and cosmologically distressing.

While progressive scholars are willing to break from the patriarchal elements of the pre-colonial Islamic tradition, they nevertheless hope to maintain a somewhat constructive relationship with that tradition. If they do not, they stand to lose authority and legitimacy in the very communities they wish to influence. In preserving some semblance of a relationship with the pre-colonial Islamic tradition, progressive scholars must make a choice: either compromise the egalitarian nature of their cosmology or recast the tradition in order to identify ethical voices that challenge patriarchy where none exist. Progressive scholars opt for the latter choice,

[160] He went on to write, "I am repelled by ugliness, and I take refuge in the gift of a mind capable of interpretation." Abou El Fadl (n 128) 175 and 178. Mubarak has argued against a violent interpretation of Q. 4:34 based on the *maqāsid* argument. This argument endeavors to locate the principle of each verse and ruling, which in the case of Q. 4:34, she declares is reconciliation. Based on this, she argues, "Hence the question becomes, would a woman's physical subjugation by means of physical abuse or disgrace help to reinstate affection and fidelity between two partners? If physical force is used against Muslim women who are well versed in their rights, it would encourage them to seek *khulʿ* and terminate their marital contract. But if the objective of this verse is to reconcile the two parties and prevent divorce, then why would it promote means, such as physical abuse, that would only impede reconciliation? Therefore, the entire objective of this verse negates the notion that God has ordered or authorized men to hit their wives." Mubarak (n 126) 281.

[161] Based on Q. 9:71, Mubarak has argued, "If men and women are to enjoin each other to enjoin justice and forbid evil, then it is necessary that each bear an equal moral responsibility over the other. This would then flagrantly contradict any notion of men's superiority to women." Mubarak (n 126) 275. Amina Wadud refers to patriarchy as "a kind of *shirk*." Amina Wadud, "Islam Beyond Patriarchy Through Gender Inclusive Qur'anic Analysis," Musawah, available at <http://www.musawah.org/sites/default/files/Wanted-AW-EN.pdf> (last accessed May 20, 2013) 109.

advocating a gender-egalitarian vision of Islam that lays claim to the Islamic tradition for authority and authenticity.

REFORMISTS: SHIFTING AUTHORITY, MAKING A NEW TRADITION

Reformist scholars sit on the opposite end of the spectrum from traditionalist scholars. Traditionalist scholars uphold a patriarchal cosmology, clinging to the pre-colonial Islamic tradition for authority, and they are suspicious and/or contemptuous of anything modern and Western. In contrast, reformist scholars unapologetically position themselves as modern, Western subjects who champion an egalitarian cosmology. Accepting this orientation requires them to reject the pre-colonial, patriarchal Islamic tradition. Reformist scholars justify this choice by historicizing the pre-colonial Islamic tradition and highlighting its human, subjective nature. Since the pre-colonial Islamic tradition was created by men who were subjects of their historical and social contexts, reformist scholars see no reason to be bound by this tradition, nor do they seek its approval. Furthermore, they argue that if the Qur'ān is truly a universal text, then it must be applicable and relevant to all historical and social conditions.

Unlike traditionalists, reformists see no reason to be ashamed of their own historical moment and its attendant subjectivities. Instead, they expect the Qur'anic text to speak to their existing idealized egalitarian cosmology. The Qur'ān should address men and women as equals and not disempower either gender. In line with this reasoning, reformist scholars cannot accept the Qur'anic text as permitting husbands to discipline their wives in any way, not to mention through violence. Any interpretation that permits the slightest bit of violence against wives is categorically unjust and therefore cannot be ascribed to a divine text that promotes justice.[162] Since reformist scholars embrace their subjectivities, they are

[162] Farid Esack demonstrates this approach well when promoting an interpretation of Q. 4:34 that does not condone violence against women. He writes, "This centering of liberation, justice and compassion in one's theology is more subversive of orthodoxy than what may appear the case from a superficial perusal. Every single dogma is subject to interrogation by the standards of gender justice and compassion and every text is read through these lenses. Every text that does not withstand this scrutiny may be subject to a host of hermeneutical devices ranging from contextualization and re-interpretation to abrogation in order to arrive at an interpretation that serves the ends of justice. Does this not constitute violence towards the text? First, none of these devices are unknown to the world of traditional Islam; the only difference is the starkness with which they are spelt out and the definitiveness of the criteria employed. Second, if a choice has to be made between violence

free to offer new interpretations of Q. 4:34 that are without any historical precedent and are unencumbered by the constraints of the pre-colonial, patriarchal Islamic tradition. The key difference between progressive and reformist scholars is that reformist scholars do not pin redemptive hope on the Islamic tradition but instead confidently shift authority from the Islamic tradition to their own critical reasoning and engagement with the Qur'anic text.

When reformist scholars jettison the patriarchal Islamic tradition, the egalitarian–authoritative dilemma comes into play. Reformist scholars who call for innovative interpretations of Q. 4:34 that correspond to the values of gender-egalitarianism are plagued with the problem of communal authority and authenticity. While some Muslims will gravitate towards the new, nonviolent interpretations of reformist scholars, mainstream Muslim communities still vest authority in scholars who can illustrate that they are somehow rooted in and continuing the rich, pristine legacy of the Islamic tradition. Reformist scholars use three methods to address this dilemma. First, they root their authority in innovative readings of the Qur'anic text rather than in the Islamic tradition, thus making the Qur'anic text central to their interpretation. It should be unsurprising, then, that reformist interpretations of Q. 4:34 are sometimes found in reformist translations of the Qur'ān.[163] Second, they justify their departure from the pre-colonial Islamic tradition on moral and ethical grounds. Why should they be beholden to a tradition that was misogynistic and violated the calls for justice in the Qur'ān? Unlike progressive scholars, reformist scholars do not seek to save the pre-colonial Islamic tradition, nor do they root their positions in or derive authority from it. Third, they

towards the text and textual legitimization of violence against real people then I would be comfortable to plead guilty to charges of violence against the text." Farid Esack, "Islam and Gender Justice: Beyond Simplistic Apologia" in J.C. Raines and D.C. Maguire (eds.), *What Do Men Owe Women? Men's Voices from World Religions* (Albany: State University of New York Press, 2001). Amina Wadud similarly argues that Muslims are empowered to say "no" to a violent reading of the Qur'anic text. She writes, "This leads me to clarify how I have finally come to say 'no' outright to the literal implementation of this passage [Q. 4:34]. This also has implications in implementing the *hudud* (penal code) ordinances. This verse, and the literal implementation of *hudud*, both imply an ethical standard of human actions that are archaic and barbarian at this time in history. They are unjust in the ways that human beings have come to experience and understand justice, and hence unacceptable to universal notions of human dignity." And also, "Here I argue against any notion that it is acceptable for a man to beat his wife. Any kind of strike, or any intention to apply the verse in that manner, violates other principles of the text itself—most notably 'justice' and human dignity, as Allah has led humankind to understand today." Amina Wadud, *Inside the Gender Jihad: Women's Reform in Islam*(Oxford: Oneworld, 2006) 192 and 200–4.

[163] See, eg, Laleh Bakhtiar, *The Sublime Qur'an* (Chicago: Kazi Publications, 2007) and Edip Yüksel, Layth Saleh al-Shaiban, and Martha Schulte-Nafeh, *Quran: A Reformist Translation* (USA: Brainbow Press, 2007).

embrace the methodology rather than the content of the Islamic tradition. If pre-colonial scholars used their own social and historical gender norms to interpret Q. 4:34, what is stopping present-day scholars from doing the same? If al-Zamakhsharī and al-Rāzī, for example, could use their social observations of men's superiority in archery or political leadership to argue that men are smarter and stronger than women—which, in turn, explained God's favor on men—why can't modern scholars conclude, based on their own observations, that neither gender is favored over the other?[164] It is important to remember that reformists embrace the methodology of the Islamic tradition only because it does not pose an ethical problem for them. If it had, it would likely be rejected.

Still, reformist scholars are acutely aware that they are writing in a highly political climate, and they must find ways to gain authority, demonstrate their commitment to Islam, and ensure that they are not viewed as betraying the believing community. They are cognizant that Q. 4:34 is used by various parties to both condemn Islam as inherently misogynist and also defend and excuse domestic violence within Muslim communities. They are also aware of multiple Muslim and non-Muslim voices that speak about domestic violence in complex ways that cannot be simplified into categories of "missionaries," "extremists," and the like. Hence, when discussing domestic violence in Islam, reformist scholars speak to multiple audiences and must balance various intersecting concerns. They must create a reasonable space to discuss domestic violence in an Islamic context without making domestic violence a uniquely Muslim problem.[165] In a *fatwā* prohibiting wife-beating in all circumstances, the Islamic Supreme Council of Canada has declared,

> Domestic violence is a huge problem across the world. We believe it is not a Muslim problem. It is a human problem. Domestic violence crosses all boundaries. Domestic violence exists in the developed and in the developing worlds. Domestic violence takes place in Christian, Jewish, Muslims, agnostic, Buddhist, Hindu, atheists, etc. houses. It is everywhere. However, as Muslims we must follow the holy Qur'an and the teachings of the Prophet Muhammad (peace be upon him) which forbids causing harm to children, wives or any

[164] Reformist scholars also cite the gendered interpretations of wifely and husbandly *nushūz* by pre-colonial scholars as evidence of medieval cultural norms influencing Qur'ān interpretation. Women's Islamic Initiative in Spirituality and Equality (WISE),"Jihad Against Violence: Muslim Women's Struggle for Peace" (July 2009), available at <http://www.wisemuslimwomen.org/images/uploads/Jihad_against_Violence_Digest(color).pdf> (last accessed Jan. 22, 2013) 6–7.

[165] Islamic Supreme Council of Canada, *Fatwā: Honor Killings, Domestic Violence and Misogyny are Un-Islamic and Major Crimes* (Feb. 4, 2012), available at <http://www.islamic-supremecouncil.com/fatwa-honour-killings-misogyny-domestic-violence.pdf> (last accessed Jan. 22, 2013).

other person due to disagreements, disputes or conflicts. All family issues must be resolved within the laws of the country we live in.

Reformist scholars complicate Muslim and non-Muslim positions on wife-beating by examining domestic violence in a framework that extends beyond Islamic and religious concerns.

Like other post-colonial scholars, reformist scholars base their understanding of an ideal Islamic marriage on Q. 30:21, which defines the central characteristics of an ideal marriage as "love and mercy." Like progressive scholars, they see the *qiwāma* of men over women as a descriptive statement relating to the historical context of seventh-century Arabia rather than as a prescription for all eternity. Laleh Bakhtiar, who has written a Qur'ān translation that reflects an egalitarian idealized cosmology, argues that husbands can be the "supporters" of their wives but under no circumstance are permitted to hit their wives.[166] As with progressive scholars, reformists interpret the obedience of righteous wives to be directed to God alone, not to their husbands. Bakhtiar does not use the English word "obedience" at all in her translation of "*qānitat*." Instead, she translates *qānitāt* as women whose behavior is "in accord with morality."[167]

Reformist scholars treat wifely *nushūz* in a manner that is similar to progressive scholars. They use Q. 4:128 as evidence that *nushūz* is a spousal infraction that can be committed by either husbands or wives. Since either spouse can commit the infraction, *nushūz* cannot mean disobedience. Instead, wifely *nushūz* is interpreted to mean marital disloyalty, marital discord, resistance, or leaving the marriage; all of these acts allow for parity between the spouses.[168] According to reformists, the Qur'ān uses the example of a wife who commits *nushūz* as a case study to exemplify divine instructions for marital reconciliation. In this case, Q. 4:34 instructs the husband to take three steps to help to save the marriage. The husband can first try to discuss the problem with his wife, reasoning with her and consulting her on methods for rapprochement.[169] Next, he may sleep in a separate bed, sexually distancing himself in order to impress the gravity of the situation at hand.[170] Of course, this second step is moot if the wife has

166 Bakhtiar (n 163) xxviii.

167 Bakhtiar (n 163) xxviii. In this, she follows the example of M. Asad, who translated *qānitāt* as "being devout." Asad (103) Q. 4:34.

168 Bakhtiar (n 163) xxviii; Faizur Rahman, "Islamic Law of Divorce," article for TwoCircles.net, <http://twocircles.net/2011may11/islamic_law_divorce.html> (last accessed Dec. 25, 2012); WISE (n 164) 7; and Yüksel et al (n 163) 20.

169 Faizur Rahman (n 168); Islamic Supreme Council of Canada (n 165) 2; and Yüksel et al (n 163) 20.

170 Faizur Rahman (n 168); Islamic Supreme Council of Canada (n 165); and Yüksel et al (n 163) 20.

already left the marital home; but if the problem is martial disloyalty or discord, then this step can still be meaningful.

Reformists grapple with the third step of *wa-ḍribūhunna* in various way. They interpret *wa-ḍribūhunna* to mean "travel," "walk away," or "leave" wives, reasoning that if consultation and separation fail, a couple has little recourse other than external arbitration or divorce.[171] Alternatively, some reformist scholars offer an innovative interpretation of Q. 4:34 altogether, while ignoring its potentially violent meanings. In this case, there is no complicated argument to be made regarding *wa-ḍribūhunna* or the Islamic tradition; the violent implications of Q. 4:34 are either denied outright or simply ignored.[172] Faizur Rahman, the Secretary-General of the Chennai-based Forum for the Promotion of Moderate Thought among Muslims, follows the latter route, altogether ignoring the violent implications of Q. 4:34. In his treatise on divorce in Islam, he lists four measures a couple can take for reconciliation before proceeding to divorce. First, they should "reason through dialogue"; then they should temporarily physically separate from each other; then they should try "more convincing" to effect reconciliation; and, finally, they should seek arbitration. By translating *wa-ḍribūhunn*a as "more convincing," Faizur Rehman entirely eliminates the potentially violent interpretations of this verse.

The Islamic Supreme Council of Canada has followed a similar approach. In its 2012 *fatwā* that prohibits all domestic violence, the Council cited several Qur'anic verses and prophetic reports to support its argument that there is no hierarchy between spouses, although husbands do bear greater responsibility for economically supporting their wives and children.[173] Marriage is supposed to be based on "mutual love, respect and care," and wives are required to be obedient to God only—obedience to husbands is not even considered as a possibility in the *fatwā*. The Supreme Council cited Q. 4:34 to demonstrate how the Qur'ān can be mistranslated to sanction violence, without admitting that this verse has been interpreted

[171] Ahmed Ali has translated *wa-ḍribūhunna* to mean "have sex with them" and re-imagines the first two steps as leading to reconciliation, and so it is permissible to have sex after the separation has proved to be effective. I place Ahmed Ali in the reformist category because he does not permit husbands to hit their wives, offers a new meaning for *wa-ḍribūhunna*, and does not draw on the Islamic tradition for the authority of this position. Ahmed Ali, *Al-Qur'an: A Contemporary Translation* (Princeton: Princeton University Press, 2004) Q. 4:34. Reformist scholars who do offer unprecedented and nonviolent interpretations for *wa-ḍribūhunna* without appealing to the Islamic tradition for legitimacy base their interpretations on the multiple meanings of the basic verbal form of *ḍ-r-b* in the Qur'anic text. Bakhtiar (n 163) xxv–xxvi; and Yüksel et al (n 163) 20.

[172] Faizur Rahman (n 168).

[173] Verses cited include 3:104, 9:71, 22:41, 30:21, 4:19, 4:32, 2:187, 2:228, and 49:13. Islamic Supreme Council of Canada (n 165) 2.

to have violent connotations in the Islamic tradition. If a wife is sexually disloyal, the *fatwā* states that husbands can "educate" their wives, separate from their beds, and then "cite" them to an authority.[174] In this interpretation of Q. 4:34, the Supreme Council has completely rejected the violent meanings of *wa-ḍribūhunna*. It does not engage the pre-colonial Islamic legal and exegetical traditions in their *fatwā* and instead blames any violent connotations of *wa-ḍribūhunna* on mistranslations.

This *fatwā* occupies a new space in Muslim discussions of domestic violence. By advocating nonviolent interpretations of *wa-ḍribūhunna*, reformist scholars join progressives in creating a legitimate Islamic space in which marital discord and Q. 4:34 can be discussed without sanctioning violence against women. This space is newfound and exciting, since it demonstrates the inception of a shift in Muslim discourse that freely rejects violence against women without getting mired in the authoritative pre-colonial Islamic tradition. If this *fatwā* is effective, it may reflect a shift in authority away from the pre-colonial Islamic tradition to living scholars.

Along with reinterpreting the Qur'anic text, reformist scholars appeal to larger religious principles that help them to articulate a holistic picture of marital reconciliation. The authors of *Qur'an: A Reformist Translation*, Edip Yüksel, Layth Saleh al-Shaiban, and Martha Schulte-Nafeh, have proposed that any interpretation of *wa-ḍribūhunna* ought to be "fair" and "just." This rules out all violent interpretations of Q. 4:34, because hitting another human being is unfair and unjust. Furthermore, since Q. 2:228 establishes that spouses have similar rights over each other, allowing husbands to hit their wives would compromise this similarity in rights. Since the Qur'ān is logical and free from inconsistencies, it is impossible that it advocates similar rights for each spouse and, at the same time, allows husbands to hit their wives, especially if wives cannot reciprocate the violence. Moreover, Yüksel et al challenge the notion that beating a wife who is sexually disloyal will solve marital problems or save a marriage.[175] Moving the conversation from a theoretical realm to a practical one, they invite readers to imagine a scenario in which a husband confronts his wife who is cheating on him.

[174] "We would also like to clarify the translation of verse 34 of Surah Al Nisa. Some translators have the Arabic word, 'wadhriboo-hunnah' translated as 'strike' OR 'hit' (with toothbrush). In our opinion, this is not the correct translation. In a case when a married woman develops a sexual relationship outside the marriage, the Qur'an requires the husband to follow three steps and not to become violent. a. First educate her, b. Second take separate beds, c. Cite her to authority." Islamic Supreme Council of Canada (n 165) 2.

[175] "Beating women who are cheating and betraying the marriage contract is not an ultimate solution, and it is not consistent with the promise of equitability and comparable rights that appears in Q. 2:228. (This is an important consideration, because the Quran proclaims, and Muslims believe, that it is utterly free from inconsistencies.) But 'striking out' the disloyal wives,—that is, separating from them—is consistent, and it is the best solution. It is also fair." Yuksel et al (n 163) 20.

The husband tries to dissuade her by reasoning with her and through sexual withdrawal, but both fail to make an impression on her. It is clear that in such a situation, it is far more reasonable for a husband to leave the marriage than aggravate the situation further by beating her.[176]

Yüksel et al have made an interesting connection between the prescription of *wa-ḍribūhunna* in Q. 4:34 and the story of Job in the Qur'ān.[177] The Qur'anic version of the story is extremely brief, so pre-colonial exegetes filled in the gaps with additional details. In their telling, Job's wife managed to upset him while caring for him, and he swore that he would beat her a hundred times when he was healed. Once he was healed, though, he found himself in a conundrum. He understood that he was bound by his oath, but he felt terrible about beating his wife, who alone supported him and cared for him through his illness. According to the exegetes, God was compassionate to Job and offered him a dispensation: he could gather a hundred twigs and hit (*fa-ḍrib*) his wife with the bundle once. This way, he could fulfill the oath and also avoid hurting his wife. This entire backstory is absent from the Qur'anic text, which makes no reference to Job's wife or his hitting her, but the Qur'ān does instruct Job to hit (*fa-ḍrib*) something, though the object of his hitting is vague. It is not even clear whether Job is to hit a person or a thing.[178] Yüksel et al have objected to the exegetical telling of the story, calling it "rather silly"; they argue instead that *fa-ḍrib* in this verse most likely means to "travel."[179] For Yüskel et al, it makes much more sense for God to instruct Job to "travel" once he was healed than to "hit" something.

In the case of Q. 4:34, Yüksel et al have proposed that when Q. 4:34 instructs men to *wa-ḍribūhunna* their wives, it intends for them to "strike out" their wives, meaning "compel a separation" from them, somewhat akin to Job's "traveling" or "striking out" on his own. Since the connotations of "striking [someone] out" in English can be problematic and

[176] In the progressive and reformist framework, the possibility that women might actually enjoy being beaten is too crass and misogynistic to be considered.

[177] Asma Barlas has made this connection as well. Barlas (n 130) 188.

[178] Yusuf Ali's translation of this story reads, "Commemorate our servant Job, Behold he cried to his Lord: 'The Evil One has afflicted me with distress and suffering!' (The command was given:) 'Strike with thy foot: here is (water) wherein to wash, cool and refreshing and (water) to drink.' And We gave him (back) his people and doubled their number—as a Grace from Ourselves, and a thing for commemoration, for all who have Understanding. 'And take in thy hand a little grass and strike (*fa-ḍrib*) therewith: and break not (thy oath).' Truly We found him full of patience and constancy: how excellent in Our service! Ever did he turn (to Us)!" Yusuf Ali (n 12) Q. 38:41–4. Yüksel et al have described this as a "rather silly story." Yüksel et al (n 163) 19.

[179] Their re-translation of Q. 38:44 reads, "Take in your hand a bundle and travel with it, do not break your oath…" Yüksel et al (n 163) 20. The organization "Sisters in Islam" has also offered the possible interpretation of *wa-ḍribūhunna* to mean "strike out on a journey." Sisters in Islam (n 129) 11.

violent, it might have been more useful for them simply to translate *wa-ḍribūhunna* as "compelling a separation." However, the fact that they do not is a reflection of the constraints that the Arabic wording of the Qur'anic text has on new interpretations of *wa-ḍribūhunna*, which cannot easily be translated to "compel a separation" without intermediary hermeneutical steps.

Laleh Bakhtiar has also proposed that *wa-ḍribūhunna* instructs husbands to "leave" or "go away from" their wives.[180] The fact that she discusses her interpretation of *wa-ḍribūhunna* in Q. 4:34 in the introduction to her translation of the Qur'ān demonstrates the importance and centrality of this issue in contemporary Islamic thought. She confidently confronts an interlocutor who might dispute her interpretation based on lack of historical precedent. How can she attribute a meaning to *wa-ḍribūhunna* that was never proposed by any Islamic scholar in the glorious Islamic tradition? She retorts that if the tradition was unjust or corrupt, as many Muslim rulers were, it is still within her right to seek justice. Hence, the authority of her interpretation is rooted in her search for justice, which she claims pre-colonial scholars lost sight of in their exegesis of Q. 4:34. For Bakhtiar, the purpose of the commentary tradition is not to limit the possible interpretations of the Qur'ān but rather to expand them.[181] Thus, she feels warranted in arguing that wife-beating, under every circumstance, should be declared criminal behavior.

Like the translators of *A Reformist Qur'an*, Bakhtiar uses "fairness" and "justice" as criteria for determining the correct meaning of the Qur'ān. She relies on prophetic practice and the Qur'anic text to argue against interpreting *wa-ḍribūhunna* as "hit them." Muḥammad's personal behavior has been described as the "embodied Qur'ān," and so believers ought to consult Muḥammad's *sunna* (exemplary behavior) when interpreting and applying a particular verse. If *wa-ḍribūhunna* was meant to instruct husbands to hit their wives, then why did Muḥammad not hit his wives?[182] Bakhtiar argues that Muḥammad never hit his wives because he understood Q. 4:34 not as a

[180] Interpreting *wa-ḍribūhunna* as "to go away from" is grammatically problematic because it requires additional qualifiers in Arabic. Bakhtiar has defended her interpretation in the face of this criticism by saying that when translating a text into another language, one must accommodate for the structure of the language into which the text is being translated. This argument is not compelling because the qualifier is needed in the Arabic text, and it is not there. Bakhtiar (n 163) xxviii.

[181] Bakhtiar writes, "If we study Islamic history, after the time of the four Rightly Guided Caliphs, we Muslims have had for almost 1500 years of uninterrupted rulership by tyrants and dictators with the exception of a few years of a pious ruler. Does that mean that we cannot go against history and demand pious, benevolent rulers? No, of course not." Bakhtiar (n 163) xxx.

[182] For a critical examination of Muḥammad's position on hitting wives, see Ayesha S. Chaudhry, "'I Wanted One Thing and God Wanted Another…': The Dilemma of the

command to hit wives but rather as instructions for husbands to leave their wives if they could not reconcile their differences after consultation and separation. That explains why, when Muḥammad had a disagreement with his wives, he removed himself from their quarters rather than hit them.[183] Since Muḥammad's own marriages were based on his love and respect for his wives, any Muslim man who desires to follow his example cannot introduce violence into his marriage. Bakhtiar also draws on Qur'anic verses to support her position against violence in marriage. Citing Q. 2:231, which prohibits men from "injuring" wives who petition for divorce,[184] Bakhtiar has highlighted the contradiction created by Q. 2:231 and Q. 4:34 if *wa-ḍribūhunna* is interpreted as "hit them." In that case, holding the two interpretations at the same time would mean that husbands are prohibited from injuring their wives when they want divorce but are permitted to hit them in order to remain married to them. Bakhtiar reckons that since the Qur'ān cannot contain contradictions, it is impossible for *wa-ḍribūhunna* to mean "hit them."[185]

In a document entitled "Jihad Against Violence," the Women's Islamic Initiative in Spirituality and Equality (WISE) Shura Council has used a multi-pronged approach to reinterpret Q. 4:34.[186] They grant that the

Prophetic Example and the Qur'anic Injunction On Wife-Beating," *Journal of Religious Ethics*,39(3) (2011) 416–39. In this article, I argued that Muḥammad's *sunna* on wife-beating is rather complex and cannot easily be described as pro- or anti-wife-beating.

183 As seen in Chapter 2, no pre-colonial scholar connected Muḥammad leaving his wives to the third imperative in Q. 4:34. Rather, they saw his behavior as reflecting the second imperative of abandonment.

184 Q. 2:231 reads, "When ye divorce women, and they fulfill the term of their ('Idda), either take them back on equitable terms or set them free on equitable terms; but do not take them back to injure them, (or) to take undue advantage; if anyone does that he wrongs his own soul. Do not treat Allah's Signs as a jest, but solemnly rehearse Allah's favours on you, and the fact that He sent down to you the Book and Wisdom, for your instruction. And fear Allah and know that Allah is well acquainted with all things." Yusuf Ali (n 12) Q. 2:231.

185 See also WISE (n 164) 8.

186 The WISE document defies easy placement in the four categories in this chapter. Although they reject violent interpretations of *wa-ḍribūhunna*,providing a new interpretation for this word, and although they consciously depart from the pre-colonial Islamic tradition, they also consider the possibility of *wa-ḍribūhunna* meaning "hit them." They defend this possible meaning using all the instruments from the neo-traditionalist toolbox: in case Q. 4:34 permits husbands to hit their wives, the hitting is severely restricted so that it is only symbolic; it must be carried out with a toothbrush or folded handkerchief; and it is meant to gradually eliminate the husbandly privilege for hitting wives. Since the WISE document intends to be read as a policy piece, it is possible that they entertained this potential meaning in order to deter men from severely hitting their wives, in case they reject the alternative interpretation offered by Bakhtiar and WISE. From a practical perspective, then, this may at least soften the implications of violence for wives. From a purely intellectual perspective, however, considering the possibility that *wa-ḍribūhunna* means "hit them" weakens their claim, potentially betraying unease and discomfort with their adherence to a new, unprecedented exegesis of *wa-ḍribūhunna*.WISE (n 164) 10.

pre-colonial Islamic tradition interpreted *wa-ḍribūhunna* to mean "beat them" by following a "sound" methodology that might have been legitimate in their own patriarchal context. However, those conclusions are no longer just or relevant to contemporary Muslim communities. Hence, WISE consciously departs from the Islamic tradition in order to adhere to Bakhtiar's interpretation of *wa-ḍribūhunna* to mean "go away from them." Just as pre-colonial scholars allowed their social and historical norms to influence their readings of Q. 4:34, the WISE Shura Council also draws on their subjectivities when interpreting Q. 4:34. In addition to the reinterpretation mentioned previously, the Council has endeavored to justify a nonviolent reading of Q. 4:34 based on the "principle objectives" (*maqāsid*) of Islamic law. The Council argues that the purpose of Islamic law is to protect the basic rights of "religion (*dīn*), life (*nafs*), mind (*ʿaql*), family (*nasl*), dignity (*ʿirḍ*) and wealth (*māl*)."[187] A law that violates any of these basic rights would undermine the very purpose of Islamic law and thus can be branded "unIslamic." Hitting one's wife obviously harms a woman's dignity and thus cannot be said to represent the divine intent.

In offering their interpretations of Q. 4:34, reformist scholars unambiguously privilege an egalitarian cosmology over a patriarchal one, arguing against the possibility that Q. 4:34 might have a violent meaning. To this end, they offer new, unprecedented, and nonviolent meanings for *wa-ḍribūhunna*. By doing so, they break from the Islamic legal and exegetical traditions, creating the egalitarian–authoritarian dilemma. Instead of trying to gain authority by rooting their interpretations in the Islamic tradition, they claim authority based on their reasoning of the Qur'anic text, asserting their subjectivity as authoritative. While some reformist scholars admit to breaking from the Islamic tradition and defend their choice on moral grounds, others strategically disregard the tradition entirely. Through different means, reformists join progressives in creating a new Islamic tradition on wife-beating in which some voices can be heard as challenging and rejecting interpretations of the Qur'ān that sanction violence against women.

CONCLUSION

Q. 4:34 is an excellent case study for exploring the diversity of post-colonial Muslim approaches to Qur'ān interpretation. Dividing these approaches into four categories—traditionalist, neo-traditionalist, progressive, and reformist—that are determined by the answer to three interrelated

[187] WISE (n 164) 9.

questions is a helpful way to capture the variety of positions available in the post-colonial period. These questions entail whether a patriarchal or egalitarian cosmology is privileged; whether the Islamic tradition is appealed to for authority; and whether it is in the end considered ethical to hit one's wife. Any answer to the three interrelated questions is necessarily fraught with political pitfalls, as the two cosmologies—patriarchal and egalitarian—are divided by the emotional and political experiences of colonialism. The way a Muslim scholar balances these two cosmologies directly impacts his or her position on the right of husbands to hit wives. Traditionalist and neo-traditionalist scholars root their authority in the Islamic tradition and therefore permit husbands to hit their wives for disciplinary purposes, albeit in an increasingly restrictive fashion. Progressive and reformist scholars distance themselves from the patriarchal positions of the pre-colonial period, arguing against the right of husbands to hit wives and offering alternative ways to think about the Qur'anic text in the contemporary period.

The struggle in modern discussions is not so much with the Qur'anic text itself but with the tradition of interpretation that attributed patriarchal meanings to the Qur'ān. All scholars, however, share a devotion to the Qur'anic text as the word of God, and they struggle to belong to and speak authoritatively in communities that share this commitment to the Qur'ān. In the end, contemporary thought about the right of husbands to hit their wives displays a great deal of variety and sophistication, and in many ways it parallels the diversity in pre-colonial scholarship on topics unrelated to gender. In fact, in providing multiple interpretations of Q. 4:34, modern scholars enrich the Islamic tradition by uncovering the polysemic nature of the Qur'anic text in areas where the tradition failed to recognize diversity. The variance of post-colonial perspectives on Q. 4:34 demonstrates that there is not one, eternally obvious, plain-sense meaning of the Qur'anic text; rather there are multiple, sometimes competing, plain-sense meanings. These meanings are shaped by the social and historical contexts, individual subjectivities, and idealized cosmologies of its readers.

5

Submissive Texts and Idealized Cosmologies

The most striking feature of post-colonial exegetical and legal approaches to Q. 4:34, especially in contrast to the pre-colonial period, is a spectacular diversity of opinions. This diversity is fueled by a new idealized cosmology that challenges and unsettles the monolithic pre-colonial idealized cosmology. Whereas the pre-colonial cosmology of Muslim scholars was unabashedly patriarchal in nature, in the post-colonial period an egalitarian cosmology has emerged which posits gender-egalitarianism as a fundamental moral good. Recall from the Introduction that an idealized cosmology refers to a worldview based on an 'if only' ideal; in the case of the Muslim scholars under study, idealized cosmologies are visions of the universe as it would exist if all humans submitted entirely to God's laws. It is the world as God intended it, as it should be, unpolluted by concerns about social reality. Idealized cosmologies are not necessarily contingent on social and historical circumstances, though they are certainly influenced by such factors. Nevertheless, an idealized cosmology represents a conception in the mind's eye that is unconstrained by experience.

In the pre-colonial period, all legal and exegetical scholars in this study shared one idealized cosmology in which the universe was created by a God who ordered all of his creation. Humans ranked above animals, and amongst humans, men had a status higher than women. God himself ranked men over women by favoring them and endowing them with superior intellectual and physical qualities. Attributing a moral character to this cosmology made it a virtue for God's creations to be content and pleased with their placement. Any discontent was viewed as a sign of rebellion, not only against the cosmology and those who ranked higher but also against God. Indeed, the normative power of the patriarchal cosmology lies in this point. As explained in earlier chapters, the pre-colonial idealized cosmology mediated women's relationships to God through their husbands. Wives pleased God by pleasing their husbands and incurred God's wrath when they angered their husbands. Hence, a wife's obedience to God and her husband were intertwined. In this framework, the disciplinary power of husbands was not only reasonable but moral, ethical, and just.

The advent of colonialism and its accompanying changes to knowledge distribution and acquisition gave rise to a new, competing egalitarian idealized cosmology that is fundamentally irreconcilable with the pre-colonial patriarchal cosmology.[1] Novel conceptions of human rights and gender-egalitarianism popularized in colonial and post-colonial contexts profoundly affected the way Muslims began to imagine themselves individually, as religious communities, and as part of a larger political world. This contributed to the emergence of an egalitarian cosmology, which in turn influenced the expectations and meanings Muslims began searching for in the Qur'anic text. In this new cosmology, the universe is created by a God who is committed to justice; a critical sign of his justice is the elimination of rankings that make one human superior to another based on essential or circumstantial characteristics. Rather, humans must all strive to distinguish themselves in God's eyes by spiritually bettering themselves. The playing field is completely leveled for attaining God's favor through good deeds, and no human has an intrinsic advantage over another based on race, gender, social status, or class. In this idealized cosmology, each human being has direct, unmediated access to the divine; both men and women stand alongside each other—on equal footing—below God. Husbands and wives can aid each other in attaining God's favor, but neither is responsible for the moral oversight of the other. Hence, it makes no sense for one spouse to have disciplinary privilege over the other, and it is never appropriate, ethical, moral, or just for a husband to hit his wife.

Comparing pre- and post-colonial approaches to Q. 4:34 based on their underlying idealized cosmologies helps to account for both the monolithic nature of pre-colonial approaches to Q. 4:34 as well as the multiplicity of perspectives in the post-colonial period. In the pre-colonial period, a

[1] Ziba Mir-Hosseini writes, "This rethinking is framed in two related contexts. The first context is that of the current encounters between two systems of values and two modes of knowledge production. The first mode is rooted in pre-modern conceptions of justice, gender and rights, which allow discrimination among individuals on the basis of faith, status and gender as found in classical fiqh rulings. The second mode is shaped by the ideals of universal human rights, equality and personal freedom, as found and advocated in international human rights documents such as CEDAW (Convention on the Elimination of All Forms of Discrimination Against Women). The second context is that of 20th-century shifts, both globally and locally, in the politics of religion, law and gender, and the changed relationship between Muslim legal tradition, state and social practice in Muslim contexts." Ziba Mir-Hosseini, "Decoding the 'DNA of Patriarchy' in Muslim Family Laws," Musawah, Mission Statement (July 23, 2012), <http://www.musawah.org/decoding-dna-patriarchy-muslim-family-laws> (last accessed Jan. 23, 2013).

patriarchal idealized cosmology enjoyed hegemony, resulting in monolithic interpretations of the husbandly privilege to physically discipline wives. Although scholars in the pre-colonial period embodied multiple subjectivities that were influenced by their significantly varied historical, social, political, theological, and legal contexts, their disparate subjectivities were not reflected in their scholarship on Q. 4:34. They were able to advance an essentially unvaried approach to marital hierarchy because they all adhered to the same idealized cosmology.

In contrast, the clash of two competing idealized cosmologies has produced creative interpretations of Q. 4:34 in the post-colonial period. Post-colonial Muslim scholars approach gendered marital hierarchy and the right of husbands to hit their wives in many ways. Some have sought to affirm the hierarchy, while others reject it outright; some have attempted to balance the two competing cosmologies and others propose alternative interpretations that sidestep the question of marital hierarchy altogether. The bedrock of this high-yielding interpretive pasture is the struggle of post-colonial scholars to reconcile competing idealized cosmologies—one patriarchal and the other egalitarian. The competition results from the difficult relationship that post-colonial scholars have to the "Islamic tradition."

The highly politicized nature of the role of the "Islamic tradition" is rooted in a post-colonial historical and social context. Many Muslim scholars see the colonial experience and loss of empire as a punishment for Muslims. Muslims lost God's favor because they had gone astray, neglecting their religious duties. Some Muslim scholars have called for a return to a pre-colonial Islam in order to reconnect with God and to restore the glory of Muslims past by reclaiming their political sovereignty.[2] As the myth of an uncorrupted, pristine pre-colonial past began to emerge, the "Islamic tradition"—which came to mean the legal and exegetical disciplines—took on an overblown authoritative status.[3] The details of the Islamic tradition that scholars

[2] The founder of the Muslim Brotherhood in Egypt, Hasan al-Banna (d. 1949), is an excellent example of a post-colonial Muslim scholar who argued for a return to a pure, Arab, pre-colonial Islam through political action. Hasan al-Banna, *Between Yesterday and Today*, available at <http://web.youngmuslims.ca/online_library/books/byat/> (last accessed Jan. 23, 2013). See also Shireen T. Hunter, "Introduction" in Shireen T. Hunter and Vartan Gregorian (eds.), *Reformist Voices of Islam: Mediating Islam and Modernity* (Armonk: M.E. Sharpe, 2008) 12; Nikki R. Keddie, *Sayyid Jamal ad-Din "al-Afghani": A Political Biography* (Berkeley: University of California Press, 1972) 130; and Qasim Zaman, *The ʿUlama in Contemporary Islam: Custodians of Change* (Princeton: Princeton University Press, 2002) 24.

[3] Sachedina has discussed the extravagant authority of the Islamic tradition in contemporary Muslim discourse: "Muslim traditionalist scholarship tends to treat any academic endeavor that questions its appropriation and interpretation of the revealed texts, whether from the Qur'an or the Tradition, in their historical contexts as an affront to the sanctity and absolute nature of Islamic revelation . . . In other words, the veracity and absoluteness of the

spoke of and continue to speak of are necessarily hazy and unfocused. The authority of this tradition is disconnected from its content. The myth of a pure Islamic tradition projects back expectations of what post-colonial scholars hope for from the Islamic tradition; it is not about actually adhering to this tradition. In this context, authority in Muslim communities is often granted to those whose voices seem rooted in the "Islamic tradition."

Meanwhile, scholars who offer new and innovative religious approaches lose religious authority on two counts: by cutting themselves off from the authoritative tradition and by appearing to be influenced by modernity, which is Western and therefore presumptively colonial. For a large portion of the Muslim world, the traumatic experience of colonialism and loss of empire after a glorious history of global expansion and leadership coincided with their encounter with modernity and enlightenment. Modern ideals and ideas thus came to represent the degrading and humiliating experience of colonialism. Moreover, since colonialists disingenuously justified their economic, political, and military conquests through the language of women's emancipation, feminism is often viewed by Muslims as part of a dangerous colonialist or neo-colonialist agenda. In this political context, calls for feminism and gender-egalitarianism can be tantamount to betraying one's community and collaborating with colonialists.[4]

In light of these realities of the post-colonial period, this chapter examines the role of idealized cosmologies in shaping the expectations that Muslims have of the Qur'anic text. How do Muslim intellectuals and activists select relevant Qur'anic verses and prophetic reports in order to justify and support their interpretations of Qur'anic texts, including Q. 4:34? In order to highlight the disparate uses of the Qur'anic text and prophetic reports to argue for opposing patriarchal and egalitarian idealized cosmologies, this chapter will compare pre-colonial legal and exegetical perspectives on Q. 4:34 with those of post-colonial progressives and reformists. Progressive and reformist scholars ultimately privilege an egalitarian idealized cosmology over the patriarchal one espoused by pre-colonial scholars. As such, progressive and reformist scholars do not permit husbands to hit their wives under any circumstance. This position sharply diverges from that of pre-colonial scholars, all of whom found a way to carve out a legitimate space for the physical disciplining of wives.

past rulings have been regarded as independent of any context and material condition for their universal applicability in the faith community." Sachedina, *Islam and the Challenge of Human Rights* (New York: Oxford University Press, 2009) 120 and 130.

[4] Margot Badran, *Feminists, Islam, and Nation: Gender and the Making of Modern Egypt* (Princeton: Princeton University Press, 1995) 20.

The fact that all of these religious scholars rely on the Qur'anic text and prophetic reports in order to justify their divergent positions provides an excellent case study for the pliability of the Qur'anic text and *aḥādīth* as authoritative sources.

THE QUR'ĀN: A PLIABLE TEXT

Post-colonial progressive and reformist scholars often level a charge against pre-colonial exegetical scholars that their method of interpreting the Qur'anic text was overly "linear and atomistic."[5] This prevented pre-colonial exegetes from comprehending the holistic message of the Qur'ān. The basic structure of Qur'ān commentaries, which analyzed the potential meanings of each word, participle, and pronoun through a line-by-line, word-by-word, verse-by-verse approach, is often held up as a point of weakness rather than strength of pre-colonial exegetical scholarship. The purpose of this criticism is twofold: first, to excuse the failure of pre-colonial scholars to discover the correct interpretation of a specific Qur'anic verse or term under study; and, second, to offer a new, "correct" interpretation by sidestepping the tradition, without having to reject it outright. Instead of the linear-atomistic approach, post-colonial scholars propose an interpretive strategy that explains individual verses in the Qur'ān through reference to other related verses. This approach is called *tafsīr al-qur'ān bi-l-qur'ān* (exegesis of the Qur'ān through the Qur'ān).[6] Those who champion this methodology see it as a sound approach to Qur'anic exegesis because it allows the Qur'ān to speak for itself when the meaning of particular verses is under question.

In the case of Q. 4:34, pre-colonial exegetes are criticized for being atomistic because they did not make what post-colonial scholars see as "obvious" connections with other verses in the Qur'ān. The three verses that are most commonly cited in progressive and reformist interpretations of Q. 4:34 are Q. 4:128, Q. 30:21, and Q. 49:13. Post-colonial scholars who seek a gender-egalitarian interpretation of the Qur'ān argue that any

[5] Asma Barlas, *"Believing Women" in Islam: Unreading Patriarchal Interpretations of the Qur'an* (Austin: University of Texas Press, 2002) 8 and Muntasir Mir, *Coherence in the Quran: A Study of Islahi's Concept of Nazm in Tadabbur-i-Quran* (Plainfield: American Trust Publication, 1986) 1.

[6] See, eg, Amina Wadud, *Qur'an and Woman* (New York: Oxford University Press, 1999) 5 and Women's Islamic Initiative in Spirituality and Equality (WISE), *Jihad Against Violence: Muslim Women's Struggle for Peace* (2009), available at <http://www.wisemuslimwomen.org/images/uploads/Jihad_against_Violence_Digest(color).pdf> (last accessed Jan. 22, 2013).

interpretation of wifely *nushūz* (in Q. 4:34) without reference to husbandly *nushūz* (in Q. 4:128) would be incomplete. Q. 4:128 reads:

> If a wife fears cruelty [*nushūz*] or desertion on her husband's part, there is no blame on them if they arrange an amicable settlement between themselves; and such settlement is best, even though men's souls are swayed by greed. But if ye do good and practise self-restraint, Allah is well-acquainted with all that ye do.[7]

Since the Qur'anic text refers to both husbandly and wifely *nushūz*, progressive and reformist scholars argue that they should not be treated in isolation from each other—as they were in the pre-colonial period. Rather, husbandly and wifely *nushūz* should be understood in light of each other. If *nushūz* is an undesirable spousal quality that both husbands and wives can exhibit, then it must have a shared meaning that can be applied to both spouses.[8] This rules out any interpretation of *nushūz* that is hierarchal, including disobedience. While pre-colonial exegetes interpreted wifely *nushūz* primarily as disobedience,[9] progressive and reformist scholars object to this interpretation because disobedience is not reciprocal. It cannot be applied to both husbands and wives; it necessitates hierarchy. Instead, they argue that the text of Q. 4:128 hints at the meaning of *nushūz* by mentioning desertion and sexual antipathy (*iʿrāḍ*) alongside *nushūz*. As such, progressive and reformist scholars prefer to interpret spousal *nushūz* as sexual disloyalty or misconduct.

Progressive and reformist scholars often use Q. 30:21 as the framing text for interpreting Q. 4:34. This verse describes spouses as signs of God and

[7] Translation by Abdullah Yusuf Ali, *The Meaning of the Holy Quran* (Beltsville: Amana Publications, 1997) Q. 4:128.

[8] Khaled M. Abou El Fadl, *Conference of the Books: The Search for Beauty in Islam* (Lanham: University Press of America, 2001) 171 and 174; Shaykh M. Hisham Kabbani and Homayra Ziad, *The Prohibition of Domestic Violence in Islam* (Washington, DC: World Organization for Resource Development and Education (WORDE), 2011), available at <http://www.worde.org/wp-content/uploads/2011/09/DV-Fatwa-Online-Version.pdf> (last accessed Jan. 22, 2013); Mohamed Mahmoud, "To Beat or Not to Beat: On the Exegetical Dilemmas over Qur'ān Q. 4:34," *Journal of the American Oriental Society*, 126(4) (2006) 549; and Hadia Mubarak, "Breaking the Interpretive Monopoly: A Re-Examination of Verse 4:34," *Hawwa*, 2(3) (2005) 273.

[9] For a comparative analysis of husbandly and wifely *nushūz* in pre-colonial exegetical and legal sources, see Kecia Ali, "Obedience and Disobedience in Islamic Discourses" in Suad Joseph (ed.), *Encyclopedia of Women in Islamic Cultures* (Leiden: Brill, 2007) 5:309–13 and Ayesha S. Chaudhry, "Marital Discord in Qur'anic Exegesis: A Lexical Analysis of Husbandly and Wifely *Nushūz* in Q. 4:34 and Q. 4:128" in S.R. Burge (ed.), *The Meaning of the Word: Lexciology and Tafsir* (forthcoming). In al-Ḥīrī's survey of the various meanings of *nushūz* in the Qur'ān, he designates "disobedience" as the meaning of wifely *nushūz* in Q. 4:34 and "sexual withdrawal" as the meaning of husbandly *nushūz* in Q. 4:128. Ismāʿīl ibn Aḥmad al-Nīsābūrī al-Ḥīrī, *Wujūh al-Qurʾān* (Mashhad: Majmaʿ al-Buhūth al-Islāmiyya, 2001) 562. See also Chapters 2 and 3 in this book.

portrays an ideal marital relationship as one that is infused with love and mercy. This verse states:

> And among His Signs is this, that He created for you mates from among yourselves, that ye may dwell in tranquility with them, and He has put love and mercy between your (hearts); verily in that are Signs for those who reflect.[10]

Progressive and reformist scholars point out that this verse (Q. 30:21) establishes the base for an ideal relationship, and as such, it poses a challenge to the acceptability of the physical disciplining of wives. How can the egalitarian and reciprocal relationship described in Q. 30:21, based on love and mercy, allow one spouse to discipline another at all, never mind through physical violence?[11] If Q. 4:34 is interpreted to permit the physical disciplining of wives, then it stands in contradiction to the spirit and letter of Q. 30:21. The pre-colonial scholars under study never mentioned Q. 30:21 in their exegetical and legal reflections on the meanings of Q. 4:34, and progressive and reformist scholars argue that this prevented them from seeing the message of Q. 4:34 in light of the larger picture of an ideal, egalitarian marriage painted through several Qur'anic verses.

Pre-colonial scholars are also accused of failing to consider the ethics of marriage within the larger ethos promulgated by the Qur'anic text in verses such as Q. 49:13. This verse is seen by progressive and reformist scholars as replacing unjust racial, gendered, and class hierarchies with a merit-based spiritual hierarchy.[12] Q. 49:13 states:

> O mankind! We created you from a single (pair) of a male and a female, and made you into nations and tribes, that ye may know each other (not that ye may despise each other). Verily the most honoured of you in the sight of Allah is (he who is) the most righteous of you. And Allah has full knowledge and is well acquainted (with all things).[13]

This verse appears to both celebrate gender and ethnic differences and remove the possibility of claiming superiority based on any of these distinctions. Progressive and reformist scholars believe this verse establishes piety, as opposed to gender or race, as the legitimate basis for differentiating between human beings. Given this egalitarian, merit-based

[10] Yusuf Ali (n 7) Q. 30:21.

[11] Laleh Bakhtiar, *The Sublime Qur'an* (Chicago: Kazi Publications, 2007) xxviii; Kabbani and Ziad (n 8); Islamic Supreme Council of Canada, *Fatwā: Honour Killings, Domestic Violence and Misogyny are Un-Islamic and Major Crimes* (Feb. 4, 2012), available at <http://www.islamicsupremecouncil.com/fatwa-honour-killings-misogyny-domestic-violence.pdf> (last accessed Jan. 22, 2013); and Sisters in Islam and Yasmin Masidi, *Are Muslim Men Allowed to Beat their Wives?* (Selangor: Sisters in Islam, 1991 and 2009) 2.

[12] See, eg, Mubarak (n 8) 275 and Islamic Supreme Council of Canada (n 11).

[13] Yusuf Ali (n 7) Q. 49:13.

social ordering, it is difficult to maintain that husbands are granted disciplinary authority in marriage based solely on their gender.[14]

Progressive and reformist scholars reason that if pre-colonial scholars had considered the potential meanings of Q. 4:34 in the context of verses like Q. 4:128, Q. 30:21, and Q. 49:13, then they would have offered less patriarchal interpretations of this verse and would have displayed overt ethical discomfort with the right of husbands to hit their wives. However, a close study of pre-colonial exegetical and juridical works demonstrates that this criticism is not entirely warranted. Pre-colonial exegesis cannot easily be labeled as "atomistic" while post-colonial progressive and reformist interpretations are seen as "holistic." In fact, since most post-colonial progressive and reformist commentaries of the Qur'ān provide commentary of only select verses and passages, their approach is arguably more atomistic than that of pre-colonial exegetes. After all, pre-colonial exegetes explored the meanings of each verse and word in the Qur'ān in the context of the entire Qur'anic text. Pre-colonial exegetes and jurists were trained in multiple disciplines, including the Qur'anic sciences, *ḥadīth* literature, Islamic law, and theology. Their exegesis of individual Qur'anic verses aligned with their overall holistic understanding of the Qur'anic text, which in turn fit in the framework of their larger idealized cosmology. If pre-colonial scholars did not cite Q. 4:128, Q. 30:21, and Q. 49:13 in their interpretations of Q. 4:34, it was not because they were unaware of these verses or unable to think of them in connection with Q. 4:34 but rather because they did not consider them relevant to Q. 4:34. This is because their idealized cosmology and thus their expectation of what the Qur'ān said about marriage differed sharply from the idealized cosmology and expectations of progressive and reformist Muslim scholars. Pre-colonial scholars simply had a different understanding of the holistic message of the Qur'ān, which in turn resulted in a divergent conception of marriage. Pre-colonial scholars understood the comprehensive message of the Qur'ān in light of a God-centered social hierarchy, where God's kingdom on Earth was composed of divinely arranged hierarchical social

[14] Riffat Hassan writes, "God, who speaks through the Qur'an, is characterized by justice, and can never be guilty of '*zulm*' (unfairness, tyranny, oppression or wrongdoing). Hence, the Qur'an, as God's word, cannot be made the source of human injustice." Riffat Hassan, *Women's Rights and Islam: From the I.C.P.D. to Beijing*(Louisville: NISA Publications, 1995) 12. See also, Lisa Hajjar, "Religion, State Power, and Domestic Violence in Muslim Societies: A Framework for Comparative Analysis," *Law & Social Inquiry*, 29(1) (2004) 11. Abdullahi An-Na'im writes, "Neither of the conditions or advantages of physical might or earning power-set by verse 4:34 as the justification for the *qawama* of men over women is tenable today." Abdullahi An-Na'im, *Dossier 14–15: Islam and Women's Rights: A Case Study*, <http://www.wluml.org/node/269> (last accessed May 22, 2013). See also, Sachedina (n 3) 121.

institutions that were ordered based on their created natures. In contrast, post-colonial progressive and reformist scholars understand the message of the Qur'ān in light of a God-centered world that is fundamentally egalitarian and where humans distinguish themselves from each other through God-consciousness and meritorious actions.

This way of thinking about the difference between the approaches of pre- and post-colonial Qur'ān interpretation leads to a rather startling conclusion. Depending on which Qur'anic verses are emphasized, the Qur'ān can be successfully used to argue for either a fundamentally egalitarian marital structure or a patriarchal one. In the business of Qur'ān interpretation, what readers expect from the text is more important than what the text actually says. This point is made well by pre-colonial scholars who did in fact draw on other Qur'anic verses to illuminate the meanings of Q. 4:34; they just selected different ones. For comparison, it is worth contrasting the post-colonial selection of Qur'anic verses with verses that pre-colonial exegetes and jurists considered most relevant to interpretation of Q. 4:34.

Three Qur'anic verses that appeared in the pre-colonial exegesis of Q. 4:34 were Q. 33:33, Q. 4:32, and Q. 20:114. While none of these verses make an appearance in the post-colonial progressive and reformist sources under study, they fit seamlessly into the idealized cosmology of pre-colonial exegetes, who understood a gendered marital hierarchy as divinely ordained and sanctioned. Since pre-colonial exegetes were untroubled by this hierarchy, their selection of Qur'anic verses either supported a hierarchal vision of marriage or did not address the hierarchy at all. According to pre-colonial exegetes, Q. 33:33 separates the social roles of men and women based on gender differentiation. This verse was further understood as discouraging women from having prominent public roles, urging them instead to be steadfast in their devotional activities and to protect their chastity.[15] Q. 33:33 reads:

> And stay quietly in your houses, and make not a dazzling display, like that of the former Times of Ignorance; and establish regular Prayer, and give regular Charity; and obey Allah and His Messenger. And Allah only wishes to remove all abomination from you, ye Members of the Family, and to make you pure and spotless.[16]

In this verse, Muḥammad's wives were instructed to be cloistered, and exegetes extended this prescription to apply to all believing women, since Muḥammad's wives were seen as exemplary models for believing women.

[15] Eg, Aḥmad ibn Muḥammad al-Thaʿlabī, *al-Kashf wa-l-bayān: al-maʿrūf Tafsīr al-Thaʿlabī* (Beirut: Dār Iḥyāʾ al-Turāth al-ʿArabī, 2002) 3:302.

[16] Yusuf Ali (n 7) Q. 33:33.

When read in light of Q. 33:33, Q. 4:34 further establishes the authority of men over cloistered women by specifying the virtuous and immoral behavior that women might exhibit within the sphere of the household. In that spirit, Q. 4:34 adds an additional authority figure for wives, alongside God and his Messenger. Whereas Q. 33:33 commands women to be obedient to both God and his Messenger, Q. 4:34 explains that wives obey God through their obedience to their husbands. In this way, Q. 4:34 and Q. 33:33 can be read as complementary texts that reinforce a gendered social order in which men rank above women.

Q.4:32 and Q. 20:114 were seen as pertinent to Q. 4:34 through the occasion of revelation (*asbāb al-nuzūl*) literature. As seen in Chapter 1, Q. 4:32 was revealed in response to Umm Salama's query about the disparity in the allotment of inheritance for men and women. According to this story, Q. 4:32 explained God's general preference for men over women. Pre-colonial exegetes saw this verse as discouraging believers from covetousness and differentiating between the spiritual rewards for men and women:

> And in no wise covet those things in which Allah hath bestowed His gifts more freely (*faḍḍala*) on some of you than on others: to men is allotted what they earn, and to women what they earn: but ask Allah of His bounty: for Allah hath full knowledge of all things.[17]

Pre-colonial exegetes read Q. 4:32 as prefacing the message of Q. 4:34. Q. 4:32 establishes the fact that God prefers some over others in general, hinting that this favor is gender-based, and calls on believers not to covet the status or favor bestowed upon others. Having established this general framework, pre-colonial exegetes saw Q. 4:34 as simply expounding on one particular instance of God's favor—that of men over women—and its instantiation in the marital relationship.[18]

Q.20:114 was also thought to be revealed in connection with Q. 4:34 but within the setting of a different cause (*sabab*) for the revelation of Q. 4:34. In this *sabab*, Muḥammad ruled for retribution in support of a woman, Ḥabība, who had been slapped by her husband. However, before this ruling

[17] Yusuf Ali (n 7) Q. 4:32.

[18] Pre-colonial exegetes who directly connected Q. 4:34 to Q. 4:32 include Muḥammad ibn Yūsuf Abū Ḥayyān, *Tafsīr al-baḥr al-muḥīṭ* (Beirut: Dār al-Kutub al-ʿIlmiyya, 1993) 3:248; ʿAbd al-Ḥaqq ibn Ghālib Ibn ʿAṭiyya, *al-Muḥarrar al-wajīz fī tafsīr al-Kitāb al-ʿAzīz* (Beirut: Manshūrāt Muḥammad ʿAlī Bayḍūn, 2001) 2:44–6; Muḥammad ibn Aḥmad al-Qurṭubī, *al-Jāmiʿ li-aḥkām al-Qurʾān: tafsīr al-Qurṭubī* (Beirut: Dār al-Kitāb al-ʿArabī, 1997) 5:162; and Fakhr al-Dīn al-Rāzī, *al-Tafsīr al-kabīr* (Beirut: Dār Iḥyāʾ al-Turāth al-ʿArabī, 1997) 4:70. In the post-colonial period, some traditionalist scholars have continued to follow this line of reasoning. Eg, Israr Ahmed saw Q. 4:32 as "mentally prepar[ing] women" for the gendered marital hierarchy in Q. 4:34. Israr Ahmed, *Dawra Tarjuma Qurʾān* (audio) (Lahore: Markazi Anjuman Khuddam-ul-Qur'an, 2008).

could be applied, Q. 4:34 was revealed, and Muḥammad's injunction was revoked. In connection with this, Muḥammad was rebuked for hastening to his ruling without first seeking divine council. This verse proclaims:

> High above all is Allah, the King, the Truth! Be not in haste with the Qur'ān before its revelation to thee is completed, but say "O my Lord! increase me in knowledge."[19]

This verse is not primarily concerned with marital hierarchy at all and was not used in service of supporting a gendered marital hierarchy. Rather, it was used to address a theological problem involving a disagreement between God and Muḥammad about the case of the slapped woman. By chastising Muḥammad for hastening to judgment before seeking God's counsel, exegetes were able to make the disagreement into a dispute about the appropriate protocol for making juridical rulings rather than a disputation about the correct legal outcome for Ḥabība.[20]

Like pre-colonial exegetes, pre-colonial jurists also cited Qur'anic verses selectively. Analyzing the Qur'anic verses referenced by legal scholars helps us to see how jurists imagined a given verse to fit into their idealized cosmology. In legal discussions surrounding the right of husbands to physically discipline wives, Q. 4:34 was used as a proof-text to support this right. According to pre-colonial jurists, Q. 4:34 instituted the right of husbands to discipline their wives, and this was absorbed into Islamic jurisprudence and affirmed as a fundamental marital right. In this way, Q. 4:34 had the tangible legal impact of sanctioning violence against women as a disciplinary measure available to husbands who wish to castigate or restrain their wives. In their discussions of the disciplinary authority of husbands over wives, pre-colonial jurists referenced Qur'anic verses that they understood to be relevant to the regulation of this husbandly privilege. The selected verses were sometimes similar to and other times different from the ones that pre-colonial exegetes drew upon. In a few instances, pre-colonial jurists cited verses that progressive and reformist Muslim scholars interpret as establishing the egalitarian ethos of marriage in the Qur'ān. However, pre-colonial jurists saw these same verses as establishing a hierarchical vision of marriage. Four verses that pre-colonial jurists used to explore the issues surrounding the right of husbands to hit wives were Q. 4:128, Q. 2:228, Q. 5:45, and Q. 5:33.

[19] Yusuf Ali (n 7) Q. 20:114.

[20] For more on this, see Chapter 1. Eg, Muḥammad ibn ʿAbd Allāh Ibn al-ʿArabī, *Aḥkām al-Qur'ān* (Cairo: Dār al-Manār, 2002) 1:493; Ibn ʿAṭiyya (n 18) 2:47; and Jalāl al-Dīn ʿAbd al-Raḥmān al-Suyūṭī, *al-Durr al-manthūr fī al-tafsīr al-ma'thūr* (Beirut: Dār al-Maʿrifa, 1970) 2:151.

Progressive and reformist scholars understand Q. 4:128 and Q. 2:228 as establishing an equitable framework for marriage in the Qur'ān. However, pre-colonial jurists saw these same verses as differentiating between the roles of husbands and wives in marriage. As seen previously, progressive and reformist scholars see the mention of husbandly *nushūz* in Q. 4:128 as confirming that *nushūz* cannot mean the "disobedience" of wives to their husbands, since both spouses can commit *nushūz*. Pre-colonial jurists quoted Q. 4:128 to argue the opposite point; based on the disparate treatments of husbandly and wifely *nushūz* in the Qur'anic text itself, they argued that the *nushūz* of husbands and wives was meant to have different meanings and consequences. In the case of husbands, *nushūz* was interpreted as meaning sexual antipathy to a wife, and wives were encouraged to address their husbands' *nushūz* by giving up some of their marital rights in order to remain married to their husbands. In contrast, wifely *nushūz* was understood to be the disobedience of wives, and the text was understood to instruct husbands to return their wives to obedience through disciplinary measures.[21]

Q.2:228 similarly has served to support opposing points for pre- and post-colonial scholars. This verse mentions that husbands and wives have similar rights to each other and also that men have a "degree" over women. When progressive and reformist scholars cite Q. 2:228, they underline the fact that the rights of both spouses are similar to each other.[22] However, in the pre-colonial period jurists saw this verse as granting husbands a "degree" over their wives.[23] This verse reads:

> Divorced women shall wait concerning themselves for three monthly periods. Nor is it lawful for them to hide what Allah hath created in their wombs,

[21] Eg, Zayn al-Dīn ibn Ibrāhīm Ibn Nujaym, *al-Baḥr al-Rā'iq, Sharḥ Kanz al-Daqā'iq* (Quetta: al-Maktaba al-Mājidīya, 1983) 4:128 and 303; Muwaffaq al-Dīn 'Abd Allāh ibn Aḥmad Ibn Qudāma, *al-Mughnī li Ibn Qudāma* (Cairo: Hajr, 1986) 10:262–3; Abū Bakr ibn Mas'ūd al-Kāsānī, *Badā'i' al-ṣanā'i' fī tartīb al-sharā'i'* (Beirut: Dār al-Kutub al-'Arabī, 1974) 3:150; and Abū Zakarīyā Yaḥyā ibn Sharaf Al-Nawawī, *Rawḍat al-ṭālibīn* (Beirut: Dār al-Kutub al-'Ilmiyya, 1992) 5:674. See also, Kecia Ali (n 9) 5:309–13. For disparate exegetical treatment of husbandly and wifely *nushūz*, see the section on *nushūz* in Chapter 2.

[22] Kabbani and Ziad (n 8). Yüksel et al have written, "Beating women who are cheating and betraying the marriage contract is not an ultimate solution, and it is not consistent with the promise of equitability and comparable rights that appears in Q. 2:228." Edip Yüksel, Layth Saleh al-Shaiban, and Martha Schulte-Nafehl, *Qur'an: A Reformist Translation* (USA: Brainbow Press, 2007) 20. See also Islamic Supreme Council of Canada (n 11).

[23] Eg, Al-Kāsānī (n 21) 2:334 and 4:15 and Ibn Nujaym (n 21) 3:385. Post-colonialist traditionalist scholars have adhered to the pre-colonial tradition on this point. Rida and Shafi used this verse to make the opposite point that is made by progressive and reformist scholars; rather than emphasizing the similarity of spousal rights they highlighted the degree of men over women. In his exegesis of the Qur'ān, Shafi discussed Q. 2:228 extensively to argue that spousal rights are reciprocal, but they need not be the same. He writes, "Despite having equal rights in many things, men have the favor (u. *fazīlat*) of rulership (u. *hākamiyyat*) over

> if they have faith in Allah and the Last Day. And their husbands have the better right to take them back in that period if they wish for reconciliation. And women shall have rights similar to the rights against them, according to what is equitable; but men have a degree (of advantage) over them and Allah is Exalted in Power, Wise.[24]

According to progressive and reformist scholars, this verse mentions two opposing points: first, that the rights of wives are "similar" to their husbands' rights, which they interpret as grounding the marital relationship on an equitable footing and, second, that men have a "degree" over women, thus characterizing the marital relationship as fundamentally hierarchical. There are many ways that these seemingly contradictory messages can be harmonized by believers. Progressive and reformist scholars privilege the "equitable" rights of spouses, while pre-colonial jurists did not believe that the "similar" rights of wives restricted husbands from having a "degree" over their wives. A reading of Q. 2:228 that underscores the status of men over women fits seamlessly with a patriarchal reading of Q. 4:34, where this rank translates into disciplinary authority for husbands.

According to some pre-colonial legal scholars, the message of Q. 5:45 is immediately relevant to any discussion of the right of husbands to discipline wives, as established by Q. 4:34. Q. 5:45 guarantees the law of retribution, and it created a problem for jurists who for the most part agreed that wives who are injured while being physically disciplined by their husbands are not entitled to retribution. To address this point, they restricted the retaliation that could be visited upon husbands to cases in which a husband severely injured his wife or killed her. In doing so, they violated the general retaliation promised in Q. 5:45, which states:

> We ordained therein for them: "Life for life, eye for eye, nose for nose, ear for ear, tooth for tooth, and wounds equal for equal." But if any one remits the retaliation by way of charity, it is an act of atonement for himself. And if any fail to judge by (the light of) what Allah hath revealed, they are (no better than) wrong-doers.[25]

Pre-colonial jurists made the case that the marital relationship is exempt from this general rule of retaliation because the Qur'anic text itself—specifically, Q. 4:34—permits husbands to discipline their wives. This

women, and women are ruled (u. *mahkūm*) and obedient (u. *tābi*ʿ)." This constitutes a theory of gender complementarity rather than equality. Muḥammad Shafi, *Maʿārif al-Qurʾān* (Karachi: Maktaba-e-Darul-Uloom, 1996) 2:395 and 401. See also Rashid Rida, *Ḥuqūq al-nisāʾ fī al-Islām: nidāʾ li-l-jins al-laṭāʾif* (Beirut: Maktab al-Islāmī, 1975) 51. Israr Ahmed also saw Q. 2:228 as establishing the degree of men over women. Israr Ahmed (n 18).

[24] Yusuf Ali (n 7) Q. 2:228.

[25] Yusuf Ali (n 7) Q. 5:45.

disciplinary power would be rendered meaningless if wives could petition the courts for retaliation against their husbands. The cause for revelation (*sabab al-nuzūl*) involving Ḥabība, who was denied retaliation as a result of the revelation of Q. 4:34, served to illustrate this point.[26]

Another connection that pre-colonial jurists made between Qur'anic texts demonstrates a distressing level of ease with marital violence. Some jurists cited Q. 5:33 to support their opinion that a husband's physical disciplining of his wife ought to be proportional to the level of her misdemeanor. A husband was to refrain from hitting his wife if admonishment would suffice and to avoid intense beating if lighter beating served the purpose of rectifying the wife's behavior. In making their case, they pointed to the analogous scenario of punishment for sedition or brigandry as described in Q. 5:33.[27] This verse reads:

> The punishment of those who wage war against Allah and His Messenger, and strive with might and main for mischief through the land is: execution, or crucifixion, or the cutting off of hands and feet from opposite sides, or exile from the land: that is their disgrace in this world, and a heavy punishment is theirs in the Hereafter.[28]

Pre-colonial jurists claimed that just as execution, crucifixion, the cutting-off of opposite limbs, and exile were all to be applied in proportion with the crime of those who "waged war against God and his Messenger," husbands should also use their discretion to apply the various disciplinary methods at their disposal in proportion to their wives' (mis)behavior. Pre-colonial jurists cited Q. 5:33 in the context of an ethical discussion pertaining to Q. 4:34. Specifically, by citing Q. 5:33, they were discouraging husbands from hitting their wives in a disproportionate manner. The fact that pre-colonial jurists found Q. 5:33 relevant to their ethical discussion of Q. 4:34, and that post-colonial progressive and reformist scholars would find this relevance morally repugnant demonstrates the impact of divergent idealized cosmologies on a given scholar's ethical standards.

The purpose of contrasting the selections of Qur'anic verses by pre-colonial exegetes and jurists with those of progressive and reformist scholars is to demonstrate that the idealized cosmologies of religious scholars influences their expectations of the message of the Qur'anic

[26] See, eg, Sulaymān ibn Al-Bājī, *al-Muntaqā: sharḥ Muwaṭṭa' Mālik* (Cairo: Dār al-Fikr al-ʿArabī, 1982) 7:79.

[27] See, eg, Muwaffaq al-Dīn ʿAbd Allāh ibn Aḥmad Ibn Qudāma, *al-Mughnī li-Ibn Qudāma* (Cairo: Hajr, 1986) 7:46; ʿAlī Ibn Muḥammad al-Māwardī, *al-Ḥāwī al-kabīr fī fiqh madhhab al-Imām al-Shāfiʿī* (Beirut: Dār al-Kutub al-ʿIlmiyya, 1994) 9:597; and Shams al-Dīn Abū ʿAbdullah Muḥammad b. ʿAbdullah al-Zarkashī, *Sharḥ al-Zarkashī ʿalā matn al-Khiraqī*ʿ (Mecca: Maktaba al-Asadī, 2009) 3:324.

[28] Yusuf Ali (n 7) Q. 5:33.

text. This in turn affects which verses they select to support their understandings of the text. Pre-colonial exegetes and jurists were able to argue compellingly that the Qur'ān supported a patriarchal marital structure, wherein husbands were permitted to physically discipline their wives. Progressive and reformist scholars have also used selections of Qur'anic verses to cogently challenge a patriarchal reading of the Qur'anic text and persuasively posit that the Qur'ān promotes an egalitarian marital ethos. The use of the Qur'anic text to argue these two opposing points confirms that the idealized cosmologies of religious scholars determine their expectations and interpretations of the Qur'anic text. In this way, the actual words of the Qur'anic text are less important in legal and ethical interpretations than the specific set of expectations that believers bring to this text.

A VERSATILE PROPHET: MUḤAMMAD MODELS FOR CONFLICTING VISIONS OF ISLAM

Just as different idealized cosmologies lead to the selection and emphasis of a contrasting set of Qur'anic verses, prophetic reports (*aḥādīth*) have also been selected to portray Muḥammad in differing ways; the man who emerges from these depictions can be a model for believers upholding irreconcilable cosmologies.

Muḥammad's example (*sunna*) is considered to be the "embodied Qur'ān,"[29] and scholars draw on prophetic reports in order to justify their various perspectives on the right of husbands to physically discipline their wives. Religious scholars who span both sides of the patriarchal–egalitarian divide cite prophetic reports in order to garner authority and legitimacy for their positions. Examining the popular selections of prophetic reports in pre- and post-colonial scholarship on Q. 4:34 brings conceptual clarity to the role of idealized cosmologies in the selective representation of prophetic practice.

In an interesting confluence of source texts, pre- and post-colonial scholars have deployed similar prophetic reports to support opposing cosmologies. In the following, we will consider the notable *aḥādīth*

[29] This argument is often articulated as a tautology, whereby a *ḥadīth* is cited to garner authority for prophetic practice. In this *ḥadīth*, 'Ā'isha was asked about Muḥammad's character, and she replied, "His character was the Qur'ān (*kāna khuluquhu al-Qur'ān*)." This point is exemplified in a series of lectures by Shaykh Abdallah Bin Biyya, a professor at King Abdul Aziz University in Saudi Arabia and a member of the Dublin-based European Council for Fatwa and Research. Abdallah b. Biyya, *His Character was the Quran* (trans. Hamza Yusuf)(2-CD set) (Oakland: Rumi Bookstore, 2007).

used in pre-colonial exegetical and juridical sources and the role these same *aḥādīth* play in progressive and reformist discussions. Four *aḥādīth* featured prominently in the pre-colonial exegesis of Q. 4:34.[30] The first prominent *ḥadīth* describes the men in Medina, represented by ʿUmar, appealing to Muḥammad for permission to hit their wives. There are various narrations of this *ḥadīth*, but the basic storyline is that Muḥammad prohibited men from hitting their wives, saying, "Do not hit the maidservants of God." This caused Meccan women to become insubordinate, which prompted ʿUmar to ask Muḥammad to retract his ban on hitting wives. Muḥammad ceded to this request, saying, "Hit them." However, when the battered wives complained to Muḥammad, he censured those who had hit their wives, saying that they were "not the best" of men.

This prophetic report helped exegetes and jurists to explore the theological problem of conflicting divine and prophetic approaches to domestic violence. Whereas Q. 4:34 describes the physical disciplining of wives as an unproblematic marital right of husbands, this *ḥadīth* illustrates that Muḥammad was conflicted about the right of husbands to hit their wives. Muḥammad's equivocation is demonstrated first by his prohibition against hitting wives, then his command to hit, and finally by his moral censure of men who hit their wives. Although some pre-colonial exegetes used this prophetic report to argue that the imperative of hitting wives in Q. 4:34 was meant to be understood as a permission rather than a command, no pre-colonial exegete saw this report as challenging the right of husbands to hit wives for disciplinary purposes. Rather, they understood the middle of this report, where Muḥammad revoked his ban on wife-beating and maintained this position despite his moral censure of men who hit their wives, as the crux of this *ḥadīth*. By doing so, they were able to present this *ḥadīth* as supporting the divine right of husbands to physically discipline their wives.[31]

Progressives and reformists reverse the strategy of pre-colonial scholars when reading this *ḥadīth*. Whereas pre-colonial exegetes (and jurists)

[30] For a survey of prophetic reports that discuss the physical disciplining of wives, see Ayesha S. Chaudhry, "'I Wanted One Thing and God Wanted Another...': The Dilemma of the Prophetic Example and the Qur'anic Injunction on Wife-Beating," *Journal of Religious Ethics*, 39(3) (2011) 416–39.

[31] Eg, see Ismāʿīl ibn ʿUmar Ibn Kathīr, *Tafsīr al-ʿaẓīm li-ibn Kathīr* (Damascus: Dar Ibn Kathir, 1994) 1:602; Al-Khāzin al-Baghdādī, *Tafsīr al-Khāzin: al-musammā Lubāb al-taʾwīl fī maʿānī al-tanzīl* (Baghdad: Maktaba al-Muthannā, 1975) 1:375; al-Rāzī (n 18) 4:70; and al-Suyūṭī (n 20) 2:155. This report also made an appearance in legal works, particularly in the Shāfiʿī school of jurisprudence. See, eg, Al-Nawawī (n 21) 5:676 and al-Shāfiʿī, *Mawsūʿat al-Imām al-Shāfiʿī al-kitāb al-Umm* (Beirut: Dār Qutayba, 1996) 11:165–6. This report is discussed in greater detail in Chapter 2.

ignored the prophetic prohibition and moral censure of wife-beating that bookend this *ḥadīth* in order to privilege the center, progressive and reformist scholars disregard prophetic permission for wife-beating in order to stress prophetic disapproval of wife-beating. They draw on the first portion of the prophetic report, where Muḥammad initially forbade believers from hitting their wives ("Do not hit the maidservants of God"), and the last portion, where he morally censured men who had adhered to his own dispensation to hit wives. These references are generally made without any mention of the middle portion of this *ḥadīth*, where ʿUmar petitioned Muḥammad for permission for husbands to hit wives and was granted this permission. When the entire report is cited, only the beginning and/or end are emphasized as morally relevant, while the center of the report is entirely ignored or excused.[32] The use of this *ḥadīth*—either to categorically forbid the hitting of wives or to morally censure men who hit their wives—fails to grasp Muḥammad's complex position on domestic violence, as well as the theological problems it raises—the very issues that pre-colonial scholars struggled with. Still, it provides progressive and reformist scholars with a categorical prophetic prohibition and/or clear moral censure against wife-beating. This is useful for granting authority to progressive and reformist positions, even when these positions find no anchor in pre-colonial scholarship. Since no pre-colonial exegete or jurist took an interpretive or legal position prohibiting wife-beating, contemporary scholars urgently require prophetic reports to forbid domestic violence. The varied treatments of this prophetic report in the pre- and post-colonial periods portray Muḥammad as two different men: one who grudgingly permits marital violence and another who categorically denounces any domestic violence. Patriarchal and egalitarian idealized cosmologies give rise to varied

[32] Eg, see Murad H. Elsaidi, "Human Rights and Islamic Law: Analyses Challenging the Husband's Authority to Punish 'Rebellious' Wives," *Muslim World Journal of Human Rights*, 7(2) (2011) 16; Fatima Mernissi, *The Veil and the Male Elite: A Feminist Interpretation of Women's Rights in Islam* (Reading, MA: Addison-Wesley, 1991) 142; and Mahmoud (n 8) 548. The Tunisian scholar M. al-Talbi has also projected contemporary conceptions back onto the Islamic tradition. In his case, he recasts the *ḥadīth* wherein ʿUmar sought permission to hit wives after Muḥammad prohibited the beating of wives. According to al-Talbi, this story represents the struggle between a pro-feminist party and an anti-feminist party in the nascent Muslim community of seventh-century Arabia. Umm Salama headed up the feminist party and received the support of Muḥammad, who married her. However, women's newfound boldness alarmed Meccan men, who, led by ʿUmar, challenged Muḥammad's support of the feminist agenda. The tensions between the two groups become so heightened and "explosive" that they threatened the internal cohesion of the newly formed religious group, which was already vulnerable in the face of internal and external enemies. In the end, Muḥammad had no choice but to allow men to hit their wives, since the very survival of the religion hung in the balance. For more, see Mahmoud (n 8) 539 and Rachel M. Scott, "A Contextual Approach to Women's Rights in the Qur'ān: Readings of 4:34," *The Muslim World*, 99 (2009) 70. See also M. Talbi, *Ummat al-wasaṭ: Al-islām wa taḥaddiyāt al-muʿāshara* (Tunis: Saras li-l-nashr, 1996) 120–3.

expectations of moral and ethical behavior from Muḥammad, and this in turn determines what Muslim scholars see and wish to emphasize about his behavior.

A second influential prophetic report in pre-colonial exegesis is Muḥammad's farewell sermon, which he delivered during his final pilgrimage.[33] There are several versions of this sermon, but in the more widespread version Muḥammad provided believers with a list of instructions for ethical, moral, and upright behavior that was meant to sum up his prophetic message. In the course of these directives, he enjoined husbands to hit their wives in a non-extreme (*ghayr mubarriḥ*) manner if the women allowed those whom their husbands disliked into their beds. In another version, he called upon husbands to hit their wives in a non-extreme manner if their wives committed openly lewd acts (*fāḥisha mubayyina*).[34]

The various narrations of this report shed light on two important questions raised by the text of Q. 4:34: what is wifely *nushūz*, and what are the limits on hitting one's wife? When the farewell sermon is read as a commentary on Q. 4:34, it defines wifely *nushūz* either as allowing someone a husband dislikes into the marital bed or as openly lewd acts. The sermon also restricts the disciplinary beating permitted to husbands by characterizing it as non-extreme (*ghayr mubarriḥ*). Interestingly, for pre-colonial exegetes, the farewell sermon seemed to be directed to the second question, but not to the first. Instead of focusing on the definition provided for wifely *nushūz*, pre-colonial exegetes saw this report as restricting the amount of permissible physical discipline. The qualification

[33] For a detailed discussion of this sermon, see Chapter 2 and Chaudhry (n 30) 429–33.

[34] Some versions of this *ḥadīth* mention the "wives are captives (*ʿawān*) of their husbands." Al-Khāzin clarified this point by stating, "[A woman] enters under her husband's command as a prisoner (*bi-l-ʿaṣīr*)." He said that hitting in a non-extreme (*ghayr mubarriḥ*) manner meant hitting them in a manner that was "not intense or hard (*al-shadīd* and *al-shāqq*)." Al-Khāzin (n 31) 375. Abū Bakr Ibn ʿArabī's version of this *ḥadīth* reads: "O people, you have rights over your wives and they have rights over you. Your rights over them are that they not give your bed to those whom you dislike and that they not engage in openly lewd behavior (*fāḥishatin mubayyina*). If they do this, then God has ordered you to abandon them in the beds and hit them in a non-extreme (*ghayr mubarriḥ*) manner. If they stop [their open lewdness], then [their rights are that] you provide for them and clothe them in an appropriate fashion (*bi-l-maʿrūf*)." Abū Bakr Ibn al-ʿArabī explained that "this narration suggests that there is no maintenance (*nafaqa*) or clothing (*kiswa*) for a wife who commits *nushūz*. Also lewdness (*fāḥisha*) is obscene/bawdy (*al-badhāʾ*) behavior, [and this is] not adultery (*zinā*), as the *ʿulamāʾ* have said." Ibn al-ʿArabī, *Aḥkām al-Qurʾān* (n 20) 1:498. In both these cases, the scholars at hand made the rights of wives over their husbands conditional on the behavior of the wives. If wives were openly lewd, then they were to be abandoned and hit in a non-extreme manner. If wives did not commit open lewdness, then they were to be provided for in an appropriate fashion (*bi-l-maʿrūf*). While the rights of husbands were absolute in this narration, the rights of wives were conditional on their good behavior. See also, ʿAbd al-Raḥmān al-Thaʿālibī, *Tafsīr al-Thaʿālibī, al-musammā bi-l-Jawāhir al-ḥisān fī tafsīr al-Qurʾān* (Beirut: Dār Iḥyāʾ al-Turāth, 1997) 2:230–1.

of non-extreme (*ghayr mubarriḥ*) became ubiquitous in pre-colonial exegesis of the imperative in Q. 4:34 to "hit them" (*wa-ḍribūhunna*). While some scholars incorporated the reference to openly lewd acts into their definitions of wifely *nushūz*, *nushūz* was never restricted to this definition. Rather, wifely *nushūz* was defined expansively to include the general disobedience of wives to their husbands.[35] In general, for pre-colonial exegetes, the farewell sermon confirmed the right of husbands to hit their wives as a fundamental right, and as such, it complied with the ruling to hit disobedient wives in Q. 4:34, in the context of a patriarchal idealized cosmology.

In the present day, progressive and reformist scholars continue to reference the farewell sermon, but they use various strategies to tackle this report so that it is brought in line with an egalitarian cosmology. One approach is to discredit this *ḥadīth*, claiming that it has a weak chain of transmission (*isnād*). Since this report allows husbands to hit their wives, however restricted this right might be, it challenges the view that wife-beating is prohibited. Hence, it is better to make it irrelevant. A second tactic is to exaggerate the pre-colonial treatment of the farewell sermon by underscoring the undesirability of hitting. The restrictions placed upon permissible physical violence in this report are understood as ushering in a gradual prohibition against wife-beating altogether. A third strategy is to see the farewell sermon as restricting both the definition of wifely *nushūz* and the nature of permissible beating. In this view, the definition of wifely *nushūz* is limited to manifest sexual lewdness (*fāḥisha mubayyina*) and/or adultery. Progressive and reformist scholars define wifely *nushūz* as adulterous behavior based on the portion of the farewell sermon that describes wives allowing those whom their husbands dislike into bed as discipline-worthy behavior. Pre-colonial exegetes understood the reference to "beds" in this phrase to mean "homes," because taking the wording of this report literally raised the bizarre possibility that it might be appropriate for a wife to allow persons whom her husband likes into her bed. Contemporary scholars who draw on this prophetic report to define wifely *nushūz* as adulterous behavior ignore the puzzling consequence of understanding beds literally rather than figuratively to mean homes.[36]

[35] ʿAbd al-Raḥmān ibn Muḥammad Ibn Abī Ḥātim,*Tafsīr al-Qurʾān al-ʿaẓīm: musnadan ʿan al-Rasūl Allāh wa-al-ṣaḥāba wa-l-tābiʿīn* (Ṣaydā: al-Maktaba al-ʿAṣriyya, 1999) 3:943; Ibn al-ʿArabī (n 20) 1:498; Ibn Kathīr (n 31) 1:602; Aḥmad ibn ʿAlī Al-Jaṣṣāṣ, *Aḥkām al-Qurʾān* (Beirut: Dār al-Kitāb al-ʿArabī, 1971) 1:375 and 2:189; al-Khāzin (n 31) 1:375; ʿAlī ibn Muḥammad Al-Māwardī, *al-Nukat wa-al-ʿuyūn: tafsīr al-Māwardī min rawāʾiʿ al-tafāsīr* (Beirut: Dār al-Kutub al-ʿIlmiyya, 1992) 1:483; al-Suyūṭī (n 20) 2:156; and al-Thaʿālibī (n 34) 2:230. See also Chapters 2 and 3.

[36] Eg, Abou El Fadl (n 8) 171 and 174 and Kabbani and Ziad (n 8).

By defining wifely *nushūz* as adultery, progressive and reformist scholars break from the pre-colonial tradition, because they seek to severely restrict the circumstances in which a husband might be permitted to discipline his wife. Pre-colonial exegetes, on the other hand, pointedly discounted adultery (*zinā*) as a definition of wifely *nushūz*, since it necessitated the application of the corporal (*ḥadd*) penalty by the state rather than simply a beating at the hands of a husband.[37]

The third report that was popular in pre-colonial exegesis provides a historical setting for the revelation (*sabab al-nuzūl*) of Q. 4:34. As seen in Chapter 1, in this report Muḥammad granted retribution to a woman who had been slapped by her husband. However, his ruling was revoked by the revelation of Q. 4:34, which confirmed the right of Ḥabība's husband to hit her. For pre-colonial exegetes, this occasion of revelation (*sabab*) indicated that the central objective of Q. 4:34 was to institute the right of husbands to physically discipline their wives. Although exegetes provided a chain of transmission (*isnād*) for this report, it was never recorded in any of the canonical books of *aḥādīth* and is therefore considered to have a weak narration. Nevertheless, the authenticity was irrelevant to pre-colonial exegetes, who never discussed it when narrating this report.[38] In contrast, contemporary scholars do not mention this report. The story contained therein is especially problematic for scholars who see the historical context of Q. 4:34 as restricting violence against wives. They argue that whereas unchecked domestic violence was the norm in seventh-century Arabia, Q. 4:34 introduced a protocol and procedure for hitting one's wife,

[37] Al-Qurtubi also wrote, "'If they [commit openly lewd behavior], then abandon them in the beds and hit them in a *ghayr mubarriḥ* manner. If they obey you (*aṭaʿnakum*) do not find a means against them. You have rights over your wives and your wives have rights over you. Your rights over your wives are that they not give your bed to anyone whom you dislike, and they not permit anyone into your homes that you dislike. And their rights over you are that you are good (*tuḥsinū*) to them in clothing (*kiswatihinna*) and feeding them (*ṭaʿāmihinna*).' [Al-Qurṭubī commented:] What is meant by openly lewd behavior (*fāḥishatin mubayyina*) is that [wives] not let those whom their husbands dislike and are angered by enter [their homes]. What is not meant by openly lewd behavior is adultery (*zinā*), since that is forbidden (*ḥarām*) and it necessitates the *ḥadd* penalty." This *ḥadīth* can be found in the collection of al-Tirmidhī, cited by al-Qurṭubī (n 18) 5:165–6. This version of the *ḥadīth* parallels Q. 4:34 more closely than the previous narration. In the context of paraphrasing the Qur'anic text, the insertion of "non-extreme" to qualify hitting is significant. Both Ibn al-ʿArabī and al-Thaʿālibī agreed that *fāḥisha* was not adultery or fornication (*zinā*), but rather it was obscene or bawdy (*badhāʾ*) behavior. Ibn al-ʿArabī (n 20)1:498; and al-Thaʿālibī (n 34) 2:230–1.

[38] For some exegetes, this report also introduced a theological problem, since Muḥammad and God appear to have disagreed regarding Ḥabība's case. Muḥammad is reported to have responded to the revelation of Q. 4:34 by stating his personal difference of opinion with the revelation, saying, "I wanted one thing and God wanted another." Chaudhry (n 30) 424; and Chapter 2 in this book.

which was meant to effectively eliminate domestic violence.[39] Ḥabība's story challenges this reading of Q. 4:34, since Muḥammad's example offers Ḥabība retaliation—based on either pre-Islamic customary practice or his own judgement—and the Qur'anic text forces Muḥammad to revoke his ruling, leaving Ḥabība without recourse.

The fourth type of prophetic report that appears in pre-colonial exegesis relates to procedure. These *aḥādīth* outline the sort of hitting that is sanctioned and forbidden to husbands. They instruct husbands to avoid hitting their wives in the face and to use a *miswāk* when hitting, and demand that the hitting be carried out in a non-extreme (*ghayr mubarriḥ*) manner. Pre-colonial exegetes understood these prophetic reports as procedural, both affirming and systemizing the correct procedure for hitting one's wife.[40] In contrast, contemporary scholars view these same prophetic reports as challenging the right of husbands to physically discipline their wives, since they represent Muḥammad's personal reticence and ethical discomfort with hitting wives. If these scholars can demonstrate that Muḥammad did not like the idea of husbands hitting their wives, then they can claim to follow his example when they prohibit husbands from hitting their wives.[41] Hence, prophetic reports that restrict the extent of physical violence permissible in marriage can be justifiably read as either prescriptive or proscriptive of wife-beating. The idealized cosmology of a particular scholar determines how these restrictions are understood.

The selection and interpretation of prophetic reports to fit the mold of pre-existing idealized cosmologies is also confirmed by the treatment of prophetic reports in pre-colonial legal works. Like pre-colonial exegetes, jurists also drew on prophetic reports to justify their positions on the disciplinary license available to husbands. The farewell sermon played a prominent role in juridical sources for characterizing acceptable marital discipline as non-extreme (*ghayr mubarriḥ*). Muslim jurists did not restrict the definition of wifely *nushūz* to openly lewd sexual acts (though they did include it in their description of wifely *nushūz*), nor did they describe it as adulterous behavior.[42] The theological implications of Muḥammad's ambivalence as recorded in the prophetic report where he first prohibited, then permitted, and finally rebuked husbands who hit their wives was of central concern for Shāfiʿī jurists. They engaged in legal

[39] Eg, WISE (n 6) 10 and Hamza Yusuf, "Sermon: Removing the Silence on Domestic Violence," (Feb. 21, 2009), video available at <http://www.youtube.com/watch?v=BDEKJDgXOU> (last accessed Sept. 5, 2013).

[40] See Chapter 2.

[41] Eg, Mubarak (n 8) 277.

[42] Ibn Nujaym (n 21) 4:128 and 303; Aḥmad ibn ʿAlī al-Jaṣṣāṣ (n 35) 1:375 and 2:189; and al-Kāsānī (n 21) 3:150.

wrangling to reconcile the contrasting divine command and prophetic reticence toward the right of husbands to physically discipline their wives. In the end, they upheld both prophetic ambivalence and divine imperative by turning the prescription of *wa-ḍribūhunna* in Q. 4:34 into a recommendation rather than a command.[43]

As can be expected, pre-colonial jurists emphasized prophetic reports that addressed the procedural nature of hitting wives. Muḥammad's directive to "hang the whip" where one's household can see it supported the disciplinary privilege and responsibility of husbands in marriage.[44] Muḥammad's statement that "for everything, there is retaliation" provided a legal backdrop for explaining why this rule did not apply to the marital relationship, within which there is no retaliation except in circumstances where wives suffer severe injuries such as broken bones, loss of limbs, or death.[45] The prophetic instruction not to lash more than ten times was applied to the beating of wives; this was seen as a necessary restriction to differentiate discretionary (*ta'zīr*) punishment from a corporal (*ḥadd*) penalty.[46]

Pre-colonial jurists also cited a *ḥadīth* in which al-Ash'ath reported that he spent a night in the Companion 'Umar's house. In the middle of the night, 'Umar began to beat his wife and al-Ash'ath came between the couple to stop the beating. At this point, 'Umar said to him, "O al-Ash'ath, remember three things from me that are from the Prophet of God, peace and blessings be upon him: A man should not be asked why he hit his wife, do not sleep without praying the *witr* [prayer] and I forgot the third." Despite the fact that the someone in the narration of this report forgot the third instruction—whether al-Ash'ath, 'Umar, or the narrator—did not dissuade pre-colonial jurists, particularly Ḥanafī and Ḥanbalī jurists, from using

[43] Al-Nawawī (n 21) 5:676 and al-Shāfi'ī (n 31) 11:165–6. For a more extensive discussion on this issue, see Kecia Ali, " 'The Best of You Will Not Strike': Al-Shāfi'ī on Qur'an, *Sunnah*, and Wife-Beating," *Comparative Islamic Studies*, 2(2) (2006) 143–55.

[44] Mālik b. Anas' (d. 179/795), "*al-Muwaṭṭa*'" in Sulaymān ibn Khalaf Al-Bājī, *al-Muntaqā: sharḥ Muwaṭṭa' Mālik* (Cairo: Dār al-Fikr al-'Arabī, 1982) 7:79. See Chapter 3 in this book.

[45] Eg, al-Haskafī and Ibn 'Ābidīn in Muḥammad Amīn ibn 'Umar Ibn 'Ābidīn, *Radd al-muḥtār 'alā al-Durr al-mukhtār sharḥ Tanwīr al-abṣār* (Beirut: Dār al-Kutub al-'Ilmiyya, 1994) 6:131. Muḥammad ibn 'Abd al-Wāḥid Ibn al-Humām, *Sharḥ fatḥ al-qadīr li-l-'ājiz al-faqīr* (Cairo: Muṣṭafā al-Bābī al-Ḥalabī, 1970) 5:345; Ibn Nujaym (n 21) 5:81; and al-Nasafī in al-Zayla'ī 'Uthmān ibn 'Alī al-Zayla'ī, *Tabyīn al-ḥaqā'iq sharḥ kanz al-daqā'iq* (Beirut: Dār al-Kutub al-'Ilmiyya, 2000) 3:633.

[46] Eg, Manṣūr ibn Yūnus Al-Buhūtī, *Irshād ulī al-nuhā li-daqā'iq al-Muntahā: ḥāshiya 'alā Muntahā al-irādāt* (Mecca: Dār Khiḍr, 2000) 2:1133; Ibn al-Humām (n 45) 5:345; Ibn Qudāma (n 27) 10:261–2; and Mar'ī ibn YūsufAl-Karmī, *Ghāyat al-muntahā fī al-jam' bayna al-Iqnā' wa-al-Muntahā* (Riyaḍh: al-Mu'assasa al-Sa'īdīyya, 1981) 2:92. This emerged from the Ḥanafī idea that *ta'zīr* must be lower than the lowest *ḥadd* penalty. For more on this, see Chapter 3 and M. Izzi Dien. "Ta'zīr (a.)" in P. Bearman, Th. Bianquis, C.E. Bosworth, E. van Donzel, and W.P. Heinrichs (eds.), *Encyclopaedia of Islam*, 2nd edn. (Leiden: Brill, 2009).

this report to discourage community members and state representatives from intervening in the domestic affairs of free men.[47] This prophetic report is rejected by progressive and reformist scholars, who recoil at the message of this *ḥadīth*.[48] The fact that either al-Ash'ath or 'Umar reported this prophetic directive among a list of three general principles, the third of which the narrator forgot, was ignored by pre-colonial jurists. However, contemporary scholars see the failure to remember the third principle as proof for the weakness and inauthenticity of this prophetic report. How can we trust a report from someone who forgot one of the three principles he was narrating? How can we know for certain that he remembered the other two correctly?

In another *ḥadīth*, Muḥammad is reported to have prohibited men from hitting their wives like slaves and then sleeping with them on the same evening.[49] Pre-colonial jurists understood this report as qualitatively differentiating the beating of wives from the beating of slaves; husbands should not hit their wives as they would hit their slaves, especially since they might desire intimacy with them. This report suggests that there is something especially crass about hitting a wife and sleeping with her the same evening that can be avoided in the hitting of a slave, with whom one does not have to sleep. Once again, pre-colonial jurists understood this report as procedural, while progressive and reformist scholars see this *ḥadīth* as an outright prohibition against hitting wives. Contemporary scholars mention several variations of this report in which Muḥammad instructs believers not to hit their wives as they would a slave or a stallion or camel.[50] In all of these cases, they suggest that whereas a man can hit his slave (or stallion and camel), he should not hit his wife. Notably, however, if this report is used to forbid wife-beating, then Muslim scholars must at least implicitly accept the right of a man to hit his slave. This raises another set of ethical problems which none of the scholars in this study have

[47] Al-Buhūtī (n 46) 2:1133; Ibn Nujaym (n 21) 3:237; Ibn Qudāma (n 27) 10:262; and al-Karmī (n 46) 2:92. This report also appeared in exegetical sources. Al-Qurṭubī also mentioned a *ḥadīth* in his exegesis in which "It is related from 'Umar that he used to beat his wife and he was rebuked/censured for this practice (*fa'udhila fī dhālika*). So he said (by way of justification), I heard Prophet Muḥammad say, 'A man is not to be asked why he beat his wife (*lā yus'alu al-rajul fī mā ḍaraba ahlahu*).' " Al-Qurṭubī (n 18) 5:166.

[48] Eg, Mubarak (n 8) 277.

[49] Al-Buhūtī (n 46) 2:1133; Ibn Qudāma (n 27) 10:261–2; and al-Karmī (n 46) 2:92. Such prophetic reports were also cited in pre-colonial exegetical literature. In one *ḥadīth*, Muḥammad told believers, "You should not whip your wife like a slave and then have intercourse with her at the end of the day." Another narration of this same *ḥadīth* reads, "Are you not ashamed that one of you might hit his wife as he would a slave in the beginning of the day and then sleep with her at night?" See Ibn al-'Arabī (n 20) 1:493–500; al-Khāzin (n 31) 1:375; and al-Suyūṭī (n 20) 2:155.

[50] El Fadl (n 8) 181; Mahmoud (n 8) 545; Mubarak (n 8) 277 and 285; and Sisters in Islam (n 11) 15.

acknowledged. It can be speculated that they do not see the permission to hit slaves as legally relevant because slavery is legislatively outlawed in all nation states in the contemporary world. Since wife-beating is not legislatively outlawed in all nation states, it is still a contestable issue in a way that slave-beating is not.

As seen previously, progressive and reformist scholars sometimes draw on the same prophetic reports that pre-colonial scholars relied on, but they interpret them differently in order to support a contrasting egalitarian idealized cosmology. To support their egalitarian interpretations of Q. 4:34, progressive and reformist scholars also call upon *aḥādīth* that were never mentioned by pre-colonial jurists and exegetes, who upheld a patriarchal idealized cosmology. For example, they draw attention to Muḥammad's personal behavior to argue against the right of husbands to hit their wives.[51] Muḥammad's example illustrates that better men do not hit their wives, so why would a Muslim man not want to follow the prophetic example? In contrast, none of the pre-colonial exegetes and jurists in this study looked to Muḥammad's treatment of his own wives in order to make a case for restricting or prohibiting the hitting of wives.

Two prophetic reports are especially influential in the post-colonial period but were rarely cited by pre-colonial exegetes and jurists. The first report is narrated from Muḥammad's youngest wife ʿĀʾisha, who described Muḥammad as never hitting anyone, not "a woman, child, or slave" except when engaged in religious warfare. A second report, cited only a few times in pre-colonial sources but repeatedly mentioned in post-colonial sources, has Muḥammad presenting himself as a model for emulation for believers and highlighting his own treatment of his wives as worthy of imitation. In this report he states, "The best of you are the best to their families, and I am the best of you to my family."[52] Both of these reports are referenced by post-colonial scholars with various positions on wife-beating—from defending a pre-colonial plain-sense reading of the Qurʾanic text that permits husbands to hit their wives, to rejecting the right of husbands to hit their wives altogether. Whatever their positions on the Qurʾanic text, post-colonial scholars agree that Muḥammad discouraged men from hitting their wives and at the very least did not engage in such violent domestic behavior himself. Progressive and reformist scholars especially highlight Muḥammad's personal behavior, as represented by these two reports, to argue that any interpretation of Q. 4:34 that permits husbands

[51] El Fadl (n 8) 169 and 186–7 and Elsaidi (n 32) 14.

[52] El Fadl (n 8) 187; Elsaidi (n 32) 14; Lisa Hajjar, "Religion, State Power, and Domestic Violence in Muslim Societies: A Framework for Comparative Analysis," *Law & Social Inquiry*, 29(1) (2004) 10–11; Mahmoud (n 8) 548–9; Sisters in Islam (n 11) 5. For more on this, see Chaudhry (n 30) 420.

to hit their wives contradicts prophetic practice outright. And since Muḥammad, who was the "embodied Qur'ān," did not hit his wives, it is not possible to interpret any Qur'anic verse to justify wife-beating. The varied interpretations of prophetic reports illustrate the central role played by the idealized cosmologies of religious scholars in the selection and interpretation of prophetic practice. Since Muḥammad is considered to be the ethical and moral model par excellence and because patriarchal and egalitarian idealized cosmologies determine morally ethical behavior in divergent ways, Muḥammad is made to model two different personalities for believers with conflicting cosmologies.

CONCLUSION

The use of Qur'anic text and prophetic practice to support opposing patriarchal and egalitarian cosmologies illustrates the malleability of these texts as well as the influence of idealized cosmology-driven expectations on the selection and interpretation of source texts. In the pre-colonial period, the uncontested reign of one patriarchal idealized cosmology resulted in generally monolithic interpretations of the prescription of *wa-ḍribūhunna* in Q. 4:34. No pre-colonial exegete or legal scholar proposed that it was unacceptable, immoral, unethical, or forbidden for husbands to hit their wives. They all interpreted the imperative *wa-ḍribūhunna* to mean that husbands could hit their wives, although most of them chose to qualify this prescription by describing the beating as non-extreme (*ghayr mubarriḥ*). Still, they were all able to imagine and rationalize a situation in which it is appropriate for a husband to hit his wife with just cause in an ethical manner. Being familiar with intelligent and strong women and witnessing male abuse of power did not make legal and exegetical scholars question the husbandly disciplinary privilege in marriage. No pre-colonial exegete or legal scholar offered an alternative meaning for *wa-ḍribūhunna* other than "hit them," even though they demonstrated methodological ease with multiple interpretations of other words and phrases in the Qur'ān. Within the text of Q. 4:34 itself, for example, they offered numerous meanings for terms such as fear (*khawf*), wifely *nushūz*, and the second imperative of abandonment (*wa-hjrūhunna*).[53]

In contrast, in the post-colonial period, competing idealized cosmologies have led to multiple interpretations of *wa-ḍribūhunna*. As seen in Chapter 4, some post-colonial scholars have interpreted *wa-ḍribūhunna* to mean that

[53] See Chapters 1 and 2.

husbands can physically discipline their wives, while others hold that they may not hit their wives at all. This creative variety is the result of picking one cosmology and defending it against other cosmologies. In all of these interpretations, the Qur'anic text and prophetic practice are called upon for authority and support. The philological structure of the Arabic text of Q. 4:34 remains intact, but its meanings are highly contested and shaped by multiple influences. Post-colonial scholars, especially progressive and reformist scholars, display a keen awareness of gender-egalitarianism and also human fallibility regarding abuse of unchecked power. Although there was no room for such considerations in the pre-colonial patriarchal cosmology, there is much more space to interact with these ideas in a world where patriarchal and egalitarian idealized cosmologies jostle for supremacy.

Conclusion

This critical survey of historical and contemporary Muslim legal and exegetical scholarship on marital violence in the context of Q. 4:34 reveals that there has been a marked shift in the interpretation of the subject. This transformation is due in large part to a new, egalitarian idealized cosmology that has caused Muslim scholars to adjust their expectations of the divine text and a just God. The juggling of competing patriarchal and egalitarian cosmologies in the post-colonial period has triggered creative and original exegetical and legal trends that have opened up avenues for understanding the Qur'ān beyond pre-colonial plain-sense readings rooted in hierarchical conceptions of gender. Furthermore, the sophisticated hermeneutical strategies of post-colonial Muslim scholarship have redemptive potential for the Islamic tradition, which stands to be enriched by contemporary discourse on marital violence and Q. 4:34. However, in order for contemporary Muslim scholarship to move beyond the egalitarian–authoritative dilemma, egalitarian readings of Q. 4:34 must be able to lay claim to religious authority. This in turn depends on the ability of Muslim scholars to allow the Qur'ān to be a performative text, so that Muslims can struggle with and determine its contemporary meanings. The greatest hurdle to transferring authority from a mythic "Islamic tradition" to the living community of believers is the "Islamic tradition" itself; its unquestioned authority has become stifling for contemporary Muslims.

A patriarchal idealized cosmology reigned supreme in the pre-colonial period, which justified the moral and disciplinary oversight of husbands over wives and sanctioned husbands to use physical discipline when necessary. In the post-colonial period, an egalitarian idealized cosmology has enabled Muslim scholars to voice ethical objections to legal and interpretive traditions that have ensconced the disciplinary rights of husbands over wives in the very foundations of the marital structure. Although pre-colonial legal and exegetical scholarship was often characterized by a multiplicity and diversity of opinions that reflected the polysemic nature of the Qur'anic text and prophetic reports, this creativity was stymied by a patriarchal idealized cosmology when it came to issues of gender. Consequently, pre-colonial legal and exegetical scholarship on the right of husbands to hit wives is monolithic, unvaried, and largely unimaginative. All pre-colonial exegetes and jurists in this study supported the right of husbands to physically discipline their wives and disagreed with each other only in terms of the limits of and liability resulting from such violence. Their differences in this regard appear tedious and stodgy in comparison to the vibrancy of modern discourse.

In contrast, discussions of marital violence in the post-colonial period are fresh, creative, and resourceful. Post-colonial scholars and activists balance multiple interests and speak to a greater variety of audiences. They negotiate the concerns of competing cosmologies by trying to balance a deeply patriarchal legal and exegetical tradition with the concerns and interests of a community that espouses gender-egalitarian values. Contemporary scholars propose multiple methods for grappling with ethically challenging religious texts and traditions, while maintaining allegiance with and speaking authentically to the believing community. The various subjectivities of post-colonial scholars are manifest in their disparate methods for rethinking and re-imagining Q. 4:34 and the right of husbands to hit their wives. Even traditionalist scholars, who endeavor to uphold the traditional plain-sense meaning of Q. 4:34 to allow husbands to ethically hit their wives, must defend their position against an egalitarian idealized cosmology. In doing so, they must recast pre-colonial positions by means of modern argumentation. In offering multiple and diverse legal and ethical positions on the right of husbands to hit their wives, contemporary scholars enrich the pre-colonial Islamic tradition in an area where it lacked creativity.

The mythologized "Islamic tradition," depicted here through the legal and exegetical traditions, is an obstacle to deriving new interpretations of Q. 4:34 that are responsive to calls for gender justice. Deriving interpretations of Q. 4:34 that do not sanction violence against wives requires a re-envisioning of the relationship that Muslims have to their collective past. One way to tackle this problem is to de-mythologize the "Islamic tradition" by shedding light on its logic and assumptions, so that Muslims can confront the fact that the pre-colonial patriarchal and modern egalitarian cosmologies are fundamentally irreconcilable with respect to gender norms and marital relations. This book aims to do exactly this with Q. 4:34. Demonstrating that pre-colonial legal and exegetical scholars did not attempt to interpret Q. 4:34 in a way that eliminated violence against wives can help Muslims to make informed decisions about whether they would like to cling to the pre-colonial Islamic tradition in an uncritical manner. It also creates authoritative space for contemporary Muslim scholars to advocate for innovative hermeneutical strategies that are responsive to the concerns of contemporary Muslim communities. In this way, authority can be transferred from a mythologized tradition to the living communities of believers.

This book examines many legal and exegetical interpretations of Q. 4:34. Post-colonial Muslim scholars have interpreted several key words in Q. 4:34 to have various plain-sense meanings and have used this text to justify both patriarchal and egalitarian cosmologies. The question nevertheless remains—what role does the Qur'ān itself play in determining its own plain-sense meaning? How does the Arabic text of the Qur'ān restrict its plausible interpretations? In the end, the argument of this book is that readers and their expectations determine the meaning of any given piece of Qur'anic text. In studying the interpretations of Q. 4:34, we learn about the idealized cosmology of its interpreters because interpretations tell us more about the interpreters than about the text itself. Q. 4:34 will always have multiple meanings because it enters human consciousness only through the individual subjectivities of its readers. In this framework, the particulars of the text of Q. 4:34 are peripheral to the expectations and needs of the believing communities with which it interacts. Hence, the challenge for Muslims is not to read Q. 4:34 in a nonviolent way—this can be done easily—but rather to read it nonviolently in the face of an authoritative tradition that only read the verse as sanctioning violence against wives.

And so we return to the fact that in order for Muslim scholars to overcome the egalitarian–authoritative dilemma, they must approach the Qur'ān as a performative text. As a performative text whose meanings are derived through its interactions with various believing communities, the Qur'ān will showcase its polysemy, whereby it can speak to various Muslim communities in multiple voices. This, however, cannot happen unless the "Islamic tradition" is de-mythologized so that Muslims can articulate and advocate for their creative interventions with authority. Once authority is transferred away from a mythically pristine tradition to the living community that interacts with, embodies, and bears the scars of violent meanings attributed to this text, contemporary Muslims will be able to authoritatively posit nonviolent meanings of Q. 4:34. Thus, contemporary Muslims may fully belong to a religious tradition that they love, in the face of enduring challenges posed by texts whose pre-colonial plain-sense meanings they cannot abide.

APPENDIX

1. Exegetes who considered the *asbāb al-nuzūl* for Q. 4:34 include Muḥammad ibn Muḥammad al-ʿImādī Abū al-Suʿūd, *Tafsīr Abī al-Suʿūd: al-musammā irshād al-ʿaql al-salīm ilā mazāyā al-Qurʾān al-Karīm* (Cairo: Maktaba Muḥammad ʿAlī Ṣubayḥ, 1952) 1:339; al-Ḥusayn ibn Masʿūd al-Baghawī, *Tafsīr al-Baghawī al-musammā Maʿālim al-tanzīl* (Beirut: Dār al-Maʿrifa, 1986) 5:422; Muḥammad ibn Yaʿqūb al-Fīrūzābādī, *Tanwīr al-miqbās min tafsīr Ibn ʿAbbās* (Beirut: Dār al-Kutub al-ʿIlmiyya, 2000) 92; Abū Bakr ibn ʿAlī al-Ḥaddād, *Tafsīr al-Ḥaddād: Kashf al-tanzīl fī taḥqīq al-mabāḥith wa-l-taʾwīl* (Beirut: Dār al-Madār al-Islāmī, 2003) 2:249; Hūd ibn Muḥakkam al-Huwwārī, *Tafsīr Kitāb Allāh al-ʿAzīz* (Beirut: Dār al-Gharb al-Islāmī, 1990) 1:377; ʿAbd al-Raḥmān ibn Muḥammad Ibn Abī Ḥātim, *Tafsīr al-Qurʾān al-ʿaẓīm: musnadan ʿan al-Rasūl Allāh wa-l-ṣaḥāba wa-l-tābiʿīn* (Ṣaydā: al-Maktaba al-ʿAṣriyya, 1999) 3:940; Muḥammad ibn ʿAbd Allāh Ibn Abī Zamanīn, *Tafsīr al-Qurʾān al-ʿazīz li-Ibn Abī Zamanīn* (Cairo: al-Fārūq al-Ḥadītha li-l-Ṭibāʿa wa-l-Nashr, 2002) 1:366; Muḥammad ibn ʿAbd Allāh Ibn al-ʿArabī, *Aḥkām al-Qurʾān* (Cairo: Dār al-Manār, 2002) 1:493; ʿAbd al-Ḥaqq ibn Ghālib Ibn ʿAṭiyya, *al-Muḥarrar al-wajīz fī tafsīr al-Kitāb al-ʿAzīz* (Beirut: Manshūrāt Muḥammad ʿAlī Bayḍūn, 2001) 2:47; Ismāʿīl ibn ʿUmar Ibn Kathīr, *Tafsīr al-ʿaẓīm li-ibn Kathīr* (Damascus: Dar Ibn Kathir, 1994) 1:601; Abū al-Faraj ʿAbd al-Raḥmān ibn ʿAlī Ibn al-Jawzī, *Zād al-masīr fī ʿilm al-tafsīr* (Damascus: al-Maktab al-Islāmī li-l-Ṭibāʿa wa-l-Nashr, 1964) 2:73; ʿAbd Allāh Ibn Wahb, *al-Jāmiʿ: tafsīr al-Qurʾān* (Beirut: Dār al-Gharb al-Islāmī, 2003) 1:41; Aḥmad ibn ʿAlī Al-Jaṣṣāṣ, *Aḥkām al-Qurʾān* (Beirut: Dār al-Kitāb al-ʿArabī, 1971) 2:188; Al-Khāzin al-Baghdādī, *Tafsīr al-Khāzin: al-musammā Lubāb al-taʾwīl fī maʿānī al-tanzīl* (Baghdad: Maktaba al-Muthannā, 1975) 1:374; ʿAlī ibn Muḥammad al-Māwardī, *al-Nukat wa-l-ʿuyūn: tafsīr al-Māwardī. Min rawāʾiʿ al-tafāsīr* (Beirut: Dār al-Kutub al-ʿIlmiyya, 1992) 1:481; Mujāhid ibn Jabr, *Tafsīr al-Imām Mujāhid ibn Jabr* (Beirut: Dār al-Fikr al-Ḥadītha, 1989) 274; Muqātil ibn Sulaymān al-Balkhī, *Tafsīr Muqātil ibn Sulaymān* (Cairo: Muʾassasat al-Ḥalabī, 1969) 1:235; Muḥammad ibn Aḥmad al-Qurṭubī, *al-Jāmiʿ li-aḥkām al-Qurʾān: tafsīr al-Qurṭubī* (Beirut: Dār al-Kitāb al-ʿArabī, 1997) 5:162; Fakhr al-Dīn al-Rāzī, *al-Tafsīr al-kabīr* (Beirut: Dār Iḥyāʾ al-Turāth al-ʿArabī, 1997) 4:70; Naṣr ibn Muḥammad Abū al-Layth al-Samarqandī, *Tafsīr al-Samarqandī, al-musammā, Baḥr al-ʿulūm* (Beirut: Dār al-Kutub al-ʿIlmiyya, 1993) 1:351; ʿAbd al-Razzāq al-Ṣanʿānī ibn Hammām al-Ḥimyarī, *Tafsīr al-Qurʾān* (Riyadh: Maktaba al-Rushd, 1989) 1:157; Muḥammad ibn Aḥmad al-Shirbīnī, *Tafsīr al-Khaṭīb*

al-Shirbīnī: al-musammā al-Sirāj al-munīr fī al-iʿāna ʿalā maʿrifat baʿḍ maʿānī kalām rabbinā al-ḥakīm al-khabīr (Beirut: Dār al-Kutub al-ʿIlmiyya, 2004) 1:346; ʿIzz al-Dīn ʿAbd al-ʿAzīz ibn ʿAbd al-Salām al-Sulamī, *Tafsīr al-Qurʾān: ikhtiṣār al-Nukat li-l-Māwardī* (Beirut: Dār Ibn Ḥazm, 1996) 1:320; Jalāl al-Dīn ʿAbd al-Raḥmān al-Suyūṭī, *al-Durr al-manthūr fī al-tafsīr al-maʾthūr* (Beirut: Dār al-Maʿrifa, 1970) 2:151; Abū Jaʿfar Muḥammad ibn Jarīr al-Ṭabarī, *Tafsīr al-Ṭabarī: al-musammā Jāmiʿ al-bayān fī taʾwīl al-Qurʾān* (Beirut: Dār al-Kutub al-ʿIlmiyya, 1999) 4:60–1; Aḥmad ibn Muḥammad al-Thaʿlabī, *al-Kashf wa-l-bayān: al-maʿrūf Tafsīr al-Thaʿlabī* (Beirut: Dār Iḥyāʾ al-Turāth al-ʿArabī, 2002) 3:302; Maḥmūd ibn ʿUmar al-Zamakhsharī, *al-Kashshāf ʿan ḥaqāʾiq ghawāmiḍ al-tanzīl wa-ʿuyūn al-aqāwīl fī wujūh al-taʾwīl* (Beirut: Dār al-Kutub al-ʿIlmiyya, 2003) 1:495.

2. Exegetes who used some form of *q-w-m* to describe the relationship between husbands and wives include Muḥammad ibn Yūsuf Abū Ḥayyān, *Tafsīr al-baḥr al-muḥīṭ* (Beirut: Dār al-Kutub al-ʿIlmiyya, 1993) 3:249; Abū al-Suʿūd, *Tafsīr Abī al-Suʿūd*, 1:338; al-Baghawī, *Maʿālim al-tanzīl*, 5:422; ʿAbd Allāh ibn ʿUmar al-Bayḍāwī, *Anwār al-tanzīl wa-asrār al-taʾwīl* (Cairo: Dār al-Kutub al-ʿArabīya al-Kubrā, 1970) 1:85; al-Ḍaḥḥāk ibn Muzāḥim, *Tafsīr al-Ḍaḥḥāk* (Cairo: Dār al-Salām li-l-Ṭibāʿa wa-l-Nashr wa-l-Tawzīʿ wa-l-Tarjama, 1999) 1:285; al-Ḥaddād, *Kashf al-tanzīl*, 2:249; Ibn al-ʿArabī, *Aḥkām al-Qurʾān*, 1:494; Ibn ʿAṭiyya, *al-Muḥarrar*, 2:47; al-Jaṣṣāṣ, *Aḥkām al-Qurʾān*, 2:188; Ibn Kathīr, *al-Tafsīr al-ʿaẓīm*, 1:601; al-Khāzin, *Lubāb*, 1:374; al-Māwardī, *al-Nukat*, 1:480; al-Nasafī, *Tafsīr al-Nasafī, al-musammā bi Madārik al-tanzīl wa-ḥaqāʾiq al-taʾwīl* (Beirut: Dār al-Qalam, 1989) 1:354; al-Qurṭubī, *al-Jāmiʿ*, 5:162; Aḥmad ibn Yūsuf al-Samīn, *al-Durr al-maṣūn fī ʿulūm al-kitāb al-maknūn* (Damascus: Dār al-Qalam, 1986) 3:670–3; al-Shirbīnī, *al-Sirāj*, 1:346; al-Suyūṭī, *al-Durr al-manthūr*, 2:151; al-Ṭabarī, *Jāmiʿ al-bayān fī al-taʾwīl al-Qurʾān*, 4:59; ʿAbd al-Raḥmān al-Thaʿālibī, *Tafsīr al-Thaʿālibī, al-musammā bi-l-Jawāhir al-ḥisān fī tafsīr al-Qurʾān* (Beirut: Dār Iḥyāʾal-Turāth, 1997) 2:229; al-Zamakhsharī, *al-Kashshāf*, 1:495.

3. Exegetes who use *musallaṭūn* to describe husbands' relationships with wives include Abū Ḥayyān, *al-baḥr al-muḥīṭ*, 3:249; al-Baghawī, *Maʿālim al-tanzīl*, 5:422; ʿAbd Allāh ibn Muḥammad al-Dīnawarī, *Tafsīr Ibn Wahb, al-musammā, al-Wāḍiḥ fī tafsīr al-Qurʾān al-karīm* (Beirut: Manshurāt Muḥammad ʿAlī Bayḍūn, Dār al-Kutub al-ʿIlmiyya, 2003); al-Fīrūzābādī, *Tanwīr*, 91; al-Ḥaddād, *Kashf al-tanzīl*, 2:249; al-Huwwārī, *Tafsīr Kitāb Allāh*, 1:377; Ibn Abī Zamanīn, *Tafsīr al-Qurʾān*, 1:366; Ibn al-Jawzī, *Zād al-masīr*, 2:73; al-Khāzin, *Lubāb*, 1:374; Muqātil, *Tafsīr Muqātil*, 1:235; al-Rāzī, *al-Tafsīr al-kabīr*, 4:70; al-Samarqandī, *Baḥr al-ʿulūm*, 1:352; al-Thaʿlabī, *al-Kashf*, 3:302.

4. Exegetes who use variations of the phrase *wa-l-akhdh ʿalā aydīhinna* to describe husbands' relationships with wives include al-Huwwārī, *Tafsīr*

Kitāb Allāh, 1:377; Ibn Abī, *Tafsīr al-Qurʾān*, 1:366; al-Khāzin, *Lubāb*, 1:374; al-Māwardī, *al-Nukat*, 1:480; Muqātil, *Tafsīr Muqātil*, 1:235; al-Rāzī, *al-Tafsīr al-kabīr*, 4:70; al-Sulamī, *Ikhtiṣār al-Nukat*, 1:320; al-Suyūṭī, *al-Durr al-manthūr*, 2:151; al-Ṭabarī, *Jāmiʿ al-bayān*, 4:59; Abū al-Ḥasan ʿAlī al-Wāḥidī Nīshābūrī, *al-Wajīz fī tafsīr al-Kitāb al-ʿazīz* (Damascus: Dār al-Qalam, 1995) 1:263.

5. Exegetes who use either the descriptor *qānitāt* or a conjugation of *ṭāʿa* to describe righteous wives include Abū Ḥayyān, *al-baḥr al-muḥīṭ*, 3:249; Abū al-Suʿūd, *Tafsīr Abī al-Suʿūd*, 1:339; al-Baghawī, *Maʿālim al-tanzīl*, 5:422; al-Bayḍāwī, *Anwār*, 1:85; al-Dīnawarī, *Al-Wāḍiḥ*, 1:151; al-Fīrūzābādī, *Tanwīr*, 91; al-Ḥaddād, *Kashf al-tanzīl*, 2:249; al-Huwwārī, *Tafsīr Kitāb Allāh*, 1:377; Ibn Abī Ḥātim, *Tafsīr al-Qurʾān*, 3:940–1; Ibn Abī Zamanīn, *Tafsīr al-Qurʾān*, 1:367; Ibn al-ʿArabī, *Aḥkām al-Qurʾān*, 1:493; Ibn ʿAṭiyya, *al-Muḥarrar*, 2:47; Ibn Kathīr, *al-Tafsīr al-ʿaẓīm*, 1:601; al-Jaṣṣāṣ, *Aḥkām al-Qurʾān*, 2:188–9; al-Khāzin, *Lubāb*, 1:374; al-Māwardī, *al-Nukat*, 1:481; Mujāhid, *Tafsīr al-Imām*, 275; Muqātil, *Tafsīr Muqātil*, 1:235; al-Naḥḥās, *Maʿānī*, 2:77; al-Nasafī, *Madārik*, 1:355; al-Rāzī, *al-Tafsīr al-kabīr*, 4:71; al-Samarqandī, *Baḥr al-ʿulūm*, 1:352; al-Ṣanʿānī, *Tafsīr al-Qurʾān*, 1:157; al-Shirbīnī, *al-Sirāj*, 1:346; al-Sulamī, *Ikhtiṣār al-Nukat*, 1:321; al-Suyūṭī, *al-Durr al-manthūr*, 2:151; al-Ṭabarī, *Jāmiʿ al-bayān*, 4:61–2; al-Thaʿālibī, *Jawāhir*, 2:229; al-Thaʿlabī, *al-Kashf*, 3:303; al-Wāḥidī, *al-Wajīz*, 1:263.

6. The version of this *ḥadīth* in al-Thaʿlabī reads, "On the authority of Abū Jaʿfar Muḥammad b. ʿAlī, on the authority of Jābir b. ʿAbd Allāh, he said, 'While we were with the Messenger and a group of his Companions, a woman came so close that she nearly stood on his head, saying, "Peace be upon you, O Messenger of God. I am a delegate to you from the women, and no woman heard of my coming to see you without being delighted by it, O Messenger of God. Indeed, God is the Lord of men and the Lord of women, and Adam is the father of men and the father of women, and Eve is the mother of men and the mother of women. So why is it that when men go out (*kharajū*) in the path of God and are killed, they will live with their Lord and be rewarded, and when they go out, the matter is as I say, but we women are confined by them, and we serve them (*nakhdumuhum*)—so do we receive any reward at all?" ' The Prophet said, 'Yes, greet the women and say to them that their obedience to their husbands and recognition of their rights will [have a result] equal to the husbands' reward, although few of you do it." Karen Bauer, "Room for Interpretation: Qurʾānic Exegesis and Gender," Ph.D. diss. (Princeton University, 2008) 79–80. According to Bauer, this *ḥadīth* illustrates the spiritual equality of men and women, since women can technically attain the reward of martyrs by being obedient to their husbands and fulfilling their rights. However, as Bauer acknowledges, this spiritual equality does not erase marital hierarchy but is attained through serving it.

7. Exegetes who argue that wives were to protect their husbands' wealth, property, and/or houses in their absence include Abū al-Suʿūd, *Tafsīr Abī al-Suʿūd*, 1:339; al-Bayḍāwī, *Anwār*, 1:85; Ibrāhīm ibn ʿUmar al-Biqāʿī, *Naẓm al-durar fī tanāsub al-āyāt wa-l-suwar* (Hyderabad: Maṭbaʿat Majlis Dā'irat al-Maʿārif al-ʿUthmāniyya, 1972) 5:270; al-Dīnawarī, *Al-Wāḍiḥ*, 1:151; al-Fīrūzābādī, *Tanwīr*, 91; al-Ḥaddād, *Kashf al-tanzīl*, 2:249, Ibn Abī Ḥātim, *Tafsīr al-Qur'ān*, 3:941; Ibn al-ʿArabī, *Aḥkām al-Qur'ān*, 1:494; Ibn ʿAṭiyya, *al-Muḥarrar*, 2:47; Ibn al-Jawzī, *Zād al-masīr*, 2:75; Ibn Kathīr, *al-Tafsīr al-ʿaẓīm*, 1:601; al-Jaṣṣāṣ, *Aḥkām al-Qur'ān*, 1:374 and 2:188; al-Khāzin, *Lubāb*, 1:374; al-Māwardī, *al-Nukat*, 1:481; Muqātil, *Tafsīr Muqātil*, 1:235; al-Naḥḥās, *Maʿānī*, 2:78, al-Nasafī, *Madārik*, 1:355; al-Qurṭubī, *al-Jāmiʿ*, 5:163; al-Rāzī, *al-Tafsīr al-kabīr*, 4:71, al-Samarqandī, *Baḥr al-ʿulūm*, 1:352; al-Shirbīnī, *al-Sirāj*, 1:346; al-Suyūṭī, *al-Durr al-manthūr*, 2:151; al-Ṭabarī, *Jāmiʿ al-bayān*, 4:62; al-Zamakhsharī, *al-Kashshāf*, 1:496.
8. Exegetes who argue that wives were to protect their own chastity in their husbands' absence include Abū al-Suʿūd, *Tafsīr Abī al-Suʿūd*, 1:339; al-Baghawī, *Maʿālim al-tanzīl*, 5:422; al-Bayḍāwī, *Anwār*, 1:85; al-Biqāʿī, *Naẓm al-durar*, 5:270; al-Dīnawarī, *Al-Wāḍiḥ*, 1:151; al-Ḥaddād, *Kashf al-tanzīl*, 2:249; al-Huwwārī, *Tafsīr Kitāb Allāh*, 1:377; Ibn Abī Ḥātim, *Tafsīr al-Qur'ān*, 3:941; Ibn Abī Zamanīn, *Tafsīr al-Qur'ān*, 1:367; Ibn al-Jawzī, *Zād al-masīr*, 2:75; Ibn Kathīr, *al-Tafsīr al-ʿaẓīm*, 1:601; al-Jaṣṣāṣ, *Aḥkām al-Qur'ān*, 1:374 and 2:188; al-Khāzin, *Lubāb*, 1:374; al-Māwardī, *al-Nukat*, 1:481; Muqātil, *Tafsīr Muqātil*, 1:235; al-Nasafī, *Madārik*, 1:355; al-Rāzī, *al-Tafsīr al-kabīr*, 4:71; al-Samarqandī, *Baḥr al-ʿulūm*, 1:352; al-Shirbīnī, *al-Sirāj*, 1:346; al-Sulamī, *Ikhtiṣār al-Nukat*, 1:321; al-Suyūṭī, *al-Durr al-manthūr*, 2:151; al-Ṭabarī, *Jāmiʿ al-bayān*, 4:62; al-Zamakhsharī, *al-Kashshāf*, 1:496.
9. Exegetes who cite the *ḥadīth* describing the "best of women" include Abū Ḥayyān, *al-baḥr al-muḥīṭ*, 3:250; Abū al-Suʿūd, *Tafsīr Abī al-Suʿūd*, 1:339; al-Baghawī, *Maʿālim al-tanzīl*, 5:423; al-Bayḍāwī, *Anwār*, 1:85; al-Ḥaddād, *Kashf al-tanzīl*, 2:249–50; Ibn Abī Ḥātim, *Tafsīr al-Qur'ān*, 3:939 and 941; Ibn ʿAṭiyya, *al-Muḥarrar*, 2:47; Ibn Kathīr, *al-Tafsīr al-ʿaẓīm*, 1:601, al-Jaṣṣāṣ, *Aḥkām al-Qur'ān*, 1:375 and 2:188–9; al-Khāzin, *Lubāb*, 1:374; al-Māwardī, *al-Nukat*, 1:481; al-Qurṭubī, *al-Jāmiʿ*, 5:163; al-Rāzī, *al-Tafsīr al-kabīr*, 4:71; al-Shirbīnī, *al-Sirāj*, 1:346; al-Suyūṭī, *al-Durr al-manthūr*, 2:151–2; al-Thaʿālibī, *Jawāhir*, 2:229; al-Thaʿlabī, *al-Kashf*, 3:303; al-Zamakhsharī, *al-Kashshāf*, 1:496.
10. Exegetes who use the terms *ta'dīb*, *adab*, *taʿlīm*, *tartīb*, or *tadbīr* or some conjugation of these words to describe husbands' responsibility in disciplining wives include al-Baghawī, *Maʿālim al-tanzīl*, 5:422; al-Biqāʿī, *Naẓm al-durar*, 5:269; al-Dīnawarī, *Al-Wāḍiḥ*, 1:151; al-Fīrūzābādī, *Tanwīr*, 91; al-Ḥaddād, *Kashf al-tanzīl*, 2:249; al-Huwwārī, *Tafsīr Kitāb Allāh*, 1:377; Ibn Abī Zamanīn, *Tafsīr al-Qur'ān*, 1:366; Ibn al-ʿArabī, *Aḥkām al-Qur'ān*, 1:499; Ibn ʿAṭiyya, *al-Muḥarrar*, 2:47; Ibn al-Jawzī, *Zād al-masīr*, 2:74; Ibn Kathīr,

al-Tafsīr al-ʿaẓīm, 1:601; al-Jaṣṣāṣ, *Aḥkām al-Qurʾān*, 2:188; al-Khāzin, *Lubāb*, 1:374; al-Māwardī, *al-Nukat*, 1:480; Muqātil, *Tafsīr Muqātil*, 1:235; al-Qurṭubī, *al-Jāmiʿ*, 5:162; ʿAbd al-Karīm ibn Hawāzin Al-Qushayrī, *Laṭāʾif al-ishārāt: tafsīr Ṣūfī Kāmil li-l-Qurʾān al-Karīm* (Cairo: Dār al-Kātib al-ʿArabī, 1968) 2:330; al-Rāzī, *al-Tafsīr al-kabīr*, 4:70; al-Samarqandī, *Baḥr al-ʿulūm*, 1:351; al-Sulamī, *Ikhtiṣār al-Nukat*, 1:320; al-Suyūṭī, *al-Durr al-manthūr*, 2:151; al-Ṭabarī, *Jāmiʿ al-bayān*, 4:59; al-Thaʿlabī, *al-Kashf*, 3:302; al-Wāḥidī, *al-Wajīz*, 1:262.

11. Exegetes who drew a parallel between the God–man and husband–wife relationships include Abū al-Suʿūd, *Tafsīr Abī al-Suʿūd*, 1:339; al-Baghawī, *Maʿālim al-tanzīl*, 5:423; al-Bayḍāwī, *Anwār*, 1:85; al-Biqāʿī, *Naẓm al-durar*, 5:272; al-Fīrūzābādī, *Tanwīr*, 91; Ibn ʿAṭiyya, *al-Muḥarrar*, 2:48; Ibn Kathīr, *al-Tafsīr al-ʿaẓīm*, 1:602; al-Khāzin, *Lubāb*, 1:376; al-Nasafī, *Madārik*, 1:355; al-Qurṭubī, *al-Jāmiʿ*, 5:166; al-Rāzī, *al-Tafsīr al-kabīr*, 4:73; al-Samarqandī, *Baḥr al-ʿulūm*, 1:352; al-Shirbīnī, *al-Sirāj*, 1:347; al-Ṭabarī, *Jāmiʿ al-bayān*, 4:71–2; al-Thaʿālibī, *Jawāhir*, 2:231; al-Zajjāj, *Maʿānī al-Qurʾān*, 2:48–9.

12. Exegetes who mention that it was not permissible to discipline a wife for not loving her husband include al-Baghawī, *Maʿālim al-tanzīl*, 5:423; al-Dīnawarī, *Al-Wāḍiḥ*, 1:151; al-Fīrūzābādī, *Tanwīr*, 91; al-Ḥaddād, *Kashf al-tanzīl*, 2:250; al-Huwwārī, *Tafsīr Kitāb Allāh*, 1:378; Ibn Abī Zamanīn, *Tafsīr al-Qurʾān*, 1:366; Ibn al-Jawzī, *Zād al-masīr*, 2:76; al-Khāzin, *Lubāb*, 1:376; al-Māwardī, *al-Nukat*, 1:483; Muqātil, *Tafsīr Muqātil*, 1:236; al-Qurṭubī, *al-Jāmiʿ*, 5:166; al-Samarqandī, *Baḥr al-ʿulūm*, 1:352; al-Sulamī, *Ḥaqāʾiq al-tafsīr*, 1:146; al-Suyūṭī, *al-Durr al-manthūr*, 2:155–6; al-Ṭabarī, *Jāmiʿ al-bayān*, 4:72; al-Thaʿlabī, *al-Kashf*, 3:303.

13. The translation of *khawf* as a cognate of *ʿilm* was preferred by Muḥammad ibn Muḥammad al-ʿImādī Abū al-Suʿūd, *Tafsīr Abī al-Suʿūd: al-musammā irshād al-ʿaql al-salīm ilā mazāyā al-Qurʾān al-Karīm* (Cairo: Maktaba Muḥammad ʿAlī Ṣubayḥ, 1952) 1:339; ʿAbd Allāh ibn Muḥammad al-Dīnawarī, *Tafsīr Ibn Wahb, al-musammā, al-Wāḍiḥ fī tafsīr al-Qurʾān al-karīm* (Beirut: Manshurāt Muḥammad ʿAlī Bayḍūn, Dār al-Kutub al-ʿIlmiyya, 2003) 1:151; Aḥmad Yūsuf Najātī al-Farrāʾ, *Maʿānī al-Qurʾān* (Cairo: al-Hayʾa al-Miṣrīya al-ʿĀmma li-l-Kitāb, 1980) 1:265; Muḥammad ibn Yaʿqūb al-Fīrūzābādī, *Tanwīr al-miqbās min tafsīr Ibn ʿAbbās* (Beirut: Dār al-Kutub al-ʿIlmiyya, 2000) 92; Abū Bakr ibn ʿAlī al-Ḥaddād, *Tafsīr al-Ḥaddād: Kashf al-tanzīl fī taḥqīq al-mabāḥith wa-l-taʾwīl* (Beirut: Dār al-Madār al-Islāmī, 2003) 2:250; ʿAbd al-Ḥaqq ibn Ghālib Ibn ʿAṭiyya, *al-Muḥarrar al-wajīz fī tafsīr al-Kitāb al-ʿAzīz* (Beirut: Manshūrāt Muḥammad ʿAlī Bayḍūn, 2001) 2:48; Abū al-Faraj ʿAbd al-Raḥmān ibn ʿAlī Ibn al-Jawzī, *Zād al-masīr fī ʿilm al-tafsīr* (Damascus: al-Maktab al-Islāmī li-l-Ṭibāʿa wa-l-Nashr, 1964) 2:75; al-Khāzin al-Baghdādī, *Tafsīr al-Khāzin: al-musammā Lubāb al-taʾwīl fī maʿānī al-tanzīl* (Baghdad: Maktaba al-Muthannā, 1975) 1:374; Muḥammad ibn Aḥmad al-Qurṭubī, *al-Jāmiʿ li-aḥkām al-Qurʾān: tafsīr al-Qurṭubī*

(Beirut: Dār al-Kitāb al-ʿArabī, 1997) 5:163; Muḥammad ibn Aḥmad al-Shirbīnī, *Tafsīr al-Khaṭīb al-Shirbīnī: al-musammā al-Sirāj al-munīr fī al-iʿāna ʿalā maʿrifa baʿḍ maʿānī kalām rabbinā al-ḥakīm al-khabīr* (Beirut: Dār al-Kutub al-ʿIlmiyya, 2004) 1:346.

14. Exegetes who include wifely disobedience as a meaning for wifely *nushūz* include Abū al-Suʿūd, *Tafsīr Abī al-Suʿūd*, 1:339; al-Biqāʿī, *Naẓm al-durar*, 5:271; ʿAbd Allāh ibn ʿUmar al-Bayḍāwī, *Anwār al-tanzīl wa-asrār al-taʾwīl* (Cairo: Dār al-Kutub al-ʿArabīyya al-Kubrā, 1970) 1:85; al-Ḥaddād, *Kashf al-tanzīl*, 2:250; ʿAbd al-Raḥmān ibn Muḥammad Ibn Abī Ḥātim, *Tafsīr al-Qurʾān al-ʿaẓīm: musnadan ʿan al-Rasūl Allāh wa-l-ṣaḥāba wa-l-tābiʿīn* (Ṣaydā: al-Maktaba al-ʿAṣriya, 1999) 3:941–2; Muḥammad ibn ʿAbd Allāh Ibn Abī Zamanīn, *Tafsīr al-Qurʾān al-ʿazīz li-Ibn Abī Zamanīn* (Cairo: al-Fārūq al-Ḥadīthah li-l-Ṭibāʿa wa-l-Nashr, 2002) 1:367; Ibn Kathīr, *al-Tafsīr al-ʿaẓīm*, 1:602; al-Jaṣṣāṣ, *Aḥkām al-Qurʾān*, 2:189; al-Māwardī, *al-Nukat*, 1:482; Muqātil, *Tafsīr Muqātil*, 1:235, al-Nasafī, *Madārik al-Tanzīl*, 1:355; al-Qurṭubī, *al-Jāmiʿ*, 5:163; al-Rāzī, *al-Tafsīr al-kabīr*, 4:72, al-Samarqandī, *Baḥr al-ʿulūm*, 1:352; Jalāl al-Dīn ʿAbd al-Raḥmān al-Suyūṭī, *al-Durr al-manthūr fī al-tafsīr al-maʾthūr* (Beirut: Dār al-Maʿrifa, 1970) 2:155; al-Ṭabarī, *Jāmiʿ al-bayān*, 4:64; al-Wāḥidī, *al-Wajīz*, 1:263; al-Zamakhsharī, *al-Kashshāf*, 1:496.

15. Exegetes that translate *nushūz* as "rising" by using *al-irtifāʿ* or a conjugation of *ʿalā*, include Abū Ḥayyān, *al-baḥr al-muḥīṭ*, 3:251; Abū al-Suʿūd, *Tafsīr Abī al-Suʿūd*, 1:339; al-Ḥusayn ibn Masʿūd al-Baghawī, *Tafsīr al-Baghawī al-musammā Maʿālim al-tanzīl* (Beirut: Dār al-Maʿrifa, 1986) 5:423; al-Bayḍāwī, *Anwār*, 1:85; al-Biqāʿī, *Naẓm al-durar*, 5:270–1; al-Ḥaddād, *Kashf al-tanzīl*, 2:50; Ibn Kathīr, *al-Tafsīr al-ʿaẓīm*, 1:602; al-Jaṣṣāṣ, *Aḥkām al-Qurʾān*, 2:189; al-Khāzin, *Lubāb*, 1:374; al-Māwardī, *al-Nukat*, 1:482; Aḥmad ibn Muḥammad al-Naḥḥās, *Maʿānī al-Qurʾān al-karīm* (Mecca: Jāmiʿat Umm al-Qurā, 1988) 2:78; al-Nasafī, *Madārik*, 1:355; al-Qurṭubī, *al-Jāmiʿ*, 5:163; al-Rāzī, *al-Tafsīr al-kabīr*, 4:72; al-Sulamī, *Ikhtiṣār al-Nukat*, 1:321;ʿAbd al-Raḥmān al-Thaʿālibī, *Tafsīr al-Thaʿālibī, al-musammā bi-l-Jawāhir al-ḥisān fī tafsīr al-Qurʾān* (Beirut: Dār Iḥyāʾ al-Turāth, 1997) 2:229; al-Ṭabarī, *Jāmiʿ al-bayān*, 4:64.

16. Exegetes who use "*nushūzahunna*" interchangeably with "ʿ*iṣyānahunna*," or "*nushūz*" with "ʿ*iṣyān*," or some conjugation thereof include Abū Ḥayyān, *al-baḥr al-muḥīṭ*, 3:251; Abū al-Suʿūd, *Tafsīr Abī al-Suʿūd*, 1:339; al-Baghawī, *Maʿālim al-tanzīl*, 5:423; al-Bayḍāwī, *Anwār*, 1:85; al-Biqāʿī, *Naẓm al-durar*, 5:271; al-Fīrūzābādī, *Tanwīr*, 91; al-Ḥaddād, *Kashf al-tanzīl*, 2:250; Hūd ibn Muḥakkam al-Huwwārī, *Tafsīr Kitāb Allāh al-ʿAzīz* (Beirut: Dār al-Gharb al-Islāmī, 1990) 1:377; Ibn Abī Zamanīn, *Tafsīr al-Qurʾān*, 1:367; al-Nasafī, *Madārik*, 1:355; al-Qurṭubī, *al-Jāmiʿ*, 5:163; al-Rāzī, *al-Tafsīr al-kabīr*, 4:72; al-Samarqandī, *Baḥr al-ʿulūm*, 1:352; al-Suyūṭī, *al-Durr al-manthūr*, 2:155; Aḥmad ibn Muḥammad al-Thaʿlabī, *al-Kashf wa-l-bayān: al-maʿrūf Tafsīr*

al-Thaʿlabī (Beirut: Dār Iḥyāʾ al-Turāth al-ʿArabī, 2002) 3:303; al-Wāḥidī, *al-Wajīz*, 1:263.

17. Exegetes who consider wifely *nushūz* to include sexual disobedience include Abū Ḥayyān, *al-baḥr al-muḥīṭ*, 3:251; al-Bayḍāwī, *Anwār*, 1:85; al-Dīnawarī, *Al-Wāḍiḥ*, 1:151; al-Fīrūzābādī, *Tanwīr*, 91; al-Ḥaddād, *Kashf al-tanzīl*, 2:250; al-Huwwārī, *Tafsīr Kitāb Allāh*, 1:377; Ibn Abī Ḥātim, *Tafsīr al-Qurʾān*, 3:942 and 944; Ibn al-ʿArabī, *Aḥkām al-Qurʾān*, 1:495; Ibn Kathīr, *al-Tafsīr al-ʿaẓīm*, 1:602; al-Jaṣṣāṣ, *Aḥkām al-Qurʾān*, 2:189; Mujāhid ibn Jabr, *Tafsīr al-Imām Mujāhid ibn Jabr* (Beirut: Dār al-Fikr al-Ḥadītha, 1989) 275; al-Qurṭubī, *al-Jāmiʿ*, 5:163 and 166; al-Suyūṭī, *al-Durr al-manthūr*, 2:156; al-Ṭabarī, *Jāmiʿ al-bayān*, 4:64–5; al-Zamakhsharī, *al-Kashshāf*, 1:496.
18. Exegetes who use a conjugation of *kh-w-f* or *t-q-w* to interpret "*fa-ʿiẓūhunna*" include Abu Bakr Ibn ʿArabī, *Aḥkām al-Qurʾān*, 1:496; al-Baghawī, *Maʿālim al-tanzīl*, 5:423; Ibn Kathīr, *al-Tafsīr al-ʿaẓīm*, 1:602; al-Jaṣṣāṣ, *Aḥkām al-Qurʾān*, 2:189; al-Khāzin, *Lubāb*, 1:374; al-Māwardī, *al-Nukat*, 1:482; al-Nasafī, *Madārik*, 1:355; al-Rāzī, *al-Tafsīr al-kabīr*, 4:72; al-Samarqandī, *Baḥr al-ʿulūm*, 1:352; al-Shirbīnī, *al-Sirāj*, 1:346; al-Sulamī, *Ikhtiṣār al-Nukat*, 1:321; al-Ṭabarī, *Jāmiʿ al-bayān*, 4:65.
19. Exegetes who consider "avoiding sex" with one's wife as a possible interpretation of *wa-hjurūhunna fī al-maḍājiʿ* include Abū Ḥayyān, *al-baḥr al-muḥīṭ*, 3:251; Abū al-Suʿūd, *Tafsīr Abī al-Suʿūd*, 1:339; al-Bayḍāwī, *Anwār*, 1:85; Ibn Abī Ḥātim, *Tafsīr al-Qurʾān*, 3:942; Ibn al-ʿArabī, *Aḥkām al-Qurʾān*, 1:496; Ibn ʿAṭiyya, *al-Muḥarrar*, 2:48; Ibn al-Jawzī, *Zād al-masīr*, 2:76; Ibn Kathīr, *al-Tafsīr al-ʿaẓīm*, 1:602; al-Māwardī, *al-Nukat*, 1:482; Muqātil, *Tafsīr Muqātil*, 1:235; al-Nasafī, *Madārik*, 1:355; al-Qurṭubī, *al-Jāmiʿ*, 5:164; al-Rāzī, *al-Tafsīr al-kabīr*, 4:72; al-Samīn, *al-Durr al-maṣūn*, 3:670–3; al-Sulamī, *Ikhtiṣār al-Nukat*, 1:321; al-Suyūṭī, *al-Durr al-manthūr*, 2:155; al-Thaʿālibī, *Jawāhir*, 2:230; al-Ṭabarī, *Jāmiʿ al-bayān*, 4:66–7.
20. Exegetes who consider "leaving the bed" as an interpretive possibility of "abandon them in beds" include al-Ḥaddād, *Kashf al-tanzīl*, 2:250; Ibn Abī Ḥātim, *Tafsīr al-Qurʾān*, 3:943; Ibn ʿAṭiyya, *al-Muḥarrar*, 2:48; Ibn al-Jawzī, *Zād al-masīr*, 2:76; Ibn Wahb, *al-Jāmiʿ*, 1:146; al-Jaṣṣāṣ, *Aḥkām al-Qurʾān*, 2:189; al-Khāzin, *Lubāb*, 1:375; al-Māwardī, *al-Nukat*,1:482; al-Qurṭubī, *al-Jāmiʿ*, 5:165; al-Samarqandī, *Baḥr al-ʿulūm*, 1:352; al-Sulamī, *Ikhtiṣār al-Nukat*, 1:321; al-Suyūṭī, *al-Durr al-manthūr*, 2:155; al-Ṭabarī, *Jāmiʿ al-bayān*, 4:67.
21. Exegetes who mention "turning one's back in bed" as a possible interpretation of *wa-hjurūhunna fī al-maḍājiʿ* include Abū Ḥayyān, *al-baḥr al-muḥīṭ*, 3:251; al-Baghawī, *Maʿālim al-tanzīl*, 5:423; Ibn Abī Ḥātim, *Tafsīr al-Qurʾān*, 3:942–3; Ibn al-ʿArabī, *Aḥkām al-Qurʾān*, 1:496–7; Ibn ʿAṭiyya, *al-Muḥarrar*, 2:48; Ibn Kathīr, *al-Tafsīr al-ʿaẓīm*, 1:602; al-Khāzin, *Lubāb*, 1:375; al-Māwardī, *al-Nukat*, 1:482; al-Nasafī, *Madārik*, 1:355; al-Qurṭubī, *al-Jāmiʿ*, 5:164; al-Sulamī, *Ikhtiṣār al-Nukat*, 1:321; al-Suyūṭī, *al-Durr*

al-manthūr, 2:155; al-Ṭabarī, *Jāmiʿ al-bayān*, 4:66; al-Thaʿālibī, *Jawāhir*, 2:230; al-Thaʿlabī, *al-Kashf*, 3:303; al-Zamakhsharī, *al-Kashshāf*, 1:496.

22. Exegetes who mention abandonment of speech as a possible interpretation of *wa-hjurūhunna fī al-maḍājiʿ* include Abū Ḥayyān, *al-baḥr al-muḥīṭ*, 3:251; al-Ḍaḥḥāk ibn Muzāḥim, *Tafsīr al-Ḍaḥḥāk* (Cairo: Dār al-Salām li-l-Ṭibāʿa wa-l-Nashr wa-l-Tawzīʿ wa-l-Tarjama, 1999) 1:285; Ibn al-ʿArabī; *Aḥkām al-Qurʾān*, 1:496; Ibn ʿAṭiyya, *al-Muḥarrar*, 2:48; Ibn Kathīr, *al-Tafsīr al-ʿaẓīm*, 1:602; Ibn al-Jawzī, *Zād al-masīr*, 2:76; al-Khāzin, *Lubāb*, 1:375; al-Māwardī, *al-Nukat*,1:482; al-Rāzī, *al-Tafsīr al-kabīr*, 4:72; al-Ṣanʿānī, *Tafsīr al-Qurʾān*, 1:158; al-Shirbīnī, *al-Sirāj*, 1:346; al-Sulamī, *Ikhtiṣār al-Nukat*, 1:321; al-Suyūṭī, *al-Durr al-manthūr*, 2:155; al-Ṭabarī, *Jāmiʿ al-bayān*, 4:66; al-Thaʿālibī, *Jawāhir*, 2:230.
23. Exegetes who mention "harsh speech" as a possible interpretation of "abandonment in bed" include Abū Ḥayyān, *al-baḥr al-muḥīṭ*, 3:252; al-Ḥaddād, *Kashf al-tanzīl*, 2:250; Ibn Abī Ḥātim, *Tafsīr al-Qurʾān*, 3:939–44; Ibn al-Jawzī, *Zād al-masīr*, 2:76; al-Māwardī, *al-Nukat*, 1:482; al-Qurṭubī, *al-Jāmiʿ*, 5:164; al-Rāzī, *al-Tafsīr al-kabīr*, 4:72; al-Samarqandī, *Baḥr al-ʿulūm*, 1:352; al-Ṣanʿānī, *Tafsīr al-Qurʾān*, 1:158; al-Sulamī, *Ikhtiṣār al-Nukat*, 1:321; al-Suyūṭī, *al-Durr al-manthūr*, 2:155; al-Ṭabarī, *Jāmiʿ al-bayān*, 4:67–8; al-Zajjāj, *Maʿānī al-Qurʾān*, 2:49.
24. Exegetes who use the qualifier "*ghayr mubarriḥ*" to limit the prescription of "*wa-ḍribūhunna*" include al-Baghawī, *Maʿālim al-tanzīl*, 5:423; al-Bayḍāwī, *Anwār*, 1:85; al-Ḍaḥḥāk, *Tafsīr al-Ḍaḥḥāk*, 1:285; al-Dīnawarī, *Al-Wāḍiḥ*, 1:151; al-Fīrūzābādī, *Tanwīr*, 91; al-Ḥaddād, *Kashf al-tanzīl*, 2:250; al-Huwwārī, *Tafsīr Kitāb Allāh*, 1:378; Ibn Abī Ḥātim, *Tafsīr al-Qurʾān*, 3:942; Ibn al-ʿArabī, *Aḥkām al-Qurʾān*, 1:498; Ibn ʿAṭiyya, *al-Muḥarrar*, 2:48; Ibn al-Jawzī, *Zād al-masīr*, 2:76; Ibn Kathīr, *al-Tafsīr al-ʿaẓīm*, 1:602; al-Jaṣṣāṣ, *Aḥkām al-Qurʾān*, 1:375 and 2:189; al-Khāzin, *Lubāb*, 1:375; al-Māwardī, *al-Nukat*, 1:483; Muqātil, *Tafsīr Muqātil*, 1:235; al-Naḥḥās, *Maʿānī*, 2:79; al-Nasafī, *Madārik*, 1:355; al-Qurṭubī, *al-Jāmiʿ*, 5:165; al-Samarqandī, *Baḥr al-ʿulūm*, 1:352; al-Ṣanʿānī, *Tafsīr al-Qurʾān*, 1:157–8; al-Shirbīnī, *al-Sirāj*, 1:346; al-Sulamī, *Ikhtiṣār al-Nukat*, 1:321; al-Suyūṭī, *al-Durr al-manthūr*, 2:155; al-Ṭabarī, *Jāmiʿ al-bayān*, 4:70; al-Thaʿālibī, *Jawāhir*, 2:230; al-Thaʿlabī, *al-Kashf*, 3:303; al-Wāḥidī, *al-Wajīz*, 1:263; al-Zajjāj, *Maʿānī al-Qurʾān*, 2:49; al-Zamakhsharī, *al-Kashshāf*, 1:496.
25. Exegetes who use *ghayr shāʾin* as an interpretation of *ghayr mubarriḥ* include Abū al-Suʿūd, *Tafsīr Abī al-Suʿūd*, 1:339; al-Baghawī, *Maʿālim al-tanzīl*, 5:423; al-Bayḍāwī, *Anwār*, 1:85; al-Dīnawarī, *Al-Wāḍiḥ*, 1:151; al-Fīrūzābādī, *Tanwīr*, 91; al-Ḥaddād, *Kashf al-tanzīl*, 2:250; al-Huwwārī, *Tafsīr Kitāb Allāh*, 1:377; Ibn Abī Zamanīn, *Tafsīr al-Qurʾān*, 1:367; al-Jaṣṣāṣ, *Aḥkām al-Qurʾān*, 2:189; al-Khāzin, *Lubāb*, 1:375; Muqātil, *Tafsīr Muqātil*, 1:235; al-Ṭabarī, *Jāmiʿ al-bayān*, 4:70; al-Thaʿālibī, *Jawāhir*, 2:230; al-Thaʿlabī, *al-Kashf*, 3:303.

26. Exegetes who consider that the three prescriptions in Q. 4:34 were to be followed sequentially as a legitimate interpretation include Abū Ḥayyān, *al-baḥr al-muḥīṭ*, 3:252; Abū al-Suʿūd, *Tafsīr Abī al-Suʿūd*, 1:339; al-ʿAyyāshī, *Tafsīr*, 1:330; al-Bayḍāwī, *Anwār*, 1:85; al-Ḥaddād, *Kashf al-tanzīl*, 2:250; Ibn Abī Zamanīn, *Tafsīr al-Qurʾān*, 1:367; Ibn al-ʿArabī, *Aḥkām al-Qurʾān*, 1:498–9; Ibn ʿAṭiyya, *al-Muḥarrar*, 2:48; Ibn al-Jawzī, *Zād al-masīr*, 2:76; Ibn Kathīr, *al-Tafsīr al-ʿaẓīm*, 1:602; al-Jaṣṣāṣ, *Aḥkām al-Qurʾān*, 2:188–9; al-Khāzin, *Lubāb*, 1:375; Muqātil, *Tafsīr Muqātil*, 1:235; al-Nasafī, *Madārik*, 1:355; al-Qurṭubī, *al-Jāmiʿ*, 5:165; al-Qushayrī, *Laṭāʾif*, 2:330; al-Rāzī, *al-Tafsīr al-kabīr*, 4:72; al-Samarqandī, *Baḥr al-ʿulūm*, 1:352; al-Ṣanʿānī, *Tafsīr al-Qurʾān*, 1:158; al-Shirbīnī, *al-Sirāj*, 1:346–7; al-Suyūṭī, *al-Durr al-manthūr*, 2:155–6, al-Ṭabarī, *Jāmiʿ al-bayān*, 4:68; al-Thaʿālibī, *Jawāhir*, 2:231; al-Wāḥidī, *al-Wajīz* 1:263; al-Zajjāj, *Maʿānī al-Qurʾān*, 2:49; al-Zamakhsharī, *al-Kashshāf*, 1:496.

Bibliography

Pre-Colonial Sources

ʿAbd ibn Ḥumayd, Abū Muḥammad, *al-Muntakhab min musnad ʿAbd ibn Ḥumayd* (Beirut: ʿĀlam al-Kutub, 1988).

Abū al-Shaykh, ʿAbd Allāh ibn Muḥammad, *Akhlāq al-Nabī wa-ādābuh* (al-Qāhira: al-Dār al-Miṣrīya al-Lebanonīya, 1991).

Abū Dāwūd, Sulaymān ibn al-Ashʿath al-Sijistānī, *Sunan Abī Dāwūd* (Beirut: Dār al-Kutub al-ʿIlmiyya, 1996).

Abū Ḥayyān, Muḥammad ibn Yūsuf, *Tafsīr al-baḥr al-muḥīṭ* (Beirut: Dār al-Kutub al-ʿIlmiyya, 1993).

Abū al-Layth al-Samarqandī, Naṣr ibn Muḥammad, *Tafsīr al-Samarqandī, al-musammā, Baḥr al-ʿulūm* (Beirut: Dār al-Kutub al-ʿIlmiyya, 1993).

Abū ʿUbayda, Maʿmar ibn al-Muthannā al-Taymī, *Majāz al-Qurʾān* (Beirut: Dār al-Kutub al-ʿIlmiyya, Manshūrāt Muḥammad ʿAlī al-Bayḍūn, 2006).

Al-Anṣārī, Zakarīyā ibn Muḥammad, *Fatḥ al-Wahhāb bi-sharḥ Manhaj al-ṭullāb* (Beirut: Dār al-Kutub al-ʿIlmiyya, 1998).

Al-Aʿwar, Hārūn b. Musā, *Al-Wujūh wa-l-naẓāʾir fī al-Qurʾān al-karīm* (Amman: Dār al-Bashīr, 2002).

Al-ʿAyyāshī, Muḥammad ibn Masʿūd, *Tafsīr* (Qom: Muʾassasat al-Baʿtha, 2000).

Al-Bābartī, Muḥammad ibn Maḥmūd Akmal al-Dīn, *al-ʿInāya sharḥ al-Hidāya* in *Sharḥ fatḥ al-qadīr li-l-ʿājiz al-faqīr* (Cairo: Muṣṭafā al-Bābī al-Ḥalabī, 1970).

Al-Baghawī, al-Ḥusayn ibn Masʿūd, *Tafsīr al-Baghawī al-musammā Maʿālim al-tanzīl* (Beirut: Dār al-Maʿrifa, 1986).

Al-Bājī, Sulaymān ibn Khalaf, *al-Muntaqā: sharḥ Muwaṭṭaʾ Mālik* (Cairo: Dār al-Fikr al-ʿArabī, 1982).

Al-Bayḍāwī, ʿAbd Allāh ibn ʿUmar, *Anwār al-tanzīl wa-asrār al-taʾwīl* (Cairo: Dār al-Kutub al-ʿArabīyya al-Kubrā, 1970).

Al-Bayhaqī, Aḥmad ibn al-Ḥusayn, *Shuʿab al-īmān* (Beirut: Dār al-Kutub al-ʿIlmiyya, 1990).

Al-Bayhaqī, Aḥmad ibn al-Ḥusayn, *al-Sunan al-kubrā* (Beirut: Dār al-Kutub al-ʿIlmiyya, 1999).

Al-Bayhaqī, Aḥmad ibn al-Ḥusayn, *Dalāʾil al-nubuwwa wa-maʿrifat aḥwāl ṣāḥib al-sharīʿa* (Beirut: Manshūrāt Muḥammad ʿAlī Bayḍūn li-Nashr Kutub al-Sunnah wa-l-Jamāʿa, Dār al-Kutub al-ʿIlmiyya, 2002).

Al-Bayhaqī, Aḥmad ibn al-Ḥusayn, *al-Ādāb* (Beirut: Dār al-Kutub al-ʿIlmiyya, 2004).

Al-Biqāʿī, Ibrāhīm ibn ʿUmar, *Naẓm al-durar fī tanāsub al-āyāt wa-l-suwar* (Hyderabad: Maṭbaʿat Majlis Dāʾirat al-Maʿārif al-ʿUthmāniyya, 1972).

Al-Buhūtī, Manṣūr ibn Yūnus, *Irshād ulī al-nuhā li-daqāʾiq al-Muntahā: ḥāshiya ʿalā Muntahā al-irādāt* (Mecca: Dār Khiḍr, 2000).

Al-Ḍaḥḥāk, ibn Muzāḥim, *Tafsīr al-Ḍaḥḥāk* (Cairo: Dār al-Salām li-l-Ṭibāʿa wa-l-Nashr wa-l-Tawzīʿ wa-l-Tarjama, 1999).

Al-Dārimī, ʿAbd Allāh ibn ʿAbd al-Raḥmān, *Sunan al-Dārimī* (Beirut: Dār al-Kutub al-ʿIlmiyya, 1996).

Al-Dīnawarī, ʿAbd Allāh ibn Muḥammad, *Tafsīr Ibn Wahb, al-musammā, al-Wāḍiḥ fī tafsīr al-Qurʾān al-karīm* (Beirut: Manshurāt Muḥammad ʿAlī Bayḍūn, Dār al-Kutub al-ʿIlmiyya, 2003).

Al-Farrāʾ, Yaḥyā ibn Ziyād, *Maʿānī al-Qurʾān* (Cairo: al-Hayʾa al-Miṣrīya al-ʿĀmma li-l-Kitāb, 1980).

Al-Fīrūzābādī, Muḥammad ibn Yaʿqūb, *Tanwīr al-miqbās min tafsīr Ibn ʿAbbās* (Beirut: Dār al-Kutub al-ʿIlmiyya, 2000).

Al-Ghazālī, Muḥammad b. Muḥammad, *Al-Wasīṭ fī al-Madhhab* (Beirut: Dār al-Kutub al-ʿIlmiyya, 2001).

Al-Ḥalabī, ʿAbd al-Raḥmān ibn Muḥammad, *Majmaʿ al-anhur* (Beirut: Dār Iḥyāʾ al-turāth al- ʿArabī, 1980).

Al-Ḥaṣkafī, Muḥammad ibn ʿAlī, *al-Durr al-mukhtār: sharḥ Tanwīr al-abṣār wa-jāmiʿ al-biḥār li-Muḥammad ibn ʿAbd Allāh ibn Aḥmad al-Ghazzī al-Ḥanafī al-Tamartāshī, fī furūʿ al-fiqh al-Ḥanafī* (Beirut: Manshūrāt Muḥammad ʿAlī Bayḍūn, 2002).

Al-Ḥaṭṭāb, Muḥammad ibn Muḥammad, *Mawāhib al-Jalīl li-sharḥ Mukhtaṣar Khalīl* (Ṭarabulus: Maktaba al-Najāḥ, 1972).

Ibn ʿĀbidīn, Muḥammad Amīn ibn ʿUmar, *Radd al-muḥtār ʿalā al-Durr al-mukhtār sharḥ Tanwīr al-abṣār* (Beirut: Dār al-Kutub al-ʿIlmiyya, 1994).

Ibn Abī Shayba, ʿAbd Allāh ibn Muḥammad, *al-Kitāb al-muṣannaf fī al-aḥādīth wa-l-āthār* (Beirut: Dār al-Kutub al-ʿIlmiyya, 1995).

Ibn Farḥūn, Ibrāhīm ibn ʿAlī, *Tabṣirat al-ḥukkām fī uṣūl al-aqḍiya wa-manāhij al-aḥkām* (Cairo: Maktabat al-Kullīyāt al-Azharīya, 1986).

Ibn Abī Ḥātim, ʿAbd al-Raḥmān ibn Muḥammad, *Tafsīr al-Qurʾān al-ʿaẓīm: musnadan ʿan al-Rasūl Allāh wa-l-ṣaḥāba wa-l-tābiʿīn* (Ṣaydā: al-Maktaba al-ʿAṣriyya, 1999).

Ibn Abī Zamanīn, Muḥammad ibn ʿAbd Allāh, *Tafsīr al-Qurʾān al-ʿazīz li-Ibn Abī Zamanīn* (Cairo: al-Fārūq al-Ḥadītha li-l-Ṭibāʿa wa-l-Nashr, 2002).

Ibn al-ʿArabī, Muḥammad ibn ʿAbd Allāh, *Aḥkām al-Qurʾān* (Cairo: Dār al-Manār, 2002).

Ibn al-Daybaʿ, ʿAbd al-Raḥmān ibn ʿAlī, *Taysīr al-wuṣūl ilā jāmiʿ al-uṣūl min ḥadīth al-Rasūl* (Beirut: Dār al-Fikr, 1997).

Ibn Ḥabīb, ʿAbd al-Mālik, *Kitāb Adab al-nisāʾ al-mawsūm bi-Kitāb al-Ghāya wa-l-nihāya*, (ed. ʿAbd al-Majid, Turki) (Beirut: Dār al-Fikr, 1992).

Ibn al-Humām, Muḥammad ibn ʿAbd al-Wāḥid, *Sharḥ fatḥ al-qadīr li-l-ʿājiz al-faqīr* (Cairo: Muṣṭafā al-Bābī al-Ḥalabī, 1970).

Ibn al-Jawzī, Abū al-Faraj ʿAbd al-Raḥmān ibn ʿAlī, *Zād al-masīr fī ʿilm al-tafsīr* (Damascus: al-Maktab al-Islāmī li-l-Ṭibāʿa wa-l-Nashr, 1964).

Ibn al-Jawzī, Abū al-Faraj ʿAbd al-Raḥmān ibn ʿAlī, *Tadhkirat al-arīb fī tafsīr al-gharīb: gharīb al-Qurʾān al-karīm* (Beirut: Dār al-Kutub al-ʿIlmiyya, 2004).

Ibn ʿAṭiyya, ʿAbd al-Ḥaqq ibn Ghālib, *al-Muḥarrar al-wajīz fī tafsīr al-Kitāb al-ʿAzīz* (Beirut: Manshūrāt Muḥammad ʿAlī Bayḍūn, 2001).
Ibn Juzayy, Muḥammad ibn, Aḥmad, *Kitāb al-Tashīl li-ʿulūm al-Tanzīl* (Beirut: Dār al-Kitāb al-ʿArabī, 1973).
Ibn al-Sari, Hannad, *Kitāb al-Zuhd* (Kuwait: Dār al-Khulafāʾ li-l-Kitāb al-Islāmī, 1985).
Ibn Bishrān, ʿAbd al-Malik ibn Muḥammad, *al-Amālī* (Riyadh: Dār al-Waṭan, 1997).
Ibn Ḥanbal, Aḥmad ibn Muḥammad, *Musnad al-Imām Aḥmad ibn Ḥanbal* (Beirut: ʿĀlam al-Kutub, 1998).
Ibn Ḥibbān, Muḥammad ʿAlī Ibn Balabān, *Al-Iḥsān bi-tartīb Ṣaḥīḥ Ibn Ḥibbān* (Beirut: Dār al-Kutub al-ʿIlmiyya, 1987).
Ibn Kathīr, Ismāʿīl ibn ʿUmar, *Tafsīr al-ʿaẓīm li-ibn Kathīr* (Damascus: Dar Ibn Kathir, 1994).
Ibn Mājah, Muḥammad ibn Yazīd, *Sunan Ibn Mājah* (Beirut: Dār al-Kutub al-ʿIlmiyya, 1998).
Ibn Manẓūr, Abī Faḍl Muḥammad b. Mukarram, *Lisān al-ʿArab* (Beirut: Dār al-Kutub al-ʿIlmiyya, 2003).
Ibn Mufliḥ al-Ḥanbalī, Abī Isḥāq Burhān al-Dīn Ibrāhīm b. Muḥammad b. ʿAbdullah b. Muḥammad, *Al-Mubdaʿ Sharḥ al-Muqniʿ* (Beirut: Dār al-Kutub al-ʿIlmiyya, 1997).
Ibn Nujaym, Zayn al-Dīn ibn Ibrāhīm, *al-Baḥr al-Rāʾiq, Sharḥ Kanz al-Daqāʾiq* (Quetta: al-Maktaba al-Mājidīya, 1983).
Ibn Qudāma, Muwaffaq al-Dīn ʿAbd Allāh ibn Aḥmad, *al-Mughnī li Ibn Qudāma* (Cairo: Hajr, 1986).
Ibn Rāhwayh, Isḥāq ibn Ibrāhīm, *Musnad Isḥāq ibn Rāhwayh* (Beirut: Dār al-Kitāb al-ʿArabī, 2002).
Ibn Taymiyya, Taqī al-Dīn, *al-Tafsīr al-kabīr* (Beirut: Dār al-Kutub al-ʿIlmiyya, 1988).
Ibn Taymiyya, Aḥmad ibn ʿAbd al-Ḥalīm, *Majmūʿ fatāwā Shaykh al-Islām Aḥmad ibn Taymīyya* (Riyadh: Dār ʿĀlim al-Kutub, 1991).
Ibn Wahb, ʿAbd Allāh, *al-Jāmiʿ: tafsīr al-Qurʾān* (Beirut: Dār al-Gharb al-Islāmī, 2003).
Al-ʿImādī, Abū al-Suʿūd Muḥammad ibn Muḥammad, *Tafsīr Abī al-Suʿūd: al-musammā irshād al-ʿaql al-salīm ilā mazāyā al-Qurʾān al-Karīm* (Cairo: Maktaba Muḥammad ʿAlī Ṣubayḥ, 1952).
Al-ʿIrāqī, ʿAbd al-Raḥīm ibn al-Ḥusayn, *Kitāb taqrīb al-asānīd wa-tartīb al-masānīd* (Beirut: Dār al-Kutub al-ʿIlmiyya, 1984).
Al-Ḥākim al-Nīsābūrī, Muḥammad ibn ʿAbd Allāh, *al-Mustadrak ʿalā al-Ṣaḥīḥayn* (Beirut: Dār al-Kutub al-ʿIlmiyya, 2002).
Al-Ḥaddād, Abū Bakr ibn ʿAlī, *Tafsīr al-Ḥaddād: Kashf al-tanzīl fī taḥqīq al-mabāḥith wa-l-taʾwīl* (Beirut: Dār al-Madār al-Islāmī, 2003).
Al-Huwwārī, Hūd ibn Muḥakkam, *Tafsīr Kitāb Allāh al-ʿAzīz* (Beirut: Dār al-Gharb al-Islāmī, 1990).
Al-Ḥīrī, Ismāʿīl ibn Aḥmad al-Nīsābūrī, *Wujūh al-Qurʾān* (Mashhad: Majmaʿ al-Buhūth al-Islāmiyya, 2001).
Al-Jaṣṣāṣ, Aḥmad ibn ʿAlī, *Aḥkām al-Qurʾān* (Beirut: Dār al-Kitāb al-ʿArabī, 1971).

Al-Karmī, Marʿī Yūsuf, *Ghāyat al-muntahā fī al-jamʿ bayna al-Iqnāʾ wa-l-Muntahā* (Riyadh: al-Muʾassasa al-Saʿīdīyya, 1981).

Al-Kāsānī, Abū Bakr ibn Masʿūd, *Badāʾiʿ al-ṣanāʾiʿ fī tartīb al-sharāʾiʿ* (Beirut: Dār al-Kutub al-ʿArabī, 1974).

Al-Khurashī, Muḥammad ibn ʿAbd Allāh, *al-Khurashī ʿalā mukhtaṣar Sīdī Khalīl wa-bi-hāmishihi Ḥāshiyat al-Shaykh ʿAlī al-ʿAdawī* (Beirut: Dār Ṣādir, 1975).

Al-Khāzin al-Baghdādī, ʿAlī ibn Muḥammad, *Tafsīr al-Khāzin: al-musammā Lubāb al-taʾwīl fī maʿānī al-tanzīl* (Baghdad: Maktaba al-Muthannā, 1975).

Al-Maḥallī, Jalāl al-Dīn Muḥammad ibn Aḥmad and al-Suyūṭī, Jalāl al-Dīn ʿAbd al-Raḥmān, *al-Qurʾān al-karīm: bi-l-rasm al-ʿUthmānī. Wa-bi-hāmishahu tafsīr al-jalalayn Jalāl al-Dīn* (Beirut: Dār al-Qalam, 1982).

Al-Marghīnānī, ʿAlī ibn Abī Bakr, *al-Hidāya: sharḥ Bidāyat al-mubtadī* (Beirut: Dār al-Kutub al-ʿIlmiyya, 2000).

Al-Mardāwī, ʿAlāʾ al-Dīn Abī al-Ḥasan Ali b. Sulaymān, *Al-inṣāf fī maʿrifa al-rājiḥ min al-khilāf ʿalā madhhab al-īmām Aḥmad Ibn Ḥanbal* (Beirut: Dār Iḥyāʾ al-turāth al-ʿArabī, 1956).

Al-Māwardī, ʿAlī ibn Muḥammad, *al-Nukat wa-l-ʿuyūn: tafsīr al-Māwardī. Min rawāʾiʿ al-tafāsīr* (Beirut: Dār al-Kutub al-ʿIlmiyya, 1992).

Al-Māwardī, ʿAlī ibn Muḥammad, *al-Ḥāwī al-kabīr fī fiqh madhhab al-Imām al-Shāfiʿī* (Beirut: Dār al-Kutub al-ʿIlmiyya, 1994).

Al-Mawṣilī, Abū Yaʿlā Aḥmad ibn ʿAlī, *Musnad Abī Yaʿlā al-Mawṣilī* (Beirut: Manshūrāt Muḥammad ʿAlī Bayḍūn, 1998).

Mujāhid, ibn Jabr, *Tafsīr al-Imām Mujāhid ibn Jabr* (Beirut: Dār al-Fikr al-Ḥadītha, 1989).

Muqātil, ibn Sulaymān al-Balkhī, *Tafsīr Muqātil ibn Sulaymān* (Cairo: Muʾassasat al-Ḥalabī, 1969).

Muslim, ibn al-Ḥajjāj al-Qushayrī, *Ṣaḥīḥ Muslim* (Beirut: Dār al-Kutub al-ʿIlmiyya, 1994).

Al-Naḥḥās, Aḥmad ibn Muḥammad, *Maʿānī al-Qurʾān al-karīm* (Mecca: Jāmiʿat Umm al-Qurā, 1988).

Al-Nasāʾī, Aḥmad ibn Shuʿayb, *Kitāb al-sunan al-kubrā* (Beirut: Dār al-Kutub al-ʿIlmiyya, 1991).

Al-Nasafī, ʿAbd Allāh ibn Aḥmad, *Tafsīr al-Nasafī, al-musammā bi-Madārik al-tanzīl wa-ḥaqāʾiq al-taʾwīl* (Beirut: Dār al-Qalam, 1989).

Al-Nasafī, ʿAbd Allāh ibn Aḥmad, *al-Baḥr al-rāʾiq, sharḥ Kanz al-daqāʾiq fī furūʿ al-Ḥanafīya* (Beirut: Dār al-Kutub al-ʿIlmiyya, 2006).

Al-Nawawī, Abū Zakarīyā Yaḥyā ibn Sharaf, *Rawḍat al-ṭālibīn* (Beirut: Dār al-Kutub al-ʿIlmiyya, 1992).

Al-Nawawī, Abū Zakarīyā Yaḥyā ibn Sharaf, *Riyād al-Ṣāliḥīn* (Beirut: Dār al-Kutub al-ʿIlmiyya, 1999).

Al-Qurṭubī, Muḥammad ibn Aḥmad, *al-Jāmiʿ li-aḥkām al-Qurʾān: tafsīr al-Qurṭubī* (Beirut: Dār al-Kitāb al-ʿArabī, 1997).

Al-Qushayrī, ʿAbd al-Karīm ibn Hawāzin, *Laṭāʾif al-ishārāt: tafsīr Ṣūfī Kāmil li-l-Qurʾān al-Karīm* (Cairo: Dār al-Kātib al-ʿArabī, 1968).

Al-Rāghib al-Iṣfahānī, Abū al-Qāsim al-Ḥusayn ibn Muḥammadī, *Muʿjam mufradāt alfāẓ al-Qurʾān* (Beirut: Dār al-Kātib al-ʿArabī, 1972).

Al-Rāghib al-Iṣfahānī, Abū al-Qāsim al-Ḥusayn ibn Muḥammadī, *al-Mufradāt fī gharīb al-Qurʾān* (Mecca: al-Maktaba, 1997).

Al-Rāzī, Fakhr al-Dīn Muḥammad ibn ʿUmar, *al-Tafsīr al-kabīr* (Beirut: Dār Iḥyāʾ al-Turāth al-ʿArabī, 1997).

Al-Ruḥaybānī, Muṣṭafā al-Ṣuyūṭī, *Maṭālib ulī al-nuhā fī sharḥ Ghāyat al-muntahā* (Damascus: al-Maktabat al-Islāmī, 1961).

Al-Rūyānī, Muḥammad ibn Hārūn, *Musnad al-Ṣaḥāba, al-maʿrūf bi-Musnad al-Rūyānī* (Beirut: Dār al-Kutub al-ʿIlmiyya, 1997).

Al-Samīn, Aḥmad ibn Yūsuf, *al-Durr al-maṣūn fī ʿulūm al-kitāb al-maknūn* (Damascus: Dār al-Qalam, 1986).

Al-Ṣanʿānī, ʿAbd al-Razzāq ibn Hammām al-Ḥimyarī, *Tafsīr al-Qurʾān* (Riyadh: Maktaba al-Rushd, 1989).

Al-Sarakhsī, Muḥammad ibn Aḥmad, *Kitāb al-mabsūṭ* (Beirut: Dār al-Maʿrifa, 1972).

Al-Shāfiʿī, Muḥammad ibn Idrīs, *Aḥkām al-Qurʾān* (Beirut: Dār al-Kutub al-ʿIlmiyya, 1975).

Al-Shāfiʿī, Muḥammad ibn Idrīs, *Mawsūʾat al-Imām al-Shāfiʿī al-kitāb al-Umm* (Beirut: Dār Qutayba, 1996).

Al-Shīrāzī, Abū Isḥāq Ibrāhīm b. ʿAlī b. Yūsuf al-Fīrūzābādī, *Al-Muhadhdhab fī fiqh al-Imām al-Shāfiʿī* (Beirut: Dār al-Kutub al-ʿIlmiyya, 1995).

Al-Shirbīnī, Muḥammad ibn al-Khaṭīb, *Mughnī al-Muḥtāj fī sharḥ al-Minā j* (Beirut: Dār al-Maʿrifa, 1997).

Al-Shirbīnī, Muḥammad ibn al-Khaṭīb, *Tafsīr al-Khaṭīb al-Shirbīnī: al-musammā al-Sirāj al-munīr fī al-iʿāna ʿalā maʿrifat baʿḍ maʿānī kalām rabbinā al-ḥakīm al-khabīr* (Beirut: Dār al-Kutub al-ʿIlmiyya, 2004).

Al-Sulamī, ʿIzz al-Dīn ʿAbd al-ʿAzīz ibn ʿAbd al-Salām, *Tafsīr al-Qurʾān: ikhtiṣār al-Nukat li-l-Māwardī* (Beirut: Dār Ibn Ḥazm, 1996).

Al-Sulamī, ʿIzz al-Dīn ʿAbd al-ʿAzīz ibn ʿAbd al-Salām, *al-Qawāʿid al-kubrā, al-mawsūm bi, Qawāʿid al-aḥkām fī iṣlāḥ al-anām* (Damascus: Dār al-Qalam, 2000).

Al-Suyūṭī, Jalāl al-Dīn ʿAbd al-Raḥmān, *al-Durr al-manthūr fī al-tafsīr al-maʾthūr* (Beirut: Dār al-Maʿrifa, 1970).

Al-Suyūṭī, Jalāl al-Dīn ʿAbd al-Raḥmān, *Al-Itqān fī ʿUlūm al-Qurʾān* (Damascus: Dār Ibn Kathīr, 2000).

Al-Suyūṭī, Jalāl al-Dīn ʿAbd al-Raḥmān, *Jamʿ al-jawāmiʿ: al-Jāmiʿ al-kabīr fī al-ḥadīth wa-l-Jāmiʿ al-ṣaghīr wa-zawāʾiduhu* (Beirut: Manshūrāt Muḥammad ʿAlī Bayḍūn, 2000).

Al-Ṭabarānī, Sulaymān ibn Aḥmad, *al-Muʿjam al-ṣaghīr li-l-Ṭabarānī* (Beirut: Dār al-Kutub al-ʿIlmiyya, 1983).

Al-Ṭabarānī, Sulaymān ibn Aḥmad, *Muʿjam al-Awsaṭ* (Beirut: Dār al-Kutub al-ʿIlmiyya, 1998).

Al-Ṭabarī, Abū Jaʿfar Muḥammad ibn Jarīr, *Tafsīr al-Ṭabarī: al-musammā Jāmiʿ al-bayān fī taʾwīl al-Qurʾān* (Beirut: Dār al-Kutub al-ʿIlmiyya, 1999).

Al-Ṭayālisī, Sulaymān ibn Dāwūd, *Musnad Abī Dāwud al-Ṭayālisī* (Beirut: Dār al-Kutubal-ʿIlmiyya, 2004).

Al-Tirmidhī, Muḥammad ibn ʿĪsā, *al-Shamāʾil al-Muḥammadīya: wa-l-khaṣāʾil al-muṣṭafawwīya* (Beirut: Dār al-Kutub al-ʿIlmiyya, 1996).

Al-Thaʿlabī, Aḥmad ibn Muḥammad, *al-Kashf wa-l-bayān: al-maʿrūf Tafsīr al-Thaʿlabī* (Beirut: Dār Iḥyāʾ al-Turāth al-ʿArabī, 2002).

Al-Thaʿālibī, ʿAbd al-Raḥmān, *Tafsīr al-Thaʿālibī, al-musammā bi-l-Jawāhir al-ḥisān fī tafsīr al-Qurʾān* (Beirut: Dār Iḥyāʾ al-Turāth, 1997).

Al-Wāḥidī Nīshābūrī, Abū al-Ḥasan ʿAlī, *al-Wajīz fī tafsīr al-Kitāb al-ʿazīz* (Damascus: Dār al-Qalam, 1995).

Al-Zajjāj, Abū Isḥāq Ibrāhīm ibn al-Sarī, *Maʿānī al-Qurʾān wa-iʿrābuhu* (Beirut: al-Maktaba al-ʿAṣriyya, 1973).

Al-Zamakhsharī, Maḥmūd ibn ʿUmar, *al-Kashshāf ʿan ḥaqāʾiq ghawāmiḍ al-tanzīl wa-ʿuyūn al-aqāwīl fī wujūh al-taʾwīl* (Beirut: Dār al-Kutub al-ʿIlmiyya, 2003).

Al-Zarkashī, Abū ʿAbdullah Muḥammad b. ʿAbdullah, *Sharḥ al-Zarkashī ʿalā matn al-Khiraqī* (Mecca: Maktaba al-Asadī, 2009).

Al-Zaylaʿī, ʿUthmān ibn ʿAlī, *Tabyīn al-ḥaqāʾiq sharḥ kanz al-daqāʾiq* (Beirut: Dār al-Kutub al-ʿIlmiyya, 2000).

Post-Colonial Sources

Abou El Fadl, Khaled, *Conference of the Books: The Search for Beauty in Islam* (New York: University Press of America, 2001)

Abou El Fadl, Khaled, "Constitutionalism and the Islamic Sunni Legacy," *Journal of Islamic and Near Eastern Law* 1(67) (2001) 1–26.

Abou El Fadl, Khaled, *Speaking in God's Name: Islamic Law, Authority and Women* (Oxford: Oneworld, 2001).

Abu-Lughod, Lila, "Do Muslim Women Really Need Saving?," *American Anthropologist*, 104(3) (2002) 783–90.

Abu-Odeh, Lama, "The Politics of (Mis)recognition: Islamic Law Pedagogy in American Academia," *American Journal of Comparative Law*, 52(4) (2004) 789–824.

Adhami, Abdullah, "Shams (sun) and Qamar (moon)" [Quote of the day on Healing Hearts Blog] (Mar. 31, 2009), <http://healing-hearts-blog.com/2009/03/31/shams-sun-and-qamar-moon> (last accessed Jan. 16, 2013).

Adler, Rachel, *Standing Again at Sinai: Judaism from a Feminist Perspective* (New York: HarperCollins, 1991).

Adler, Rachel, *Engendering Judaism: An Inclusive Theology and Ethics* (Philadelphia: Jewish Publication Society, 1998).

Ahmed, Israr, *Dawra Tarjuma Qurʾān (audio)* (Lahore: Markazi Anjuman Khuddam-ul-Qurʾan, 2008).

Ahmed, Leila, *Women and Gender in Islam: Historical Roots of a Modern Debate* (New Haven: Yale University Press, 1992).

Ahmed, Rumee, "The Ethics of Prophetic Disobedience: Q. 8:67 at the Crossroads of the Islamic Sciences," *Journal of Religious Ethics*, 39(3) (2011) 440–57.

Ahmed, Rumee, *Narratives of Islamic Legal Theory* (Oxford: Oxford University Press, 2012).

Ali, Abdullah Yusuf, *The Meaning of the Holy Qur'an* (Beltsville: Amana Publications, 1997).

Ali, Ahmed, *Al-Qur'an: A Contemporary Translation* (Princeton: Princeton University Press, 2004).

Ali, Kecia, *Money, Sex, and Power: The Contractual Nature of Marriage in Islamic Jurisprudence of the Formative Period*, Ph.D. thesis (Duke University, 2002).

Ali, Kecia, "Women, Gender, Ta'a (Obedience), and Nushūz (Disobedience) in Islamic Discourses" in Suad Joseph (ed.), *Encyclopedia of Women and Islamic Cultures* (Leiden: Brill, 2003).

Ali, Kecia, "'A Beautiful Example': The Prophet Muhammad as a Model for Muslim Husbands," *Islamic Studies*, 43(2) (2004) 273–91.

Ali, Kecia, *Sexual Ethics and Islam* (Oxford: Oneworld, 2006).

Ali, Kecia, "The Best of You Will Not Strike," *Comparative Islamic Studies*, 2(2) (2006) 143–55.

Ali, Kecia, "Obedience and Disobedience in Islamic Discourses" in Suad Joseph (ed.), *Encyclopedia of Women in Islamic Cultures* (Leiden: Brill, 2007) 309–13.

Ali, Kecia, *Marriage and Slavery in Early Islam* (Cambridge, MA: Harvard University Press, 2010).

Anderson, Benedict, *Imagined Communities: Reflections on the Origin and Spread of Nationalism* (London: Verso, 2003).

An-Na'im, Abdullahi, *Dossier 14–15: Islam and Women's Rights: A Case Study*, <http://www.wluml.org/node/269> (last accessed May 22, 2013).

Ansari, Zaynab (a.k.a. Umm Salah), "Is It a Distortion to Say that Wife-Beating Is Allowed in Islam?" [Q&A, online forum] (Feb. 22, 2005), <http://www.ummah.com/forum/archive/index.php/t-51317.html> (last accessed Jan. 17, 2013).

Arkoun, Mohammed, "Discours islamiques, discours orientalistes et pensée scientfique" in "As Others See Us: Mutual Perceptions, East and West Bernard Lewis" (special issue) (ed. Edmund Leites and Margaret Case), *Comparative Civilizations Review*, 13–14 (1985–6).

Asad, Muhammad, *The Message of the Qur'an* (Watsonville: Book Foundation, 2003).

Aulette, Judy Root and Wittner, Judith, *Gendered Worlds*, 2nd edn. (New York: Oxford University Press, 2012).

Aune, David, *Westminster Dictionary of the New Testament and Early Christian Literature* (Louisville: Westminster John Knox Press, 2003).

Austin, J.L., *How to Do Things with Words* (Oxford: Oxford University Press, 1962).

Awda, Abdul Qadir, *al-Tashrī' al-Jinā'ī al-Islāmī* (Cairo: Dār al-turāth, 1985).

Badawi, Jamal A., *Gender Equity in Islam: Basic Principles* (Plainfield: American Trust Publications, 1995).

Badran, Margot, *Feminists, Islam, and Nation: Gender and the Making of Modern Egypt* (Princeton: Princeton University Press, 1995).

Bakhtiar, Laleh, *The Sublime Qur'an* (Chicago: Kazi Publications, 2007).

Al-Banna, Hasan, *Between Yesterday and Today*, translation (Prelude, 1997), available at <http://web.youngmuslims.ca/online_library/books/byat/> (last accessed Jan. 29, 2013).

Barlas, Asma, *"Believing Women" in Islam: Unreading Patriarchal Interpretations of the Qur'an* (Austin: University of Texas Press, 2002).

Bauer, Karen, "'Traditional' Exegeses of Q. 4:34," *Comparative Islamic Studies*, 2(2) (2006) 129–42.

Bauer, Karen, "*Room for Interpretation: Qur'ānic Exegesis and Gender*," Ph.D. diss. (Princeton University, 2008).

de Biberstein-Kazimirsky, A., *Dictionnaire arabe-français* (Paris: G.P. Maisonneuve, 1960).

Biyya, Abdallah b., *His Character was the Qur'an* (trans. Hamza Yusuf), 2-CD set (Oakland: Rumi Bookstore, 2007).

Brown, Jonathan A.C., *Hadith: Muhammad's Legacy in the Medieval and Modern World* (Oxford: Oneworld, 2009).

Browning, Don S., Green, M. Christian, and Witt, John Jr. (eds.), *Sex, Marriage and Family in World Religions* (New York: Columbia University Press, 2006).

al-Bukhārī, Muḥammad Ibn Isma'īl, *Summarized Ṣaḥīḥ al-Bukhārī* (trans. Muhammad Mohsin Khan) (Riyadh: Maktaba Dār al-Salām, 1994).

Calder, Norman, "*Tafsīr* from Ṭabarī to Ibn Kathīr: Problems in the Description of a Genre, Illustrated with Reference to the Story of Abraham" in G.R. Hawting and Abdul-Kader A. Shareef (eds.), *Approaches to the Qur'ān* (London: Routledge, 1993) 101–40.

Chaudhry, Ayesha S., "The Problems of Conscience and Hermeneutics: A Few Contemporary Approaches," *Comparative Islamic Studies*, 2(2) (2006) 157–70.

Chaudhry, Ayesha S., "*Wife-Beating in the Pre-Modern Islamic Tradition: An Inter-Disciplinary Study of Ḥadīth, Qur'anic Exegesis, and Islamic Jurisprudence*," Ph.D. diss. (New York University, 2009).

Chaudhry, Ayesha S., "The Ethics of Marital Discipline in Pre-Modern Qur'anic Exegesis," *Journal of the Society of Christian Ethics*, 30(2) (2010) 123–30.

Chaudhry, Ayesha S., "'I Wanted One Thing and God Wanted Another...': The Dilemma of the Prophetic Example and the Qur'anic Injunction on Wife-Beating," *Journal of Religious Ethics*, 39(3) (2011) 416–39.

Chaudhry, Ayesha S., "Women" in *Encyclopedia of Islamic Political Thought* (Princeton: Princeton University Press, 2012) 595–9.

Chaudhry, Ayesha S., "Lexical Definitions of *Nushūz* in Qur'anic Exegesis: A Comparative Analysis of Husbandly and Wifely *Nushūz* in Q. 4:34 and Q. 4:128" in S.R. Burge (ed.), *The Meaning of the Word: Lexicology and Tafsīr* (forthcoming).

Davis, Nancy J. and Robinson, Robert V., "The Egalitarian Face of Islamic Orthodoxy: Support for Islamic Law and Economic Justice in Seven Muslim-Majority Nations," *American Sociological Review*, 71(2) (2006) 167–90.

Dien, M. Izzi, "Ta'zīr (a.)" in P. Bearman, Th. Bianquis, C.E. Bosworth, E. van Donzel, and W.P. Heinrichs (eds.), *Encyclopaedia of Islam*, 2nd edn. (Leiden: Brill, 2009).

Dien, M. Izzi and Walker, P.E., "Wilāya (a.)" in P. Bearman, Th. Bianquis, C.E. Bosworth, E. van Donzel, and W.P. Heinrichs (eds.), *Encyclopaedia of Islam*, 2nd edn. (Leiden: Brill, 2009).

Elsaidi, Murad H., "Human Rights and Islamic Law: Analyses Challenging the Husband's Authority to Punish 'Rebellious' Wives," *Muslim World Journal of Human Rights*, 7(2) (2011) 1–25.

Esack, Farid, "Islam and Gender Justice: Beyond Simplistic Apologia" in J.C. Raines and D.C. Maguire (eds.), *What Do Men Owe Women? Men's Voices from World Religions* (Albany: State University of New York Press, 2001).

Fadel, Mohammad, "Two Women, One Man: Knowledge, Power, and Gender in Medieval Sunni Legal Thought," *International Journal of Middle East Studies*, 29 (1997) 185–204.

Fadel, Mohammad, "Public Reason as a Strategy for Principled Reconciliation: The Case of Islamic Law and International Human Rights," *Chicago Journal of International Law*, 8(1) (2008) 1–20.

Fadel, Mohammad, "Is Historicism a Viable Strategy for Islamic Legal Reform? The Case of 'Never Shall a Folk Prosper Who Have Appointed a Woman to Rule Them,'" *Islamic Law and Society* (2011) 1–64.

Grossman, Maxine and Berlin, Adele (eds.), *The Oxford Dictionary of the Jewish Religion* (New York: Oxford University Press, 2011).

Haddad, G.F., "Wife Beating," *Living Islam: Islamic Tradition website article* (Feb. 12, 2000), <http://www.livingislam.org/fiqhi/fiqha_e32.html> (last accessed Jan. 26, 2013).

Haddad, G.F., "Marriage and Men's Cruelty," Q&A on "Qibla" website (2008), <http://spa.qibla.com/issue_view.asp?HD=7&ID=3438&CATE=1> (last accessed Jan. 17, 2012).

Hajjar, Lisa. "Religion, State Power, and Domestic Violence in Muslim Societies: A Framework for Comparative Analysis," *Law & Social Inquiry*, 29(1) (2004) 1–38.

Haleem, M.A.S., *The Qur'ān: A New Translation* (Oxford: Oxford University Press, 2004).

Hansrot, Luqman and Desai, Ebrahim, Answer to question posted on "Ask Imam" website (Aug. 21, 2009), <http://www.askimam.org/public/question_detail/18235> (last accessed Jan. 17, 2013).

Hashmi, Farhat, "Tafseer: Surah Nisā' 33–35" (audio), available at <http://www.farhathashmi.com/quran/tafsir/> (last accessed Jan. 25, 2013).

Hassan, Riffat, *Women's Rights and Islam: From the I.C.P.D. to Beijing* (Louisville: NISA Publications, 1995).

Hava, J.G., *Arabic–English Dictionary* (Beirut: Catholic Press, 1951).

Al-Hibri, Azizah, "An Introduction to Muslim Women's Rights" in Gisela Webb (ed.), *Windows of Faith* (Syracuse: Syracuse University Press, 2000).

Hidayatullah, Aysha, *Women Trustees of Allah: Methods, Limits, and Possibilities of 'Feminist Theology' in Islam*, Ph.D. diss. (University of California, Santa Barbara, 2009).

Hunter, Shireen T. and Gregorian Vartan (eds.), *Reformist Voices of Islam: Mediating Islam and Modernity* (Armonk: M.E. Sharpe, 2008).

Ibn, Baaz, "My Husband Curses and Abuses Me," Advice given on "Fatwa-Online" website (undated), <http://www.fatwa-online.com/fataawa/marriage/maritalrelations/0000206_6.htm> (last accessed Jan. 25, 2013).

Ibn Baaz, "My Husband Does Not Treat Me in a Good and Proper Fashion," Advice given on "Fatwa-Online" website (undated), <http://www.fatwa-online.com/fataawa/marriage/maritalrelations/0000206_5.htm> (last accessed Jan. 25, 2013).

Ibn Rushd, *The Distinguished Jurist's Primer* (trans. Imran Ahsan Khan Nyazee) (Reading, UK: Ithaca Press, 2000).

Islamic Supreme Council of Canada, *Fatwā: Honour Killings, Domestic Violence and Misogyny are Un-Islamic and Major Crimes* (Feb. 4, 2012), available at <http://www.islamicsupremecouncil.com/fatwa-honour-killings-misogyny-domestic-violence.pdf> (last accessed Jan. 22, 2013).

Islam Q & A Team, "His Wife Is Not Very Interested in Intercourse . . .," answer to question posted on "Islam Online" website (July 24, 2007), <http://islamonline.com/news/articles/3/His_wife_is_not_very_interested_in_intercourse_so_.html> (last accessed Dec. 21, 2012).

Islam Q & A Team, "Husband Forcing His Wife to Have Intercourse," advice posted on "Islam Q & A" website (undated), <http://islamqa.info/en/ref/33597/> (last accessed Jan. 16, 2013).

Islamweb Team, "Explanation of Surah al-Nisa': 4:34," answer to question posted on "Islamweb English" website (2002), <http://www.islamweb.net/emainpage/index.php?page=showfatwa&Option=FatwaId&Id=84120> (last accessed Jan. 29, 2013).

Juynboll, G.H.A., *Muslim Tradition: Studies in Chronology, Provenance, and Authorship of Early Ḥadīth, Cambridge Studies in Islamic Civilization* (Cambridge: Cambridge University Press, 1983).

Kabbani, M. Hisham and Ziad, Homayra, "The Prohibition of Domestic Violence in Islam," World Organization for Resource Development and Education (WORDE) (Washington, DC, 2011), available at <http://www.worde.org/wp-content/uploads/2011/09/DV-Fatwa-Online-Version.pdf> (last accessed Jan. 22, 2013).

Al-Kawthari, Muhammad Ibn Adam, "Question #07275472: Can My Brother Beat Up My Abusive Husband?," answer to question posted on "Daruliftaa.com" (Mar. 5, 2004), <http://www.daruliftaa.com/question?txt_QuestionID=q-07275472> (last accessed Jan. 15, 2013).

Al-Kawthari, Muhammad Ibn Adam, "Question #07335282: Can a Wife Refuse Her Husband's Call to Bed?," answer to question posted on "Daruliftaa.com" (Mar. 5, 2004), <http://www.daruliftaa.com/question?txt_QuestionID=q-07335282> (last accessed Jan. 15, 2013).

Keddie, Nikki R., *Sayyid Jamal ad-Din "al-Afghani": A Political Biography* (Berkeley: University of California Press, 1972).

Khalifa, Rashad, *Qur'an: The Final Testament* (Fremont: Universal Unity, 2001).

Kueny, Kathryn, *The Rhetoric of Sobriety: Wine in Early Islam* (Albany: State University of New York Press, 2001).

Lander, Mark, "Germany Cites Koran in Rejecting Divorce," *The New York Times* (Mar. 22, 2007).

Leemhuis, Fred, "Origins and Early Development of the Tafsir Tradtion" in Andrew Rippin (ed.), *Approaches to the History of the Interpretation of the Qur'ān* (Oxford: Clarendon Press, 1988).

Macfarlane, Julie, *Islamic Divorce in North America: A Shari'a Path in a Secular Society* (Oxford: Oxford University Press, 2012).

MacIntyre, Alasdair, *Whose Justice? Which Rationality?* (Notre Dame: University of Notre Dame Press, 1988).

Mahmoud, Mohamed, "To Beat or Not to Beat: On the Exegetical Dilemmas over Qur'ān, 4:34," *Journal of the American Oriental Society*, 126(4) (2006) 537–50.

Marín, Manuela, "Disciplining Wives: A Historical Reading of Qur'ān 4:34," *Studia Islamica* (2003) 5–40.

Maududi, Abul ala, *Tafhīm al-Qur'ān* (Lahore: Islamic Publications, 1962).

Memon, Kamran, "Wife Abuse in the Muslim Community," online article (undated), <http://www.zawaj.com/articles/abuse_memon.html> (last accessed Jan. 20, 2013).

Mernissi, Fatima, *The Veil and the Male Elite: A Feminist Interpretation of Women's Rights in Islam* (New York: Basic Books, 1991).

Meron, Ya'akov, "The Development of Legal Thought in Hanafi Texts," *Studia Islamica*, 30 (1969) 72–118.

Mir-Hosseini, Ziba, "Justice, Equality and Muslim Family Laws: New Ideas, New Prospects" in Ziba Mir-Hosseini, Kari Vogt, Lena Larsen, and Christian Moe (eds.), *Gender and Equality in Muslim Family Law: Justice and Ethics in the Islamic Legal Tradition* (London: I.B. Taurus, 2013).

Mir, Muntasir, *Coherence in the Qur'an: A Study of Islahi's Concept of Nazm in Tadabbur-i-Qur'an* (Plainfield: American Trust Publication, 1986).

Mir-Hosseini, Ziba and Anwar, Zainah, "Decoding the 'DNA of Patriarchy' in Muslim Family Laws," online article (May 21, 2012), <http://www.musawah.org/decoding-dna-patriarchy-muslim-family-laws> (last accessed Jan. 29, 2013).

Mohsin, Khan, *The Noble Qur'an: Interpretation of the Meanings of the Noble Qur'an in the English Language* (Riyadh: Dar-us-Salam Publications, 1999).

Moosa, Ebrahim, "Allegory of the Rule (Hukm): Law as Simulacrum in Islam," *History of Religions*, 38(1) (1998) 1–24.

Moosa, Ebrahim, "The Debts and Burdens of Critical Islam" in Omid Safi (ed.), *Progressive Muslims: On Justice, Gender and Pluralism* (Oxford: Oneworld, 2003).

Moosa, Ebrahim, "Colonialism and Islamic Law" in Muhammad Khalid Masud, Armando Salvatore, and Martin van Bruinessen (eds.), *Islam and Modernity: Key Issues and Debates* (Edinburgh: Edinburgh University Press, 2009) 158–81.

Mubarak, Hadia, "Breaking the Interpretive Monopoly: A Re-Examination of Verse 4:34," *Hawwa*, 2(3) (2005) 261–89.

Ochs, Peter, *Peirce, Pragmatism and the Logic of Scripture* (Cambridge: Cambridge University Press, 1998).

Panipati, Sanaullah, *al-Tafsīr al-Mazharī* (Quetta: Baluchistan Book Depot, 1983).

Pickthall, Marmaduke William and ʿAshshī, ʿArafāt Kāmil, *The Meaning of the Glorious Qurʾan: Text and Explanatory Translation* (Beltsville: Amana Publications, 1994).

Al-Qaradawi, Yusuf, *The Lawful and Prohibited in Islam (Al-Halal wa-l-Haram fī al-Islām)* (Indianapolis: American Trust Publications, 1984).

Al-Qaradawi, Yusuf, *Sharīʿa and Life,* television programme (Oct. 15, 1997).

Qutb, Sayyid, *"Fī Ẓilāl al-Qurʾān,"* commentary on verses 4:24–34 (undated), <http://altafsir.com/Tafasir.asp?tMadhNo=0&tTafsirNo=53&tSoraNo=4&tAyahNo=34&tDisplay=yes&UserProfile=0&LanguageId=1> (last accessed Jan. 25, 2012).

Qutb, Sayyid, *In the Shade of the Qurʾān* (Rajshahi: Islamic Cultural Centre, 1981).

Rabbani, Faraz, "Is It Not a Form of Sexual Abuse for a Husband to be Able to Force His Wife to Have Sex?," Q & A on "Qibla" website (2008), <http://spa.qibla.com/issue_view.asp?HD=11&ID=1830&CATE=117> (last accessed Jan. 17, 2013).

Rabbani, Faraz, "Marriage: 'Demanding Sex' as Abuse or Rape," Q & A on "Qibla" website (2008), <http://spa.qibla.com/issue_view.asp?HD=11&ID=4087&CATE=117> (last accessed Jan. 17, 2013).

Rabbani, Faraz, "What Does It Mean to Hit the Wife Lightly?," Q & A on "Qibla" website (2008), <http://spa.qibla.com/issue_view.asp?HD=11&ID=4758&CATE=121> (last accessed Jan. 20, 2013).

Rahman, Faizur, "Islamic Law of Divorce," article for TwoCircles.net (May 11, 2011), <http://twocircles.net/2011may11/islamic_law_divorce.html> (last accessed Jan. 29, 2013).

Rahman, Fazlur, *Major Themes in the Qurʾan* (Minneapolis: Bibliotheca Islamica, 1980).

Rahman, Fazlur, *Islam and Modernity: Transformation of an Intellectual Tradition* (Chicago: University of Chicago Press, 1984).

Rapoport, Yossef, *Marriage, Money and Divorce in Medieval Islamic Society* (Cambridge: Cambridge University Press, 2005).

Rida, Rashid, *Ḥuqūq al-nisāʾ fī al-Islām: nidāʾ li-l-jins al-laṭāʾif* (Beirut: Maktab al-Islāmī, 1975).

Rippin, Andrew, *Approaches to the History of the Interpretation of the Qurʾān* (Oxford: Clarendon Press, 1988).

Rippin, Andrew, "The Function of Asbāb al-Nuzūl in Qurʾānic Exegesis," *Bulletin of Oriental and African Studies*, 51(1) (1988) 1–20.

Rippin, Andrew, "*Tafsīr Ibn ʿAbbās* and Criteria for Dating Early *Tafsīr* Texts," *Jerusalem Studies in Arabic and Islam*, 18 (1994) 38–83.

Rispler-Chaim, Vardit, "Nušūz between Medieval and Contemporary Islamic Law: The Human Rights Aspect," *Arabica*, 39(3) (1992) 315–27.

Sachedina, Abdulaziz, *Islam and the Challenge of Human Rights* (Oxford: Oxford University Press, 2009).

Sadeghi, Behnam, *The Structure of Reasoning in Post-Formative Islamic Jurisprudence*, Ph.D. diss. (Princeton University, 2006).

Saleh, Walid A., *The Formation of the Classical Tafsīr Tradition: The Qur'ān Commentary of Al-Thaʿlabī (D. 427/1035)* (Boston: Brill, 2004).

Sands, Kristin Zahra, *Ṣūfī Commentaries on the Qur'ān in Classical Islam* (London: Routledge, 2006).

Schacht, J., "*Ḳiṣāṣ*" in P. Bearman, Th. Bianquis, C.E. Bosworth, E. van Donzel, and W.P. Heinrichs (eds.), *Encyclopaedia of Islam*, 2nd edn. (Leiden: Brill, 2009).

Scott, Joan W., "Fantasy Echo: History and the Construction of Identity," *Critical Inquiry* 27(2) (2001) 284–304.

Scott, Rachel M., "A Contextual Approach to Women's Rights in the Qur'ān: Readings of 4:34," *The Muslim World*, 99 (2009) 60–85.

Shafaat, Ahmad, "Tafseer of Surah an-Nisa, Ayah 34," online article (1984, revised 2000), <http://www.islamicperspectives.com/quran-4-34.htm> (last accessed Jan. 15, 2013).

Shafi, Muhammad, *Maʿārif al-Qur'ān* (Karachi: Maktaba-e-Darul-Uloom, 1996).

Shaikh, Sa'diyya, "Exegetical Violence: Nushuz in Qur'anic Gender Ideology," *Journal for Islamic Studies*, 17 (1997) 49–73.

Shaikh, Sa'diyya, "A Tafsir of Praxis: Gender, Marital Violence, and Resistance in a South African Muslim Community" in Dan Maguire and Sa'diyya Shaikh (eds.), *Violence against Women: Roots and Cures in World Religions* (Cleveland: Pilgrim Press, 2007).

Shakir, M.H., *The Qur'an* (Elmhurst: Tahrike Tarsile Qur'an, 1990).

Silvers, Laury, "'In the Book We have Left Out Nothing': The Ethical Problem of the Existence of Verse 4:34 in the Qur'an," *Journal of Comparative Islamic Studies*, 2(2) (2006) 171–80.

Sisters in Islam and Masidi, Yasmin, *Are Muslim Men Allowed to Beat their Wives?* (Selangor: Sisters in Islam, 1991 and 2009).

Sonbol, Amira El Azhary, *Women, the Family, and Divorce Laws in Islamic History* (Syracuse: Syracuse University Press, 1996).

Stowasser, Barbara F., *Women in the Qur'an: Traditions and Interpretations* (New York: Oxford University Press, 1994).

Taylor, Charles, *Modern Social Imaginaries* (Durham, NC: Duke University Press, 2004).

Talbi, M., *Ummat al-wasaṭ: Al-islām wa-taḥaddiyāt al-muʿāshara* (Tunis: Saras li-l-nashr, 1996).

Thanvi, Ashraf Ali, *Bayān al-Qur'ān* (Multan: Idara ta'lifāt Ashrafiyya, n.d.).

Trible, Phyllis, *Texts of Terror: Literary-Feminist Readings of Biblical Narratives* (Philadelphia: Fortress Press, 1984).

Tucker, Judith, *In the House of the Law: Gender and Islamic Law in Ottoman Syria and Palestine* (Berkeley: University of California Press, 1998).

Tucker, Judith, *Women, Family and Gender in Islamic Law* (Cambridge: Cambridge University Press, 2008).

Tyan, E., "Diya" in P. Bearman, Th. Bianquis, C.E. Bosworth, E. van Donzel, and W.P. Heinrichs (eds.), *Encyclopaedia of Islam*, 2nd edn. (Leiden: Brill, 2009).

Umar, (first name unknown), "Rebuttal to Qur'an on Beating Wives," response to http://answering-islam.org/Authors/Arlandson/contact.htm James M.

Arlandson (Dec. 5, 2008), <http://www.answering-christianity.com/umar/beating_rebuttal.htm> (last accessed July 12, 2013).

Van Buren, Abigail, "Tried and True Rules for a Happy Marriage," *Chicago Tribune* (Feb. 1, 1996), available at <http://articles.chicagotribune.com/1996-02-01/features/9602010300_1_dear-abby-dear-readers-name-calling> (last accessed Jan. 26, 2013).

Wadud, Amina, *Qur'an and Woman* (New York: Oxford University Press, 1999).

Wadud, Amina, *Inside the Gender Jihad: Women's Reform in Islam* (Oxford: Oneworld, 2006).

Wadud, Amina, "Islam Beyond Patriarchy Through Gender Inclusive Qur'anic Analysis," Musawah (undated), available at <http://www.musawah.org/sites/default/files/Wanted-AW-EN.pdf> (last accessed May 20, 2013).

Wansbrough, John E., *Qur'anic Studies: Sources and Methods of Scriptural Interpretation* (Oxford: Oxford University Press, 1977).

Wehr, Hans, *Arabic–English Dictionary: The Hans Wehr Dictionary of Modern Written Arabic* (Ithaca: Spoken Language Services, 1994).

Weiss, Bernard G., *The Search for God's Law* (Salt Lake City: University of Utah Press, 1992).

Wensinck, A.J., "Miswāḳ" in P. Bearman, Th. Bianquis, C.E. Bosworth, E. van Donzel, and W.P. Heinrichs (eds.), *Encyclopaedia of Islam*, 2nd edn. (Leiden: Brill, 2009).

Wheeler, Brannon, *Prophets in the Qur'ān: An Introduction to the Qur'ān and Muslim Exegesis* (London: Continuum, 2002).

Women's Islamic Initiative in Spirituality and Equality (WISE), "Jihad Against Violence: Muslim Women's Struggle for Peace," (July 2009), available at <http://www.wisemuslimwomen.org/images/uploads/Jihad_against_Violence_Digest(color).pdf> (last accessed Jan. 22, 2013).

Yüksel, Edip, al-Shaiban, Layth Saleh, and Schulte-Nafeh, Martha, *Qur'an: A Reformist Translation* (USA: Brainbow Press, 2007).

Yusuf, Hamza, "Sermon: Removing the Silence on Domestic Violence," (Feb. 21, 2009), video available at <http://www.youtube.com/watch?v=BDEKJDgXOU> (last accessed Sept. 5, 2013).

Yusuf, Hamza, *Men and Women, audio CD* (Hayward: Alhambra Productions, 2003).

Zaman, Muhammad Qasim, *The Ulama in Contemporary Islam: Custodians of Change, Princeton Studies in Muslim Politics* (Princeton: Princeton University Press, 2002).

Index

INTRODUCTORY NOTE

References such as '178–9' indicate (not necessarily continuous) discussion of a topic across a range of pages. Wherever possible in the case of topics with many references, these have either been divided into sub-topics or only the most significant discussions of the topic are listed. Because the entire work is about 'Islam' and the 'women', the use of these terms (and certain others which occur constantly throughout the book) as entry points has been restricted. Information will be found under the corresponding detailed topics.